9781113845832

THE NEW WORLD ORDER

THE NEW WORLD ORDER

INTERNATIONAL ORGANIZATION
INTERNATIONAL LAW
INTERNATIONAL COÖPERATION

BY

FREDERICK CHARLES HICKS
A.M., LL.B.
LAW LIBRARIAN OF
COLUMBIA UNIVERSITY

GARDEN CITY   NEW YORK
DOUBLEDAY, PAGE & COMPANY
1920

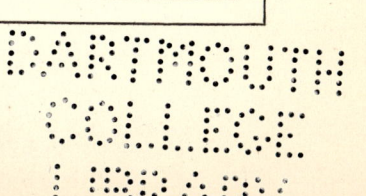

Gift of Carn. End. Int. Peace.

COPYRIGHT, 1920, BY
DOUBLEDAY, PAGE & COMPANY
ALL RIGHTS RESERVED, INCLUDING THAT OF
TRANSLATION INTO FOREIGN LANGUAGES,
INCLUDING THE SCANDINAVIAN

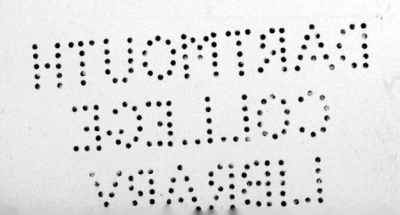

PREFACE

IN the Summer Session of 1919, the author gave a course of lectures on International Organization and Coöperation, in the Department of Public Law, Columbia University. The lectures were supplemented by discussions and written reports by members of the class on various phases of the subject. The general purpose was to examine the League Covenant analytically in its relation to (1) international organization, (2) international law, and (3) international coöperation, using the comparative method whenever precedents could be found.

The substance of these lectures and discussions was put into form in August, 1919. During the period up to March 31, 1920, the manuscript was kept abreast of events in connection with the League and the Treaty of Versailles. As the purpose was to analyze the Covenant and Treaty at first hand and not to defend a thesis, or support policy with regard to any particular state, the failure of the United States to become an original member of the League has in no way disturbed the plan of the book. On November 19, 1919, the United States Senate defeated ratification by a vote of 55 to 39, and again on March 19, 1920, by a vote of 49 to 35. On March 20, 1920, the Treaty of Versailles was returned to President Wilson. Whether or not the United States remains outside of the League, or becomes a member with reservations, the League Covenant is in force as to the present members; and, unless it fails utterly of its purposes, will affect the foreign relations of the United States both in the matter of peaceful coöperation and in settling disputes which might lead to a rupture. Moreover, the wisdom of the reservations proposed by the United States Senate can be appraised only by such a study as has here been attempted.

For the most part, the facts have been allowed to speak for themselves, opinions and prophecies rarely being hazarded; but the study has resulted in the author's personal conviction that the League of Nations should be supported not merely because it provides means for putting war a few steps farther in the background, but because it emphasizes the necessity for coöperation between sovereign states. International coöperation is an end in itself, the benefits of which are felt directly by the people of all participating states, and incidentally it tends to decrease the number of disputes likely to lead to a rupture.

The author is indebted to many writers whose works have been consulted and quoted and to whom credit is given in the footnotes, the chapter references, and the selected Bibliography (Appendix 8). Particularly is he grateful to Mr. Henry F. Munro, Lecturer in International Law, Columbia University, who examined and criticized all of the manuscript; and to Miss Elsie Basset, of the Catalogue Staff of the Columbia University Law Library, who verified all references, dates, and quotations.

FREDERICK C. HICKS.

Columbia University,
 March 31, 1920.

TABLE OF CONTENTS

I. INTERNATIONAL ORGANIZATION

CHAPTER		PAGE
I.	THE SOCIETY OF NATIONS IN 1914	3
II.	THE BALANCE OF POWER AND THE CONCERT OF EUROPE	17
III.	HOW THE LEAGUE OF NATIONS WAS BORN	34
IV.	SALIENT FEATURES OF THE LEAGUE COVENANT	49
V.	PROPOSALS FOR A LEAGUE OF NATIONS	66
VI.	FORMER LEAGUES OF NATIONS	79

II. INTERNATIONAL LAW AND THE LEAGUE

VII.	CUSTOMARY INTERNATIONAL LAW AND TREATY-MADE LAW	95
VIII.	THE LEAGUE AND THE DEVELOPMENT OF INTERNATIONAL LAW	108
IX.	INTERNATIONAL LAW OF PEACE	121
X.	INTERNATIONAL COMMISSIONS OF INQUIRY	134
XI.	INTERNATIONAL ARBITRATION	147
XII.	INTERNATIONAL TRIBUNALS WITH PERMANENT PERSONNEL	164
XIII.	INTERNATIONAL ADMINISTRATION OF TERRITORY	176

III. INTERNATIONAL COÖPERATION AND THE LEAGUE

XIV.	INTERNATIONAL COÖPERATION DURING THE WAR	201
XV.	DIPLOMACY AS A MEANS OF INTERNATIONAL COÖPERATION	212
XVI.	TREATIES AND COÖPERATION	227
XVII.	COÖPERATION IN NATIONAL LEGISLATION	242
XVIII.	PUBLIC INTERNATIONAL UNIONS	256
XIX.	THE INTERNATIONAL LABOR ORGANIZATION	270

TABLE OF CONTENTS

CHAPTER | PAGE
XX. PRIVATE INTERNATIONAL CONFERENCES AND ASSOCIATIONS 280

IV. APPENDICES

1. TREATY OF PEACE WITH GERMANY 297
   (a) The Covenant of the League of Nations . . . 303
   (b) Selected Articles from the Treaty 315
   (c) Labor Organization 366
2. THE TRIPLE ALLIANCE 383
   (a) Dual Alliance, October 7, 1879 383
   (b) Triple Alliance, May, 1882 386
3. RUSSO-FRENCH ALLIANCE 388
   (a) Projet de Convention Militaire, December, 1893 388
   (b) Convention Navale, July 16, 1912 390
4. THE HOLY ALLIANCE ACT 391
5. CENTRAL AMERICAN TREATIES, December 20, 1907 . 393
   (a) General Treaty of Peace and Amity 393
   (b) Convention for the Establishment of a Central American Court of Justice 399
   (c) Convention for the Establishment of an International Central American Bureau 406
   (d) Convention Concerning Future Central American Conferences 409
6. HAGUE CONVENTIONS AND DRAFTS, 1907 411
   (a) Convention for the Pacific Settlement of International Disputes 411
   (b) Draft Convention Relative to the Creation of a Judicial Arbitration Court 431
   (c) Convention Relative to the Creation of an International Prize Court 438
7. TREATY FOR THE ADVANCEMENT OF PEACE BETWEEN THE UNITED STATES OF AMERICA AND GUATEMALA, September 20, 1913. 455
8. BIBLIOGRAPHY 457
   INDEX 491

PART I
INTERNATIONAL ORGANIZATION

INTERNATIONAL ORGANIZATION

I. The Society of Nations in 1914
II. The Balance of Power and the Concert of Europe
III. How the League Was Born
IV. Salient Features of the League Covenant
V. Proposals for a League of Nations
VI. Former League of Nations

CHAPTER I

THE SOCIETY OF NATIONS IN 1914

THE expression "League of Nations" as the name for the new international régime which was created by Part I of the Treaty of Versailles was not adopted without some dissent. Leagues of the past have not all had a beneficent influence, and some of the bloodiest wars in history have been waged in their name. To France particularly the term is of sinister meaning, associated as it is with her devastating religious wars of the sixteenth century. Her statesmen preferred the name "society" to indicate a voluntary association of equals drawn together for a common purpose. *Société*, not *ligue*, is therefore used in the French version of the treaty as the equivalent of "league." A society is something more than an association by agreement. It is the result of natural development; while a league has connected with it something of the idea of politics. Usage justifies the use of the word "nations" as synonymous with the word "states" to signify the politically organized communities which enter into international relations. Up to the time of Jeremy Bentham the rules applicable to these relations were collectively called the law of nations, and the expression coined by him, international law, apparently settled the usage for all time. But, legally speaking, a state and a nation are not the same. This is now a commonplace in popular works on the League of Nations as it has long been in technical works on international law.

A state is defined as a sovereign political unity. It occupies a specified territory inhabited by people who owe allegiance to it, are protected by it, and who, as a unity, have no means of expressing themselves except through the agencies of state organization. A nation is less easily defined. By itself, it is neither sovereign, political, nor organized. Its unity comes from ties of blood, language, religion, customs, literature, and history. Races are neither states nor nations; they are ethnographical divisions of the world's population, such as the Caucasian, Mongolian, Ethiopian, and Malay races, and they are so widely scattered that scarcely any state or any nation is wholly composed of one race. It is possible, of course, for a nation to be organized into a state, thus adding the characteristics of one to the other. The attempt has been made in the re-mapping of Europe to make states out of national groups, and France was already an example of a state almost co-terminous with a nation. On the other hand, the British Empire is made up of many nationalities; so also is the United States. Switzerland is an example of a small state made up of several well-defined national groups, the chief of which have undoubted ties of blood, language, and literature with Germany, Italy, and France respectively. These have not yet been completely amalgamated into a Swiss nation, but the status of Switzerland as a state is not thereby affected.[1]

In the Preamble of the League of Nations Covenant the word "nation" is synonymous with "state". It speaks of just and honorable relations between "nations", of the dealings of "organized peoples", and rules of conduct for "governments" which are the political organs of states. Only self-governing states, dominions, or colonies may be members of the League, thus excluding from direct representation national groups which are not sepa-

---

[1] Ruyssen (International Conciliation, March, 1917, p. 71–72) distinguishes between nation and nationality. "Nationality," he says, "in the abstract sense, is the characteristic of that which is national. But it is also, especially in the concrete sense, the totality of those ethnical elements which aspire to the dignity, the risks and the thrilling experiences of national life. Nationality is the nation in power, the nation attempting to realize itself and to play a part in history. It is made of similar but dissevered elements which would unite to form a common body and give it the functions necessary to a common life, in a word, to achieve unity and political sovereignty.

"Unquestionably, the distinction between these ideas is frequently vague; 'nation' and 'nationality' may be used interchangeably to designate the same ethnic group. We may give the name of nation not only to existing states, where political unity visibly corresponds with a unity of homogeneous ethnical characteristics, but also to those states which have been deprived by the accident of history of this unity within such comparatively recent times that its memory still remains as an ideal for restoration."

rately organized. These must be satisfied with representation through the states to which they belong.

It is perhaps fortunate for the English-speaking world that the name "Society of Nations" was not used, for thus some confusion is avoided. There already was a Society or Family of Nations which will continue to exist, whatever may be the fortunes of the League. Germany, for instance, is still a member of the Society of Nations although not yet admitted to the League. Mexico, although not yet invited to join the League, is still a member of the Society of Nations. Canada, Australia, South Africa, New Zealand, and India do not belong to the older Society, and membership in the League does not admit them to it. The two expressions are obviously not used in the same sense. There are no two rival organizations with slightly different names, each subscribing to a different agreement. The older Society of Nations has no written Covenant, no officers, no seat of government or administration, and when a state has once been admitted there is no means of escaping the obligations of membership. It is an inchoate, indefinite Society, but a very real one. When we speak of states as members of the Society of Nations we refer to states as defined in international law. The Central and South American republics, after their revolt from Spain, set up governments and each for its own people exercised the powers of a state. They were states in fact, *de facto* states, but not in the full sense of the word. Before the modern era, it was possible for some organized peoples to live in practical isolation from the rest of the world. These also were states in a constitutional sense. They had their own laws, forms of government, officials, and military forces. Such isolation is no longer possible; but still there may be territories and peoples politically organized which have only a *de facto* status. These may come into existence through civil wars, or revolution, or through the consent of the states of which they formerly were parts. It is not, however, until evidence of stability is produced, either by continued existence, or by appeal to their history while dependent peoples, that their statehood is fully accepted in international law. The technical process by which a state ceases to be merely *de facto* and becomes *de jure* is Recognition. In the Treaty of Versailles the formal creation of Poland and other states is contemporaneous with their recognition by Germany and other signatories. For a brief period prior to the signing of the treaty they were *de facto* states, and as to some of the victorious Allies, *de jure* states. Recognition gives to states the right of legation, of sending and receiving diplomatic agents; and it acknowledges them as equal, sovereign, independent states having the right to exist. They acquire not only rights but duties, and among the latter is the all-important obligation to respect the rules of international law.

Just what this international law is there will be occasion to discuss later on. Suffice it to say for the present that it is a body of rules which, through usage, custom, and common consent, the members of the Family of Nations consider binding on themselves. They are not rules imposed by a world legislature, for no such body at any time has been in existence. There is no such body for the old Society of Nations and none has been created for the new League. The entire theory of international relations would have to be reconstructed to admit of this, and we should have a confederation similar to the United States of America, in place of sovereign independent states. If we go back in history to the time when Rome was the head of a universal empire, we find the nearest approach to a world legislature that history records. But it was not an international legislature, because all of the subdivisions of the empire were vassal states, not free, sovereign, and independent. The Holy Roman Empire, on the other hand, was an empire only in name, with no authority over the member states, and doomed to disappear. Napoleon had a dream of world empire which came near to realization, but if he had succeeded, he would have destroyed the Society of Nations by substituting for it one state. Napoleon's attempt at universal dominion was itself an occasion for intensified reassertion of the rights of states to live. There was indeed an attempt to create something like a confederation of these states for mutual protection, but even this broke down after twenty years of half-hearted experimentation.

The modern world consists of a circle of states each aspiring to

THE SOCIETY OF NATIONS IN 1914

greatness, seeking wealth, influence, increase of territory, outlets for growth of population into colonies and undeveloped lands, and each asserting its absolute sovereignty, and its legal equality with all the others. This situation has been described by advocates of a new order as international anarchy. The phrase is without justification, for it implies absolute disrespect for law on the part of all states. The world has just witnessed the best demonstration that the greater part of it has a respect for law for which it is willing to fight. Nevertheless, it is evident that there is something wanting in an international system which can be maintained only by four years of war. Of what value to the world is the Society of States, with its recognition of the sovereignty, independence, and equality of its member states? Are these realities or merely fictions? Should they be abandoned and some new doctrine be substituted for them, or must they be preserved to serve a better purpose under new conditions?

Sovereignty, independence, and equality are attributes of states so closely connected that it is difficult to define them separately. They are different facets of the same jewel—the right to exist. They are the terms by means of which each state describes its legal right to the full enjoyment of its statehood, limited only by its duty to the other states. Where supposed rights conflict, the obligation lies equally on all states to refrain from their assertion until by agreement a compromise can be effected. If they had been universally content to do this, an ideal situation would have existed; but the ideal is never attained. On the contrary, conflict of rights has ever been with states, as with persons, the occasion for renewed assertion of those rights. With states the danger of such a situation has been that independence and equality include the right to decide when and on what provocation war shall be resorted to as a means of maintaining those very rights. Thus the fatal circle is complete. With such a system, power is evidently the arbiter of justice, a doctrine even more discreditable to international law than it would be to municipal law. But this situation is not the unethical result of a conspiracy of powerful brigand states; it is the result of evolution. From doctrines put forth for the benefit of all, the weak as well as the strong, have flowed consequences not at all anticipated. This may be illustrated by the development of the doctrine of the equality of states.[1]

For almost three centuries writers on international law have included among fundamental principles the juristic equality of states. "All sovereign states," they say, "without respect to their relative power, are, in the eye of international law, equal, being endowed with the same natural rights, bound by the same duties, and subject to the same obligations." The doctrine is said to possess both a philosophical and historical sanction, and its truth until recent years has seldom been questioned.

Philosophically, the principle was given form by Hugo Grotius. Universal sovereignty having ceased to be even theoretically possible, national states emerged, warring with each other for supremacy, and with no restraint except physical weakness. To relieve this situation Grotius invoked the so-called law of nature. As people were said to have been in a state of nature before the organization of governments, and though free, to have obeyed certain laws discovered to them by their own reason, so states, freed from any control from above, were now in a state of nature with respect to each other. By analogy the law of nature was applicable to the relations of states. To explain the meaning and content of the law of nature, recourse was had to the Roman law in which the *jus gentium* and the *jus naturale* were identified. A favorite dogma of the *jus gentium* was the equality of men. Grotius adopted this conception and so made the absolute equality of states a fundamental principle of his legal system.

Modern political theorists have satisfied themselves that historically there never was a state of nature such as Grotius premised. There certainly never was a law of nature that could be treated as a positive code; and the equality of men living according to a law of nature was a misconception. Liberty and equality for men did not exist until the organization of political communities. Until that time men had only such liberty as they could win from nature

---

[1] Summarized from the author's address printed in the Proceedings of the American Society of International Law, 1909, p. 238-247.

and each other by the exertion of powers. Equality is not, therefore, really a postulate of the law of nature and could not properly be said to become an attribute of states on the philosophical grounds which Grotius laid.

But the doctrine doubtless would never have been accepted by the world of the seventeenth century had it not been for this erroneous appeal to the law of nature. The adoption of any principle by all states was a great stride in the world's progress, tending to bring order out of chaos, and set up standards of conduct which to this day are viewed with respect. Judged by its results in the years immediately following its promulgation, its justification is so strong that it should not be discredited merely by abstract reasoning. It gave to weak states an admitted principle to which to appeal when dealing with strong states, and stayed the hand of those accustomed to crush without mercy.

Yet there came a time when states began to find numerous occasions for disregarding the principle. The law of nature seemed less and less a valid reason for a steadfast recognition of equality. It was then that there was brought forth the alternative and supplementary ground for equality which the far-seeing Grotius had advanced. He had asserted that states are bound by rules which have received the assent of all or most of their number. Whatever might have been the ground for the original consent, an appeal to history cumulating examples amounting to a custom was sufficient to establish the validity of a rule. Thus, the great states of the world having agreed among themselves that recognition of the sovereignty of a state carries with it all the international rights and duties which they possess themselves, the rule is binding and cannot be controverted. This undoubtedly is the sounder reason for asserting that all sovereign states are equal in international law. It is, in fact, a statement of the modern doctrine that international law is based on practice. Sovereignty having been defined as the absolute political independence of a state, the recognition of this attribute theoretically establishes the equality of states and admits them into the Family of Nations.

Now it is undoubtedly the practice of statesmen to assert that all sovereign states are equal. By Article 81 of the Treaty of Versailles, Germany "recognizes the complete independence of the Czechoslovak State", and thus concedes that in law the new state is equal to all others in the Family of Nations. But beyond this formal recognition, practice is far from uniform. It was said in 1907, concerning the equality of states, that "a crowd of international incidents goes to prove the principle to be one almost more active and better known in its breach than its observance,"[1] and the last twelve years have furnished many more examples. Nevertheless, in our own courts from Chief Justice Marshall down, the doctrine has served as the basis for decisions involving states; and it has recently been solemnly reasserted by the American Institute of International Law. Article 3 of the Declaration of the Rights and Duties of Nations, adopted by the Institute at its Washington meeting on January 6, 1916, says that "Every nation is in law and before law the equal of every other nation belonging to the Society of Nations, and all nations have the right to claim and, according to the Declaration of Independence of the United States, 'to assume among the Powers of the earth, the separate and equal station to which the laws of nature and of nature's God entitle them.'"[2] It is the weak states that are most anxious that the doctrine shall not be lost sight of. At the Hague Conferences, and at the Paris Peace Conference, it was the so-called minor powers that appealed to the principle, when representation on courts and committees was under discussion. In a dispute between a great and a minor power the latter has found legal equality to be of little avail; nevertheless it has been the only safeguard of the smaller states. They have been obliged to save their *amour propre* by acquiescence, with or without a show of force by their powerful opponents. For instance, Colombia found it best to agree to the creation of Panama as an independent state, protesting at the same time that an act of injustice had been done. Some states owe their very existence to agreement to a virtual limitation of their sovereignty and equality.

---

[1] American Journal of International Law, 1:419.

[2] Scott: The American Institute of International Law: Its Declaration of the Rights and Duties of Nations, p. 88.

Cuba is legally equal to the United States, but she obtained this recognition only by agreeing to the so-called Platt amendment, which was embodied in the treaty of May 22, 1903.[1] By this treaty the exercise of Cuba's sovereign powers was by "voluntary" agreement materially restricted. The practice of the past shows that the doctrine of equality is effective chiefly when two powers are nearly equal in fact, whether the two be Great Powers or minor powers. As between a Great Power and a small power, it has seldom prevented the former from accomplishing its object, but has left a basis for a subsequent claim by the latter which under certain conditions may be effectively asserted. And all of this has been done under the forms of equality, jealously guarded by the minor states.

There is no evidence at the present time that the assertion of the principle of equality is to be discontinued; and it may be that at last practice and theory are about to be united. The unrestricted right to declare war was the logical result of the doctrine, and at the same time its chief enemy. With war restrained and held only as an ultimate recourse, equality may become in some true sense a fact. As in a society of individual persons, freedom, liberty, equality of opportunity come only by limitation of extreme claims, so also with a society of individual states. Actual equality comes only from innate characteristics. But states, though unequal in power and influence, may under an agreed rule have equal opportunity of presenting their claims and demanding recognition of rights which the facts support. They may have equal access to the formularies and rules of procedure by means of which intercourse is maintained. It is possible that, freed from the fear of sudden and unprovoked war, even the Great Powers may now do from another motive that which the minor powers have been forced to do, and without discarding their ultimate sovereign and equal rights, consent to forego the extreme exercise of them.

Such was not the situation in 1914. The sovereign states in the Family of Nations did not stand on equal ground, and the doctrine conceived as the succor of the weak had become the excuse for oppression. Not power in the aggregate, not the collective power

[1] Malloy: Treaties, 1:362–364.

of a world society, but power concentrated in individual states was the ruling force. And since power so placed was the ultimate sanction or enforcing power in the Society of Nations, it was inevitable that this family of legally equal states should in practice be ruled on matters of policy by a few powerful states, whose position is well described by the phase, the "Primacy of the Great Powers". When the European war broke out the Great Powers were Great Britain, France, Germany, Austria-Hungary, Italy, Russia, Japan, and the United States of America. Japan was recognized as a Great Power early in the twentieth century. Spain, in the day of her strength as an exploring and colonizing state, was a Great Power. Russia, still with enormous territory and population, is no longer a Great Power. China, more populous than any other, never has been considered a Great Power. An example of the Great Powers ruling the lesser is that of Austria-Hungary in 1908 annexing Bosnia and Herzegovina in violation of Article 25 of the Treaty of Berlin. Two minor powers, Serbia and Montenegro, protested, not as parties to the treaty, but as sovereign states whose interests were affected. Austria refused to receive the protests, and the Great Powers did not intervene.

It should not be inferred, however, that the control of the Society of States was effected solely by combination of Great Powers opposed to the minor powers. The Great Powers themselves needed some restraints, and since there was no organized power above them, that restraint naturally developed through groupings within the eight powers, each group being supported by an alignment of the minor powers. Thus in 1914, the European leadership was divided between Germany, Austria-Hungary, and Italy on the one hand, and Great Britain, France, and Russia on the other. In Asia, Japan was the predominant power, and in the Western Hemisphere, the United States. There was supposed to exist an equipoise in interstate relations by which no state or group of states could obtain an unfair advantage over the others. This equilibrium is known as the Balance of Power.

The Society of Nations which we have been describing is not politically organized. It lacks nearly all of those elements which are associated with the conception of government. It is a headless association which is the outgrowth of evolution. It therefore has no controlling conscience, and no common purpose to which its members are devoted. Furthermore, it should be reiterated that it is not intended to prevent war. On the contrary, it could not exist without contemplating war as always not far in the background, the ultimate recourse and sanction. This does not mean that exponents of international law advocate war; with few exceptions they look for the time when occasions for war will have disappeared. Every state exists with revolution as a possibility; but revolution is not recommended as the customary means of recording state action.

What then justifies the statement that there already was and still is a Society of Nations distinct from the League? First, that there is a generally accepted body of international law; second, that there is a well-organized official means of intercourse for the ordinary relations of states, viz., the diplomatic services; third, there is a well-tried means of settling certain classes of differences without recourse to war, viz., arbitration and commissions of inquiry; and fourth, there are rules for the conduct of war.

As a Society, it has been most successful in carrying on intercourse during peace. Its chief weakness lies in the fact that nothing but self-interest can, under the theory of absolute sovereignty, restrain a powerful state from declaring war. And war, once begun, removes most of the value of the Society, for the time being, even for those states which are not concerned as belligerents. Its value to the world is seen in the general advance in civilization which has come from legitimate rivalry between states. The world has gone forward faster because of the era of national competition which culminated finally in the European war, since no means, save war, existed for limiting the aspirations of one state within reasonable bounds.

Has the era of unbridled state competition now come to an end, to be followed by a rational era of coöperation? The same question has been asked at the end of each cataclysmic war. After the Napoleonic wars, the answer was made by a renewed appeal by

European states to the Balance of Power as a practical means of control. But this did not go to the root of the matter, namely the right of a powerful state in virtue of its sovereignty to declare war, being itself legally the sole judge whether the war was in support of law or in violation of it. In 1919 the attempted answer was the League of Nations, but let us not imagine that this is a new conception produced by the latest necessity for something better than had yet been devised. The hopeful thing about the old Society of Nations is that, like all living organisms, its members have never been satisfied with it, and they have never ceased to seek some means of removing its manifest imperfections. For four hundred years leaders of thought have been seeking remedies, proposing substitutes, and on paper erecting systems of intercourse and international settlement; and for a shorter period states have been coming to agreement on details which have been put into practice. These experiments have met with varying degrees of success; some have failed absolutely, others have been satisfactory within a limited field, and all have added to the experience of the world in international statesmanship, without which a successful league of nations could not be maintained.

It is for this reason that a preliminary chapter on the Society of Nations has been thought necessary. In the study of the League Covenant, the existing law so far as it is unchanged by positive declaration must be kept constantly in mind. Moreover, and this is perhaps more important, we must expect to find most of the old elements of policy persisting. The war, overwhelming as it is in its lessons, has probably not essentially changed the nature of man, nor the aspirations of states. The same dangers are to be guarded against, and the same forces will be at play. Fervently desiring, as well-thinking men and women, that the League may succeed, we shall make this more possible if we do not immediately expect too much of it. Considering facts alone, and not merely aspirations, we must see the League as a new manifestation of the desire to give more definite organization to the existing Society of Nations upon which it is based and out of which it has grown. For instance, observing that since the advent of national consciousness, states have grouped themselves to further their own interests, we may expect the same phenomenon to appear in the operation of the Society now headed by the League. In fact, this new organization will give more opportunity to the Great Powers, and lessen the influence of the weak, if a counteracting influence is not nourished.

It is a matter of observation in the case of private corporations that men and interests which forge to the front under a loose organization have increased power when a closer organization is effected. The small holder who votes by proxy has little influence unless actual wrong-doing can be brought home to the leaders. Then an appeal to the law gives, in recent years, adequate remedy. The League will bring to the lesser states a formula for protest and appeal for justice and redress; but this will not be sufficient. The spirit of coöperation must make itself manifest. As will be shown later on, international coöperation has organized itself in many ways both official and unofficial, and has tended to offset the dangers of unrestrained state ambition. Much less emphasis has been placed by protagonists of the League on the organization of international coöperation than on matters of more immediate interest, e. g., the prevention of war, disarmament, arbitration, a court of justice, and the Assembly, Council, and Secretariat. The organization of peaceful daily state intercourse may turn out to be much more important. Coöperation is not essentially a matter of law; it is a matter of policy, self-interest, and spiritual attitude. Its organization, forms, and agencies are already partly law, and may become much more so under the leadership of the League. If this organization does not itself become stereotyped and lifeless, on the one hand, or a mere handmaiden of political statecraft on the other, it may solve what has been the insoluble problem under the old Society of Nations, and which is equally a problem under the League. This problem is summed up in the word Sovereignty, with its synonyms Independence and Equality, and the logically deducible right to declare war. This right has never been relinquished by the world of states. Sporadic attempts have been made; two states at a time, as for instance the United States and France, and small groups, such as the Central American states, have mutually agreed to a limitation of the right. Such attempts, however, have been and will ever be ineffective. The agreement must be general. Even where agreement has been reached, except in one notable group of treaties, the relinquishment has excepted matters involving national honor and vital interests. These terms are difficult to define, and leave wide latitude to any state in interpreting its obligations. They are differently defined at different times by the same state, and they vary with a state's conception of the word Sovereignty.

Now Sovereignty, with some meaning or other, is so firmly fixed in the minds of men and the consciousness of states that we may not expect it to disappear. Moreover, no assembly of representatives of states will attempt to re-define it; and even less will any single state venture to limit by positive statement its right to appeal to the attribute of sovereignty. It will be only in practice that modifications of the extreme doctrine will appear, and these without legally limiting it. Just as the weaker states have found it expedient to relinquish the exercise of some of their legal rights, under the form of voluntary agreement, so the Great Powers, under the lash of a great need and with the conviction that the time for unrestricted competition has passed, will coöperate, here and there, piece by piece, in limiting the exercise of their sovereign rights. And among these Great Powers the example must be set by the most powerful few.

References for Chapter I

OPPENHEIM. International Law, 1912, 1:3-20. The League of Nations, p. 4–11.

STOWELL AND MUNRO. International Cases, 1:153–168.

WILSON AND TUCKER. International Law, p. 45–54.

LAWRENCE, T. J. The Society of Nations, p. 1–57.

WULF, MAURICE DE. The Society of Nations in the Thirteenth Century.

(International Journal of Ethics, 29:210–229, January, 1919.)

DUGGAN. The League of Nations, p. 161–183 (Chapter by H. E. Barnes).

CHAPTER II

THE BALANCE OF POWER AND THE CONCERT OF EUROPE

THE old Society of Nations has no constitutional organs, and the Primacy of the Great Powers in it is without legal standing. It is, however, an historical and ever-present fact. In all international conferences and in all important international affairs during both peace and war, it is the Great Powers that control. Only Great Powers are able to acquire spheres of influence in other states; no minor powers are represented in the consortium to finance the new Chinese Republic[1]; the Great Powers controlled in the prosecution of the European war; made the terms of the armistice; organized and controlled the Peace Conference; were chiefly responsible for the League of Nations Covenant; and will have the dominant position in the League itself. The Great Powers, when acting together, form a rudimentary organ of government, control and administration—an organ which has sometimes operated effectively, and at other times failed completely. The failures came because unity of purpose was lacking; because consistent, continued coöperation cannot be had without a highly developed organization. Organization places artificial restraints on self-interests which shift and fluctuate according to natural laws.

In following the operations of the Great Powers in the Society of Nations, we may therefore expect to find few evidences of concerted action for the benefit of all members, and equally few of consistency as regards themselves alone. Following inevitable tendencies, states as naturally as men form themselves into groups according to their predominant interests. From the beginning of

---
[1] Moore, F.: Control of Foreign Loans and Concessions in China (The Messenger of the New York Peace Society, v. 2, no. 1, December, 1918).

time, men have been drawn together to further their common aims, thus forming social groups. When these groups are organized into states, the persons composing them re-group themselves politically and socially within the states. But each state as a collective entity now has a consciousness which leads it to seek association on equal terms with other states for mutual protection and commercial, economic, and social advancement. No two states at any given time are of equal power. Their relative power continually varies according to their internal development, enterprise, the character of their leaders, and the increase of population. They may become more nearly equal by accession of territory, or less equal because one gains and the other loses territory. A single state may also by a definite policy of military preparation acquire at an abnormal rate the means of exerting power. There is a continuous fluctuation in comparative force, and no actual balance at any time. One state may become exceptionally strong and still not produce any uneasy reactions in other states. The accident of geographical position and just policies in dealing with less powerful neighbors may contribute to this confidence. The United States, although dominant in the Western Hemisphere, has not aroused any great fear that it will misuse its power. On the contrary, through the Monroe Doctrine, it has served as a protector of the other independent states of the Western Hemisphere. But if the powerful state is contiguous to others, so that they are exposed to sudden onslaught and if they live in fear of it, then they tend to combine against the single great state for mutual protection. The first state then seeks alliances or understandings with other states as a counterpoise, and the process goes on until two or more groups are formed, each made up of Great Powers surrounded by minor powers. If all states in a given area, for instance Europe, were in one or the other of these groups, and if the groups were of exactly equal power, there would be at that moment an exact balance. But because of the changes in actual power of the constituent states, this balance would not long remain. If all states were not grouped, then the balance would be only between those in alliance, and outside would be a state or states which "held" the balance of power. By throwing

THE BALANCE OF POWER

its weight to one side of the scales the balance would be destroyed. The same result could be obtained if a state went from one group to another. If now, for the hypothesis of actual equality at any given time, we substitute a condition which only approaches equality, and if we think of this power wherever placed as rising and falling, ever changing, we have the conception of a gently oscillating balance in which first one side, then the other, is slightly heavier. There is a play of forces with a movement of comparatively slight amplitude.

Alliances are political facts. They may represent, at the time of their making, groups nearly equal in power, but they tend to become obsolete because the states which form the groups are not static. They may soon cease to represent equality and serve only as a cloak for inequality. Therefore each state jealously watches all the others, and from time to time statesmen attempt to provide by fresh alliances for new or anticipated conditions. It becomes a race in which the ability to make political forecasts is an important element for success. Not only to the swiftest but to the wisest is the victory. Victory means in this case not the destruction of individual states, nor the restriction of them to a given status, but the formation of new relations which will offset changes of power in the states and consequently in the groups to which they belong. What is sought is the maintenance of the international *status quo*. This desire is natural, and based on the right, recognized in international law, of self-preservation.

In continental Europe, where many rival states are side by side, separated by no large bodies of water or other geographical barriers, it has long been a recognized policy to combine not only to counterbalance existing inequalities, but to anticipate and forestall possible or expected combinations of power. Around this policy has been developed a doctrine or theory called the Balance of Power, which Bernard says[1] is "a short expression of the political maxim that no single state ought to be suffered to become strong enough to overbear the aggregate strength of the rest, or some considerable but undefinable proportion of their aggregate strength. But since it is

[1] Four Lectures on Subjects Connected with Diplomacy, p. 97-98.

impossible to fix with anything like precision the point at which this excessive preponderance is reached, or to make sure how many of the lesser Powers will actually throw their weight into the opposite scale, it has come to mean more than this: every aggrandizement likely to jeopardize the actual state of possession has been treated as a displacement *pro tanto* of the equilibrium; and the equilibrium itself meant such a distribution of force among the different countries of Europe as offered a security for the existing state of possession."

This was the conception of the doctrine as it was fully developed in 1865 when Bernard wrote. It is a doctrine philosophically sound and it has in the past, on the whole, been applied for the good of the world. It prevented any state from attaining to a hegemony in Europe, and safeguarded the life of weak states. In judging of its validity as a doctrine we must not forget that its purpose is not to prevent war. Like international law, it takes cognizance of the fact that under certain circumstances war is justified, and although it results in rivalry of power, it was the best known means of decreasing the fear of sudden aggressive war, of making struggles more equal and less frequent, because less profitable. It accepts war in the last analysis as inevitable, but does not admit that might lodged in a single state makes right. On the contrary, it seeks to neutralize this might—to make it a possession of less value.

Although the Balance of Power is a modern doctrine, Hume has shown[1] that the idea was known to the ancient Greeks and the Persians. Athens at the height of her power was opposed by a league which produced the Peloponnesian wars. When the Thebans and Lacedemonians were rivals, the Athenians stood ready to join the weaker. They helped the Thebans conquer the Spartans, and then, to restore the balance, allied themselves with the vanquished. Rome, on the other hand, furnishes few evidences that the policy was relied on. The *Pax Romana*, embracing the whole known world, admitted not of a balance between states, but of a balance within the empire. It is recorded, however, that King Hiero, of Syracuse, though an ally of Rome, sent assistance

[1] Philosophical Works, v. 3, pt. II, Essay VII, Of the Balance of Power.

to the Carthaginians, "esteeming it requisite both in order to retain his dominions in Sicily, and to preserve the Roman friendship, that Carthage should be safe." "And here he acted with great wisdom and prudence," for, said Polybius, "never ought such a force be thrown into one hand, as to incapacitate the neighboring states from defending their rights against it."[1]

In the Middle Ages feudalism and the system of free cities retarded the growth of national unity until power became centred in each political group in the hands of kings. This concentration of power made possible alliances between monarchs rather than between peoples, and brought wars which were not based on conflict of national interests. Not until the Peace of Westphalia, which ended the Thirty Years' War, was the basis laid for the working of the Balance of Power as a system. The Treaties of Osnaburg and Münster were drawn up by the first of the great European congresses. In it were represented all of the Christian powers except Great Britain, Russia, and Poland. By these treaties, Switzerland and the Netherlands were given full political status, and the 355 states which belonged to the German Empire were made practically independent. The leadership of the Holy Roman Empire and the Pope was broken, and there were now numerous new states claiming independence and equality as members of the Family of Nations. Without leadership wars were inevitable, and they were legion. The most far-reaching of these was the war of the Spanish Succession, between France and Spain on the one hand, and Great Britain, Holland, Portugal, and Savoy on the other. It was ended by the Peace of Utrecht, 1713, which brought forth a flood of treaties. In some of them the principle of the Balance of Power was specifically recognized. For instance, in the treaty between Great Britain and Spain, its purpose is stated to be "for the establishment of a peace, for Christendom, by a just equilibrium of power." This formal recognition did not, however, give it a place in international law. It is, and always has been, a matter of policy asserting itself in various forms according to the natural law of self-preservation. The latter is recognized in international law as a

---
[1] Hume. Philosophical Works, v. 3, p. 352.

right, but the particular method of preservation known as the Balance of Power has not been so recognized.

The European Balance of Power from 1715 to 1789 has been described as "merely a temporary immobility produced by exhaustion after long wars." It began with a quadruple alliance (1718) between the Emperor Charles VI and France, Great Britain, and Holland to maintain the Peace of Utrecht. It saw Russia recognized as a Great Power (1721), and several wars between Austria and Prussia, in which Great Britain, France, Spain, Bavaria, Saxony, and Holland were involved. The peace treaties of Aix-la-Chapelle (1748), Hubertsburg (1763), and Paris (1763) made readjustments intended to be permanent, but they gave little stability to the international situation. Within a few years Europe was to be upset by the activities of Napoleon. His rocket-like career, which at its height made all of Europe except Russia and Great Britain subordinate to him, filled the chancelleries of Europe with discussion of the necessity for a new Balance. And yet, after his fall, it was from France, which for a quarter of a century had been the disturber of Europe, that a new definition of the Balance of Power came. It was contained in the instructions to Talleyrand for his conduct at the Congress of Vienna.

It is a combination of the mutual rights and interests of the Powers, by means of which, Europe aims at securing the following objects:

1st. That no single Power, nor union of Powers, shall have the mastery in Europe.
2nd. That no single Power, nor union of Powers, shall be at liberty to infringe the actual possession and recognized rights of any other Power.
3rd. That it shall no longer be necessary, in order to maintain the established state of affairs, to live in a state of imminent or actual war, and that the proposed combination shall secure the peace and repose of Europe against the efforts of a disturber, by diminishing his chances of success.[1]

---
[1]Gerard, J. W.: The Peace of Utrecht, p. 393, translated from correspondence between Prince Talleyrand and Louis XVIII.

THE BALANCE OF POWER

The agreements and events of the next twenty years may be thought of either as the constitution and operation of a Confederation of Europe,[1] or as the beginning of the Concert of Europe. The latter had its inception in a common fear of France as early as July 17, 1791, when Count Kaunitz in a circular letter "impressed upon the Imperial ambassadors the duty of all the Powers to make common cause for the purpose of preserving 'public peace, the tranquillity of states, the inviolability of possessions, and the faith of treaties'; and based his appeal on the fact that the nations of Europe, united by ties of religion, institutions, and culture, formed but a single family."[2] When Napoleon had been defeated and normal conditions restored, France was admitted to the European Concert which in 1818 consisted of Great Britain, France, Austria, Russia, and Prussia. Great Britain, however, following her policy of isolation, tended to hold aloof except when her immediate interests were touched. Her chief care was that her colonial policy might be prosecuted undisturbed and that the Low Countries might not come under the control of one of the great continental powers. The purpose of the Concert was not merely to maintain the relative *status quo* among states, but to provide a policy for the whole of Europe. It was based on the assumption that the Great Powers, now that the Napoleonic menace was removed, would find a common basis for coöperation, and would stand together for the promotion of the general good. The principle of progress to which it was devoted might, however, be used as an excuse for aggression; in the hands of states whose membership in the Concert was due only to the possession of power, the temptation was great to find reason for interfering in the affairs of other states. Thus the right of intervention became sanctified in place of the modern obligation of non-intervention. For the first half of the century, the legitimacy of existing sovereigns was the chief ground given for interventions. The proposed intervention by European Powers to aid Spain in winning back her American colonies produced the Monroe Doctrine. Later, the preservation of the rights of nationalities

---
[1] For the development of this idea, see Chapter VI.
[2] Phillips: Confederation of Europe, p. 39.

was given as a reason for intervention. The intervention of Great Britain, France, and Russia in the Graeco-Turkish war, 1827, led to the independence of Greece; Belgium became independent in 1830 through the intervention of Great Britain, Austria, France, Prussia, and Russia; the Russo-Turkish war of 1853 became the Crimean War of 1854–56 through the intervention of Great Britain, France, and Sardinia on the side of Turkey; when Russia defeated Turkey in 1877, the Powers intervened after the treaty of peace to save Turkey from being driven out of Europe; after the victory of Japan over China, she was stripped of her spoils by the intervention of European Powers; in 1897, Turkey's grip on Crete was loosened by aid given to Greece.

During the nineteenth century the Concert exerted its influence in a number of international congresses. Those of Aix-la-Chapelle, Troppau, Laibach, and Verona are described in Chapter VI. At the Congress of Paris, 1856, the Black Sea was neutralized, and the integrity of Turkey guaranteed. In 1871, the Black Sea settlement was revised at the Conference of London; and in 1878, the Berlin Congress dealt with the situation in the Balkans. Other congresses and conferences were held, but they are not illustrations of the workings of the European Concert.

It is possible to present an impressive array of evidences of unity in the control of Europe; but one can find also many centrifugal forces. After the Congress of Berlin, the Balance of Power within the Concert began to take the shape which it was to keep until the year 1914. Germany and Austria-Hungary were drawn together by common interests in the Near East, resulting in the alliance of 1879, the terms of which were not published until 1888, when announcement was made as a check to Russia. By its terms, the two powers bound themselves to support each other "with the whole of their imperial military power" if either should be attacked by Russia. If the attack should be made by any other power, each agreed to observe a "benevolent neutrality," and not to uphold the aggressor. But if Russia should give assistance to the aggressor then Germany and Austria-Hungary agreed to give each other the same military support as if the attack had been made by Russia in the first instance.[1] The treaty was declared to be purely defensive in purpose, and "in conformity with its pacific character and to avoid all false interpretation" was to be kept secret, unless it was necessary to make it known to Russia in order to restrain her military preparations. This Dual Alliance became the Triple Alliance when it was joined in 1882 by Italy, as a protest against the colonial policy of France in Morocco.[2] The result was that Russia and France began to find common interests. By 1890 an indefinite understanding had been arrived at, the tenor of which is shown by a note by M. de Giers, Russian Minister of Foreign Affairs, who said, "The entente cordiale which has so happily been established between France and Russia is the best guarantee of peace. While the Triple Alliance is ruining itself with armaments, the intimate accord of the two countries is necessary for the maintenance in Europe of a proper balance of forces."[3] Out of this entente grew eventually two definite Conventions, one having to do with military and the other with naval coöperation. After much correspondence and many ambassadorial conversations a project for the Military Convention was drawn up and signed in St. Petersburg by military representatives of the two states on August 17, 1892. On the following day General Boisdeffre, the French representative, was received by the Russian Emperor, who approved in principle the project of a convention. Formal ratification by the Russian Emperor was communicated on December 15/27, 1893, and by the French Government on December 23, 1893;/January 4, 1894.[4] By this treaty, it was agreed that if France was attacked by Germany, or by Italy supported by Germany, Russia would employ all the forces at her command against Germany. And if Russia was attacked by Germany, or by Austria supported by Germany, France would employ all her forces in fighting Germany. In case of mobilization of the forces of the Triple Alliance, or of one of its members, France and

---

[1] For text of the treaty, see Appendix 2 (a).

[2] For the published parts of the agreement, see Appendix 2 (b).

[3] Documents Diplomatiques; L'Alliance Franco-Russe, Paris, 1918, p. 3.

[4] For the text of the Convention, see Appendix 3 (a); the letters announcing its ratification are contained in Documents Diplomatiques; L'Alliance Franco-Russe, Paris, 1918, p. 127-129.

Russia agreed to mobilize immediately and simultaneously all of their forces and place them as near as possible to their frontiers. Against Germany, France was to employ 1,300,000 men and Russia 700,000 to 800,000. The military staffs, it was agreed, should in time of peace mutually inform each other concerning the armies of the Triple Alliance. Neither state was to conclude a separate peace, and the Convention was to remain in force during the life of the Triple Alliance.[1] Great Britain, however, held aloof, fearing the designs of Russia on India, the Persian Gulf, and Constantinople. Since the Crimean War, she had found it to her interest to stand back of Turkey. Her alliance with Japan in 1902 was a momentous event. By it she effectually checked Russian aspirations in China and Thibet, and paved the way for the Russo-Japanese war of 1904. The treaty stipulated that either state was to come to the aid of the other, if it was attacked by more than one power. It was, however, advisable for Great Britain to clear up her differences with France, and this was done by an agreement of April 8, 1904. The Newfoundland fisheries question was settled once for all, and a compromise was reached on colonial problems in Africa and elsewhere. Great Britain agreed to support France in Morocco, and France to withhold her hand in Egypt. After the defeat of Russia by Japan, the atmosphere was cleared for an understanding between Great Britain and Russia. By the treaty of 1907, the sphere of each in Persia, Thibet, and Afghanistan was recognized. Thus came into being the Triple Entente, a three-cornered arrangement, not based on one convention as was the Triple Alliance, but on a Franco-Russian defensive alliance, and a friendly understanding between Russia and Great Britain.

From 1907 to 1914, there were three wars, the Turco-Italian war of 1911, and two Balkan wars beginning in 1912. Italy's belligerent action was a menace to the Triple Alliance, because Germany had become the protector of Turkey in succession to Great Britain. It served to show that Italy was not bound very

---

[1] The Naval Convention was not signed until July 16, 1912. For text of the Convention, see Appendix 3 (b). Announcement of ratification by the Russian Emperor was made in a letter dated August 2/15, 1912. For this letter see Documents Diplomatiques; L'Alliance Franco-Russe, Paris, 1918, p. 138.

closely by her alliance, and that she might follow her own policies, even through an understanding with France, if occasion demanded. War in the Balkans was barely averted in 1909. The revolution of the Young Turks upset German and Austrian plans, and caused Great Britain again to make her influence felt in Turkey. As a counter-stroke, Germany supported Austria's proclamation of October 7, 1908, annexing Bosnia and Herzegovina. As this was in violation of Article 25 of the Treaty of Berlin, Russia and Serbia protested, with the support of Great Britain. Austria stood her ground and Germany then demanded that Article 25 of the Berlin treaty be abrogated, otherwise Austria would invade Serbia. As Russia, Great Britain, and France were not ready for war, Russia yielded, and Serbia was obliged to accept the situation. Thus Germany reëstablished her influence in Turkey, and felt assured that she might pursue her own policies without immediate danger of interference by the Triple Entente.

At the outset of the first Balkan war, when Bulgaria, Greece, Serbia, and Montenegro were arrayed against Turkey, the Concert of Europe took a hand. By a collective note of October 8, the Balkan allies were told that in the event of war no modification of the *status quo* would be permitted. But the warning had no restraining effect, an aggressive war was carried on, and Turkey, defeated, was compelled to give up Macedonia and most of her territory in Europe. The Concert deliberated in ambassadorial conferences in London and agreed that Albania should be autonomous, that Serbia should have commercial access to the Adriatic coasts; and that Skutari should not be retained by Montenegro. These arrangements were not satisfactory to either Serbia, Albania, or Montenegro, and moreover, no apportionment among the Balkan allies of the territory won from Turkey had been made. A dispute now arose over the division of the spoils of war, which precipitated the second Balkan conflict. Eventually Serbia, Greece, Rumania, Montenegro, and Turkey were arrayed against Bulgaria, forcing the latter to accept the Treaty of Bucharest, August 10, 1913, by which she yielded most of her new possessions to Greece, Serbia, Rumania, and Turkey. Serbia, encouraged by her successes, now began to plan a greater Serbia to include the portions of Bosnia and Herzegovina inhabited by Serbians.

If these were the only wars, they were not the only ones that were from time to time imminent. War between Germany and France had been threatened in 1905, when the German Emperor interfered in the plans of France in Morocco, where she had established herself with the consent of Great Britain. War was averted by reference of the questions involved to a conference of the powers at Algeciras, in January, 1906. It was attended by representatives of Great Britain, France, Germany, Belgium, Holland, Italy, Austria-Hungary, Portugal, Russia, Sweden, Spain, and the United States, and it drew up commercial regulations to become operative in Morocco, the independence of which was recognized. Germany's claims were not upheld, and the entente between Great Britain and France was strengthened. The solution was by no means final, for in 1908 France and Germany were at odds over the Casablanca affair, in which German officials were involved. The dispute was settled by reference to the Permanent Court of Arbitration at the Hague.[1] Again in 1911, trouble impended when Germany sent a warship to Agadir to protect her citizens in Morocco. French and British warships also were immediately stationed there, and for four months the situation was tense. Finally a compromise was reached in which Germany recognized Morocco as a French Protectorate in return for territorial concessions by France in West Africa.

After the Treaty of Bucharest, Austria-Hungary put into force extreme measures to suppress the Pan-Serbian movement in her Bosnian territory, but her police were powerless to prevent the formation of secret societies which were organized in Serbia for operation in Bosnia. This made more tense the already strained relations between Austria and Serbia, and when the Archduke Franz Ferdinand, heir to the Austrian throne and the man chiefly responsible for the annexation of Bosnia in 1908, visited Serajevo, Bosnia, on June 28, 1914, he and his morganatic wife were assassinated. On July 23, Austria sent a note to Serbia, which, after com-

---
[1]Wilson: Hague Arbitration Cases, p. 82–101.

THE BALANCE OF POWER

plaining of the "culpable tolerance" of the Serbian Government toward anti-Austrian propaganda and activities in Serbia, and after accusing Serbian officers and functionaries of having instigated and carried through the assassination of the Archduke, demanded a formal disapproval and repudiation of these activities by the Serbian Government. It made detailed demands which were inconsistent with the existence of Serbian sovereignty, and called for a reply within forty-eight hours. Efforts were made by the European Powers to obtain an extension of time for Serbia, but Austria refused. On July 25, Serbia returned an humble and apologetic note which, however, was unsatisfactory to Austria. Diplomatic relations were broken off immediately, and on July 28 Austria declared war. An attempt was now made to secure mediation through the Concert of Europe. On July 24, Great Britain had suggested that Germany, Italy, France, and Great Britain work together simultaneously at Vienna and St. Petersburg to prevent an open rupture, and on July 26, she definitely proposed a conference at London of the ambassadors of Germany, Italy, France, and Great Britain "for the purpose of discovering an issue which would prevent complications." Until the conclusion of the conference all military activity was to be suspended. France and Italy accepted the proposal, but Germany and Austria refused. Further efforts also brought no results, and it soon became patent that neither the Balance of Power nor the Concert of Europe would be able to prevent a general European conflict.

When the end of the Great War came by the collapse of Germany, something like a world balance had been established, and by steps which will be recounted in the next chapter a League of Nations was set up to maintain this balance. During the armistice period, while the Paris Peace Conference was in session, there was much discussion of the relative merits of the old European system and the proposed League as a means of preserving peace.

President Wilson in his address before Congress on February 11, 1918, had already taken a stand against what he termed "the great game, now forever discredited, of the balance of power." At Manchester, England, he told his audience that "if the future had nothing for us but a new attempt to keep the world at a right poise by a balance of power, the United States would take no interest, because she would join no combination of power which is not a combination of us all." A day later an apparently opposite point of view was taken by Premier Clemenceau in the French Chamber of Deputies. "There is an old system," he said, "which appears condemned to-day and to which I do not fear to say that I remain faithful at this moment." That he remained faithful even to the end of the Congress of Versailles is shown by the fact that on the same day that the peace treaty with Germany was signed, two other treaties between France and Great Britain and France and the United States respectively were signed. These treaties are so important in connection with the League itself that one of them is herewith reproduced in full:

CONSIDERING that the United States of America and the Government of the French Republic are equally animated by a desire to maintain the peace of the world, so happily restored by the treaty signed at Versailles on June 28, which put an end to the war begun by the aggression of the German Empire and terminated by the defeat of that power, and

Considering that the United States of America and the Government of the French Republic are fully convinced that an unprovoked aggression directed by Germany against France would not only violate both the letter and spirit of the Versailles treaty, to which the United States and France are parties, thus exposing France anew to the intolerable burden of unprovoked war, but that such aggression would be regarded by the Treaty of Versailles as being against all the powers signatory to the treaty and calculated to disturb the peace of the world, involving inevitably and directly the states of Europe and indirectly the entire world, as experience has amply and unhappily demonstrated, and

Considering that the United States of America and the Government of the French Republic apprehend that the stipulations concerning the left bank of the Rhine cannot assure immediately to France, on the one hand, and to the United States, on the other, as signatory powers to the Treaty of Versailles, appropriate security and protection:

Consequently, the United States of America and the Government of the French Republic, having decided to conclude a treaty to realize these necessary ends, Woodrow Wilson, President of the United States of America, and Robert Lansing, Secretary of State, specially authorized to that end by the President of the United States of America, and Georges Clemenceau, President of the Council of Ministers and Minister of War, and Stephen Pichon, Minister of Foreign Affairs, specially authorized to that end by Raymond Poincaré, President of the French Republic, have agreed upon the following:

Article 1.—The following stipulations concerning the left bank of the Rhine are contained in the Peace Treaty signed with Germany at Versailles, June 28, 1919, by the United States of America, by the Government of the French Republic, and by the British Empire, among other powers:

Article 42.—Germany is forbidden to maintain or construct any fortifications either on the left bank of the Rhine or on the right bank to the west of a line drawn fifty kilometers to the east of the Rhine.

Article 43.—In the area defined above the maintenance and the assembly of armed forces, either permanently or temporarily, and military manœuvres of any kind, as well as the upkeep of all permanent works for mobilization, are in the same way forbidden.

Article 44.—In case Germany violates in any manner whatever the provisions of Articles 42 and 43 she shall be regarded as committing a hostile act against the powers signatory of the present treaty and as calculated to disturb the peace of the world.

In case these stipulations should not assure immediately to France appropriate security and protection, the United States of America shall be bound to come immediately to her aid in case of any unprovoked act of aggression directed against her by Germany.

Article 2.—The present treaty, couched in terms analogous to those of a treaty concluded on the same date and to the same end between Great Britain and the French Republic, a copy of which is hereto annexed, will not enter into force until the moment when the latter is ratified.

Article 3.—The present treaty must be submitted to the Council of the League of Nations and must be recognized by the Council, deciding if occasion arise by majority, as an engagement in conformity with the Covenant of the League. It will remain in force until, upon demand of one of the parties to the treaty, the Council deciding if occasion arise by a majority, finds that the League itself assures sufficient protection.

Article 4.—The present treaty shall before ratification be submitted to the Chambers of the French Parliament for approval and it shall be submitted to the Senate of the United States of America at the same time as the treaty of Versailles shall be submitted for assent to ratification. Ratifications shall be exchanged at the time of deposit in Paris of the ratifications of the treaty of Versailles, or as soon afterward as possible.[1]

The agreement between Great Britain and France corresponds with the above except that there is an additional provision that the treaty imposes no obligation upon any of the dominions of the British Empire unless and until it be approved by the Parliament of each dominion interested.

The publication of these treaties, according to the press, immediately produced a reaction in Italy.[2] Resentment was shown in government circles that Italy has been omitted from the alliance, and it was stated that since "it had always been an axiom of European statesmanship that no continental power can exist alone," Italy might for self-protection be forced into an alliance with Germany and Russia.

It has been argued that this new triple alliance is inconsistent with the principles of the League of Nations and that it may even destroy it. An opposite argument may with equal cogency be advanced. If we have rightly conceived the nature of the Balance of Power, it was inevitable that there should be opposing groups within the League. Just what these treaties foreshadow was in fact predicted by Professor Oppenheim[3] when he said, "It is a fact—I make this statement although I am sure it will be violently contradicted—that, just as hitherto, so within a League of Nations some kind of Balance of Power only can guarantee the independence and equality of the smaller states. For the Community of Power, on which the League of Nations must rest, would at once disappear if one or two members of the League became so powerful that they could disregard the combined power of the other members." In his view, the two are not only consistent but correlative. The Balance of Power within the League should operate under restraints

---

[1] Current History, 10:273–274, August, 1919; Living Age, 302: 396-398, August 16, 1919.
[2] New York Times, July 8, 1919.
[3] The League of Nations and Its Problems, p. 21.

which will remove its objectionable features and give play to natural forces as long as they contribute to the good of all.

REFERENCES FOR CHAPTER II

STOWELL, E. C. Diplomacy of the War of 1914, 1:3-37.

OPPENHEIM. International Law, 1:59-83.

WILSON AND TUCKER. International Law, p. 81-87.

BERNARD, M. Lectures on Subjects Connected with Diplomacy, p. 61-109.

DUGGAN. The League of Nations, p. 273-288 (Chapter by H. F. Munro).

OAKES AND MOWAT. Great European Treaties of the Nineteenth Century. Oxford, Clarendon Press, 1918.

CHAPTER III

HOW THE LEAGUE OF NATIONS WAS BORN

It is not necessary to relate the rapid succession of events which followed Austria's declaration of war, among which were the invasion of Belgium, the withdrawal of Italy from the Triple Alliance, the ranging of Turkey and Bulgaria on the side of the Teutons, and the entrance of Great Britain into the war. Before the final collapse of Germany, twenty-five states were fighting against the Central Powers, four had broken off diplomatic relations with them, and seventeen, though neutral, were almost as profoundly affected as if they had become belligerents. It was the Central European Powers against the world. Moreover, on account of their position, stretching like a barrier across the continent from the North and Baltic seas to the Bosphorus and beyond, and on account of centralized control of their military forces and economic resources, they were winning the war.

Opposed to them was a potentially overwhelming force, but for three years a force without central organization or control. Even the various allied states were without complete control over the individual units of which they were composed. The self-governing dominions of Great Britain, which with the mother country represented 434,286,650 people and 13,123,712 square miles of territory, were not united into a war-making machine. They represented within one empire the situation which existed among the independent states aligned with the Allies. The British Government could not with authority call upon them for a specific quota of men or supplies. Conscription could not constitutionally be applied to the whole empire without the consent of the dominions. Organization for war was needed, and this was accomplished, first, by forming a British War Cabinet, whose members were to concern them-

HOW THE LEAGUE WAS BORN

selves solely with problems of the war; and second, by a unique body called the Imperial War Cabinet. In the past there had, on special occasions, been meetings of representatives of the various dominions in Imperial Conferences. The occasion for summoning an Imperial War Cabinet gave it special significance. It consisted of the British War Cabinet together with the prime ministers, or their representatives, of Canada, Australia, New Zealand, Newfoundland, and South Africa, a representative of the Government of India, and the Secretary of State for the Colonies who spoke on behalf of the Crown Colonies and Protectorates. This Cabinet devoted itself strictly to problems involved in the conduct of the war and the larger issues of imperial policy connected with the war. The Overseas Representatives met also, under the presidency of the Secretary of State for the Colonies, as an Imperial War Conference to discuss non-war problems or questions connected with the war but of lesser importance.[1] Adjustments for war purposes were made within the other allied sovereign states, none of them, however, involving anything analogous to the Imperial War Cabinet. Then followed by various steps the organization of a better coöperative system among the states themselves. This development is described more fully in Chapter XIV. Suffice it to say here that, through the Paris Conference of 1917, attended by representatives of seventeen states, plans were made and organs created for removing elements of conflict in the operations of the Allies, both as to military and economic matters, with results which were most in evidence when the armistice with Germany was signed on November 11, 1918. The coöperative efforts of the Allied governments were coördinated by a Supreme War Council created in November, 1917. Meanwhile, there had been going on practically throughout the world a determined agitation for the creation, at the end of the war, of some general agency for world coöperation by which future wars might be prevented. The resulting proposals are summarized at the end of Chapter V. The effect of this propaganda, combined with the logic of events, was that when the armistice was signed, the world, including the Teutonic Powers, was ready for

[1] The War Cabinet, 1917, p. 5-11.

some kind of league. War-weary, and foreseeing perhaps a century which must be devoted to recuperation, the states saw in cooperation for mutual protection, as well as for mutual rehabilitation, the primary need of the world. This conviction was by no means unique in history, except that it was more widespread than ever before. It was, in fact, a repetition of phenomena which have appeared after nearly every great war of the last four centuries. But it was now felt by many that the Balance of Power had been discredited, that treaties of guarantee were not alone sufficient, and that something new and more definite must be invented. The difficulty lay in deciding how, when, where, and by whom the new scheme should be drafted, and when drafted, how it should be put into operation.

Here begins the story of the Peace Conference itself; for the method by which the peace terms were drafted, including the League Covenant, the way in which the initiative was taken, in whom lay the real power to act, are significant equally with the organization for the conduct of the war, as examples of how international affairs are carried on, and how the League is likely to work.

The Supreme War Council drew up the terms of the armistice in conference with the representatives of other Allied Powers, but the real decision was made by the Great Powers by whose arms and resources the war had been won. As later stated by Premier Clemenceau, when the smaller powers were demanding fuller representation in the committees of the Peace Conference, these Great Powers could have acted regardless of the opinion of all the others. "The five Powers," he said, "are obliged to say that they are in a position to justify their attitude. At the time of the Armistice they had together 12,000,000 men under arms on the battlefields. Their dead can be counted by millions. If the great idea of a Society of Nations did not shape the whole of our work here, it would have been possible for us five Great Powers to consult only ourselves in the settlement. That would have been, after all, our right. Well, that has never been our thought. We have asked all the nations interested in a settlement to meet us here. We

HOW THE LEAGUE WAS BORN

have asked them to give us their coöperation and their help."[1] The Supreme War Council, after renewing the armistice, resolved itself into a Supreme Council to deal with the terms of peace, and either officially or in informal conferences made the preliminary plans for the Peace Conference. It decided when the Conference should meet, what states should be admitted to it, and how they should be represented. It decided on forms of procedure, the organization of the Conference, both temporary and permanent, and in short all of the matters which an official committee on arrangements would have attended to. When the first meeting of the Conference was held on January 18, 1919, at the Quai d'Orsay, the regulations to govern its work were ready for distribution. Although they were varied from time to time, they should here be printed in full as the only official statement that was issued.

Official Statement of the Regulations Governing the Work of the Conference:[2]

I. The Conference assembled to fix the conditions of peace, first in the preliminaries of peace and then in the definite treaty of peace, shall include the representatives of the belligerent Allied and associated Powers. The belligerent Powers with general interests (the United States of America, the British Empire, France, Italy, and Japan) shall take part in all sittings and commissions. The belligerent Powers with particular interests (Belgium, Brazil, the British Dominions and India, China, Cuba, Greece, Guatemala, Haiti, Hedjaz, Honduras, Liberia, Nicaragua, Panama, Poland, Portugal, Rumania, Serbia, Siam, and the Czecho-Slovak Republic) shall take part in the sittings at which questions concerning them are discussed. The Powers in a state of diplomatic rupture with the enemy Powers (Bolivia, Ecuador, Peru, and Uruguay) shall take part in the sittings at which questions concerning them are discussed. Neutral Powers and States in process of formation may be heard either orally or in writing when summoned by the Powers with general interests at sittings devoted especially to the examination of questions directly concerning them, but only so far as these questions are concerned.

II. The Powers shall be represented by Plenipotentiary Dele-

---

[1] Current History, 9:389, March, 1919.
[2] Text as published by the London Times, Monday, January 20, 1919.

gates to the number of five for the United States of America, the British Empire, France, Italy, and Japan; three for Belgium, Brazil, and Serbia; two for China, Greece, Hedjaz, Poland, Portugal, Rumania, Siam, and the Czecho-Slovak Republic; one for Cuba, Guatemala, Haiti, Honduras, Liberia, Nicaragua, and Panama; one for Bolivia, Ecuador, Peru, and Uruguay. The British Dominions and India shall be represented as follows: Two delegates each for Australia, Canada, South Africa, and India (including the Native States); one delegate for New Zealand. Although the number of delegates may not exceed the figures above mentioned, each delegation has the right to avail itself of the panel system. The representation of the Dominions (including Newfoundland) and India may besides be included in the representation of the British Empire by the panel system. Montenegro shall be represented by one delegate, but the rules concerning the designation of this delegate shall not be fixed until the moment when the political situation of this country shall have been cleared up. The conditions of the representation of Russia shall be fixed by the Conference at the moment when the matters concerning Russia are examined.

III. Each delegation of Plenipotentiaries may be accompanied by technical delegates properly accredited and by two stenographers. The technical delegates may be present at the sittings for the purpose of furnishing information which may be asked of them. They shall be allowed to speak for the purpose of giving any desired explanations.

IV. The delegates take precedence according to the alphabetical order in French of the Powers.

V. The Conference will be declared open by the President of the French Republic. The President of the Council of French Ministers will be invested temporarily with the Chairmanship. Immediately after this, a Committee, composed of one Plenipotentiary of each of the great Allied or associated Powers, shall proceed at once to the authentication of the credentials of all members present.

VI. In the course of the first meeting, the Conference will proceed to appoint a permanent President and four Vice-Presidents chosen from the Plenipotentiaries of the Great Powers in alphabetical order.

VII. A Secretariat appointed from outside Plenipotentiaries and composed of one representative of the United States of America, one of the British Empire, one of France, one of Italy, and one of Japan, will be submitted to the approval of the Conference by the

HOW THE LEAGUE WAS BORN

President, who will be the controlling authority responsible for its operations. This Secretariat will be entrusted with the task of drafting protocols of the meetings, of classifying the archives, of providing for the administrative organization of the Conference, and generally of ensuring the regular and punctual working of the services entrusted to it. The head of the Secretariat will have charge of, and be responsible for, the protocols and archives. The archives will always be open to the members of the Conference.

VIII. The publicity of the proceedings shall be ensured by official communiqués which shall be prepared by the Secretariat for publication. In case of disagreement as to the drafting of these communiqués the matter shall be referred to the principal Plenipotentiaries or their representatives.

IX. All documents intended for inclusion in the protocols must be handed in in writing by the Plenipotentiaries presenting them. No document or proposition may be submitted save by one of the Plenipotentiaries or in his name.

X. Plenipotentiaries wishing to make a proposal unconnected with the questions on the agenda or not arising from the discussion shall give notice of the same twenty-four hours in advance in order to facilitate discussion. However, exceptions can be made to this rule in the case of amendments or secondary questions, but not in the case of substantive proposals.

XI. Petitions, memoranda, observations, or documents forwarded to the Conference by any person other than Plenipotentiaries must be received and classified by the Secretariat. Such of these communications as are of political interest will be briefly summarized in a list to be distributed to all the Plenipotentiaries. This list will be kept up to date as analogous communications are received. All such documents will be deposited in the archives.

XII. The discussion of the questions to be decided will comprise a first and a second reading. The first will consist of general discussion with the object of obtaining agreement on matters of principle. Subsequently, there will be a second reading for more detailed examination.

XIII. The Plenipotentiaries shall have the right, subject to the agreement of the Conference, to authorize their technical delegates to submit technical explanations on such points as may be deemed useful. If the Conference thinks it advisable, the technical examination of any particular question may be entrusted to a committee of technical delegates, whose duty it will be to report and suggest solutions.

XIV. The protocols drawn up by the Secretariat shall be printed and distributed in proof to the delegates in the shortest possible time in order to expedite the work of the Conference. The communication thus made in advance shall take the place of the reading of the protocols at the beginning of each meeting. If no alteration is proposed by the Plenipotentiaries, the text shall be deemed approved and be entered in the archives. If any alteration is proposed, its text shall be read by the President at the beginning of the following meeting. In any case, the protocol must be read out in full at the request of any Plenipotentiary.

XV. A committee shall be formed for drafting the resolutions adopted. This committee shall concern itself only with questions which have been decided. Its sole duty shall be to draw up the text of the decisions adopted and to present it for the approval of the Conference. It shall be composed of five members not forming part of the Plenipotentiary Delegates, and composed of one representative of the United States of America, one of the British Empire, one of France, one of Italy, and one of Japan.

Throughout these regulations it will be observed that prominence is given to "belligerent Powers with general interests," states which in the Peace Treaty are designated as the "principal Allied and Associated Powers," viz., the United States, the British Empire, France, Italy, and Japan.

At the first Plenary Session of the Conference, the inaugural speech was made by President Poincaré, and President Wilson, seconded by Lloyd George, nominated Premier Clemenceau as President of the Conference. The latter then briefly outlined the programme of work and announced that the first questions to be considered were (1) responsibility of the authors of the war, (2) penalties for crimes committed during the war, (3) international legislation in regard to labor. The members of the Conference were invited to send written memoranda on these questions to the Secretariat, and then the session adjourned.

The constructive work of the Peace Conference was done through councils and commissions. The chief of these was the Supreme Council which consisted of the two ranking delegates from each of the five principal Allied and Associated Powers, and was popularly known as the Big Ten. Even this small group proved at times during the Conference to be too large, and so there were formed other groups successively known as the Big Five, The Big Four, and the Big Three. First, the second ranking delegates were eliminated, leaving a council of five, then Japan's representative dropped out, leaving four members, and then Italy, for a time, leaving three. The Big Ten as an organ of the Conference seems to have been retained in spite of these changes so that if need be the conclusions of the smaller groups could be submitted to it; and, moreover, since a state of war still existed this Supreme Council of the Conference sometimes sat as a Supreme War Council of the allied belligerents with military members present. On February 9, an Inter-Allied Supreme Economic Council was created to consider certain matters connected with the Armistice. After this time the Armistice Commission with civilian members added reported to this Council.

Ultimately, numerous commissions, with technical experts as members, were formed. The principal powers had, before the Armistice, been at work individually in preparation for the problems of the peace terms, and their plenipotentiaries were accompanied by corps of specialists. Besides the commissions on territorial problems, the Conference appointed commissions on Responsibility for the War; Reparation for Damages; International Labor Legislation; International Control over Ports, Waterways, and Railways; Economic Drafting; Financial Drafting; and a Commission on the Formation of a League of Nations.

The second Plenary Session of the Paris Conference was held on January 25, 1919. Its first business was the unanimous adoption of a resolution read by Premier Clemenceau, which had been drafted by the Supreme Council, and which contained the following provision for a Committee on the formation of a League of Nations:

> It is essential to the maintenance of the world settlement which the associated nations are now met to establish that a League of Nations be created to promote international obligations and to provide safeguards against war.
> This League should be created as an integral part of the general treaty of peace and should be open to every civilized nation which can be relied on to promote its objects.

The members of the League should periodically meet in international conference and should have a permanent organization and secretaries to carry on the business of the League in the intervals between the conferences.

The Conference therefore appoints a committee, representative of the associated Governments, to work out the details of the constitution and the functions of the League and the draft of resolutions in regard to breaches of the laws of war for presentation to the Peace Conference.[1]

After the reading of the resolution, addresses were made in support of it by President Wilson; Premier Lloyd George; Signor Orlando, Italian Premier; Leon Bourgeois, French delegate; and representatives of other states. The Belgian delegate M. Hymans, however, requested an explanation of the last clause of the resolution relating to the appointment of a committee. In reply, Premier Clemenceau announced the decision that the committee was to be made up of two representatives for each of the five Great Powers and five to be elected by all the other powers. He then named the delegates chosen by the Great Powers and suggested that the nineteen other powers should meet on the following Monday to elect their delegates. It was at this point that the whole question of the representation of the minor powers on the Conference Committees was raised, delegates from Belgium, Brazil, Greece, Canada, Czechoslovakia, Rumania, Siam, China, and Poland participating in the discussion. They were answered by M. Clemenceau in a significant speech, from which the above quotation was made. This set all official protest at rest, and the representatives of the small powers met on January 27, with M. Jules Cambon, French delegate, presiding. For the League Commission, they selected as their joint representatives one delegate each from Belgium, Brazil, China, Serbia, and Portugal. Thus the complete Commission on the Formation of a League of Nations consisted of the following:

United States—President Wilson (Chairman) and Col. House.
British Empire—Lord Robert Cecil and Lieut. Gen. J. C. Smuts (South Africa).

[1] Current History, 9:383, March, 1919.

France—Leon Bourgeois and M. Larnaude.
Italy—Premier Orlando and Senator Scialoja.
Japan—Viscount Chinda and M. Ochiai.
Belgium—Paul Hymans.
Brazil—Epitacio Pessoa.
China—Wellington Koo.
Serbia—M. R. Vesnitch.
Portugal—Jaime B. Reis.

The first meeting of the Commission was held on February 3, President Wilson presiding. It had before it for discussion a printed text of a draft of a League Covenant, which had been agreed to before the organization of the Commission by President Wilson, Lord Cecil, General Smuts, and Premier Orlando. Daily sessions were held until February 13, when the tentative draft was adopted by the Commission. On the following day President Wilson read the draft at the third Plenary Session of the Peace Conference, and spoke in support of it. The document in full was made public, and the suspension of sessions of the Commission, on account of President Wilson's return to the United States, gave opportunity throughout the world for criticism, discussion, and debate. This interval was of the greatest importance, especially for those states where treaties must be ratified by the legislature, since the League Covenant, in accordance with the resolution of January 25, was to "be created as an integral part of the general treaty of peace." President Wilson reached Boston on February 24 and addressed a meeting in Mechanics' Hall. While he was on the ocean, discussion of the League draft began in the United States Senate, objections being made that it was a surrender of United States sovereignty, that it disregarded the Monroe Doctrine, and that it committed the United States to a policy of entangling alliances with the power of decision in the hands of foreign states. The criticisms were summed up by Senator Lodge on February 28 and by Senator Knox on March 1. The opposition culminated in a resolution presented by Senator Lodge but not put to vote. It was signed by thirty-nine Republicans who would be members of the Senate when the Treaty would be presented for approval, and it stated that "the constitution of the League of Nations in the form now proposed to the Peace Conference should not be accepted by the United States." Immediately after this incident President Wilson, on March 4, addressed an audience in New York, and sailed for Europe. He landed at Brest on March 13.

Daily sessions of the League Commission were resumed on March 18. Thus far, only belligerents had had an opportunity to express opinion on the League draft, and since it was the intention to invite all states eventually to join, an invitation was sent out by the Peace Conference to all the neutral nations in Europe, Asia, and South America to attend a private and unofficial conference in Paris on March 20. A sub-committee of the League Commission was appointed to receive the neutral delegates. Thirteen states sent representatives. A number of proposed amendments were submitted, one by Switzerland being intended to safeguard the Monroe Doctrine.

The result of all this discussion and revision was an amended draft of a League Covenant, which was adopted by the Plenary Session of the Conference on April 28, 1919. The adoption was of course not final or binding on the respective states, because the Covenant was to form part of the Peace Treaty, which itself was yet to be drawn up, signed by the representatives of the states, and formally ratified by the states themselves. In order, however, to make preparations for the preliminary organization of the League, President Wilson introduced the following resolutions, which were adopted:

Mr. President—I take the opportunity to move the following resolutions in order to carry out the provisions of the covenant: You will notice that the covenant provides that the first Secretary-General shall be chosen by this conference. It also provides that the first choice of the four member States who are to be added to the five great powers on the Council is left to this conference.

I move, therefore, that the first Secretary-General of the Council shall be the honorable Sir James Eric Drummond, and, second, that, until such time as the assembly shall have selected the first four members of the League to be represented on the Council in accordance with Article IV of the covenant, representatives of

HOW THE LEAGUE WAS BORN

Belgium, Brazil, Greece, and Spain shall be members, and, third, that the powers to be represented on the Council of the League of Nations are requested to name representatives who shall form a committee of nine to prepare plans for the organization of the League and for the establishment of the seat of the League and to make arrangements and to prepare the agenda for the first meeting of the assembly, this committee to report both to the Council and the Assembly of the League.[1]

The organization committee did not meet until May 5, but in the meantime informal conferences were held, at which the work of the committee was mapped out. These plans included the organization of temporary headquarters in London during the summer of 1919, preparations for the first meeting of the League which was to have been called by President Wilson to meet in Washington in October, 1919, and the establishment of the permanent headquarters at Geneva, Switzerland. The committee itself at its first meeting in Paris, May 5, was attended by the following: Stephen Pichon, France; Col. E. M. House, United States; Lord Robert Cecil, Great Britain; Marquis Imperiali, Italy; Viscount Chinda, Japan; Rolin Jacquemyns, Belgium; Eleutherios Venizelos, Greece; Guinones de Leon, Spain; and Antonio O. de Magalhaes, Brazil. On motion of Col. House, M. Pichon was elected chairman.

Meanwhile, the stage was being set for the Versailles Peace Congress of 1919. On May 1 the German delegates presented their credentials, and received those of the Allies, and on May 7, the anniversary of the sinking of the *Lusitania*, the Treaty of Peace was presented to them. Part I consists of the League of Nations Covenant, while there are references to the Covenant in many of the other sections. The Treaty is the longest ever drafted. It contains about 87,000 words, divided into fifteen parts, with 440 Articles, not including numerous Annexes. It was produced by over 1,000 experts working continuously for three and a half months. It is printed in parallel pages of English and French, both texts having equal validity. It does not deal with questions affecting Austria, Bulgaria, and Turkey except in so far as it binds

---
[1] Current History, 10:506, June, 1919.

Germany to accept any agreements reached with her former allies. The signatures of the High Contracting Parties were affixed in the Hall of Mirrors in the Palace of Versailles, at 3:15 P.M., Paris time, on June 28, 1919. Article 440 of the Treaty makes arrangements for its ratification. "The deposit of ratification," it says, "shall be made at Paris as soon as possible. Powers of which the seat of the government is outside Europe will be entitled merely to inform the government of the French Republic through their diplomatic representatives at Paris that their ratification has been given; in that case they must transmit the instrument of ratification as soon as possible. A first procès-verbal of the deposit of ratifications will be drawn up as soon as the Treaty has been ratified by Germany on the one hand and by three of the Principal Allied and Associated Powers on the other. From the date of this first procès-verbal the Treaty will come into force between the High Contracting Parties who have ratified it. For the determination of all periods of time provided for in the present Treaty this date will be the date of the coming into force of the Treaty.

"In all other respects the treaty will enter into force for each power at the date of the deposit of its ratification."

These plans for the ratification of the Treaty and the institution of the League were not destined to be carried out as rapidly as had been anticipated; and after ratification by Germany and three of the Principal Allied Powers, the deposit of the ratification documents in Paris and the issuance of the procès-verbal of the deposit were delayed in the hope that the League might come into being with the United States as one of its original members. Eventually, it became necessary to proceed without the United States, and therefore Germany and fourteen Allied Powers exchanged ratifications and finished signing the procès-verbal in the Clock Hall of the French Ministry of Foreign Affairs, Paris, at 4:11 P. M., on January 10, 1920. Immediately thereafter, Premier Clemenceau announced "The protocol between the Allied and Associated Powers and Germany has been signed. The ratifications of the treaty with Germany have been deposited. From this moment the treaty enters into effect. It will be enforced in all its terms." The original

HOW THE LEAGUE WAS BORN

members of the League of Nations were therefore the fourteen Allied Powers who had ratified the Treaty, together with the British Dominions and India, viz., British Empire, Canada, Australia, South Africa, New Zealand, India, France, Italy, Japan, Belgium, Bolivia, Brazil, Guatemala, Panama, Peru, Poland, Siam, Czechoslovakia, and Uruguay. Other states mentioned in the Annex to the Covenant, in rapid succession, either ratified the treaty or acceded to the Covenant.

During the period between the signing and the exchange of ratifications of the Treaty, the prospective Secretary-General of the League and the Committee on organization of the League were at work in London and elsewhere. The Supreme Council of the Peace Conference having set the date, President Wilson in accordance with Article 5 of the Covenant, on January 12 issued the summons for the first meeting of the League Council to be held in Paris on January 16, 1920, at 10:30 A. M. at the French Ministry of Foreign Affairs. The meeting was held in the Clock Hall, the following representatives being present: Bourgeois (France), Curzon (British Empire), Matsui (Japan), da Cunha (Brazil), Venizelos (Greece), Ferraris (Italy), de Leon (Spain), and Hymans (Belgium). The first action of the Council was the election of M. Bourgeois as permanent chairman, who immediately formally installed Sir Eric Drummond as Secretary-General. The second meeting of the Council was held in London in the Picture Gallery of St. James Palace, February 11 to 13.

Thus was the League of Nations born, and thus did it begin its work without the participation of the United States.

References for Chapter III

THE WAR CABINET. Report for 1917.
Documents Regarding the Peace Conference.
  (International Conciliation, No. 139, June, 1919.)
THE SUPREME WAR COUNCIL.
  (Current History, 7: pt. 1, p. 434-346, December, 1917.)
INTERALLIED CONFERENCE AT PARIS.
  (Current History, 7: pt. 2, p. 89-91, January, 1918.)

FENWICK, C. G. Organization and Procedure of the Peace Conference. (American Political Science Review, 13:199-212, May, 1919.)

MUNRO, H. F. The Berlin Congress. Washington, 1918.

DUGGAN. The League of Nations, p. 50-63 (Chapter by J. P. Cotton and D. W. Morrow).

CHAPTER IV

SALIENT FEATURES OF THE LEAGUE COVENANT

THAT the Covenant of the League of Nations is an epoch-making document is now a commonplace. Gladstone's phrase so often quoted concerning the Constitution of the United States, that it is "the most wonderful work ever struck off at a given time by the brain and purpose of man," must now be applied to the League Covenant, if it be worthy of the great purposes which drew it forth. With such purposes and such a document, one can approach the task of describing it only with trepidation. Many years will pass before any one can form a true estimate of its character, its functions, its practicability, and its wisdom. But it is the duty of everyone to make the attempt lest its good features be made of no avail through ignorance, and its bad features be perpetuated through inertia. At best it is an experiment worthy of a fair trial; and at worst, it can prove only a failure from which fruitful lessons may be drawn. It may be that ardent advocates of the League are doomed to disappointment because too much is expected of an agreement not well understood; and on the contrary, the practical working of the League may win over its most positive opponents. Whether the plan set forth in the Covenant be good or bad, one thing is certain: its success or failure depends on the wisdom, ability, and character of the men and women in whose hands the functioning of the League is placed. Even a poor plan may be made to work well, if wisely administered; and likewise the best-laid plans may fail for want of master minds. Never in the political history of the world has so much depended on the right choice of representatives by the respective states. They must be persons who know the history, national characteristics, and aspirations of their own states, but who have vision to look into the future, courage to make precedents as well as follow them, strength to combat opposition with logic, industry to acquire facts, and loyalty to a cause even when they are in the minority. Character and ability combined were never so necessary in the political affairs of men.

Probably no document in the world's history has brought forth so much in the nature of commentary as this Covenant is destined to produce. In every state, throughout the world, whether original members of the League or not, the minds and pens of men are at work; and the reactions produced by points of contact and conflict between the constitutions, laws, decisions, religions, morals, and customs of the respective states and the League Covenant are of infinite variety. No one mind can grasp the many-sided aspects of the truth; but all must try. Here, therefore, are pointed out some of the salient features of the Covenant—those which stand out as obviously important for study. Positive or dogmatic statements cannot be made; but only the bare outlines of a study with many questions left unanswered.

Before attempting a general survey of the document itself, let us consider its nature apart from its contents. Unquestionably it forms part of a treaty and will be open to construction along with the rest of the Treaty of Peace with Germany. It is also part of the treaties of peace with Austria, Turkey, and Bulgaria, and thus forms a connecting link between all four treaties. By these treaties the four states assent to the League Covenant, but do not immediately become members of the League itself. All the other signatories to the treaties, subject to ratification, are original members. Its character as an integral part of a treaty imposed on vanquished enemies is thus emphasized. For them, it was quite as obligatory as a prerequisite to peace as any other section of the Treaty. While it was drawn up and adopted by the Peace Conference as a separate document, it now appears as Part I, in twenty-six articles, of each of the peace treaties. When we examine the Treaty with Germany, we find that the Covenant and the other parts are inextricably interwoven. But with one exception the references are from the other parts to the Covenant, and not *vice versa*. The one exception is in Article 5, relating to voting and procedure. "Except where otherwise expressly provided in the Covenant, *or by the terms of the present Treaty*," this article reads; and the italicized phrase was inserted after the draft of the Covenant was completed. After reading the draft at the Plenary Session of the Peace Conference on April 28, 1919, President Wilson moved the insertion of the words, explaining that "in several parts of the Treaty of which this Covenant will form a part, certain duties are assigned to the Council of the League of Nations. In some instances it is provided that the action they shall take shall be by a majority vote. It is therefore necessary to make the covenant conform with the other portions of the Treaty by adding these words."[1]

In the rest of the Treaty, on the other hand, we find the League of Nations referred to by name seventy-one times. It is, in fact, one of the agents of the signatories for making the Treaty effective so that it may be in very truth not merely a scrap of paper. It was a burning question at the Peace Conference as in the United States whether peace should not first be made and then the League constituted. The Conference committed itself to the plan followed when at its second session, January 25, 1919, it resolved that "this League should be created as an integral part of the general Treaty of Peace"; and it assigned to the League so many duties in connection with the return to peace and the reconstitution of Europe that these alone justify its creation. If there had been no league, then other agencies must have been created for the same purpose; and these would have operated without the unifying influence of a permanent organization.

There can be no doubt that the Covenant is an integral part of the treaty; but it stands in many respects on a different footing from the other provisions. Its permanence is a distinguishing characteristic. It will remain in force, if the intention is carried out, long after the other sections have been executed. When the duties specifically assigned to it in connection with the return to peace have been done, its primary functions will still remain to be

[1] International Conciliation, June, 1919, p. 848.

performed. The League will in fact continue its life much as though it had been created by a separate treaty. It is not static; provision is made for change; and it is self-perpetuating. Something new in the history of international relations has happened. The League has many of the characteristics of an offensive and defensive alliance. Certainly the members agree to support each other even by war when specified contingencies arise; and there are those who contend that the chief effect of the Covenant is to organize the control already in the hands of the five Great Powers. But that is to say that words do not have their plain meaning, that nothing has been learned by the European war, and that as of old "to the victor belong the spoils." If only an alliance were intended, why admit other states? Power was and is in the hands of the United States, Great Britain, France, Italy, and Japan. They could have made the peace and their alliance without regard to other states. Did they form a league in order more completely to organize their power over the world, or were they distrustful of each other? No one is competent to answer; but as has been shown, the idea of a balance of power cannot be eliminated. It will exist informally if not formally. For a mere alliance, much unnecessary machinery has been created; machinery which would retard the movements of an alliance and bring into the reckoning many disturbing elements.

Taking the Covenant at its face value, it is something more than a treaty of alliance. According to one group it has produced only an efficient organ for coöperation, which binds no state except by its own consent; while equally authoritative students contend that there has been reared a corporation of tremendous power controlling not only its members, but stretching out its hands to the entire world. The Covenant, says Dr. David J. Hill,[1] "creates a new legal person, acting by itself in a manner to be determined by itself, and in accordance with rules to be adopted by itself. It creates a body, at first called the Executive Council, which, in turn, chooses and directs its own organs of action, defines their rights and duties, and confers new authority upon them. It creates obli-

---
[1] Present Problems in Foreign Policy, p. 111–112.

FEATURES OF LEAGUE COVENANT

gations on the part of the nations composing the League which these nations owe not to one another but to the League, as a distinct and separate legal person, who can call them to account for non-performance of duty and inflict punishment upon them. It attributes to the League as a corporate entity powers which, under international law, the separate states do not, either singly or in combination, themselves possess; thus creating an *imperium* over states not belonging to the League, which is empowered to coerce and punish them for not submitting to its decisions. The duties of the officers of the League are duties to the League, not to the component states, which cannot separately hold them to accountability or punish them for excesses or disobedience."

Another form of attack on the League is to liken it to a "voting trust" in which the majority of the stock of several corporations is transferred to a central committee or board of trustees, which while issuing to the stockholders certificates showing their interests and rights to dividends, exercises the voting power of the stock in electing boards of directors for the various associated corporations, and thus directs their policy for the common object of lessening competition and increasing profits. The Council of the League is the object of attack by the above critics because in it is concentrated most of the power which the League possesses. Sometimes it is urged, not that power is itself a danger, but that the League is not a good example of a central world organization endowed with power. It is contended, with very cogent arguments, that in the present League not only has the Council, and to a lesser degree the Assembly, legislative and executive power, but judicial power also. This contention has reference chiefly to the provisions of Article 15.

The advocates of the League see none of these dangers inherent in the Covenant. If power is granted, it is by agreement as far as it affects the member states; and with regard to non-members, it is justified by the interest of the world in the maintenance of peace. They see no infringement of national sovereignty, or if admitting it, foresee liberty for states as a result of limitation of rights. Something of this viewpoint is evidenced by the title of the document. It is a covenant, not a constitution. Constitutions have association with politically organized states and are law. A covenant, in law, is a special form of contract. It is both written and under seal, and thus is the most formal and binding of all contracts. But the word in a more general use has a moral or religious sense, meaning a solemn mutual agreement to strive for high ends. In the interpretation of covenants the prime motive is to give effect to the intention of the covenanters. If the League of Nations Covenant is both legally and morally a solemn agreement for the accomplishment of ends admitted to be in themselves worthy, then its advocates and their opponents really recruit themselves from those who accept, on the one hand, or doubt, on the other, the sincerity of the states which have associated themselves in the League. Distrust can only be removed by demonstration of sincerity, and so there devolves on the world the duty of giving to the League membership, and particularly to the dominant five, the opportunity of proving that in certain great matters the general interests are for them predominant over the special interests—the international over the national.

The League Covenant is in form a mutual agreement to accomplish the purposes stated in the Preamble. These purposes are not new to international society. Coöperation, peace, and security, fair dealings between states, respect for law, and the keeping of treaty obligations—these are fundamental in the theory of international relations. But the machinery for bringing practice more nearly at one with these ideals has never been operated on so large a scale as is now proposed. What, then, is this organization set up to promote international coöperation, peace, and security?

The League of Nations is an organization in which the members are either self-governing states, colonies, or dominions. They do not therefore all possess complete external sovereignty. Among the original members are Canada, Australia, South Africa, New Zealand, and India. These British dominions and possessions not only are members of the League, but they had accredited representatives at the Peace Conference who participated in its deliberations and committee work, and signed the Peace Treaty with

Germany.[1] The contemplated original members of the League numbered thirty-two. Thirteen other states listed in the Annex were invited to join. They did so by acceding without reservations to the Covenant by depositing declarations with the Secretariat of the League within two months of the coming into force of the Covenant (Art. 1). Among the states not original members, or specifically invited to join, are Germany, Austria, Turkey, Bulgaria, Russia, Mexico, Costa Rica, Santo Domingo, and Luxemburg. They, if deemed to be self-governing, may gain admittance through a two-thirds vote of the Assembly, if they give "effective guarantees" of their sincere intention to observe their international obligations, and if they accept the regulations of the League in regard to their military, naval, and air forces, and armaments. A member may withdraw, after two years' notice, "provided that all its international obligations and all its obligations under this Covenant shall have been fulfilled at the time of its withdrawal" (Art. 1). There are thus two classes of obligations to be considered: first, those between states without reference to the League, and second, those incurred by the act of agreement to the Covenant. By Article 9, a permanent commission is created to advise the Council concerning the provisions of Article 1. The Council apparently must decide whether a state which has given notice of withdrawal has fulfilled all of its obligations. If there should be a dispute on this point, it probably would be referred to the Assembly or to a court of arbitration. There is another method of release from the League which seems to be inconsistent with the foregoing. By Article 16, it is declared that "any member of the League which has violated any covenant of the League may be declared to be no longer a member of the League by a vote of the Council concurred in by the representatives of all the other members of the League represented thereon."

---

[1] It should be noted, however, that they are not named in the Preamble of the Treaty, except among the representatives of the "British Empire." The latter expression is now used for the first time in an international treaty. "His Majesty the King of the United Kingdom of Great Britain and Ireland and of the British Dominions beyond the Seas, Emperor of India" was represented at the signing of the Treaty by five plenipotentiaries, and in addition by others who signed in his name "for" Canada, Australia, South Africa, New Zealand, and India.

Does this mean that expulsion would release a member from its obligations under the Covenant? This does not seem likely, and doubtless such a member on expulsion would find itself at war with the League if it refused to meet its outstanding obligations. Finally, a state may cease to be a member by dissenting from an amendment duly made to the Covenant in accordance with Article 26. In this case we are left to assume that a state, all of whose obligations had been met, would immediately be released from membership. The requirement of two years' notice would not apply; but it is not clear what the situation would be if the state were not free of all obligations.

Membership of states and governments in an international organization, no matter what be its character, can only be effected through the agency of human beings. In the Family of Nations, intercourse is carried on through exchange of diplomatic representatives who reside at the seats of government of the respective states. This method, having many advantages, is fortunately in no way affected by the creation of the League. Every full-fledged state will continue to maintain permanent representation in every other such state; but colonies and dominions have the right neither to send nor receive diplomatic representatives. In diplomatic intercourse each state deals directly with every other, a means effective for that purpose, but cumbersome and slow when concerted action between many states is desired. In the deliberative and executive organs of the League we find representation given to non-sovereign dominions, and a means of direct contact for the representatives of all members at one and the same time. The representatives of the members of the League are not substitutes for their diplomatic officers; but they doubtless will reach agreements to be formally concluded by regular diplomatic means. Members of the League will therefore always participate in it through agents specially appointed by the states themselves to be associated in the organs of the League. These organs are (1) an Assembly, (2) a Council, (3) a Permanent Secretariat, (4) Permanent Commissions, and (5) a Permanent Court of International Justice later to be created.

FEATURES OF LEAGUE COVENANT

The Assembly (Art. 3) is the largest body created by the Covenant. Each member state may have not more than three representatives in it, but it may have less if it so desires. The number of the representatives does not affect the voting powers of a state. Each state has only one vote. The Assembly meets "at stated intervals and from time to time as occasion may require at the seat of the League" or at another place if it is so decided. The first meeting of the Assembly and of the Council "shall be summoned by the President of the United States" (Art. 5).

The Council (Art. 4), at the outset, was to consist of one representative from each of nine states. Five of these are the United States, the British Empire, France, Italy, and Japan, which, as denominated in the Treaty, are "the principal Allied and Associated Powers." These are always to have representatives on the Council. Until action is taken by the Assembly, the four other states represented are Belgium, Brazil, Spain, and Greece. With the approval of a majority of the Assembly, the Council may name additional permanent members, and with like approval, it may increase the number of states to be selected by the Assembly for transitory membership. No limit is placed on the number that may be added by such action, and therefore it would be possible for the Assembly and Council to raise the latter into a large body. This, however, is evidently not the intention. For the four transitory members named, four others may be substituted by the Assembly "from time to time in its discretion." When the Council is considering matters specially affecting a state not represented in it, that state "shall be invited to send a representative to sit as a member." It is not stated that this state will be given a vote, but "to sit as a member" perhaps implies this. The Council must meet at least once a year, and may meet oftener if occasion requires. Its regular meeting-place is the seat of the League, but other places may be chosen. As in the Assembly, each state has one vote. There is no arrangement for weighing or valuing the votes. All are of equal effect.

In both the Assembly and Council except where otherwise provided in the Covenant or in other parts of the Treaty, decisions require the agreement of all members represented at the meetings (Art. 5). This is a recognition of the legal equality of states. The exceptions to the unanimity rule in the Covenant are the following: (1) all matters of procedure including the appointment of committees of investigation may be regulated by majority vote of those present (Art. 5); (2) admission of new members requires only a two-thirds vote of the Assembly (Art. 1); (3) a majority of the Assembly may approve the designation by the Council of additional permanent and transitory members of the Council (Art. 4); (4) the Assembly may by majority vote approve the Council's appointment of a Secretary-General (Art. 6); (5) the Council by majority vote may decide to publish a report on an international dispute which it has not been able to settle (Art. 15); (6) in considering disputes involving a member or members of the Council, the votes of those members are not counted in the Council meetings (Art. 15); (7) in case a dispute is referred to the Assembly, its report must be concurred in by the representatives of those members of the League represented on the Council and by a majority of the other members exclusive in each case of the representatives of the parties to the dispute (Art. 15); (8) the Covenant may be amended when ratified by a majority of the members of the League represented in the Assembly, with the concurrence of all members whose representatives compose the Council (Art. 26). The amendments are effected by diplomatic ratifications, apart from the League organization, but the preliminary agreements would probably be made at meetings of the Council and Assembly, and the inference is that the Assembly might approve draft amendments by majority vote.

The general powers of the Council and Assembly are defined in identical terms. They may deal at their meetings "with any matter within the sphere of action of the League or affecting the peace of the world" (Arts. 3, 4). Definite powers and duties are also mentioned for each. The Assembly[1] specifically (1) may admit

---

[1] In listing the powers and duties of the Assembly and Council, and the obligations of the members, the order in which the provisions appear in the Covenant has been retained.

states as new members of the League (Art. 1); (2) shall select the four transitory members of the Council (Art. 4); (3) may approve enlargement of the Council (Art. 4); (4) shall regulate its own procedure and appoint its own committees (Art. 5); (5) shall approve or disapprove the Secretary-General appointed by the Council (Art. 6); (6) may receive information concerning circumstances affecting international relations which threaten the peace of the world (Art. 11); (7) shall consider and report within six months on disputes referred to it by the Council (Art. 15); (8) may advise the reconsideration by members of the League of treaties which have become inapplicable, and the consideration of international conditions whose continuance might endanger the peace of the world (Art. 19); (9) may, it is inferred, express its opinion on proposed amendments to the Covenant (Art. 26).

The specific powers and duties of the Council are more numerous. It (1) may propose increase in its membership to be approved by the Assembly (Art. 4); (2) shall invite parties to a dispute to sit at its meetings as members during consideration of that dispute (Art. 4); (3) shall regulate its own procedure and appoint committees (Art. 5); (4) shall appoint the Secretary-General for approval by the Assembly (Art. 6); (5) may change the seat of the League (Art. 7); (6) shall formulate plans for reduction of national armaments for acceptance by the states (Art. 8); (7) may give or withhold permission to exceed the limits agreed upon (Art. 8); (8) may revise the plans as to reduction of armaments at least every ten years (Art. 8); (9) shall advise how the evil effects of private manufacture of munitions and implements of war can be prevented (Art. 8); (10) shall advise the members of the League how to deal with any threat or danger of external aggression affecting the territorial integrity and existing political independence of a member (Art. 10); (11) may receive information concerning circumstances affecting international relations which threaten the peace of the world (Art. 11); (12) shall report within six months on disputes submitted to it (Arts. 12, 15); (13) shall propose steps to give effect to arbitral awards which have not been carried out by the parties (Art. 13); (14) shall formulate plans for the establishment of a

Permanent Court of International Justice (Art. 14); (15) may direct the publication of relevant facts and papers relating to a dispute submitted to it (Art. 15); (16) shall prepare and publish statements and reports of disputes settled by it (Art. 15); (17) shall publish a report on disputes submitted to it but not settled (Art. 15); (18) shall decide whether a matter submitted to it is solely within the domestic jurisdiction of a state (Art. 15); (19) may in any case refer disputes to the Assembly and shall do so on the request of either party made within fourteen days after the submisssion of the dispute to the Council (Art. 15); (20) shall recommend to the several governments what effective military or naval forces shall severally be contributed by them to the armed forces to be used to protect the covenants of the League (Art. 16); (21) may, by a vote unanimous except for the offending member, expel members from the League for violation of its covenants (Art. 16); (22) shall determine the conditions under which non-members engaged in disputes may be invited to accept the obligations of membership for the purposes of the dispute (Art. 17); (23) shall institute inquiries concerning disputes involving non-members who have accepted the invitation (Art. 17); (24) may take measures and make recommendations to prevent hostilities and settle disputes involving two non-members who refuse to accept the obligations of membership (Art. 17); (25) shall, if not previously agreed upon, define the degree of authority, control, or administration to be exercised by Mandatories (Art. 22); (26) shall receive the annual reports of the Mandatories (Art. 22); (27) may authorize the Secretariat to collect and distribute all relevant information and render other assistance in matters of international interest regulated by general coventions but not placed under the control of international bureaus or commissions (Art. 24); (28) may include in the expenses of the Secretariat, those of any bureau or commission which is placed under the direction of the League (Art. 24).

The third organ of the League is the Permanent Secretariat. It is the only organ of the League which functions continuously, and its duties are chiefly of a ministerial character. It is the business office of the League; but it has other functions involving the

FEATURES OF LEAGUE COVENANT

exercise of discretion. For a detailed description of it in connection with its prototypes, the reader is referred to Chapter XVIII.

Some of the activities of the League depend on an accurate and detailed knowledge of complex facts which can only be collected and digested by experts. Provision is therefore made in two instances for permanent commissions to assist the Council. The first of these is constituted to advise the Council on admissions to the League and withdrawals from it under Article 1, and to advise on reduction of armaments under Article 8, and on military and naval questions generally (Art. 9). The second is created to receive and examine the annual reports of the Mandatories, and to advise the Council on all matters relating to the observance of the mandates (Art. 22).

The fifth organ of the League is yet to be created. It is the judicial organ for which plans are to be formulated by the Council to be submitted to the members of the League for adoption. It is to be known as the Permanent Court of International Justice. No details concerning its probable constitution or membership are given; but two of its functions are stated. "The Court shall be competent," says Article 14, "to hear and determine any dispute of an international character which the parties thereto submit to it. The Court may also give an advisory opinion upon any dispute or question referred to it by the Council or by the Assembly." Since international courts are subsequently discussed in detail,[1] no extended notice is needed here. It should be observed, however, that the proposed court will have no jurisdiction over disputes without the consent of the parties. Its institution cannot therefore be used to prove that a world state has been created. On the contrary, it tends to indicate that the independence of states is to be respected.

Already reference has been made to the general purposes which the members of the League agree to promote (Preamble). We may now summarize the specific obligations and duties which are placed on the members by the Covenant, leaving a fuller treatment to subsequent chapters. The members agree (1) to pay their

[1] Post, Chapters XI and XII.

proportion of the expenses of the Secretariat (Art. 6). The expenses of representatives in the Council and Assembly are to be paid by the states represented, since neither these nor the means of supporting the two permanent commissions are provided for in the Covenant. They agree (2) not to exceed the limits of armaments to which they have consented, without the concurrence of the Council (Art. 8); (3) "to interchange full and frank information as to the scale of their armaments, their military and naval programmes and the condition of such of their industries as are adaptable to warlike purposes" (Art. 8); (4) "to respect and preserve as against external aggression the territorial integrity and existing political independence of all members of the League" (Art. 10); (5) in case of any war or threat of war to "take any action that may be deemed wise and effectual to safeguard the peace of nations" (Art. 11); (6) to submit disputes between them likely to lead to a rupture either to arbitration or to inquiry by the Council, and "in no case to resort to war until three months after the award by the arbitrators or the report by the Council" (Art. 12); (7) to submit to arbitration disputes recognized by them as suitable for submission to arbitration and which cannot be settled by diplomacy (Art. 13); (8) to carry out in good faith any award rendered, and not to "resort to war against a member of the League which complies therewith" (Art. 13); (9) to submit to the Council for investigation all disputes likely to lead to a rupture, which have not been submitted to arbitration, and to communicate to the Secretary-General as promptly as possible statements of their case with all relevant facts and papers. (Art. 15); (10) not to go to war with a party to a dispute which complies with the recommendations of the report of the Council unanimously adopted except by parties to the dispute (Art. 15); (11) to subject a covenant-breaking state to severance of all trade or financial relations, and the prohibition of all intercourse between the nationals of that state and the nationals of all other states, whether members of the League or not (Art. 16); (12) to contribute in a proportion to be recommended by the Council to the armed forces to be used to protect the covenants of the League (Art. 16); (13) mutually to support one another in the financial and economic measures taken, in order to distribute the losses and expenses, and to assist one another in resisting "any special measures aimed at one of their number by the covenant-breaking state" (Art. 16); (14) to afford passage through their territory to the forces of a coöperating member (Art. 16); (15) to register with the Secretariat every treaty or international engagement hereafter entered into by them, agreeing that otherwise they will not be binding (Art. 18); (16) to consider as abrogated all obligations or understandings inconsistent with the Covenant, and not hereafter to enter into any such inconsistent engagements (Art. 20); (17) to consider the well-being and development of backward peoples a sacred trust of civilization (Art. 22); (18) to endeavor to secure and maintain fair and humane conditions of labor for men, women, and children in all countries, and for that purpose to maintain the necessary international organizations (Art. 23); (19) to undertake to secure just treatment of the native inhabitants of territories under their control (Art. 23); (20) to intrust the League with the general supervision over the execution of agreements with regard to the traffic in women and children and in opium and other dangerous drugs (Art. 23); (21) to intrust the League with the general supervision of the trade in arms and ammunition wherever the control of this trade is a matter of common interest (Art. 23); (22) to make provision to secure and maintain freedom of communication and of transit and equitable treatment for the commerce of all members of the League (Art. 23); (23) to endeavor to take steps in matters of international concern for the prevention and control of disease (Art. 23); (24) to place under the direction of the League all International Bureaus or Commissions hereafter constituted for the regulation of matters of international interest (Art. 23); (25) to encourage and promote the establishment and coöperation of duly-authorized voluntary Red Cross organizations having as purposes improvement of health, the prevention of disease, and the mitigation of suffering throughout the world (Art. 25). The whole list of obligations is summed up by reiterating the two primary functions of the League, namely to promote international coöperation and to achieve international peace and security.

To secure action under most of these obligations it is not necessary that the organs of the League shall first take some step. The obligations either now exist, or will come into force on the happening of a stated contingency. This feature has caused it to be said of the League that it is automatic rather than delegated in form. Mr. Lowell,[1] comparing the two forms, says:

The automatic form is more simple, more primitive, but not ill-adapted to sovereign states whose duties to the League are so few that they can be specifically enumerated in a covenant. It consists in prescribing definitely the obligations which the members assume, or will assume on the happening of a certain event, and giving no authority to any representative body to exercise its discretion in issuing orders binding upon them. Suppose, for example, that a nation declares war on any member of the League; under the delegated form the representative body would meet, discuss the situation, determine the action to be taken by the members of the League, and issue its directions accordingly; while under the automatic form all the members of the League would be under an immediate obligation to perform the acts prescribed in the agreement, such as to cut off all intercourse with the offending state, to come in arms to the defense of the member attacked, or whatever the provision of the agreement for such a case might be, and they would do so without waiting for, without regard to, any action by a representative body of the League. . . . The automatic form of league has, therefore, the advantage that it provides a more effective guaranty of peace. Such a compact to combine for armed resistance against an aggressor on any one member would certainly have prevented Germany from making this war; whereas the delegated form of league might not have done so. . . .

Another advantage of the automatic form is that the obligations of the members are specifically stated, so that they know precisely what duties they assume under any conditions that may arise; while the delegated form leaves their obligations uncertain, to be determined at some future time by a representative body which may go further or less far than some of the members desired. Vigorous objection has been made in the United States to partnership in a league that would have authority to order this country what to do in case of an attack against another member of the League. The objection is not without cogency; but it does not apply to the Covenant of Paris, either in its original or its amended

---

[1] Duggan: League of Nations, p. 101-104.

form; for that Covenant has adopted as its basic principle the automatic type of league, fixing the obligations of the members and the sanctions for violation in the pact itself, instead of leaving them to be determined by a representative body. The Council of the League is, indeed, at liberty, and even enjoined, to advise or recommend further action by the members; but this each member undertakes only if it chooses to do so. The language is in that respect perfectly clear and consistent, unless we are to construe such words as "advise," "propose," and "recommend," in a sense quite contrary to their ordinary meaning.

Fortunately this automatic action is not confined to wars and threats of wars. It relates also to many vital matters which need attention during peace. By many, this function of the League is considered more important than that which relates directly to war. This phase of the subject is treated at length in Part III, *post*.

References for Chapter IV

ACADEMY OF POLITICAL SCIENCE. Proceedings, 8:no. 3, p. 15-49.
THE COVENANTER. N. Y., Doubleday Page & Co., 1919.
DUGGAN. The League of Nations, p. 96-111 (Chapter by A. L. Lowell).
HILL, D. J. Present Problems in Foreign Policy.
LEAGUE OF NATIONS. Comparison of the plan for the League of Nations, showing the original draft . . . together with the Covenant as finally reported.
(Senate Doc. no. 46. 66th Cong. 1st Sess.)

CHAPTER V

PROPOSALS FOR A LEAGUE OF NATIONS

THE long path which war has worn through the world's history is strewn with discarded plans for world organization and the preservation of peace. From time to time, either during the conflict or just after its close, men turn their minds to measures of prevention. "In the contraries of peace," said William Penn, "we see the beauties and benefits of it . . . It is a great mark of the corruption of our natures . . . that we cannot . . . know the comfort of peace, but by the smart and penance of the vices of war."[1] In the past, the desire for some new adjustment of state relations has tended to become quiescent as soon as peace has returned and men are again going about their daily tasks. But many of the proposals for change were committed to printing and were preserved for later study. They form a group of projects and schemes and visions that were never put to the test, and which existed only in the minds of men and in the books written by them. The books which embody these abortive schemes cannot be disregarded, for they trace the development of the idea of peace and of internationalism. When looked at in their proper setting of events, they acquire significant application to present-day problems, and form a background for the League of Nations of to-day.

Only a few of the plans can be noted here. They are set forth and commented on at length in Ter Meulen's Gedanke der Internationalen Organisation, published at The Hague, 1917.[2]

The first of the schemes of world organization which has been selected for comment is of importance not so much for its own sake as because of the great book which it produced. In 1513 there were not

---
[1] Essay Toward the Present and Future Peace of Europe, Section 1.
[2] For a list of books containing the earlier proposals see Appendix 8.

only rumors of war but there was war itself. The English King Henry VIII was at odds with both France and Scotland; France was invading Italy, and just ending a conflict with Spain. In 1514 Wolsey made peace with France, and the Treaty of Bologna (1516) ended the French war with Italy a year after Francis I came to the throne. It was a natural time for propounding a scheme to prevent war, and during these wars one was brought forward by William of Ciervia, and John Sylvagius, Chancellor of Burgundy. We learn about it in a letter written by Erasmus,[1] who says that the plan was to assemble a Congress of Kings at Cambray, to consist of Maximilian the Emperor, Francis the First of France, Henry the Eighth of England, and Charles of the Low Countries. They were to enter into a permanent agreement to maintain the peace of Europe. "But certain persons," says Erasmus, "who get nothing by peace, and a great deal by war, threw obstacles in the way, which prevented this truly kingly purpose from being carried into execution. After this great disappointment, I sat down and wrote, by desire of John Sylvagius, my Querela Pacis, or Complaint of Peace. But, since that period," he continues, "things have been growing worse and worse; and I believe I must soon compose the Epitaph, instead of the Complaint of Peace; as she seems to be dead and buried, and not very likely to revive." Of this great book, first issued in 1516, many editions were printed. The first American edition appeared in Boston in 1813, and the last in Chicago, 1917.

The peace between England and France was, however, the occasion for a treaty of alliance between some of the monarchs mentioned above for securing a lasting peace. It was signed in St. Paul's Cathedral, London, on October 2, 1518, by Henry VIII and the French plenipotentiaries; and Charles of Spain and Pope Leo X later acceded to it. A league was formed whose members were to be "friends of the friends and foes of the foes" of any of them. If any state bound by the treaty should invade, attack, or injure the dominions of any member, all the others agreed to take arms against that state within two months, and in certain cases to furnish fleets of war-ships. The treaty expressly excepted from its

[1] See the preface to his Complaint of Peace, Boston, 1813, p iii-iv.

scope civil wars unless instigated by one of the contracting parties. All of the members agreed to allow passage through their territory of the troops of their confederates. Within eight months all Christian princes were at liberty to join the league.[1]

Erasmus' Complaint and Wolsey's league seem to have had little effect. When a century had passed, Europe was in the throes of the Thirty Years' War. France had fought her four wars with Austria (1521-1544), and survived her eight successive civil wars (1562-1598); the great Henry of Navarre had come to the throne (1589) and been assassinated by Ravaillac (1610); and Queen Elizabeth had ended her long reign (1603) to be succeeded by James I.

Thus was Europe situated when in 1623 a book appeared in Paris which contained the first distinct printed proposal for substituting international arbitration for war. It did not propose disarmament, but provided for a "Congress of Ambassadors" to act both as an international legislature and a court whose decrees were to be enforced by the national armies. The book is entitled Le Nouveau Cynée, and although both the first and second editions indicate the author's name in abbreviated form, his real name was not known until 1890. Until then bibliographies listed the work under Emery La Croix, a different person from the author, Emeric Crucé, who was a French monk living in Paris, and the author of several other works. We are indebted for our information to Mr. Ernest Nys, the eminent French authority on international law, whose account of the discovery is given in the introduction to the translation of the work by Thomas W. Balch, published in Philadelphia, 1909. Only two copies of the first edition are known. One is in the Bibliotheque Nationale and the other in the library of Harvard College. The latter copy belonged to Charles Sumner. It had been found on a Paris book stall by his brother, George Sumner, and it came to Harvard in 1874 along with the Sumner library. The title of the book recognizes the wisdom of Cineas, a Thessalian orator, who counselled King Pyrrhus against war.

[1] For the text of this treaty and comment on it, see The Nation (N. Y.), 108: 372, March 8, 1919.

Two years after Crucé's "Cynée" was published, Hugo Grotius, then an exile in France, issued his "De Jure Belli ac Pacis," but as this work did not propose any plan of world organization it does not fall within this present study. All unknown to the world there had, however, been formed an ambitious plan conceived some twenty years prior to the publication of Crucé's work. Our whole knowledge of it comes from the memoirs of a man who was forty years old when Henry IV came to the throne and who, dying in 1641, came within two years of outliving Louis XIII. This was Maximilien de Béthune, duc de Sully, Minister of Finance to Henry IV, and his confidant and friend. During his long official career, Sully kept a journal, from which, soon after Henry's death (1610), he began to dictate his memoirs. Two volumes, covering the years 1570-1610, were printed in 1638, the third and fourth volumes being prepared by secretaries after his death. They were published in Paris in 1662. At the end of the last volume is a special chapter devoted to the "Great Design of Henry IV" for a Christian republic whereby the peace of Europe might be preserved. Throughout the Memoirs, however, are references to the scheme, especially the accounts of conferences which Sully had with Queen Elizabeth in 1601 and with James I in 1603, for the purpose of enlisting their coöperation in his sovereign's design. According to Sully, or rather, let us say, according to his "Memoirs" issued by other hands twenty-one years after his death, the design was not only worked out in detail, but about to be put into operation at the time of Henry's death. It was by no means a disinterested scheme, for its principal object was to reduce to impotence the House of Austria. It is, however, conceded to have been the first plan of a comprehensive character for the federation of Europe. After the subjugation of Austria, Europe was to have been divided among fifteen powers, whose commissioners were to legislate as a Great General Council. This council and a system of minor councils were to act as international courts, whose decisions were to be enforced by the national armies acting in concert. Boundary disputes and disputes over the election of monarchs of the Holy Roman Empire were to be settled by arbitration.

It is an interesting puzzle to know why no reference to so ambitious a scheme is found in any work prior to Sully's. Did Henry really conceive the plan and gain adherents to it as the "Memoirs" relate? Or was it a work of Sully's imagination, or of the editors of his journal after his death? These are questions about which historians and the editors of the successive editions of the "Memoirs" are at odds, and about which at least one university dissertation has been written. There is still room for higher criticism of manuscripts and texts, and for the discovery of historical data with which to illumine a doubtful question.

Volumes I and II of Sully's "Memoirs" were published before the Peace of Westphalia, and volumes III and IV two years after the Peace of the Pyrenees, which ended the war between France and Spain. Louis XIV's determination to extend the French frontier to the Scheldt, however, soon precipitated the Devolution War of 1667–1668, England and Holland already being at war. The Dutch war of 1672 and that of the League of Augsburg, 1688–1697, followed, and the stage was being set for the War of the Spanish Succession. Meanwhile, England had fought her civil wars, beheaded her king, experimented with her Commonwealth and Protectorate, and welcomed back her hereditary monarch. The time was ripe for another protest and plan for the prevention of war by world organization. It came from William Penn, who was born in London five years before Charles I was beheaded. In 1693 was published his "Essay toward the present and future peace of Europe." England, he says, cannot lay claim to the honor of originating the plan, because "it was not only the design, but glory of one of the greatest princes that ever reigned," Henry the Great. The merit of Penn's plan lies in the fact that it was disinterested, and not like Henry's, to be preceded by a political manœuvre. Moreover, it was the first to advocate limitation of armament to national needs. He proposed a "General Dyet, Estates or Parliament," to meet periodically as a legislature and as a court, whose judgments were to be enforced by the combined strength of all the sovereignties.

In spite of Penn's logical argument against war and his construc-

PROPOSALS FOR A LEAGUE

tive plan for peace, he was destined to see war continue—in fact, to outlive the Spanish Succession War of 1702–1713. He had at least one convert, however, in his friend and co-religionist, John Bellers. Bellers was always engaged in some scheme for the betterment of his fellow-men—the education of the poor, the care of the sick, the improvement of the prisons—and in 1710 he addressed an elaborate proposal to Parliament for a confederation of states to do away with war. It contained also a proposal for a convocation of all religions.

Penn had the satisfaction also of knowing that another mind in France had been at work on a similar project. Two years after the appearance of Bellers's pamphlet, in 1712, the Abbé Saint-Pierre issued in Paris his "projet de traité pour rendre la paix perpetuelle." The copy in the British Museum Library once belonged to the Cardinal de Rohan, and contains the autograph of the author and of Robert Southey. It was printed without title page and with many passages blank, which in this copy are filled up by the author in manuscript. The project was an elaboration of the great design of Henry IV, to whom full credit is given by the author. It was, however, so great an advance over its prototype as to merit consideration as an original scheme. It called for a permanent seat of world government, a Congress of Deputies to legislate and act as a court and as a tribunal of arbitration, a generalissimo of all the armies, which, however, were to remain intact, and it now proposed for the first time an international executive, in the form of an Executive Council of five. When the Peace of Utrecht (1713) ended the War of the Spanish Succession, this book was in print. Two years later a translation was published in London, to be followed by several editions in Holland. It challenged the attention of the great scholars of Europe, and moved Leibnitz in 1715 to write Saint-Pierre a letter of approval. In 1717 the Triple Alliance between France, England, and Holland was formed, and in 1728–1729 the Congress of Soissons was held. The war of the Austrian succession and the war between England and Spain filled men's minds from 1739–1748, and then came the Seven Years' War, 1756–1763. It was during this war, in 1761, that Saint-Pierre's project was revived by Rousseau, who published a summary of the project extracted from manuscripts given him in 1754 by M. le Comte de Saint-Pierre, a nephew of the Abbé Saint-Pierre. In the same year it was translated into English and published in London, with a second English edition in 1767. To this extract was added later Rousseau's "Jugement sur la paix perpetuelle."

In 1769 Napoleon Bonaparte was born, an event which boded ill for the peace of the world; in 1772 came the first partition of Poland; from 1775 to 1783 the American Revolution was fought; and in 1789 the French Revolution broke out. In that year Jeremy Bentham was forty-one years of age, and beginning with the year 1786 he had been writing about international law. His "Principles of International Law" were, however, never published in his lifetime. Not until Bowring's great edition of 1843 were Bentham's notes edited and printed. On pages 535 to 560 of volume II are four essays on international law "now first published from the original manuscripts," which were dated 1786 to 1789. The essays are built up by the editor from notes of Bentham, which consisted of incomplete projected paragraphs, completed paragraphs, and fragments. The fourth essay is entitled "A plan for an universal and perpetual peace." To remove the causes of war, Bentham proposed a reduction of armaments and the elimination of the colonial system. For the maintenance of peace he proposed (1) general and perpetual treaties, limiting the size of armies, and (2) "the establishment of a common court of judicature for the decision of differences between the several nations, although such court were not to be armed with any coercive powers." Enforcement of decrees was to be had by public opinion through the press and printed manifestos. As a last resort, a state was to be put "under the ban of Europe."

Bentham's scheme, remaining in fragmentary manuscript form for thirty-four years, had no influence on passing events. But the work of another great thinker, published on the Continent, attracted immediate attention. It will be noticed that all of the projects thus far noted emanated either from Holland, France, or England. Germany was not yet represented on the side of peace, but, like the rest of the world, was deep in war. In 1793 began the French reign of terror; in the same year England began her great war with France, which was already waging war on Austria and Prussia. In 1795 the Peace of Basel ended for a time the war between Germany and France. It was in this year that Immanuel Kant published in Königsberg his Zum ewigen Frieden. Fifteen hundred copies were sold within a few weeks, and a second edition was printed in 1796. At the same time an English translation was published in London, and a French edition in Königsberg. Edition followed edition, and critical comment piled up a voluminous literature. In fact, from a bibliographical standpoint, Kant's little work holds place along with Sully's Memoirs and Saint-Pierre's Projet. Kant's three constructive principles are (1) that the civil constitution of every state shall be republican, (2) that all international right must be grounded upon a federation of free states, and (3) that right between nations must be limited to the conditions of universal hospitality. He proposed a permanent international congress, representing a federation of states, the abolition of standing armies, and the creation of world citizenship in addition to national citizenship. By "republican" government, Kant meant constitutional government, with a representative legislative body.

The first section of his essay lays down preliminary articles which he thinks are essential as a basis for perpetual peace. Some of them have a familiar sound to-day. They are:

1. No conclusion of peace shall be held to be such, which is made with the secret reservation of the material for a future war.
2. No state having an independent existence, whether it be small or great, may be acquired by another state, through inheritance, exchange, purchase, or gift.
3. Standing armies shall after a time be entirely abolished.
4. No national debts shall be contracted in connection with the foreign affairs of the state.
5. No state shall interfere by force in the constitution and government of another state.
6. No state at war with another shall permit such kinds of hostility as will make mutual confidence impossible in time of future

peace; such as the employment of assassins, of poisoners, the violation of capitulation, the instigation of treason, in the state against which it is making war.

When we enter the nineteenth century, we find no dearth of wars. We find, however, that the desire for world peace has crossed the Atlantic and given itself expression in the formation of the American Peace Society in 1828. This Society was directly responsible for the production of an epoch-making work, which added the element needed to give precedent for nearly every item in the programme of a League of Nations proposed in the year 1919. William Ladd's Essay on a Congress of Nations was printed in Boston in 1840. Forty-five years had elapsed since the publication of Kant's essay, but these years were dotted with new editions and reprints of the books which have already been noted; and in the United States there had been a deluge of essays, no one of which had made for itself a permanent place. Many of these essays were submitted in competition for a prize offered by the American Peace Society for the best essay on a Congress of Nations, but the prize was never awarded because two successive committees were unable to agree. The result was that in 1840 the Society printed five of the best essays, together with a sixth by Ladd, "containing all the matter relevant to the subject which was elicited by the rejected essays," with original material which distinguishes his plan from all those which preceded him. He proposed an international legislative congress, enforcement by good will and public opinion only (armies being used internationally only for police duty); and, as an entirely distinct feature, a Court of Nations, made up of two judges appointed by each state. Henry IV, Crucé, Penn, Saint-Pierre, and Rousseau had given judicial functions to the legislative body, acting as a court. Ladd's plan provided for a separate court. He had been preceded in this conception by Bentham in 1789, but as Bentham's plan was not published until 1843, Ladd could not have been indebted to him for the idea. Moreover, we see the genesis of Ladd's independent thought in his essay of 1827 under the pseudonym "Philanthropos."[1]

---
[1] The Essays of Philanthropos on Peace and War. Exeter, N. H., 1827.

PROPOSALS FOR A LEAGUE

From Ladd's time to the present there has been a rapid increase of interest in plans for a new world order for the purpose of maintaining peace. For the most part, the new proposals are based on those which have already been mentioned. But the successive schemes tend to become more complete and detailed because each draws from the whole group of its predecessors. In three synopses which have been prepared the[1] features of the various plans are tabulated under the headings (1) International Legislation, (2) International Courts and Their Jurisdiction, (3) Arbitration and Conciliation for Non-justiciable Disputes, (4) Sanctions, (5) International Executive, (6) Armaments, (7) Territorial Changes, and (8) Diplomatic Relations. Under headings (3) and (4) we find matter not found in the older schemes. The distinction between justiciable and non-justiciable disputes is of recent origin and not common to all the new plans. The use of economic pressure as a sanction for a league before resort to war and not merely as an incident of it is new also. We find in addition that there is emphasis on the need of permanent international courts to supplement temporary or occasional courts of arbitration. Some of the recent plans are the work of individual writers, for example, Lorimer[2] and La Fontaine,[3] but most of them were produced by the combined efforts of societies or study groups. The important British plans were drawn up by the Fabian Society,[4] by the so-called Bryce Group,[5] and by the League of Nations Society.[6] In the United States, proposals were made by the American Peace Society,[7] by the Marburg Study Group,[8] by the League of Free

---

[1] Levermore, Plans for International Organization (American Peace Society); Levermore, Synopsis of Plans for International Organization (in Advocate of Peace, July, 1919); and Synopsis of Plans for International Organization (Messenger of the New York Peace Society, January, 1918).

[2] Institutes of the Law of Nations, 1883-1884.

[3] The Great Solution, 1916.

[4] See Woolf, International Government, p. 371-410.

[5] See Bryce, Proposals for the Prevention of Future Wars, 1917.

[6] See Bibliography, Appendix 8.

[7] See Advocate of Peace, any number after May, 1917.

[8] See Marburg, Draft Convention for League of Nations, 1918.

Nations, and by the League to Enforce Peace. The latter Society was organized in June, 1915, to promote the following programme:

First: The submission of all justiciable questions, not settled by negotiation, to a judicial tribunal for hearing and judgment.
Second: The submission of all other questions to a Council of Conciliation for hearing and recommendation.
Third: The signatory powers shall use their economic forces against any one of their number that refuses to submit any question to an international tribunal or Council of Conciliation before issuing an ultimatum or threatening war. They shall follow this by the joint use of their military forces against that nation, if it proceeds to make war or invade another's territory.
Fourth: To hold conferences between the signatory powers to formulate and codify rules of international law, which shall govern the decisions of the Judicial Tribunal.

After the signing of the armistice with Germany, the Society expanded the above into a "Victory Programme" which it adopted on November 23, 1918. As an illustration of development from a general plan to a more detailed scheme, and in order that it may be compared with the League Covenant, it is given below:

The war now happily brought to a close has been above all a war to end war, but in order to ensure the fruits of victory and to prevent the recurrence of such a catastrophe there should be formed a League of Free Nations, as universal as possible, based upon treaty and pledged that the security of each state shall rest upon the strength of the whole. The initiating nucleus of the membership of the League should be the nations associated as belligerents in winning the war.

The League should aim at promoting the liberty, progress, and fair economic opportunity of all nations, and the orderly development of the world.

It should ensure peace by eliminating causes of dissension, by deciding controversies by peaceable means, and by uniting the potential force of all the members as a standing menace against any nation that seeks to upset the peace of the world.

The advantages of membership in the League, both economically and from the point of view of security, should be so clear that all nations will desire to be members of it.

For this purpose it is necessary to create—

1. For the decision of justiciable questions an impartial tribunal whose jurisdiction shall not depend upon the assent of the parties to the controversy; provision to be made for enforcing its decisions.

2. For questions that are not justiciable in their character, a Council of Conciliation, as mediator, which shall hear, consider, and make recommendations; and, failing acquiescence by the parties concerned, the League shall determine what action, if any, shall be taken.

3. An administrative organization for the conduct of affairs of common interest, the protection and care of backward regions and internationalized places, and such matters as have been jointly administered before and during the war. We hold that this object must be attained by methods and through machinery that will ensure both stability and progress; preventing, on the one hand, any crystallization of the status quo that will defeat the forces of healthy growth and change, and providing, on the other hand, a way by which progress can be secured and necessary change effected without recourse to war.

4. A representative Congress to formulate and codify rules of international law, to inspect the work of the administrative bodies, and to consider any matter affecting the tranquillity of the world or the progress or betterment of human relations. Its deliberations should be public.

5. An Executive Body, able to speak with authority in the name of the nations represented, and to act in case the peace of the world is endangered.

The representation of the different nations in the organs of the League should be in proportion to the responsibilities and obligations they assume. The rules of international law should not be defeated for lack of unanimity.

A resort to force by any nation should be prevented by a solemn agreement that any aggression will be met immediately by such an overwhelming economic and military force that it will not be attempted.

No member of the League should make any other offensive or defensive treaty or alliance, and all treaties of whatever nature made by any member of the League should at once be made public.

Such a League must be formed at the time of the definitive peace, or the opportunity may be lost forever.[1]

---

[1] *International Conciliation*, January, 1919, p. 48-50.

On the assembling of the Peace Conference, representatives of the societies in the various states met in Paris and attempted to agree on a single plan which might be recommended to the Conference. The French and British governments also were prepared with schemes drafted by official committees, and an important contribution was made by General J. C. Smuts,[1] of South Africa. His proposal and explanation of a system of Mandatories for the control of undeveloped territory and peoples throws much light on Article 22 of the League Covenant.

REFERENCES FOR CHAPTER V

DUGGAN. The League of Nations, p. 18-49 (Chapter by C. J. H. Hayes).
MORROW. Society of Free States, p. 12-33.
For further references, see Bibliography, Appendix 8, section 3.

---

[1] See The Nation (N. Y.), 108: 225-237, February 8, 1919.

CHAPTER VI

FORMER LEAGUES OF NATIONS

ALTHOUGH popular and theoretical interest in world organization survived throughout centuries of discouragement, there were but two actual experiments of sufficient scope to warrant comparison with the new League of Nations. The Society of Nations described in our first chapter is indeed the foundation for every such league, but it is not itself a closely knit organization. On the other hand, confederations such as the United States of America, Switzerland, and the former German Empire are not leagues in the international sense, but single states having a particular form of internal organization. The British Empire, with its autonomous dominions, has much in common with an international confederation; but even here we have no precedent for a league, because the dominions are not sovereign. The recent developments within the British Empire, evidenced by the permanent establishment of periodic Imperial Conferences, and those which are foreshadowed by the admission to the League of Nations of the self-governing dominions and possessions, are indications, however, of a tendency to give to non-sovereign governments so much of the essence of sovereignty as in effect recognizes the existence of a real Confederation.

To constitute an international league in the modern sense, there must be sovereign independent states which by voluntary act enter into arrangements to accomplish general aims of common interest. Mere alliances for mutual protection against other states and alliances to guarantee adherence to a treaty are not such leagues. There must be, in addition to a general bond of union, organs through which the league may act. A fully-developed league would have a permanent administrative bureau; a deliberative representative body meeting at stated intervals; a governing body with power to make decisions under specified conditions; and some agreed means of settling disputes, viz., either occasional or permanently constituted courts. To hold the league together there must be penalties for violation of its agreements, but in international relations these penalties never yet have been enforced by an international standing army.

The Confederation of Europe

Of all the earlier alliances and so-called leagues, the only one which bears any resemblance to the League of Nations is that which existed from 1814 to 1823, often loosely described as the Confederation of Europe. It is worthy of study because the circumstances of its origin and development are strikingly similar to those which have given birth to the present League, and the causes of its failure are warnings of the dangers which beset the path of the new League. In 1814 it was the necessity of subduing France and keeping her in leash which drew the rest of Europe into alliance. In 1919, it was the aggressions of Germany which brought about united offensive action against her and her allies, and which was the incentive for the formation of a permanent League. In 1818, France was formally readmitted to the Councils of the Great Powers of Europe, and by 1820 the Confederation began to break up. This happened in spite of the Holy Alliance Act professing the most altruistic purposes. In 1920, provision is already made for the return of Germany to the fold under a Covenant conceived in sincerity and good faith. France was not responsible for the disruption of the Confederation, nor need Germany destroy the League. There were inherent weaknesses in the plans of 1814, and what is more to the point, the European world did not as a whole want a confederation. Have we builded better in 1920, and does the world desire the League sufficiently to make workable the present plan even though it may be imperfect?

The two outstanding figures of this period are Napoleon Bonaparte and Alexander I of Russia. The latter, of course, was a pigmy in intellect compared to the former, yet he represents the antithesis of Napoleon's doctrine of conquest and universal dominion. It was the persistence of his idealism which, after Waterloo, injected into the existing alliances something of morality and justice, and for a brief period gave to Europe some of the aspects of a confederation. Far different would have been the result if the Treaty of Tilsit (1807) between France and Russia had not been broken by Alexander in 1811. Alexander came to the throne in 1801 and Napoleon in 1804. The world was weary with wars which had not been checked by the shifting alliances made in the hope of preserving the Balance of Power. In 1805 we find Russia joined with England, Austria, and Sweden in Pitt's Third Coalition. France, prevented from invading England by the battle of Trafalgar, snatched victory out of defeat by crushing Austria and Russia at Austerlitz, and then in 1806 the Confederation of the Rhine was formed by Napoleon. Russia soon went over to the victorious side, and in 1809 we find her making common cause with France against Austria. But the pendulum swings, and in 1813 we find Russia and Austria both at war with France. In January of that year Alexander crossed into Prussia, proclaiming his mission as the Liberator of Europe, and offering "his assistance to all the peoples which, to-day forced to oppose him, shall abandon the cause of Napoleon and henceforth follow only their own interests." He made a direct appeal to nationality, promising, after the destruction of Napoleon, "to restore to each nation the full and entire enjoyment of its rights and of its institutions; to place all, including ourselves, under the safeguard of a general alliance, in order to guarantee ourselves and to save them from the ambitions of a conqueror."[1] In December the allies invaded France, and on March 1, 1814, the Treaty of Chaumont was signed by Great Britain, Russia, Prussia, and Austria. Its purposes were the successful prosecution of the war and a collective guarantee of the territorial arrangements to be agreed upon. The alliance was to last twenty years, during which time the four Powers were to concert for mutual protection against attacks by France; to provide "amicable intervention" in such an event; and, if intervention should fail, each was immediately to put 60,000 men in the field. Interpreted in the

[1] Phillips: Confederation of Europe, p. 64-65.

light of Alexander's proclamation of 1813, we have here the first step in the formation of a general league under the guidance of the Powers. After the abdication of Napoleon, Alexander entered the French capital, and the first Treaty of Paris was signed (May 30, 1814) by eight Powers: Great Britain, Russia, Prussia, Austria, France, Spain, Portugal, and Sweden. The treaty dealt not only with the terms of peace, but with other matters, among which was the regulation of navigation on the Rhine and other navigable rivers which separate or traverse different states.

To the Congress of Vienna were left the details of the new territorial arrangements. Attended by representatives of most of the European states, it purported to be a real European parliament; but it was in fact, as Von Gentz has said, a "collection of negotiators," under the dominance of the Quadruple Alliance, and influenced by the astute diplomacy of Talleyrand. The latter found a hearing for the claims of legitimacy as opposed to Alexander's plea for nationality, and the Final Act of the Conference (June 9, 1815) restored Europe as far as possible to its situation prior to Napoleon's conquests. In the meantime, Napoleon had returned from Elba, and on June 18 he was defeated at Waterloo. In July, Paris was occupied a second time by the allies and Louis XVIII was again seated on the throne. France was in a turmoil, isolated parts of the army holding out for months, and the dismemberment of France was more than probable. Again Alexander entered Paris, and true to his theory that war had not been made against the French people but against Napoleon, he held the forces of disintegration in check. Arrangements were made for joint military occupation and for an informal European executive which received in common all communications from the French. The ministers of the four Powers of the Alliance met daily in the British embassy at Paris and until the withdrawal of the allied armies in 1818 acted as a "Big Four," not unlike a more recent group. The second Treaty of Paris (November 20, 1815) renewed the Treaty of Chaumont and provided for periodic meetings of the four Powers. "To facilitate and to secure the execution of the present Treaty," reads Article VI, "and to consolidate the connections, which at the present moment so closely unite the four Sovereigns for the happiness of the World, the High Contracting Parties have agreed to renew their Meetings at fixed periods, either under the immediate auspices of the Sovereigns themselves, or by their respective Ministers, for the purpose of consulting upon their common interests, and for the consideration of the measures which at each of those periods shall be considered the most salutary, for the repose and prosperity of Nations, and for the maintenance of the Peace of Europe."[1] Thus was added a new element of organization to the Quadruple Alliance already committed by the Treaty of Chaumont to peaceful and, if necessary, armed intervention. Moreover, the Alliance was no longer directed exclusively against France, but against any disturber of the peace. If we add to these arrangements a parallel agreement made two months earlier, we have the full text of the League covenant of that time, under which four conferences were held. This earlier agreement is the famous Act of the Holy Alliance.[2]

For the origin of this Act we must go back to the year 1804, shortly after Napoleon became emperor. Alexander, under the guidance of La Harpe, had read the project of Saint-Pierre and the criticism of it by Rousseau. The latter's objection to the French monk's plan was that it would require a Henry IV to carry it out. Why should not Alexander play the part of Henry IV? Why should he not free the world from fear of France as Henry had planned to free Europe from the menace of Austria? Why should he not then set up a league by which the sacred rights of humanity would be secured? He put his idea on paper in instructions to his minister Novosiltsov, whom he sent on a special mission on September 11, 1804, to lay the plan before Pitt. England and Russia could unite, he said, only if the countries to be freed from Napoleon were to remain free from the old abuses. Justice and humanity must be regarded; national rights must be respected; Poland, Sardinia, and Switzerland must be restored, and Holland made independent; the French people must be shown that the war was not against them but against the Corsican; and Christian peoples

---
[1] British and Foreign State Papers, 3:279.
[2] For the text of this Act see Appendix 4.

must be freed from the yoke of the Turk. Pitt's reply was cold to the idealism of Alexander, but receptive of a plan of union to secure sovereign rights, to establish a system of public law in Europe, and first of all to subdue France. Napoleon kept the subsequent allies busy until 1815 pursuing this last project. When that was accomplished, Alexander again put forth his dream. This time he carried with him every Christian sovereign of Europe except the Pope, even Great Britain, though still true to her policy of "splendid isolation," assenting in principle. The act was signed by Russia, Austria, and Prussia on September 14, 1815, and was announced by Alexander at a review of allied troops near Châlons on September 26, when all Christian nations were invited to join. The form and religious sentiments of the document were due to the acquaintance of Alexander with Baroness von Krüdener, a religious enthusiast whom he brought with him to Paris, and who conducted nightly prayer-meetings in a building adjoining Alexander's house. In the name of the Most High and Indivisible Trinity, the three monarchs based their agreement on "the sublime truths which the holy religion of our Saviour teaches." They agreed to act toward each other as brothers, to regard themselves as fathers of their subjects, to consider themselves as three members of one Christian nation under the Sovereign God; and to receive into the Holy Alliance all powers which would avow the sacred principles to which they were bound. It was a strange treaty, unique in history; but if we translate it into modern terms of diplomatic intercourse, we find it to be a general treaty of amity, seeking international coöperation. It was fundamentally sound, for no league, either then or now, can survive without the spirit of coöperation in international affairs. We have every reason to believe that Alexander was sincere in urging this treaty upon Europe, and it is not accurate to characterize it at the outset as a reactionary movement intended merely to maintain reigning sovereigns on their thrones and to preserve their territories intact. On the contrary, assuming that these existing governments had been made safe by the Treaties of Chaumont and Paris, it placed a duty on their chiefs to govern wisely and deal fairly with their neighbors. It is the irony of fate that the ill-advised policies of the later days of the Alliance have associated the Holy Alliance more with its failure than with its original purpose. How easily might a similar fate befall any modern League of Nations!

To summarize the loose organization which has been called the Confederation of Europe, we find therefore a covenant made up of (1) the Treaty of Chaumont, renewed at the Congress of Vienna, (2) the second Treaty of Paris, and (3) the Holy Alliance Act. Under these treaties jointly considered, we find a quadruple alliance bound for twenty years to keep France in check by armed force if necessary; an agreement for periodic meetings to deal with new conditions and maintain the general peace of Europe; and a solemn avowal by all Christian states that they will govern wisely and seek the common good of all peoples. Meanwhile, there was a joint military occupation of France, and an international council of ministers meeting regularly in Paris.

That these arrangements did not constitute a United States of Europe is plain from the steadfast opposition of Great Britain to such an interpretation; and Alexander's attempts to broaden the scope of the treaties to include all European states were frustrated by the diplomacy of Metternich and Castlereagh. Nevertheless, four international conferences were held which may be considered either as the acts of an incipient confederation, or as meetings of the European Concert. At the Conference of Aix-la-Chapelle, which began on September 30, 1818, the three questions of immediate importance were the withdrawal of the allied armies of occupation from France, security for the payment of indemnity by France, and the admission of France to the Alliance of Chaumont. France was represented by Richelieu, although he was not admitted to the Conference, and he succeeded in obtaining a declaration by which France might attend subsequent Conferences, under Article VI of the Treaty of Paris (November 20, 1815). As a protection against France, the Quadruple Alliance was continued in force. But the Conference acted also as a kind of European representative assembly, considering such important questions as the suppression of the slave trade which had been abolished in principle at Vienna;

the suppression of the Barbary pirates; and the proposed intervention to preserve the revolting American colonies to Spain. On these larger matters the Conference was able to come to little agreement; but on many minor questions presented in the form of petitions from the lesser states or their peoples, it acted the part of dictator. On November 15, 1818, it agreed to a declaration, which France was allowed to sign, stating the objects of the "intimate union established among the monarchs," and their resolution "never to depart, either among themselves or in their relations with other states, from the strictest observation of the principles of the right of nations."

The Conference did not, however, inaugurate a period of peace and fraternity, but one of revolution and reaction. There was unrest throughout Europe, and revolt in Spanish America. Intervention in France was threatened, and Alexander was suspected of an intention to attack Austria. While professing liberal views, he began to feel misgivings as to the gratitude of the masses for the intended benignity of his rule; and he felt that the whole system to which he was committed depended on the permanency of existing governments. He therefore took that step which presaged the break-up of the Confederation, the proposal of April 19, 1820, that the five Great Powers should meet at Madrid because "the Spanish revolution," he said, "fixes the attention of two worlds; the interests to be decided are those of the universe . . . and involve the future of all civilized peoples." No result would have come from this declaration had not revolution broken out in Naples. As a consequence, a second conference assembled at Troppau on October 29, 1820, at which we find Alexander in a new rôle. Since 1804, he had been the apostle of liberalism, and the leader in that sort of internationalism which was possible to a hereditary absolute monarch. Now mutiny in his own guard at St. Petersburg and the turmoil of the world drove him to the opposite extreme. Great Britain and France were represented at Troppau only by ministers, and so Russia, Austria, and Prussia acted independently in issuing the Preliminary Protocol of Troppau, which changed the spirit of the Holy Alliance and foreshadowed its future. "States which have undergone a change of Government due to revolution," it reads, "the results of which threaten other states, *ipso facto*, cease to be members of the European Alliance, and remain excluded from it until their situation gives guarantees for legal order and stability. If, owing to such alterations, immediate danger threatens other states, the Powers bind themselves, by peaceful means, or if need be by arms, to bring back the guilty state into the bosom of the Great Alliance."[1] Great Britain refused to sign this document, and therefore the three originators of it withdrew their signatures. The impression made on the world could not, however, be withdrawn. In order that the King of Naples might attend, the Conference was adjourned to Laibach in the middle of January, 1821, and discussion of the Protocol was continued, but neither Great Britain nor France would agree to it. The three other Great Powers consequently came to an understanding to act independently.

The fourth of the "periodic" conferences growing out of the Treaty of Paris, 1815, was held at Verona in October, 1822, attended by a great concourse of sovereigns and their suites. Here the breach between Great Britain and the allies was widened, on the question of intervention in Spain, and the use of force to restore her colonies. The direct result of the Conference was armed intervention by France in Spain, by means of which Ferdinand VII was restored to the throne; and the indirect consequences were the recognition by Great Britain of the independence of the Spanish colonies, and the proclamation of the Monroe Doctrine by President Monroe. Thus ended Alexander's attempt to create a Confederation of Europe.

CENTRAL AMERICAN LEAGUE OF NATIONS

Curiously enough, we must look to some of those very Spanish-American colonies on which the Holy Alliance split, for the only other general experiment in international government sufficiently definite to repay study. The present Central American states were originally subject to Spain as the Vice-royalty of Guatemala.

---
[1] Phillips: Confederation of Europe, p. 222.

When they declared their separation from Spain in 1821, the provinces did not immediately set up separate governments. All but Costa Rica threw in their lot with Mexico; but in 1823 they all reasserted their independence, only to consolidate in November, 1824, under the "Constitution of the Federation of Central America." This Federation was dissolved by its own Congress in 1838, and then began a series of attempts to refederate, sixteen in number, which lasted from 1839 to 1906. From that time on the movement had for its object, under the suggestion of the United States of America and of Mexico, not so much to create a federated state out of five as to form a close league of independent republics through a general treaty of Amity and Friendship.

A long succession of revolutions, violent changes of government, and misunderstandings between states led up to the Washington Peace Conference of 1907, which was necessitated because of two conflicting systems for maintaining peace. The first of these systems was inaugurated at Corinto, Nicaragua, in 1902, when the five republics negotiated a treaty establishing obligatory arbitration. This was reinforced by an additional treaty of 1903, and a proclamation of 1904 in which four of the states guaranteed the peace of Central America by military force, if necessary. In spite of all these precautions, war between Honduras, Guatemala, and Salvador was begun in 1906. It was brought to a speedy end by the joint intercession of the United States and Mexico, and peace was reëstablished by a treaty signed on board the U. S. S. *Marblehead* by representatives of all Central American states except Nicaragua. A further treaty was signed at San José within a month, in which an agreement was made to submit subsequent differences to the Presidents of the United States and of Mexico, as umpires. The Corinto agreement also remained in force. There were therefore two rival peace systems, by one of which all except Costa Rica were bound to submit differences to Central American arbitration, and by the other of which all except Nicaragua were committed to American-Mexican mediation. The Corinto plan failed when put to the test in 1907, and the United States and Mexico again took a hand, Nicaragua now adhering to the plan. The outcome was the Central American Peace Conference which convened in Washington on November 13, 1907. When after five weeks it adjourned, the Central American League of Nations was in being. The representatives of the United States and Mexico were present as mediators, but the Conference devoted itself, not to the settlement of old difficulties, but to constructive work to promote peace and understanding in the future. Seven conventions were signed. The first of these contained an agreement for ten years to submit all differences, of whatever nature, to a court of justice; neutralized Honduras; provided for permanent diplomatic relations; for non-intervention; and for constitutional reforms in the respective states. The second of these created, also for ten years, the Central American Court of Justice, which will be discussed in Chapter XII. The third related to extradition; the fourth established for fifteen years an International Central American Bureau; the fifth created for fifteen years a Pedagogical League and a Central American Pedagogical Institute; the sixth provided for annual conferences for at least five years; and the seventh had to do with international railroad connections. The treaties constituted a system of organization and coöperation. The international organization was made up of an International Bureau, an International Court of Justice, international commissions, and periodic diplomatic conferences. These organs were to function by virtue of coöperation in regard to education, finance, communications, agriculture, customs, administration of justice by the national courts, extradition of criminals, and permanent diplomatic relations.

Although the Court of Justice no longer exists, a league was actually in operation for ten years; the Bureau arranged six conferences at which important treaties were signed; the Court decided nine cases; progress has been made toward educational unity, and since 1907 no international war has taken place. The International Bureau and the Pedagogical Institute are still in existence, as well as the agreement to hold conferences.[1]

The Central American League of Nations involved agreement

[1] For text of four of the treaties see Appendix 5.

between only five states, contiguous in territory, using the same language, originally part of the same Vice-royalty, and from the time of their separation from Spain recognizing the need of common action. Throughout their state existence they have been protected from foreign aggression by the Monroe Doctrine, and they have not been forced to maintain large armies and navies. The conditions therefore were of the best for the formation of a League; and the ease with which it was done under the guidance of the United States and Mexico provided no precedent for similar action by the entire world. The discontinuance of its most significant organ, the Court of Justice, which was vested with unusual competence, may even be used as an unfavorable augury for the League of Nations. If the Central American League formed under favorable circumstances was found to be unworkable, how much more difficult is the problem before the whole family of states. On the other hand, it may be urged that the very fact that the little League had no control over the relations of its members with non-members predestined it to failure. If this is true, the larger membership of the League of Nations, even though they be so diverse in character, creates by exclusion of causes of dispute a fundamental condition of success. Whichever view is correct, we may still find in the Central American experiment much that should be emulated. At the same time that administrative, deliberative, and judicial organs were set up, arrangements were made to lay a basis for coöperation. The unification of educational methods was sought, communications were to be improved, and criminals were to be extradited between all the states for the suppression of lawlessness. The spirit which prompted these arrangements is one which must obtain throughout the world to-day in order that life may be kept in the new-born organism.

To Central America we must, up to the present League, look for the most clear-cut illustration of international organization. In the Confederation of Europe we find, on the other hand, an experiment tried under conditions more analogous to the world situation of today. It was, however, scarcely developed into an organization, and therefore, as a precedent, it must be used with caution. As

Phillips has said,[1] "a discriminating judgment is necessary in applying the lessons of history to practical politics." If we may hope that the world has genuinely advanced since the days of Alexander I, and if in the present League of Nations there are combined the best elements of the two experiments which we have just described, then the Great Experiment now dedicated to the Sovereignty of Right has an even chance of success.

REFERENCES FOR CHAPTER VI

PHILLIPS. Confederation of Europe, p. 43-85, 148-156.
  The Peace Movement and the Holy Alliance. (Edinburgh Review, 215: 405-433, April, 1912.) National Federations and World Federation. (Edinburgh Review, 226: 1-27, July, 1917.)
EUROPEAN BACKGROUND OF THE MONROE DOCTRINE.
  (A League of Nations, 1: no. 5, p. 266-285.)
FERRERO, G. Problems of Peace, 1919, p. 29-64.
ZACHARIAH, K. Historical Antecedents of the League of Nations. (Calcutta Review, no. 296, p. 160-188, April, 1919.)
CENTRAL AMERICAN LEAGUE OF NATIONS.
  (World Peace Foundation. Pamphlet Series, 7: no. 1.)
RAMIREZ PENA, ABRAHAM. Conferencias Centroamericanas, 1909-1914. San Salvador, Imprenta Nacional, 1916.

---

[1] Edinburgh Review, 215:409.

PART II

INTERNATIONAL LAW AND THE LEAGUE

INTERNATIONAL LAW AND THE LEAGUE

VII. CUSTOMARY INTERNATIONAL LAW AND TREATY-MADE LAW
VIII. THE LEAGUE AND THE DEVELOPMENT OF INTERNATIONAL LAW
IX. INTERNATIONAL LAW OF PEACE
X. INTERNATIONAL COMMISSIONS OF INQUIRY
XI. INTERNATIONAL ARBITRATION
XII. INTERNATIONAL TRIBUNALS WITH PERMANENT PERSONNEL
XIII. INTERNATIONAL ADMINISTRATION OF TERRITORY

CHAPTER VII

CUSTOMARY INTERNATIONAL LAW AND TREATY-MADE LAW

THE statement has already been made that the background of the League of Nations is the Society of States, and that this Society connotes the existence of international law. This fact is recognized in the Preamble of the League Covenant in which one of its purposes is said to be "to promote international coöperation and to achieve international peace and security . . . by the firm establishment of the understandings of international law as the actual rule of conduct among Governments." Two questions are raised by this quotation: first, what are the understandings of international law; and second, have they not been the actual rule of conduct among governments? In the same paragraph we find that another purpose is the maintenance of "a scrupulous respect for all treaty obligations in the dealings of organized peoples with one another." This leads to the further query: What relation have treaties to international law; are they a part of it, or something distinct from it, since they are separately mentioned?

It has repeatedly been said during the late war that there is no such thing as international law—that there are no rules of importance upon which an agreement has been reached, and that the so-called "law" is broken at will. To the latter statement, it is sufficient to say that the breach of international law does not destroy it any more than the safe-breaker destroys the criminal law. Punishment eventually is meted out to the criminal; and so also Germany is now suffering the penalty for the breach of international law. Yet it must be confessed that there is a disconcerting indefiniteness about the law of nations which leaves it open to attack. It is difficult to give a convincing answer when one is asked who makes international law, and who enforces it? Certainly it is not made by a legislature, and certainly there is no police force to give it sanction. It must be admitted then that it is not statute law—not rules made by a superior body, for universal application to political subordinates. Nor does it consist of rules which have been built up by the decisions of courts having international authority comparable to the authority of national courts.[1] Statutes and court decisions are the most obvious sources of the rules enforceable in a state. In the first case, power is delegated to a body of men to lay down in advance regulations for the conduct of citizens. The courts, in doubtful cases, construe these rules, and often find it necessary under conditions not anticipated by the statutes to expand their scope and apply them in such ways as virtually to change their meaning. These decisions are preserved, and form precedents for subsequent decisions under the principle accepted in English-speaking countries of *stare decisis* —let it stand, having been decided. Thus what has been called judge-made law comes into existence. In both of the above cases the whole force of the state stands back of the rules and requires respect for them. There is in existence, however, much law which can be traced neither to a source in statutes nor in decisions. The decisions themselves often recognize a rule as existent through immemorial custom. This is the common law of a country; the decisions of courts do not create it but merely express and apply it. National law in democracies is based on the consent of the governed. Consent to statute law and judge-made law is given indirectly through representatives and by public opinion. Law which is the outgrowth of custom is the direct creation of the citizenry and has their consent in advance.

The Austinian theory of law does not take into consideration the consent of the governed, and recognizes as legal rules only those which emanate from a sovereign body and are impressed on subjects. The force of custom is disregarded, and the element of

---

[1] The nearest approach to such courts are the various national prize courts which apply the rules of international law, and whose decisions are commonly used as precedents.

command is emphasized to the exclusion of consent. Austin's definition is: "Every positive law or every law simply and strictly so called is set directly or circuitously by a sovereign person or body, to a member or members of the independent political society wherein that person or body is sovereign or supreme. Or (changing the expression) it is set directly or circuitously by a monarch or sovereign number, to a person or persons in a state of subjection to its author."[1] The theory does not square with the facts of modern political life in which democracy and representative government are essential features. On Austin's hypothesis there could be no such thing as international law because there would be no source from which it might come. Without doubt customary law based on consent exists in democracies as truly as positive law exists in the older monarchies which might be cited as the best examples in support of Austin's contention; and we need not limit ourselves to his theory in trying to find analogies between national law and international law.

If now we substitute for persons in a democratic commonwealth independent states in a Society of Nations we will find that there is only one basis for law between them, namely, Common Consent. Since there is no international statute law, and since the principle of *stare decisis* does not apply to decisions of International Courts of Arbitration, we must turn to custom and other evidences of consent to establish the existence of international law. Consent may be either expressed or tacit. In the case of custom it is tacit.

International law in the most restricted sense is that body of rules which sovereign states by common consent, as the result of custom, consider legally binding on themselves. By custom we mean not merely habit or usage but these developed into a rule which is adhered to in the conviction that an obligation exists.[2] That a customary rule exists can be learned only from the conduct of states, and the opinion of men who have devoted themselves to the study of interstate phenomena. The development of the custom

---

[1] The Province of Jurisprudence Determined, ed. 1861, Lecture VI. For a discussion of this theory of law see Willoughby, Nature of the State, p. 162-165.
[2] Oppenheim: International Law, 1:22-23.

may be traced in the agreements made between states, and their reaction when a supposed custom is violated whether or not an express agreement has been made. Ordinarily, the precise time when a usage becomes a custom and a custom becomes a rule of law cannot be determined. Perhaps the only circumstance that would positively mark the final transition would be a universal treaty which in terms would be declaratory of existing law. Tacit consent would then be replaced by expressed consent. Such a treaty would not create the rule, but be a means of recording that common consent upon which all international law is based. Neither would it preserve the rule from change, for the very nature of custom is that it is the creature of evolution. Such a treaty can therefore declare only the law as it exists at a given time, and may itself become obsolete as a declaration through customary variation in the rule.

The "understandings" of customary international law may therefore be sought by each state and each person in the records of history, which itself is open to various interpretations. For this reason the opinions of writers on the law of nations have more weight than corresponding treatises on national law. Only by patient study can any one hope to gather from diplomatic documents, arbitral awards, decisions of prize courts, applications of the law of nations by national courts, municipal statutes, and treaties, the data on which to base an opinion. And when experts disagree, we may assume that usage has not yet fully developed into custom. There are enough rules based on customs which are generally observed to constitute a genuine body of law. Isolated examples of disobedience to it may be found, but the rules remain and develop as actual rules of conduct. As matters now stand the non-observance of supposed customary rules by a large group of states over a considerable period would argue not violation of law, but either the absence of a rule or the development of a new rule.

The historical development of international law is usually treated as dividing itself into three periods,[1] (1) that prior to the

---
[1] See Wilson and Tucker: International Law, p. 13-27.

Christian era, (2) the middle period extending to the year 1648, and (3) the modern period, from 1648 to the present. In the early period we find only the germs of an international law, chiefly relating to maritime commerce, and by analogy with rules which were common to all parts of the Roman Empire. In the middle period we find Rome still the dominant power down to the sixth century, when its place was taken by the Church as a unifying influence. Feudalism, which was the antithesis of the Roman system, laid the basis for the idea of territorial sovereignty. The Crusades then helped to develop the idea of common interests and devotion to a common cause; while the extention of commerce developed well-recognized maritime codes which applied not merely in one state but in the dealings of merchants of different states. Many modern rules of maritime law can be traced to the Amalfitan Tables, the Consolato del Mare, the Laws of Oleron, the laws of Wisby, and the laws of the Hanseatic League. Consuls were sent to reside in foreign countries, and though their functions were purely commercial, they were the forerunners of our present diplomatic system. The period ended with the Peace of Westphalia, 1648, terminating the Thirty Years' War, during which was published Hugo Grotius' De Jure Belli ac Pacis (1625).

The modern period is punctuated with international congresses which hastened the development of law. It was in this period that the modern system took shape based on a widely recognized conception of national states possessing territorial sovereignty. The great congresses referred to not only made international settlements necessitated by wars, but came to agreements as to their own future conduct. They gave expressed consent to rules which were to be applied in their relations one with another. Did the parties by signature to those agreements make international law? Was any non-signatory state bound by those agreements? Certainly not in any legal sense. International law cannot be *created* by treaty unless all sovereign states in the Family of Nations are parties; in no case was every such state a party; therefore law was not *created*. But such treaties are evidences of the evolution of rules, which by subsequent accession, adhesion, or approbation of other powers, or by mere adoption in practice, may grow into genuine international law of universal application. The consent necessary for the existence of law would then be expressed as to some states and tacit as to others. The signatory states might in cases where treaties expire by limitation, help to fix the rule by retaining it to guide their conduct after the obligation had ceased. They might do this in the conviction that custom together with the treaty had made new and binding law.

Most treaties are not, however, in terms either declaratory of international law or evidences of the growth of custom. The rules according to which treaties are made, kept, and denounced are parts of the law of nations, but their subject matter is not necessarily law. When therefore the League Preamble speaks of "a scrupulous respect for all treaty obligations," it refers to definite engagements between states somewhat similar to contracts between persons. The analogy is helpful, though not perfect. Both treaties and contracts are voluntary engagements, both are intended to be kept, and both may be broken if the parties, viz., one of the states and one of the contractors respectively, are willing to suffer damages. But in the case of treaties there has been no supreme tribunal to assess these damages as there is in the case of a private contractor. In the case of treaties, it can logically be deduced from the absolute sovereignty of states that a state is at liberty at any time to abrogate its contracts. Here, however, enters the customary rule of law which lays down the general injunction that treaties are binding, and then recognizes exceptions to the rule. It is well understood that a treaty may expire from lapse of time according to its own terms, by which a definite period is set, or on the occurrence of named circumstances; or it may be dissolved by mutual consent; or because another treaty is substituted for it. A perpetual treaty may not be terminated at the mere will of one state; yet even here there is a way out, for a "vital change of circumstances" is said to justify withdrawal even from such a treaty. All treaties are concluded under the tacit reservation *rebus sic stantibus;* for a state is not presumed to agree to an engagement by which its independence and existence may be endangered. In general, treaties are terminated by war between the contracting parties, but there are exceptions to this rule.[1]

It is sometimes said that treaties as well as custom are sources of international law. If we consider the true nature of treaties, we see that this can be true only in a special sense. Every rule of international law must be binding on all members of the Family of Nations. Treaties are binding only on the states which are parties to them. Third states can acquire neither rights nor duties under treaties between two other states. They may from policy act as though they were legally bound, or they may under certain conditions accede or adhere to a treaty, but they are under no obligation to do so. They may, according to some authorities, even intervene to prevent the operation of such a treaty if it violates an accepted rule of international law, or when it affects their safety, or when it violates rights previously acquired by treaty. The precepts of international law are the tests of the validity of treaties and not *vice versa*. In what sense, then can it be said that treaties make law?

At the outset we may eliminate the great majority of treaties which deal with boundaries, mutual guaranty, commerce, communications, extradition, copyright, weights and measures, customs, sanitation, labor, agriculture, industry, and the like. Most of these have no effect on the development of law regarding their subject matter. But there is a class which for want of a better term have been called law-making treaties. These are such as are entered into by large groups of states which agree to general rules of conduct. As above explained these may develop into universal law either by expressed or tacit consent; but even before this happens they are of extremely great importance especially when most of the Great Powers are involved. To this class of rules some publicists[2] have given the name General International Law, in contradistinction to Universal International Law. The acceptance of this arbitrary terminology will clarify the conception of what international law is, what treaties are, and how one reacts on the

---

[1] See Lawrence: Principles of International Law, 6th ed., p. 360-365:
[2] See Oppenheim; International Law, 1:23.

other. It retains the fundamental idea of consent as the only basis for both international law and treaties, is in conformity with the doctrines of sovereignty and equality, distinguishes between ordinary and "law-making" treaties, recognizes the force of custom, and provides for the evolution of law through expressed as well as tacit consent. We shall find the concept of General International Law of service in discussing the possible effect of the League of Nations on the growth of international law.

Oppenheim[1] briefly summarizes the great treaties, declarations, and conventions which he considers to have been law-making in character. Their generality is indicated by the number of states which signed them or later acceded or adhered to them. The most important are: (1) the Final Act of the Congress of Vienna, June 9, 1815, signed by eight states which agreed to the neutralization of Switzerland, freedom of navigation on international rivers, the desirability of abolishing the negro slave-trade, and a classification of diplomatic envoys; (2) the Protocol of the Congress of Aix-la-Chapelle, November 21, 1818, signed by five states, which recognized a fourth class of diplomatic envoys, viz., Ministers Resident; (3) the Treaties of London, November 15, 1831, and April 19, 1839 (five states), by which Belgium was neutralized; (4) the Declaration of Paris, April 13, 1856 (seven signatory states, with adhesion by eighteen others), which laid down four rules for maritime war; (5) the Geneva Convention, August 22, 1864, revised July 6, 1906 (all except three states), which provided for the amelioration of the condition of the wounded of armies in the field; (6) the Treaty of London, May 11, 1867 (eight states), by which Luxemburg was neutralized; (7) the Declaration of St. Petersburg, November 29, 1868 (sixteen states), which regulated the use of projectiles in war; (8) the Treaty of Berlin, July 13, 1878 (seven states), which, according to Oppenheim, was "law-making with regard to Bulgaria, Montenegro, Rumania, and Servia"; (9) the General Act of the Congo Conference of Berlin, February 26, 1885 (fourteen states), which provided for freedom of navigation in the Congo basin and on the Congo and Niger rivers, the prohibition of slave transport in the

[1] International Law, 1: 587-595.

CUSTOMARY INTERNATIONAL LAW

Congo basin, neutralization of the Congo territories, and notification to each other of future occupations by the signatory powers on the coast of Africa; (10) the Treaty of Constantinople, October 29, 1888 (nine states), neutralizing the Suez Canal and giving freedom of navigation in it; (11) the General Act of the Brussels Conference, July 2, 1890, revised November 3, 1906 (seventeen states), which restricted the liquor traffic and suppressed the slave trade in Western Africa; (12) Final Act of the First Hague Conference, July 29, 1899 (twenty-six states); (13) Final Act of the Second Hague Conference, October 18, 1907 (forty-four states); (14) the Declaration of London, February 26, 1909 (ten states). This last Declaration was, however, never ratified.

To this list we must now add the Treaty of Versailles, June 28, 1919, of which the part constituting the League Covenant is discussed in the next chapter. The two Hague Conferences and the International Naval Conference of London met under conditions favorable for concluding law-making treaties. They met not as a consequence of any particular war, but to attempt in time of peace to formulate rules for the amicable settlement of disputes, and to draw up regulations for the conduct of war on land and sea. The call for the First Hague Conference was issued by Czar Nicholas II of Russia who was impelled by a desire to rid his country of the burden of armaments. The Conference of 1907 was first proposed by President Roosevelt, but he withdrew so that the Russian Emperor might have the honor of calling both Conferences. The First Conference was attended by delegates of twenty-six states, and the second by delegates of forty-four states. At the Versailles Peace Congress only twenty-eight states were represented, so that the Second Hague Conference remains the largest ever assembled. The two Hague Conferences were organized on identical lines. In each case an unofficial "steering committee" made up of the first delegates of the Great Powers set the machinery in motion. Provision was made for plenary sessions and for commissions to work out the details of the programme and prepare drafts for submission to the plenary sessions. In all meetings a unanimous vote was required for action. Each state had one vote no matter how large its delegation might be. The Conferences elected their own presidents, and there were secretaries who were not members of the Conferences. The Commissions of the First Conference had to do with (1) armaments, (2) laws and customs of war, (3) arbitration, (4) petitions, and (5) editing. The Second Conference appointed Commissions on (1) arbitration, with a sub-commission on maritime prizes, (2) land warfare, with sub-committees on (a) laws and customs of war, and (b) neutrals and declaration of war, (3) maritime war, with sub-commissions on (a) bombardment of ports, use of submarine mines and torpedoes, and (b) belligerent ships in neutral ports, and the revision of the Geneva Red Cross Convention, (4) maritime law, (5) petitions, (6) editing. The work of the First Conference was embodied in three conventions, on (1) pacific settlement of international disputes, (2) laws and customs of war on land, and (3) adaptation to maritime warfare of the principles of the Geneva Convention of August 22, 1864. There were three Declarations prohibiting (1) the launching of projectiles and explosives from balloons, (2) the use of asphyxiating gas, and (3) the use of expanding bullets. *Voeux* were adopted concerning (1) the revision of the Geneva Convention, 1864, (2) rights and duties of neutrals, (3) limitation of the effectiveness of arms, (4) limitation of armaments, (5) inviolability of private property at sea, and (6) prohibition of bombardment of coast towns and villages. The Second Conference adopted thirteen conventions concerning (1) pacific settlement of international disputes, (2) limitation of the employment of force for the recovery of contract debts, (3) opening of hostilities, (4) laws and customs of war on land, (5) rights and duties of neutral powers and persons in case of war on land, (6) status of enemy merchant ships at the outbreak of hostilities, (7) conversion of merchant ships into war-ships, (8) laying of automatic submarine contact mines, (9) bombardment by naval forces, (10) adaptation to maritime warfare of the principles of the Geneva Convention, (11) restriction of the exercise of the right to capture in naval war, (12) creation of an International Prize Court, and (13) rights and duties of neutral powers in naval war. There was a new Declaration prohibiting the discharge of projectiles and explo-

CUSTOMARY INTERNATIONAL LAW

sives from balloons, since the Declaration of the First Conference was for five years only. Each Conference adopted a Final Act which is an official summary of the proceedings. All of the above conventions and declarations, so far as ratified, were in force at the outbreak of the European war; but those relating to war contained clauses to the effect that they bound belligerents only when ratified by them, and then only if all the belligerents are contracting powers. This had the effect of releasing all the belligerents from them and explains why the Hague Conferences appear to have had so little influence. In fact, the failure to observe the conventions was in conformity to the letter of the rule concerning their applicability; and it cannot therefore be used as an illustration of the weakness of international law-making treaties. The situation rather emphasized the difficulty of agreeing to such treaties.

The Declaration of London is the direct result of the action of the Second Hague Conference in adopting a Convention Relative to the Creation of an International Prize Court.[1] Article 7 of this Convention relating to the law to be applied by the Prize Court reads:

"If a question of law to be decided is covered by a treaty in force between the belligerent captor and a power which is itself or whose subject or citizen is a party to the proceedings, the court is governed by the provisions of the said treaty.

"In the absence of such provisions, the court shall apply the rules of international law. If no generally recognized rule exists, the court shall give judgment in accordance with the general principles of justice and equity."

Because of the indefiniteness of the second paragraph, it was proposed by the British Government that a conference assemble in London "with the object of arriving at an agreement as to what are the generally recognized principles of international law within the meaning of paragraph 2 of Article 7 of the convention." Accordingly the Conference, participated in by ten maritime powers, met on December 4, 1908, and completed its labors on February 26, 1909, when the Declaration of London Concerning the Laws of Naval

---
[1] For the text of this convention see Appendix 6 (c).

War was signed. The Declaration did not purport to create new law even as between the parties. The Preliminary Provision, on the contrary, specifically states that "The Signatory Powers are agreed that the rules contained in the following chapters correspond in substance with the generally recognized principles of international law." Great Britain was not able immediately to ratify the Declaration because some of its provisions conflicted with her statute law. The Naval Prize Bill, intended to remove this difficulty, was defeated in the British Parliament on December 12, 1911, through the efforts of opponents of the Declaration. In 1914, a second bill was introduced, but it had not been passed when the war broke out. On August 6, 1914, the United States Government suggested to the belligerent states that they apply the provisions of the Declaration during the war; but as they could not all agree to do this without modifications of the Declaration, the suggestion was withdrawn in October, 1914. Here again, as in the case of the Hague Conventions, we find not that the Declaration was violated during the war, but that it was not in force.

In these instances we have illustrations of the difficulty, on the one hand, of creating law, and on the other, of agreeing as to what existent law is. If the Second Hague Conventions and the Declaration of London had been in force we should have had true examples of general treaty-made law. As between states which were not belligerents the conventions relating to war passed by the Second Hague Conference are still applicable, but the Declaration of London is not binding on any state. As between Germany and the Allied and Associated Powers, the Hague Conventions are not revived by the Treaty of Versailles. We can now see these great conventions and the Declaration of London, the product of the best minds of the signatory states, merely as steps in the development of international law—evidences as far as they go of the growth of custom in relation to the laws of war. The Final Act of the Second Hague Conference contains the following:

The conference recommends to the Powers the assembly of a Third Peace Conference, which might be held within a period corresponding to that which has elapsed since the preceding conference, at a date to be fixed by common agreement between the Powers, and it calls their attention to the necessity of preparing the programme of this Third Conference a sufficient time in advance to ensure its deliberations being conducted with the necessary authority and expedition.

It now remains to be seen whether the creation of the League of Nations has made a Third Hague Conference unnecessary. For the conclusion of treaties diplomatic powers are required. If the delegates of the members of the League are given diplomatic powers, the Assembly may serve as a diplomatic congress; otherwise it may be wise to call a Third Hague Conference to make effective the recommendations of the Assembly in regard to the development of international law. To many publicists the latter course seems preferable; for one reason, in order that all sovereign states, nonmembers of the League as well as members, may be invited. In any case the work of the two Hague Conferences and of the International Naval Conference ought not to be lost. In the light of a new and unparalleled experience, their product should be revised, if only to attempt anew to record the progress of custom and the common consent on which all international law is founded.

References for Chapter VII

LAWRENCE, T. J. Principles of International Law, 6th ed., p. 360–365.

OPPENHEIM. International Law, 1:20–83, 587–595.

WILSON AND TUCKER. International Law, p. 13–42.

FOULKE, R. R. Treaties (Columbia Law Review, 18:422-458, May, 1918).

ROXBURGH, R. F. International Conventions and Third States.

CHAPTER VIII

THE LEAGUE AND THE DEVELOPMENT OF INTERNATIONAL LAW

AS BETWEEN the signatories, the treaties of peace between the Allied and Associated Powers and the four defeated belligerents respectively are law-making treaties creating and declaring General International Law. Of these the most important is the Treaty with Germany. Not only does it, in common with the three other treaties, contain the League of Nations Covenant, but also what has been called the Labor Charter. The principles laid down relating to labor and the organization created will be discussed in Chapter XIX. In addition, there are provisions of a law-making character abrogating the treaty of 1839 by which Belgium was neutralized; creating new states and the free city of Danzig; providing for the internationalization of rivers and waterways, and for freedom of navigation on them; and setting up regulations for aërial navigation. We are here concerned, however, only with that part of the Treaty which creates the League of Nations.

The League Covenant might contribute to the development of international law in two ways: first, by itself stating new rules or restating existing rules; and second, by setting up machinery potentially capable of making law.

At this time, one can venture only with great hesitancy on the task of prophesying what the legal effect of the Covenant will be. Here follows, therefore, only a series of questions raised by reading the document in the light cast by the preceding chapters.

THE COVENANT AS A LAW-MAKING TREATY

Passing by the Preamble for the present, we find in Article 8 what appears to be a statement of a new rule. "The members of the League recognize," it says, "that the maintenance of peace requires the reduction of national armaments to the lowest point consistent with national safety and the enforcement by common action of international obligations." Since the maintenance of peace is one of the primary objects of the League, the word "requires" stands out with prominence. No mere statement of policy is made, but an agreement which, put in the form of a rule, might read: No state may maintain an army for the purpose of foreign aggression. Armies and navies may be maintained only to protect the state and to assist other states in preserving the peace of the world. In order to make this rule effective, some details are specified. The Council is authorized to work out a plan for the proportional reduction of armament, which plan, however, when adopted by the states, is subject to reconsideration and revision at least every ten years, but during that period no state may exceed the limit set without the permission of the Council. A subordinate rule not stated in positive terms is that munitions and implements of war should not be manufactured by private enterprise. This might itself grow into an international rule to the effect that only states may manufacture the means of carrying on war. Information as to the scale of the armaments of the various nations and their military and naval programmes must be made public as a safeguard for the observance of the above rules concerning disarmament, and there is provided a permanent military commission to advise the Council concerning the execution of the rule. We find also, glancing forward to Article 23, that the principle is expressly recognized that the traffic in arms and ammunition in countries where its control is necessary is a matter of common interest. In fact, under this rule of proportional disarmament we find an indication of a new attitude which accounts for the other rules which follow. We find the idea of public utilities, which is well known in municipal law, developing into an international concept. Throughout the Covenant we find the reiteration of the idea that matters which affect the peace and comfort of the world or any of its members, even its subject peoples, are matters of public concern calling for joint action on the initiative of one or many states.

In Article 10 we find expression of the rule that every state is entitled to security for its territory from external aggression. This is declaratory of the rule which lays down the obligation of non-intervention, a rule, however, which has not been fully recognized in theory or acquiesced in in practice. In fact, as we have seen, the principle of intervention for certain purposes was during the Holy Alliance expressly recognized as legitimate. We now find, however, agreement on a rule that security of territory from external aggression is a matter of public concern.[1]

The third rule, not new in theory but new in practice, is contained in Articles 11, 12, 13, 14, 15, and 17. The rule may be briefly stated as follows: No state, whether a member of the League or not, may go to war without first attempting to settle the dispute either by diplomacy, by submission to a commission of inquiry, or by arbitration. It may be considered that such a moral rule already existed, but unquestionably there was no such rule of law. The Covenant now states specifically that "any war or threat of war, whether immediately affecting any of the members of the League or not, is hereby declared a matter of concern to the whole League." (Art. 11.) Certain processes which must precede the beginning of hostilities are laid down in Articles 12, 13, 14, and 15, and by Article 17 the application of the rule is extended to non-members. Perhaps the whole purport of this rule might be summed up in the words, the world is entitled to peace; war in the future is to be the exception and peace the rule.

[1] In interpreting Article 10, it may be helpful to compare it with the corresponding Article (3) of the American draft covenant submitted by President Wilson to the League of Nations Commission of the Peace Conference. "The Contracting Powers unite in guaranteeing to each other political independence and territorial integrity against external aggression; but it is understood between them that such territorial readjustments, if any, as may in the future become necessary by reason of changes in present racial conditions and aspirations or present social and political relationships, pursuant to the principle of self-determination, and also such territorial readjustments as may in the judgment of three-fourths of the delegates be demanded by the welfare and manifest interest of the people concerned, may be effected if agreeable to those people and to the States from which the territory is separated or to which it is added and that territorial changes may in equity involve material compensation. The Contracting Powers accept without reservation the principle that the peace of the world is superior in importance to every question of political jurisdiction or boundary." (The Independent, July 5, 1919, p. 15.)

But war under certain circumstances is still justified. In fact, we now find suggested a new rule contrary to the legal development of the last three centuries but reminiscent of Grotius. Just wars are legal and unjust wars are illegal; states as well as persons may commit crimes; state crimes must be punished by the only means available among sovereign states, namely, war. The history and vicissitudes of a similar rule stated by Grotius in 1604 are followed in a recent book by Vollenhoven.[1] In 1603 and 1604 the Portuguese took the law into their own hands when they came into contact with Dutch navigators and traders, carrying off as booty whatever they could. In protest against this, Grotius wrote a book entitled On the Right of Capture. A part of it, *Mare Liberum*, was published in 1609, but the rest of it was unknown until 1864. In it he contended that, in the interest of society, state crime must be punished not only by the offended state, but by all others not directly concerned. The world at large was not affected by this unpublished book; but when De Jure Belli ac Pacis was issued in 1625, it contained a long list of crimes of which a state may be guilty, with the manner in which punishment should be inflicted. "The right of making war, not the right to conclude peace, is first mentioned in the title of his book," says Vollenhoven (p. 13), "and this right of making war (he is never weary of repeating it) stands or falls with the right and the duty to grapple with state crime and state injustice as much as with crime and injustice of citizens. The lawful war, according to Grotius, is that which is meant for punishment and with namby-pamby wars he will have nothing to do (although war should always be conducted on principles of humanity); in such a war literally everything ought to be allowed that may be required to get the upper hand of the criminal nation." In order to judge of the conduct of states, Grotius conceived of a complete, comprehensive set of state duties, and while recognizing the independence and equality of states, limited their right to declare and conduct war except for punishment of crime. It was a fatality to the world that the great writers who followed Grotius, among whom the most prominent was Vattel, did not carry forward and

[1] The Three Stages in the Evolution of the Law of Nations.

develop the limitation on the right to declare war along with the right of states in every other respect, to conduct themselves as sovereign. The contrary doctrine was developed as an attribute of sovereignty, legally though not morally justified, that a state has unbridled liberty to wage war for the sake of paramount power. It was the chief purpose of the Hague Conferences to put a check on the exercise of this right; but the effort failed. It took such a catastrophe as the European war to bring us back to the complete doctrine of Grotius, and to impel the states to set up by a binding agreement a means of determining when war may and when it may not be legally waged.

It has always been considered a legal rule that either when war is threatened or during its progress one nation may tender its "good offices" to the states at war, in order to prevent a conflict or bring it to an end. In Article 11 we find an expansion of this rule. It is declared "to be the friendly right of each member of the League to bring to the attention of the Assembly or of the Council any circumstance whatever affecting international relations which threatens to disturb international peace or the good understanding between nations upon which peace depends." It is therefore a rule of law here recognized that it is not an unfriendly act to take up with third parties the affairs of two contending states. Under the rule of good offices the offer had to be made to the belligerents or disputants themselves.

In Article 13 we find a new rule foreshadowed, if it is not actually stated. It has always been a question to be solved only by states themselves whether a particular dispute is suitable for decision by arbitration. States have always been particularly sensitive on this point. Full discussion of it will be found in Chapter XI. Here we may merely state that in Article 13 an attempt is made to define in general terms those disputes which are suitable for arbitration. A rule of law might read something like the following. According to the law of nations the following disputes are in general suitable for submission to arbitration: 1st, those concerning the interpretation of a treaty; 2nd, concerning any question of international law; 3rd, concerning the existence of any fact which if established would constitute a breach of an international obligation; 4th, concerning the existence and nature of the reparation to be made for a breach of an international obligation.

In Article 16 we find formal recognition of international ostracism and joint boycott as legitimate means of dealing with recalcitrant states. Whether or not these are intended as means of carrying on war or whether they should be classed in the group known as "measures short of war" is not clear. At any rate, the agreement not to have intercourse with a state under the ban of the League whether it be a member of the League or not will probably vitally affect the rules of warfare according to which it is legitimate to carry on trade even in munitions with a belligerent, subject to the penalties to be enforced by the belligerents themselves.

Article 16 contains also the implication of another rule, namely, that in case of just wars conducted by the League the financial and economic losses of the participants must be equitably distributed among the members of the League, so that the burdens will not fall heaviest upon nations least able to bear them.

Articles 18, 19, and 20 lay down new rules concerning treaties. These rules perhaps might read as follows: Secret treaties hereafter made are not binding. All treaties must be published. Every treaty must be registered in a public place under the auspices of the League where it may be examined by the accredited representatives of all sovereign states. In the latter provision we find a sort of Torrens system established for treaties. Their authenticity, binding force, and content are no longer a matter of concern merely to the parties. These matters are now of public concern. This idea is enforced in a rule contained in Article 20 to the effect that all treaties must be consistent with the principles upon which the League is founded. Treaties inconsistent with these principles must be abrogated. In fact, signature to the Covenant by the agreement in Article 20 automatically abrogates such treaties and provision is made in Article 19 for occasional revision of the treaties at the suggestion of the Assembly of the League in order that consistency may be maintained. For clarity's sake Article 21 explains that treaties of arbitration are not in any case inconsistent with the League Covenant. Whether or not this same article when it says "Nothing in this covenant shall be deemed to affect the validity of . . . regional understandings like the Monroe Doctrine for securing the maintenance of peace" is a formal recognition of the Monroe Doctrine as a rule of international law, or whether it merely defines this doctrine as a "regional understanding" "for securing the maintenance of peace" is a matter of controversy. It may be well contended historically that the primary purpose of the Monroe Doctrine was not to maintain peace, and this section has been the object of very searching and pertinent attack by the opponents of the League. It is contended by many that no protection whatsoever to the Monroe Doctrine is given. We will have occasion later in this chapter to recur to this point. If, however, the Monroe Doctrine is itself now recognized as a rule of law, the original wording of the document should be quoted here:[1]

At the proposal of the Russian Imperial Government, made through the minister of the Emperor residing here, a full power and instructions have been transmitted to the minister of the United States at St. Petersburg, to arrange, by amicable negotiation, the respective rights and interests of the two nations on the northwest coast of this continent. A similar proposal has been made by his Imperial Majesty to the Government of Great Britain, which has likewise been acceded to. The Government of the United States has been desirous, by this friendly proceeding, of manifesting the great value which they have invariably attached to the friendship of the Emperor, and their solicitude to cultivate the best understanding with his Government. In the discussions to which this interest has given rise, and in the arrangements by which they may terminate, the occasion has been judged proper for asserting as a principle in which the rights and interests of the United States are involved, that the American continents, by the free and independent condition which they have assumed and maintain, are henceforth not to be considered as subjects for future colonization by any European powers.

. . . The citizens of the United States cherish sentiments the most friendly in favor of the liberty and happiness of their fellow-men on that side of the Atlantic. In the wars of the Euro-

---

[1] Richardson: A Compilation of the Messages and Papers of the President, p. 778, 786-788.

pean powers in matters relating to themselves we have never taken any part, nor does it comport with our policy so to do. It is only when our rights are invaded or seriously menaced that we resent injuries or make preparation for our defense. With the movements in this hemisphere we are, of necessity, more immediately connected, and by causes which must be obvious to all enlightened and impartial observers. The political system of the allied powers is essentially different in this respect from that of America. This difference proceeds from that which exists in their respective Governments. And to the defense of our own, which has been achieved by the loss of so much blood and treasure, and matured by the wisdom of their most enlightened citizens, and under which we have enjoyed unexampled felicity, this whole nation is devoted. We owe it, therefore, to candor, and to the amicable relations existing between the United States and those powers, to declare that we should consider any attempt on their part to extend their system to any portion of this hemisphere as dangerous to our peace and safety. With the existing colonies or dependencies of any European power we have not interfered and shall not interfere. But with the Governments who have declared their independence, and maintained it, and whose independence we have, on great consideration and on just principles, acknowledged, we could not view any interposition for the purpose of oppressing them, or controlling in any other manner their destiny, by any European power, in any other light than as the manifestation of an unfriendly disposition toward the United States. In the war between these new Governments and Spain we declared our neutrality at the time of their recognition, and to this we have adhered and shall continue to adhere, provided no change shall occur which, in the judgment of the competent authorities of this Government, shall make a corresponding change on the part of the United States indispensable to their security.[1]

In Section 22, which relates to the control of colonies and territories by means of the mandatory system, a rule is laid down and a principle stated that the well-being and development of backward peoples constitute a sacred trust of civilization. They may not be

---

[1] The successive interpretations and expansions of this Doctrine in the messages of Presidents subsequent to Monroe are collected in A League of Nations (World Peace Foundation), v. 1, no. 5, June, 1918. The story of the formulation, development, and effect of the Doctrine is told in Latané, From Isolation to Leadership, p. 19-53, 131-148.

exploited for the benefit of one state. The backward peoples themselves have rights which must be respected and from this flows another rule, namely, that all such communities not now sovereign have the right, when they are capable of it, to become independent, self-governing states. Rules of far-reaching importance are laid down in Article 23 which may be grouped as follows. Conditions of labor, the prevention of disease, the control of the traffic in women and children, in opium and dangerous drugs, are matters of common interest to all states and all peoples. They are of international concern and are subject to international supervision. It may be considered a rule accepted in Article 24 that the permanent offices or bureaus of public international unions hereafter created must be under international direction. This does not mean that the unions themselves are controlled by the League, but that their administrative commissions and ministerial and secretarial bureaus are to be controlled by the League. Finally we find a specific recognition in Article 25 that the improvement of health, prevention of disease, and the mitigation of suffering throughout the world are matters of public concern. Reference is made particularly to voluntary Red Cross organizations, but only to those which devote themselves to the purposes above enumerated. No rule apparently is laid down that Red Cross organizations devoting themselves entirely to work during war time are matters of public concern, although doubtless this would be a justifiable inference.

Has the League Legislative Power?

We now come to the question whether the League Covenant has erected any organs through which legislative power may be exercised. A legislature in its ordinary meaning is a body of persons in a state invested with the power to make and repeal laws. The word "legislator" comes from two Latin words meaning "law" and "to bear," the whole expression meaning a bearer or proposer of law. Legislation is the enactment of rules for the regulation of future conduct, rights, and controversy. In a state the legislature is one of the three departments of government and is to be distinguished from the executive and the judicial departments. Its powers are limited by the fundamental law of the state whether it be a written or unwritten constitution. It is part of a system and its efficacy depends not merely on the promulgation of laws but upon the means of interpreting them and enforcing them. Is there any such organization created by the Covenant? Is there, in fact, a world state with departments of government? The answer is in the negative. In the League we do not find a full-fledged system of government to be enforced by international police. There is no power, therefore, to make rules which may be imposed upon the world. Municipal legislation within a state presupposes a sovereign power which lays down rules of conduct, but in international society such rules of conduct can be created only by agreement, since the states are all sovereign and independent. What then has been provided in the League to permit international legislation used in this figurative sense either by proposing rules or by laying them down? Articles 3 and 4 dealing with the Assembly and the Council of the League set up what some writers have called a bi-cameral legislature and they point out that both bodies are representative of the members of the League, the Council being similar to a senate and the Assembly to a house of representatives. What, however, is the function of these two bodies? For both of them we find the same statement: "The Assembly (or Council) may deal at its meetings with any matter within the sphere of action of the League or affecting the peace of the world." The Preamble to the Covenant throws light on what is considered within the sphere of action of the League. We find two main purposes, (1) to promote international coöperation and (2) to achieve international peace and security. These two ends are to be accomplished (a) by the acceptance of obligations not to resort to war, (b) by the prescription of open, just, and honorable relations between nations, (c) by the firm establishment of the understandings of international law as the actual rule of conduct between governments, (d) by the maintenance of justice, and (e) by a scrupulous respect for all treaty obligations. Anything which has to do with these matters is therefore within the scope of the Assembly and Council and we have already in this chapter considered in detail the specific rules which were laid down for the accomplishment of these purposes. Now the Council and Assembly are not empowered to produce international legislation by formally enacting it, nor are they specifically authorized to make agreements. If the latter were the case they would be making treaties. Are the representatives of the members of the League qualified and authorized to make treaties? In Article 7 we find the statement that "representatives of the members of the League and officials of the League when engaged on the business of the League shall enjoy diplomatic privileges and immunities." This does not, however, give these representatives the status of plenipotentiaries, that is to say, persons with full power to conclude treaties binding upon their states when subsequently ratified. Unless such powers are given the representatives by amendments to the League or by separate agreement, they cannot therefore enter into treaties. They might, however, agree upon draft conventions which after submission to the various states could be concluded by a diplomatic congress or by direct state action, and finally ratified by the states.

There are no articles of the Covenant which directly give to either the Council or Assembly anything like legislative power. In Article 15 it is provided that the Council shall make no report or recommendation in disputes arising out of matters which by international law are solely within domestic jurisdiction, but the decision whether a matter is by international law solely within the domestic jurisdiction of a party is left to the Council and the Council may reach a decision binding upon the parties if all of its members with the exception of parties to the dispute are unanimous. Suppose, for instance, that a dispute arose as to the admission of Orientals to British Colombia contrary to her immigration laws. Could an Eastern state, for example, raise the question with the League as to whether such exclusion was a matter solely within the domestic jurisdiction of Canada, and if so, could the Council unanimously, except for the vote of Canada and the Eastern state, declare immigration to be a matter coming under international law? If so, it would perhaps be laying down a special rule which would be applicable to Canada alone, under specific circumstances; but it would not be making general rules. Its action would be more nearly judicial than legislative in character. Similarly it has been contended that under this power of the Council, Article 21, which mentions the Monroe Doctrine, gives in fact no protection to it. It is contended that in any dispute a difference of opinion may well arise as to whether the Monroe Doctrine applies and if so, the Council would be in a position by successive determinations to redefine the Monroe Doctrine, changing its meaning and its detailed application. Here, again, its function is judicial only.

Attention should be paid also to the method provided for amending the League Covenant. Article 26 provides that amendments "will take effect when ratified by the members of the League whose representatives compose the Council and by a majority of the members of the League whose representatives compose the Assembly." The League Covenant is itself part of a law-making treaty, and if the Council and Assembly together could amend it, these two organs of the League would have power to make new law. They have, however, power only to propose amendments for ratification by the states in their sovereign capacity. This situation is emphasized by a clause which was added at the request of the Brazilian delegation in order to avoid constitutional difficulties. "No such amendment shall bind any member of the League which signifies its dissent therefrom, but in that case it shall cease to be a member of the League." Although it is agreed that an amendment, that is a treaty, shall take effect when only a majority of the members have ratified it, a member will tacitly assent to it if it does not avail itself of the privilege of withdrawing. There is, therefore, no hint of legislation in the method of making amendments. These are binding only with the consent of the members.

References for Chapter VIII

Baker, Ernest. The Constitution of the League of Nations: Legislative.
   (New Europe, 10: 180–184, March 6, 1919.)
Oppenheim. The League of Nations, p. 41–55.

DUGGAN. The League of Nations, p. 289–303 (Chapter by E. Kimball).

EDMUNDS, S. E. International Law Applied to the Treaty of Peace.

A LEAGUE OF NATIONS (World Peace Foundation) 1: no; 5, 1918.

LATANÉ. From Isolation to Leadership, p. 19–53, 131–148.

CHAPTER IX

INTERNATIONAL LAW OF PEACE

There is no place in these pages for an extended discussion of international law. Its nature, content, history, and application are set out at length in many authoritative treatises, some of which are listed at the end of this chapter. We are justified here in referring only to those phases of international law which have special relations to the League of Nations. Even these phases can be treated only in outline. The subject is usually divided into three parts, the international law (1) of peace, (2) of war, and (3) of neutrality. For the last five years the laws of war have been uppermost, even those of neutrality sinking into subordination. If the League of Nations accomplishes all that is claimed for it, the laws of war and of neutrality will both lose much of their importance. They will come into play rarely, and will be subject to supervision and scrutiny while in operation such as they have not hitherto received. They may thus in time completely change their character; but as matters now stand they remain practically untouched by the League Covenant. If, therefore, the League goes to war with one of its members, or with a non-member, or if two members are at war, or a member with a non-member, or two non-members, they will be governed by existing rules of international law. Moreover, non-members who are not parties to a conflict will be neutrals and governed by the rules of neutrality. The rules applicable are largely codified in the conventions of the two Hague Conferences and in the Declaration of London. So far as they have been accepted by the several states, they will apply hereafter, unless changed by some future conference.

The law of peace, of the amicable settlement of disputes, and of so-called non-hostile redress, is the phase of international law whose "understandings" the League is designed firmly to establish "as the actual rule of conduct among Governments." The rules of international relations in peace are destined to become all important. They should have this position not only for progress, comfort, convenience, and culture generally, but because a conscientious observance of them will prevent occasions for conflict from arising. Merely as a suggestion for further reading it is therefore appropriate to summarize from reliable sources the chief rules which form the background to the League.

We have already seen (Chapter I) that states which are members of international society have certain attributes, which are expressed by the terms sovereignty, independence, equality. While these are attributes of the states, there exists a rule of law that these attributes shall be respected. Only when a state misuses its rights and directly or indirectly infringes the rights of others, do correlative rules come into play. Intervention in the affairs of another state is justifiable only on grounds of self-preservation. There is otherwise no right of intervention, but on the contrary an obligation not to intervene. Nevertheless, interventions have been justified in practice on several other grounds, all of which are subject to grave abuses. These grounds are, to prevent acts illegal under the law of nations; to carry out the provisions of a treaty; to preserve the Balance of Power; to safeguard the rights of humanity. Henceforth we must assume that there is no justification for intervention except under the aegis of the League. An alternative has been provided through the obligation to submit disputes either to arbitration or inquiry. These are agreed means by which members of the League may test the need for intervention and safeguard their independence. But states still have the right to employ means of self-help. This right as now defined in international law will probably survive. It is not necessarily an occasion for war, although it is close to it. The right exists, as stated by Daniel Webster, only when there is "a necessity of self-defence, instant, overwhelming, leaving no choice of means, and no moment for deliberation." The act must be "limited by that necessity and

INTERNATIONAL LAW OF PEACE

kept clearly within it." A classic example of self-help is found in the Caroline case.[1]

The distinctive rules of peace are those which relate to rights of property, jurisdiction, and intercourse.

PROPERTY

A state has the ultimate title to all territory within its boundaries. This includes all land and water. In certain circumstances land which has come under private ownership may revert to the state, and it may be appropriated for compensation under the right of eminent domain. Ordinarily, and as against individuals, the state does not make claim under its ultimate title, except through taxation; but as against other states it continuously asserts and maintains the right. Within its own territory it may own and hold in immediate possession land and the buildings thereon, such as the public grounds and buildings in the District of Columbia. It may, in its state capacity, own property in foreign states, such as its foreign embassies; and it may as a private individual possess property either at home or abroad. The state may and usually does own ships of war and other public vessels such as hospital, light, and coast-survey ships. It also may own ships used for non-public purposes, as passenger and freight ships.

The capacity in which the state is owner, whether as a public or a private person, affects the status of the property in both war and peace, and in the case of ships, their immunity from jurisdiction in foreign ports.

The distinction between private and public ownership is many times recognized in the Treaty of Versailles. Articles 297-298, with the Annex, relate to private Property, Rights, and Interests. The property of the German states is separately treated. For instance, by Article 256, states to which German territory is ceded acquire all property and possessions situated therein belonging to the German Empire or to the German states. The value of the property is to be paid by the new owners to the Reparation Commission to apply as money paid for reparation by Germany. Such

---
[1] Stowell and Munroe: International Cases, 1: 121-123.

payments are not required of France for public property in Alsace-Lorraine, or of Belgium on account of property in territory ceded to her. In the former case, the exception is made "in view of the terms on which Alsace-Lorraine was ceded to Germany in 1871."

No state has ownership over the open sea or beyond three marine miles from its shores except in bays specially designated, and in other bays whose mouths, according to different authorities, are from six to ten miles wide. It may be questioned whether a state has ownership over marginal waters from low tide to the three-mile limit. This is a mooted question. The strip of water is, however, not subject to private ownership, and as against other states, the riparian state would possess title. Some writers use the word domain to include both marginal waters and the air spaces above a state's possessions, thus avoiding the application of the term territory to land on the one hand, and to waters and the air on the other hand. The control over the latter two is less absolute than over territory, indicating a limitation on ownership. Control of them is incident to the possession of territory. Territory may be acquired by a state in five ways: (1) by occupation, which completes the inchoate title obtained by discovery of land. Occupation involves the establishment of responsible local authority; (2) by prescription, through uninterrupted and uncontested possession for many years; (3) by accretion, through additions to land area by action of rivers or marginal waters, or by artificial means; (4) by conquest, which is the forcible acquisition of territory. It remains to be seen whether this form of acquisition has become obsolete under Article 10 of the League Covenant; (5) by cession, which is transfer of territory by treaty as a result of conquest, or by gift, sale, or exchange.

A state, obviously, has no ownership in the persons who are its subjects. Allegiance and nationality involve mutual rights and duties between the state and its citizens.

Jurisdiction

Jurisdiction is the right of a state to exercise control. It may or may not be accompanied by ownership. With respect to a state's own land areas, the two are coincident; with regard to marginal waters and aërial spaces, jurisdiction is not dependent on absolute ownership; and with regard to persons, and to territory controlled but not owned, the two are completely disassociated.

With exceptions to be noted, a state's jurisdiction extends to all persons and things within its boundaries. This includes not only citizens but aliens, and the latter may be excluded wholly or in part through national immigration laws. Jurisdiction follows a state's citizens and their property to all places not under the complete jurisdiction of other states, as the high seas. It may also be exercised in territory under foreign sovereignty or in territory the status of which is not yet decided. In the case of leased territory, such as the Panama Canal Zone, sovereignty does not reside in the state exercising jurisdiction. By the treaty of 1903[1] (1) the United States guaranteed the independence of Panama, (2) Panama granted to the United States the perpetual use, occupation, and control of the ten-mile Canal Zone, and (3) "all the rights, power, and authority within the zone . . . which the United States would possess and exercise if it were the sovereign of the territory." There are numerous instances of exercise of jurisdiction over leased Chinese territory; the one most notable to-day being that of Kiao-Chau. China refused to sign the Treaty of Versailles because Germany's jurisdictional rights under the treaty of 1898 were transferred to Japan (which state had expelled Germany in 1914), and not immediately returned to China, which throughout possessed sovereignty over the territory in dispute.

Under the mandatory system of the League of Nations, the Mandatories exercise jurisdiction without possessing sovereignty. Apparently, the sovereignty in the case of the German colonies rests in the five Great Powers to whom it was transferred by the peace treaty.[2] A somewhat different situation exists when undeveloped, but hitherto independent territory is jointly occupied or practically controlled by two states. In these instances, sovereignty, for a

[1] Malloy: Treaties, 2: 1349-50.
[2] See Treaty of Versailles, Art. 119. For a discussion of sovereignty in relation to the Mandatories see Chapter XIII.

time at least, is usually admitted to remain with the native chiefs, since neither state is willing to admit the claims of the other; but their authority is gradually superseded and the question of sovereignty remains in abeyance until agreement can be reached by the occupying states. In the meantime, they exercise jurisdiction jointly. This was the history of joint occupation in Samoa, and several steps in a similar development have been made in the New Hebrides.[1]

A state possesses unqualified jurisdiction over inland seas and lakes entirely within its boundaries. Examples of such bodies of water are Lake Baikal, the Aral Sea, the Dead Sea, Lake Winnipeg, and Lake Michigan. Conflict of jurisdiction may occur when inland waters are surrounded by land belonging to several states. In such instances, for example, Lakes Ontario, Erie, and Huron, the limits of jurisdiction are usually determined by treaty. Similar rules apply to rivers wholly within the boundaries of a state, and to those which form the boundaries of several states. In the former case, the owner-state's jurisdiction is complete, and in the latter case, it is either limited by treaty, or is understood to extend to the centre of the main channel. Rivers which flow through several states are under the jurisdiction, within their boundaries, of the respective states. A discussion of so-called international rivers under the League and in general practice will be found in Chapter XIII.

The history of the open sea and its major branches as regards jurisdiction shows a progressive development of international law. In antiquity the open sea was common to all mankind since there was no law of nations. But in 138 A. D. the Roman Emperor said of himself, "being emperor of the world, I am consequently the law of the sea." His successors in the Holy Roman Empire styled themselves "Kings of the Ocean." In the Middle Ages, when piracy was rampant, states began to assert jurisdiction over stretches of the sea as a matter of protection. By Papal bulls of 1493,[2] Alexander VI recognized Venice as paramount in the Adria-

---

[1] See post, Chapter XIII.
[2] See Davenport: European Treaties bearing on the History of the United States, p. 56-83.

tic, Portugal in the Indian Ocean and in the Atlantic south of Morocco, and Spain in the Pacific and in the Gulf of Mexico. Sweden and Denmark claimed jurisdiction in the Baltic. In these cases not only jurisdiction but sovereignty was claimed; maritime ceremonials such as dipping the flag were demanded, tolls were collected, and fishing prohibited. In 1580 Queen Elizabeth contested Spain's claim to the Pacific, asserting it to be common to all nations. Yet Great Britain was then claiming sovereignty over the North Sea and over the Atlantic from the North Cape to Cape Finisterre. As late as 1805 she required foreign ships in these waters to strike their topsails and take in their flags as a ceremonial. Three great books were produced as a result of conflicting claims. Grotius in 1609 wrote his Mare Liberum, contending that the Dutch had the right to navigate the Indies without permission of Portugal. The opposite view was taken by Selden in his Mare Clausum, published in 1635, and Bynkershoek, supporting Grotius, wrote De Dominio Maris in 1702. The last of these brought out the doctrine that national jurisdiction ends with the effective force of arms exerted from the shore.

The open sea is now defined as the ocean and all connecting arms and bays not within the territorial limits of any state. It thus includes such bodies as the Black Sea, the Irish Sea, the North Sea, the Gulfs of Mexico and California, the Mediterranean and the Adriatic seas. Either by custom or by treaty certain large bays, such as Delaware, Chesapeake, and Conception bays, are considered to be under territorial jurisdiction.

According to Oppenheim the "maritime belt is that part of the sea which, in contradistinction to the Open Sea, is under the sway of the littoral states. But no unanimity exists with regard to the nature of the sway of the littoral states,"[1] or as to the exact breadth of the belt. When Bynkershoek advanced his theory, the effective range of cannon shot was three miles. To-day the range is many times wider, yet the most common claim is for three miles. The length of these miles varies, however, according to the systems used in different states. There is difference of opinion also whether the

---
[1] International Law, 1:255.

measurement should begin from high or low water, from the point where the water ceases to be navigable, or from the last point where coast batteries could be erected. The weight of opinion is in favor of the low-water mark.

The high seas are open to free navigation for all states, and a qualified right exists in most other waters. Coast navigation involving the use of the maritime belt is usually restricted to ships under the registry of riparian states; but there is free passage for merchantmen, subject to police and pilotage regulations. Port and light dues are often required for anchorage privileges. Fishing is under the control of the bordering states, except beyond the maritime belt.

Every vessel must be under some state jurisdiction. Pirates are the enemies of mankind and may be destroyed by any state. Vessels are either public or private in character. Public vessels are war-ships, mail ships, revenue cutters, lighthouse tenders, dispatch boats, and the like. Private vessels are owned by individual persons or corporations. The nationality of a ship depends on the flag which it is entitled to fly. If a false flag is used, the ownership determines nationality. On the high seas all vessels are under national jurisdiction. In foreign waters presumption, although practice varies, is in favor of local jurisdiction with regard to private ships, and in favor of the state whose flag is flown with regard to public ships.

Theory concerning jurisdiction over air spaces above a state's territory and above the open sea is much the same as that concerning the maritime belt and the high seas. Freedom of navigation is admitted under regulations of the respective states. Part XI, Articles 313 to 320, of the Treaty of Versailles, relates to aërial navigation, and insures to the aircraft of the Allied and Associated Powers full liberty of passage and landing over and in the territory and waters of Germany, subject to such regulations as are made for German air-ships.

Jurisdiction applies not only to territory, to marginal waters, to air spaces, and to ships and aircraft, but to persons. Persons in a state are either nationals or aliens. In a general sense, all per-

INTERNATIONAL LAW OF PEACE

sons within a state are, for the time being, subjects of it because they are under its control, but citizens are more completely controlled than are aliens. For certain purposes, states assert jurisdiction over their nationals in foreign states, but this assertion can only be made effective through state coöperation. Nationality, as summarized by Professor Wilson,[1] can be acquired (1) by general law, (2) by marriage, (3) through act of parents, (4) through general transfer of allegiance by treaty of cession, purchase, etc., (5) through transfer of allegiance by conquest, (6) in consequence of certain special service, (7) by admission of new territory to a state, (8) by special act of legislation, and (9) by election. Naturalization laws vary greatly in different states, some of which maintain also that nationality is inalienable. The subject of transfer of nationality is dealt with in the peace treaties ending the European War in connection with the transfer of territory and the erection of new states.

A fruitful source of international negotiation is in regard to protection of citizens abroad. This is effected through diplomatic exchanges and agreements. It is only when discrimination is made against aliens so that they are on a different footing from nationals that a basis for claims is created. This subject is exhaustively treated in Borchard's "Diplomatic Protection of Citizens Abroad." He discusses the right of diplomatic protection as indicated by the legal relations existing (1) between the state and its citizens abroad, (2) between the alien and the state of residence, and (3) between the two states concerned with respect to their mutual rights and obligations.

To the foregoing generalizations concerning jurisdiction there are important exceptions. Foreign sovereigns and heads of state, with their suites, while visiting a country in an official capacity, are exempt from local jurisdiction. As representatives of the sovereign, diplomatic agents are for most purposes likewise exempt. Their persons are inviolable, unless they are actually plotting against the security of the state, and they are exempt from both civil and criminal process. Their property and the houses in which

[1] Handbook of International Law, p. 127.

they live are also largely exempt, but this exemption is subject to its appropriate use. Under the League Covenant, representatives of the members of the League and its officials when engaged on the business of the League enjoy diplomatic privileges and immunities. The buildings and other property occupied by the League, or by its officials and representatives, are inviolable (Art. 7). Public armed forces of a foreign state within the territory of another state when peace exists between the two are exempt from local jurisdiction; but permission to enter must be had either specially or by general agreement. Article 16 of the League Covenant contains a general agreement to "take the necessary steps to afford passage through their territory to the forces of any of the members of the League which are coöperating to protect the covenants of the League." During this passage, the troops will not be amenable to local law, but their officers will be responsible for their good behavior.

Public ships in foreign territorial waters are exempt from local jurisdiction. Unless they themselves use violence they cannot legally be expelled by force, and they do not need special permission before entering. Private ships in foreign territorial waters are for most purposes under local jurisdiction, but this jurisdiction does not extend to internal discipline or to offenses committed on board unless the tranquillity of the port is disturbed. In certain Oriental states whose systems of jurisprudence are different from those of Western states, extra-territorial jurisdiction exists. This means that by treaty, aliens are in certain respects exempt from local jurisdiction and are entitled to have legal controversies in which they are involved tried in a consular court according to the laws of the state to which they belong.

INTERCOURSE

The interdependence of states is now so complete that the existence of a right of intercourse is unquestioned. The means of intercourse for persons are continually increasing; not only ships, railroads, telephone; telegraph on land, under the sea and in the air; but air-ships may now be used. All these raise questions of international law. Intercourse between states is carried on by the above physical means, and by diplomatic negotiation. The most tangible results of the latter are international treaties, the nature of which has already been described (Chapter VII). Diplomacy as a means of international coöperation is discussed in Chapter XV.

NON-HOSTILE REDRESS

When intercourse between states has resulted in misunderstandings which are likely to lead to a rupture, there are recognized means of attempting amicably to settle the disputes. These are discussed in Chapters X, XI, XII. States may, however, seek other means of redress without an actual resort to war. We have seen that in certain circumstances self-help may be used; but there are other means sometimes called non-amicable measures of redress short of war. These are of several kinds. (1) A state may sever diplomatic relations without prohibiting intercourse between its nationals and the nationals of the other state. This is a form of public protest giving notice to the world that in some respect it is claimed that international obligations have been neglected. (2) If one state, acting entirely within its rights, so conducts itself as incidentally to affect another state or its citizens unfavorably, the injured state may make retaliation in kind. This is known as retorsion. Such acts might consist of vexatious immigration laws, or unusual, discriminative tariffs. A retaliation in kind often results in the repeal of the obnoxious legislation. (3) If the act complained of is an actual taking of the person or property of a citizen while in a foreign state, the state to which the injured citizen owes allegiance may perform acts of reprisal. This is not merely retaliation in kind, but the use of any means whereby discomforts and deprivations are placed upon the citizens of the offending state. This form of redress should not be confused with reprisals during war; and, moreover, it has almost entirely disappeared in practice. (4) Embargo is another means of redress. It consists either in the detention of the goods and ships of another state, or in the detention of its own ships in order to prevent their seizure by another state. The former is hostile and the latter civil or pacific embargo. Neither is looked upon with favor to-day. (5) Closely related to pacific embargo is non-intercourse, which is more general in scope. It consists in interdicting practically all intercourse, both commercial and social, between the nationals of one state and the nationals of an offending state. The last two forms of redress are developed in the League Covenant into a virtual boycott (Art. 16). Whether the imposition of economic pressure on a state under this article will technically be considered war, or a measure short of war, is not entirely clear. It is certainly a non-amicable measure, but its purpose is to bring to a close war begun in violation of the Covenant. The Article provides that in such a case, all members will subject the offending state to the severance of all trade and financial relations, and prohibit intercourse between the nationals of that state with the nationals of all other states whether or not they are members of the League. (6) Sometimes a state will make a display of force without in any way using it. This is in the nature of a threat, the effectiveness of which depends entirely on the relative strength of the powers involved. (7) A final form of redress is so close to war that some authorities refuse to classify it as non-hostile. It is known as pacific blockade. It consists in blockading the ports of a state without declaring war, but usually only with respect to the ships of the offending state and of the blockading state.

There is a considerable body of law relating to the preliminaries to the opening of hostilities. These have to do with declaration of war, notification to neutrals, and the status of neutral and enemy ships both public and private in neutral and enemy ports at the outbreak of hostilities. Many of these rules are codified in the Hague Conventions and the Declaration of London.

Most of the rules on the above matters, especially those relating entirely to peace, are untouched by the League Covenant. It is important to bear them in mind at this time because they specify the conditions under which the League will operate.

References for Chapter IX

HALL, W. H. International Law, 6th ed., p. 101–369.
LAWRENCE, T. J. Handbook of Public International Law, p. 39–87.

OPPENHEIM. International Law, v. 1.
WILSON, G. G. Handbook of International Law, p. 55-237.
WILSON AND TUCKER. International Law, p. 73-230.
BORCHARD, E. M. Diplomatic Protection of Citizens Abroad.
STOWELL AND MUNRO. International Cases.

> Measures short of War, 1:107-121.
> Self-help, 1:121-125.
> Jurisdiction, 1:373-393.
> Reprisals, 2:3-24.
> Outbreak of War, 2:25-35.
> Liquidation of Peace, 2:35-48.

CHAPTER X

INTERNATIONAL COMMISSIONS OF INQUIRY

THE underlying purpose of the League is the promotion of international coöperation and the achievement of international peace and security. The final section of this book is devoted to international coöperation. We now will consider in the remaining chapters of Part II some of the means of preventing war as provided in the League Covenant and as already recognized by international law and treaties.

The League Covenant provides two methods of settling international disputes without recourse to war, viz., arbitration, and investigation of the facts involved in a dispute either by the Council or the Assembly. These two methods we will take up in inverse order. By Article 12, "the members of the League agree that if there should arise between them any dispute likely to lead to a rupture they will submit the matter either to arbitration *or to inquiry by the Council*, and they agree in no case to resort to war until three months after the award by the arbitrators or the report by the Council." The arbitral award must be made within a reasonable time and the report of the Council within six months after the submission of the dispute. If a dispute is not submitted to arbitration, the members agree, by Article 15, that they will submit the matter to the Council. "Any party to the dispute may effect such submission by giving notice of the existence of the dispute to the Secretary-General, who will make all necessary arrangements for a full investigation and consideration thereof." Each party to the dispute agrees promptly to submit to the Secretary-General a statement of the case, with all relevant facts and papers, which the Council is authorized to publish. The Council must then endeavor to effect a settlement and if successful must publish the result with facts and explanations. If the Council is unsuccessful, it must, a majority concurring, publish a report containing its recommendations and explanations. If the Council does not so vote, any state represented on the Council may issue a statement of the facts of the dispute and its conclusions regarding them. In case the members of the Council with the exception of the representatives of one or more parties to the dispute are unanimous as to the report, the members of the League agree "that they will not go to war with any party to the dispute which complies with the recommendations of the report." If agreement by the Council as above cannot be had, "the members of the League reserve to themselves the right to take such action as they consider necessary for the maintenance of right and justice." It is not clear whether this provision refers to the "members of the League" collectively or individually. In the first case, the Council could even at this stage refer the dispute to the Assembly in order to obtain a further delay. In the second case, either the parties to the dispute could alone go to war, or the other members take sides with them, thus precipitating a general war.

The Council will make no recommendations concerning matters solely within the domestic jurisdiction of a state. The Council may in any case refer the dispute to the Assembly, and it must so refer it at the request of either party if the request is made within fourteen days of its submission to the Council. When referred to the Assembly, its powers are identical with those of the Council except that the report must be concurred in by the representatives of those members of the League represented on the Council, and of a majority of the other members of the League, exclusive in each case of parties to the dispute. The above provisions relate to disputes between members of the League. Disputes between two states outside of the League, or between one such state and a member of the League, are provided for by Article 17. In the event of a dispute, the state or states outside of the League "shall be invited to accept the obligations of membership" upon such conditions as the Council may deem just, and for this purpose the Council may modify the provisions of Articles 12 to 16. The Council appears to be given no discretion as to whether it shall or shall not invite non-members temporarily to accept the obligations of the League; but it is conceivable that there may be a difference of opinion within the Council as to whether a dispute likely to lead to a rupture exists. Moreover, there may be disagreement as to the conditions under which the invitation should be extended. Thus, it is possible that one or more members, under the unanimity rule, might prevent the Council from taking any action until an open rupture had occurred. The Council begins its investigation as soon as it has extended the invitation to states outside the League, not waiting for acceptance.

The penalty for failure to comply with the above provisions of the Covenant is set forth in Article 16 and the concluding paragraphs of Article 17. Should a member of the League, or a state invited to accept the obligations of membership in regard to a dispute with a member state, resort to war in violation of the Covenant, "it shall *ipso facto* be deemed to have committed an act of war against all the other members of the League," and it will be subjected to severance of all trade and financial relations, prohibition of all intercourse between it and any other state, and military and naval coercion on the recommendation of the Council. When two states outside the League refuse to accept the obligations of membership in the League in order to deal with a dispute between them, the measures to be taken and recommendations to be made will be decided upon by the Council. Any member of the League which violates one of its covenants may be expelled from membership "by a vote of the Council concurred in by the representatives of all the other members of the League represented thereon" (Art. 16).

It should be noted that the above provisions relate to disputes which the parties consider cannot be settled by arbitration, and which cannot be satisfactorily settled by diplomacy. Deferring the discussion of these two means of settlement to later chapters, let us examine more in detail the method of settlement or recommendation by means of reference to the Council or to the Assembly. Three classes of disputes are provided for, (1) those between members of the League, as A and B, (2) those between a member and a non-member, as A and X, and (3) those between non-members, as X and Y. In disputes belonging to the first class, A and B have by signature to the Covenant contracted to accept the assistance of the Council or of the Assembly; but neither A nor B is bound to accept the recommendation made in the report, and if both reject it, they may go to war three months after the submission of the report. As six months are allowed in which to make the report, the League may therefore delay hostilities in such a case for nine months. If, however, the report is unanimously adopted by the Council, with the exception of the representatives of A and B (who according to Article 4 will be present as members even though not permanently there), or by the Council and a majority of the other members of the League, with the exception of A and B, and if A, for instance, complies with the recommendation, then B and all other members agree not to go to war with A. If, however, B begins hostilities, the whole League will be arrayed against it, and it will be subject in the discretion of the Council to expulsion from membership (Art. 16). If the Council or Assembly cannot reach an agreement as above indicated, for instance if the report is approved only by a majority of the Council, then A and B, at the expiration of three months from the issuance of the report, may (1) try to settle their dispute by diplomacy, or (2) submit it to arbitration which, however, is hardly likely, or (3) go to war. If the last method were chosen then the other members of the League could individually tender good offices or offer to mediate, or intimate that they would take sides in order to bring hostilities to a close. The contrary result would be produced if the preponderance of power were not on one side, for the threat would only bring more parties into the contest. The Council might also, even at this stage, by unanimous vote, refer the dispute to the Assembly in the hope that by publicity, open debate, and personal influence, a report acceptable to one disputant might be agreed upon with a sufficient number of votes to make it effective.[1]

---

[1] It is scarcely possible that a unanimous vote of the Council for submission to the Assembly could be obtained; yet unanimity would be required because this is not named as an instance in which the unanimity rule does not apply.

If, when the dispute first came up in the Council, either A or B claimed that it arose out of a matter solely within domestic jurisdiction, the Council would pass upon this claim, and if it proved to be well-founded, no report would be made. This might not, however, settle the dispute; it might even aggravate it, if A still pressed its claim. A and B would be left to their own resources, and might resort to non-hostile means of redress, to diplomacy, or to arbitration. War has, therefore, not been prohibited between A and B, except under very definite circumstances. The restraints do not infringe sovereign rights because A and B agree to a limitation of the exercise of their right to declare war when they join the League. The regulations are self-imposed.

A difficult question, doubtless now of academic interest only, might be raised if a dispute should arise between Great Britain and one of her dominions, a member of the League. Suppose Australia should become seriously at variance with the mother country. Could Great Britain claim that the dispute was solely within her domestic jurisdiction? That perhaps would depend on the matter out of which the dispute arose; for Australia could with justice claim that to some extent her status was changed when she was admitted to full League membership. Civil war is not within the purview of the League; yet Australia is a full-fledged member, and she could assert the right to have her disputes, even with Great Britain, considered by the League.

In disputes of the second and third classes a new situation is created. If a dispute arises between A and X, X will be invited to act in the matter as if she were a member of the League. She may do this voluntarily and thus preserve the theory of her sovereignty. By this means a small non-member state might get the protection of the League against the overpowering might of a member state. But if X rejects the invitation of the League, and makes war on A regardless of the provisions of the Covenant, X will be subjected to economic boycott and military and naval pressure. She will have imposed on her a set of rules to which she has not given assent. This seems to be a violation of her sovereignty. On the other hand, war is still a legal remedy under international law, and it is open to the

League as rightfully as to non-members. For the purpose of bringing to a speedy end war begun by non-members, or as a deterrent to such wars, it may and indeed must still be used. The League, in order to prevent as far as possible the formation of powerful alliances outside the League, was forced to announce in advance what it would consider a *casus belli*.

Again, if X and Y are at odds, and both reject the League's invitation, "the Council may take such measures and make such recommendations as will prevent hostilities and will result in the settlement of the dispute." In order, therefore, to prevent war between X and Y, non-members of the League, the League may itself go to war with both X and Y. If X accepted the invitation of the League and Y rejected it, the same rules would apply as between A and X, when X refused to accept temporary membership. The cases where X, or X and Y, refuse to accept the obligations of the League may be few in number; or it may be that all sovereign states will become members of the League, thus removing the difficulty as to sovereignty, but if any powerful state should remain or become a non-member, the success of the League might be jeopardized by this provision. If the penalty clause did not apply to non-members refusing temporary membership, the arrangement would be strictly in conformity with rules of international law regarding amicable settlement of international disputes.

As regards members of the League, admirable provision is made for publicity and for delay in taking up arms, both of which make for peace. And the penalty clause, by agreement, properly applies to them as a guarantee of adherence to the Covenant. We may learn something of the probable operation of the plan as regards members of the League by surveying former attempts of a like character.

The normal way of settling international disputes is by diplomatic negotiation. It is dependent for its success on a spirit of coöperation and conciliation and on the skill of the negotiators. Its weakness arises from the pressure of uninformed public sentiment when calmness is required, and it is evident that at times a dispute gets beyond the point where it can directly be discussed by the parties to it. Therefore international law has long recognized as lawful the interposition of third parties for certain limited purposes. Thus a third state may tender its good offices to two disputing states for the purpose of beginning or renewing negotiations, or it may serve as mediator between the states, taking active part in the negotiations. Good offices and mediation may be tendered either before hostilities, or for the purpose of ending them. For example, the Russo-Japanese war was brought to an end through the good offices of President Roosevelt. Except where treaties so stipulate, a state is not bound to accept a tender of good offices or of mediation; but the tender is not considered an unfriendly act. The revised Hague Convention for the Pacific Settlement of International Disputes provides for Good Offices and Mediation, but recourse to them is not required.[1]

The Hague Convention contains a second method of preventing recourse to war; namely, International Commissions of Inquiry, the purpose of which is the elucidation of the facts involved in a dispute.[2] These commissions were to be created by voluntary act of the states after a dispute had arisen, and therefore have no permanent character; and it was assumed that states would be unwilling to resort to them in cases involving national honor or vital interests. There is, however, no reason why a state may not, if it desires, submit such cases to inquiry. It may do so with perfect safety, since the Hague Convention provides that "the report of the commission is limited to a statement of facts, and has in no way the character of an award. It leaves to the parties entire freedom as to the effect to be given to the statement" (Art. 35).

The efficacy of the kind of Commission of Inquiry provided for by the Hague Convention of 1899 was put to the test in 1904 in the course of the Russo-Japanese war. On the night of October 21, the Russian fleet was passing through the Dogger Bank fishing grounds in the North Sea on its way to the Far East, and under the impression that Japanese torpedo boats were about to attack it, fired on some trawlers of the Hull fishing fleet. One trawler was

[1] See Appendix 6 (a).
[2] *Ibid.*

COMMISSIONS OF INQUIRY

sunk, five were damaged, two men were killed and six wounded. The Russian fleet continued on its way without rendering assistance to the injured trawlers, and made no report until it reached Vigo, Spain, on the 26th. When the surviving fishermen reached England, and the facts became known, indignation ran high. On account of the Anglo-Japanese alliance of 1902, there was danger that Great Britain might enter the war, and the situation was tense, preliminary orders being issued to the British fleet. Diplomatic representations were made by both parties, but the testimony of the fishermen and of the Russian officers who made the attack were totally at variance. The Russian Admiral Rozhdestvensky insisted that two Japanese torpedo boats had been seen and that the trawlers had been unavoidably injured in repelling an attack. The fishermen denied that any except Russian war-ships had been present. Under these circumstances, on the suggestion of France, which tendered good offices, agreement was reached within a week to institute an inquiry into the facts. A formal agreement was signed at St. Petersburg on November 25, to proceed in accordance with Articles 9 to 14 of the Hague Convention. Great Britain, Russia, France, and the United States each chose one commissioner, and the four jointly chose a fifth, an Austrian admiral. The Commission sat intermittently in Paris from December 22, 1904, to February 25, 1905. Its first task was to formulate rules of procedure, none having been included in the Hague Convention of 1899. It concluded its labor, after hearing testimony, by publishing a report concurred in by a majority of the Commission. The report, finding that no Japanese ships had been on the Dogger Bank on the night of October 21, declared the attack unjustifiable and placed the responsibility on the Russian Admiral. Although this was not an arbitral award, and was binding on neither party, Russia accepted the finding and paid an indemnity of £65,000. The experience showed that even the brief and timid recommendation of the First Hague Conference provided a real means of preventing war, and that the idea was worthy of further development.[1]

---

[1] For report of the Commission, see Scott: Hague Court Reports p. 403-412, 609-615.

At the Second Hague Conference the Convention for the Pacific Settlement of International Disputes was revised and strengthened. The six Articles (9 to 14) of the Convention of 1899, relating to Commissions of Inquiry, were expanded into twenty-eight (Articles 9 to 36). Most of the new provisions relate to procedure which in the main followed the rules adopted by the Dogger Bank Commission. The phraseology of Article 9 was changed from a mere recommendation to a statement that the contracting powers "deem it expedient and desirable" that recourse be had to International Commissions of Inquiry. The exception of disputes involving national honor and vital interests was retained. During the Turco-Italian war the practical value of these commissions was again demonstrated. On January 25, 1912, the French mail steamer *Tavignano* was seized by the Italian torpedo boat *Fulmine* off the coast of Tunis and conducted to Tripoli under suspicion of having contraband-of-war on board. None being found she was released the next day. On January 25 also two Tunisian mahones, the *Camouna* and *Gaulois*, were fired upon by the Italian torpedo boat *Canopo*. Indemnity was claimed by France for these acts, which were justified by Italy on the ground that they took place on the high seas and not in the territorial waters of Tunis as claimed by France. Agreement was made on April 15 and May 20, 1912, to submit the question of fact to a Commission of Inquiry made up of three naval officers appointed by France, Italy, and Great Britain respectively. The report of the Commission, made on July 23, was indefinite and it was then agreed to submit the case to the Permanent Court of Arbitration. Subsequently, however, the dispute was settled by negotiation, the two governments being anxious "to show the spirit of cordial friendship which mutually animates them." Italy paid an indemnity of 5,000 francs.[1]

Commissions of Inquiry as international instruments next received official attention when the Taft administration negotiated treaties of arbitration with France and Great Britain. Although they were never ratified they mark a stage of development. By the first article of these treaties, the parties would have agreed to

[1] Scott: Hague Court Reports, p. 413-421, 616-623.

settle by arbitration all differences "which it has not been possible to adjust by diplomacy, relating to international matters—which are justiciable in their nature by reason of being susceptible of decision by the application of the principles of law or equity." The next two articles contained an agreement "to institute as occasion arises," Joint High Commissions of Inquiry composed of six members, three from each state, for elucidating the facts, defining the issues, and making recommendations in a dispute. The report, however, was, as formerly, not to be regarded as a decision or as having the character of an award. The provisions of the Hague Convention so far as applicable were to apply. The disputes to be investigated were, however, not to be limited to those not involving national honor or vital interests. They might include so-called "justiciable" questions before their submission to arbitration, or non-justiciable questions. The treaty failed of ratification by the United States Senate because of a further provision that the question whether a dispute was or was not justiciable should be referred to the Commission. If all or all but one of the commissioners agreed and reported that the difference was justiciable, then it was to be referred to arbitration. This provision gave to the Commission a power of decision on what states have always considered a vital question.

Within six weeks after the beginning of the first Wilson administration, negotiations were begun by Secretary of State Bryan for a new set of treaties. Following up an idea which he had presented to the London conference of the Interparliamentary Union in July, 1906, he proposed to all governments represented in Washington the conclusion of a series of bipartite treaties by which the parties would agree to submit all questions of every character and nature for investigation by permanent International Commissions, refraining from hostilities until a report had been made. The Commissions were to begin their investigations as a matter of course, upon their own initiative, without waiting for the formality of a request from either party. The report, however, was to have no binding force. The plan was intended to provide three things, (1) investigation of the facts of a dispute, (2) time for calm consideration before beginning hostilities, and (3) opportunity for the expression of public opinion. The proposal was favorably received by the foreign representatives, and was approved in advance by the United States Senate Committee on Foreign Relations. Thereupon, treaties were drawn up, and between April 24, 1913, and the present, thirty-five states have ratified or signed or accepted in principle one of the treaties with the United States. The plan differs from all others which were put into operation in that (1) there are no limitations on the character of the questions to be submitted for investigation, (2) the Commissions are permanent and not to be created after a dispute has come, (3) the Commissions may spontaneously offer their services, or be called in by either party, (4) the parties agree not to begin hostilities or declare war before the report is made, which must be within one year. It is like the Hague schemes in that the report when submitted has no binding force. Lange[1] has well summarized the treaties[2] as follows: "The parties agree to refer 'all disputes, of every nature whatsoever,' 'which diplomacy shall fail to adjust,' to a Commission of five, instituted before the origin of the dispute, 'for investigation and report.' The report shall be completed, as a general rule, within one year, and the parties agree 'not to declare war or begin hostilities during such investigation and before the report is submitted.' The conclusions of the report, however, are not binding upon the parties: 'The High Contracting Parties reserve the right to act independently on the subject matter of the dispute after the report of the Commission shall have been submitted.' The treaties are concluded for a limited period of five years; if not denounced, they will be in force for a prolonged period." None of the treaties preclude preparation for war during the progress of the investigation.

It was Mr. Bryan's plan not only that the United States should conclude such treaties with all other states, but that each state should conclude a similar treaty with every other. Thus there would be upward of a thousand nearly identical treaties and as

[1] The American Peace Treaties, p. 61-62.
[2] For example of a treaty, see Appendix 7.

many permanent Commissions of Inquiry, a cumbersome system, surely; but according to experience up to that time, easier to accomplish than joint agreement to a universal treaty.

In what situation then does a state bound by the Hague Convention, a Bryan treaty, and the League Covenant find itself in relation to International Commissions of Inquiry? The Convention adopted at the Second Hague Conference and many of the Bryan treaties are still in force. "Nothing in this Covenant," says Article 21, "shall be deemed to affect the validity of international engagements such as treaties of arbitration . . . for securing the maintenance of peace." In case of a dispute with a state not bound by the Bryan treaty, the first state would be free to submit the dispute for investigation to a specially instituted Commission. Where a treaty exists, the dispute might be submitted to the permanent Commission, under the obligation not to resort to war prior to the submission of the report. But in either case, after investigation and report, the state would not now be free to go to war. Here the League Covenant would exert its influence. If the dispute was with a member of the League, and the Council with the exception of the representatives of the two states was unanimous in its report, and the other state accepted the recommendations, the first state could not then go to war without thereby being at war with the League itself. If the dispute was with a non-member of the League which temporarily accepted the obligations of the League, the situation would be the same. If, by any chance, the first state should cease to be a member of the League it would then be subject to coercion by the League, whether its dispute was with a member or a non-member.

The Bryan treaties could voluntarily be denounced as unnecessary, as could also the Hague Convention, and it is possible that the Assembly may by virtue of Article 19 recommend this.

Part XIII of the Treaty of Versailles, relating to an International Labor Organization, contains provisions for the investigation of disputes by Commissions of Inquiry. They are described in Chapter XIX, where the whole Labor Organization is discussed.

References for Chapter X

BAKER, ERNEST. The Constitution of the League of Nations: Judicial.
   (New Europe, 10: 196–203, March 13, 1919.)
FINCH. The Bryan Peace Treaties.
   (American Journal of International Law, 10: 882–890.)
HULL. The Two Hague Conferences, p. 267–297.
LANGE. The American Peace Treaties.
MYERS. The Conciliation Plan of the League to Enforce Peace, with American Treaties in Force.
   (World Peace Foundation. Pamphlet Series, 6: no. 5.)
OPPENHEIM. International Law, 2: 10–15.
SCOTT. Hague Court Reports, p. 403–421, 609–623.
STOWELL AND MUNRO. International Cases, 1: 98–106.

CHAPTER XI

INTERNATIONAL ARBITRATION

The members of the League, and non-members when invited, have the choice of submitting disputes to inquiry by the Council or Assembly, or to arbitration (Art. 12), and the members agree "in no case to resort to war until three months after the award by the arbitrators or the report of the Council." The award must be made "within a reasonable time," and not within six months as in the case of the report of the Council or Assembly. The dispute may be referred to any court chosen by the parties, either by special agreement or in accordance with any convention existing between them. Thus, they may set up a special tribunal for the particular dispute, selecting the judges by agreement; or they may do so by virtue of an arbitration treaty already made; or they may avail themselves of any existing court, such as the Permanent Court of Arbitration at the Hague, or in time, the Court of International Justice, plans for which are to be made by the Council (Art. 14). In order to study the possibilities with regard to arbitration, let us, as in the last chapter, indicate two members of the League by A and B; a member and a non-member by A and X; and two non-members by X and Y. In a dispute between A and B which has not been settled by diplomacy, and which has not been referred to the Council or Assembly for inquiry, they both have agreed by Article 12 to submit it to arbitration, and not to go to war until three months after the award which must be made within a reasonable time. They both agree by Article 13 to carry out the award; but if A refuses to do so, and B accepts the award, then the whole League including A agrees not to go to war with B. If A, however, does go to war with B, this will be considered an act of war on the League, and all the penalties of Article 16 will apply. In case either A or B or both fail to carry out the award, but still do not go to war, then "the Council shall propose what steps should be taken to give effect thereto" (Art. 13). Attention should be paid to the wording of the last paragraph of Article 13, with particular reference to the antecedent of the pronoun "they." "The *members* of the League," (i. e., all of them) "agree that *they*" (i. e., all members) "will carry out in full good faith any award that may be rendered and that they" (i. e., all of them, and particularly the members which do not accept the award) "will not resort to war against a member of the League which complies therewith." If the dispute is between A and X, it is provided that X shall be invited to proceed as though it were a member, and if it accepts, the case is precisely like the preceding one, the Council having power, however, to prescribe the terms which apply to X while acting as member. In this case, however, arbitration is always to be preceded by investigation by the Council, which shall "recommend such action as may seem best and most effectual in the circumstances" (Art. 17). If X refuses the invitation, and goes to war against A, then X has made war on the League. This means, of course, that A could immediately commence hostilities.

If the dispute is between X and Y, both must be invited temporarily to enter the League, and if they accept, the Covenant applies to them. If both refuse, then the Council may, but is not obliged to, "take such measures and make such recommendations as will prevent hostilities and will result in the settlement of the dispute." The decision apparently may be made to let X and Y fight. It is the evident intention that the award of the arbitration tribunal shall be final, and that states whether members of the League or not must settle disputes either by negotiation, or mediation, or investigation, or arbitration. The penalty for not so deciding disputes is war, for the ultimate resource of the League, whether in forcing submission of a dispute, or compliance with an award, is war. It is important to notice, however, that when a dispute has once been submitted to arbitration, the right of the parties to carry on a bipartite war has been relinquished. After arbitration, the only war recognized as possible is a war by the League to punish a

INTERNATIONAL ARBITRATION

Covenant breaker, viz., one which fails to comply with the award. States will therefore consider carefully what disputes they submit to arbitration.

Is there any means of determining whether a difference is a proper subject for arbitration? Article 13 gives a partial answer. It contains the agreement to submit to arbitration disputes which the parties "recognize to be suitable for submission to arbitration and which cannot be satisfactorily settled by diplomacy." It then enumerates some of the matters which the parties agree in advance to be generally suitable. "Disputes as to the interpretation of a treaty, as to any question of international law, as to the existence of any fact which if established would constitute a breach of any international obligation, or as to the extent and nature of the reparation to be made for any such breach, are declared to be among those which are generally suitable for submission to arbitration." This language is an elaboration and extension of Articles 16 and 38[1] of the Hague Conventions of 1899 and 1907 respectively. By them, the powers recognized arbitration as the most effective and equitable means of settling disputes "of a legal nature, and especially in the interpretation or application of international conventions." Both the League Covenant and the Hague Convention are more definite as far as they go than the unratified Taft treaties of 1911, by which the signatories would have been bound to submit to arbitration all differences "which it had not been possible to adjust by diplomacy, relating to international matters in which the High Contracting Parties are concerned by virtue of a claim of right made by one against the other under treaty or otherwise, and which are justiciable in their nature by reason of being susceptible of decision by the application of the principles of law and equity." We have seen that the Taft treaties failed of ratification because the United States Senate was unwilling to leave to a Court of Inquiry the decision as to what differences are justiciable. The Taft treaties were themselves an attempt to avoid the definite limitations which were contained in the arbitration treaties of 1908 with France and Great Britain. Article 1 of both of these treaties reads as fol-

[1] See Appendix 6 (a).

lows: "Differences which may arise of a legal nature or relating to the interpretation of treaties . . . and which it may not have been possible to settle by diplomacy, shall be referred to the Permanent Court of Arbitration established at the Hague . . . provided, nevertheless, that they do not affect the vital interests, the independence, or the honor of the two Contracting States, and do not concern the interests of third Parties."[1] In so far as the treaties of 1908 bound the parties to submit to arbitration disputes of definite categories, they marked a forward step; but if they are considered as placing limitations on the classes of disputes that might be arbitrated, they were backward steps. Before that time, on numerous occasions beginning with the arbitrations under Article 7 of the Jay Treaty of 1794[2] and ending with the Pious Fund Case of 1902 submitted to the Permanent Court of Arbitration at the Hague[3] the United States had arbitrated without reservation matters involving vital interests and national honor. Whether or not this practice could have been continued, we now have emphasized by the League Covenant the fact that some disputes will probably not be recognized by the parties as suitable for arbitration. It will be noticed that the League Covenant does not use the words vital interests, independence, and national honor, as reservations in relation to the enumerated disputes suitable for submission to arbitration. In other words, the interpretation of all treaties, all questions of international law, all proved facts constituting a breach of international obligations, and the extent of reparation to be made, are subject to arbitration. Any one of these matters may be considered by a member of the League as involving its vital interests or honor or independence, yet there is no escape from the agreement unless the word "generally" provides a loophole.[4] How sweeping an agreement this is may be seen by reference to the debates in the committees of the Second

[1] Malloy: Treaties, 1:814-815.
[2] Malloy: Treaties, 1:596.
[3] Wilson: Hague Arbitration Cases, p. 1-11.
[4] It has been suggested that the word "generally" is here used in a sense not common to-day, namely, as meaning collectively, as a whole, without omissions. The usual meaning of the word is "extensively," though not universally.

INTERNATIONAL ARBITRATION

Hague Conference. There the attempt was made to include in the Convention for the Pacific Settlement of International Disputes a list of classes of treaties the interpretation of which was subject to obligatory arbitration. Twenty-four classes of treaties were separately voted upon, and none of them received a unanimous vote for inclusion. It was argued that any one of the classes, even treaties concerning, for instance, literary and artistic copyright, might involve political and economic as well as judicial questions and therefore be unsuitable for obligatory arbitration.[1]

International disputes are usually classed into those of a legal and those of a political nature. In practice it is difficult to maintain the distinction. An instance of a legal question would be a dispute over the exemption from local jurisdiction of a foreign warship in territorial waters of another state. A political question would be one involving the conflicting colonial policies of two states. In either case, no opinion could be formed without an investigation of the facts, perhaps by a Commission of Inquiry; and in either case honor or vital interests might by either party be thought to be involved. Under the League, the first question would be subject to arbitration, while the latter would not. Perhaps the only generalization concerning non-justiciable questions that can be made is to characterize them as those which cannot be settled by an award of damages. Such cases are those involving a state's territory, insult to its flag, its power to receive political refugees, and freedom of thought and religion. It might be well to adopt the suggestion made by Barclay in 1907[2] as an explanation of the terms vital interest and national honor. For them he would substitute the phrase "affecting neither the independence nor territorial integrity nor the internal laws or institutions" of a power. The Covenant does not exclude from arbitration matters involving domestic jurisdiction, although it does preclude investigation of them by the Council (Art. 15).

"International arbitration," according to the Hague Conven-

[1] Hull: Two Hague Conferences, p. 332-335.
[2] Problems of International Practice.

tions, "has for its object the settlement of disputes between states by judges of their own choice and on the basis of respect for law."[1] In this statement there are three essential points: first, the disputes are to be settled or decided; second, by judges chosen by the parties; third, on the basis of respect for law. These, in the opinion of the members of both Hague Conferences, are the characteristics of arbitration tribunals, and there is no hint in the words that all three points are not of equal force. Yet on the last point a very considerable difference of opinion has arisen. According to Scott[2] the statement that the settlement is to be made on the basis of respect for law, "does not mean necessarily that the decision is to be reached by the impartial and passionless application of principles of law, as in the case of municipal courts, but the decision is to be reached 'on the basis of respect for law,' which may be a very different matter." How may it be a very different matter? Would an international arbitration tribunal be justified in rendering an award on the basis of *disrespect* for law? If so, it is difficult to understand the care with which the convention in its next article (38), as has already been pointed out, recognizes the effectiveness of arbitration in the settlement of questions "of a legal nature and especially in the interpretation or application of international conventions." Is not the legal or judicial character of arbitration here pointedly emphasized? It cannot be denied that the opposite view has received considerable support, especially by the members of the Society for the Judicial Settlement of International Disputes, and by the advocates of the Court of Arbitral Justice. They appear, however, according to other eminent authorities, in the ardor of advocacy to have done injustice to a time-honored institution, even overlooking the technical meaning of the word arbitration. A host of support could be marshalled for the contention that arbitral settlement is one and the same thing as judicial settlement, the distinction being not between law and arbitration, but between arbitration and mediation. The authorities have been collected by Balch in an article entitled "'Arbitration' as a Term

---

[1] See Appendix 6 (a).
[2] Hague Court Reports, p. xvii.

of International Law"[1] wherein the use of the term in international law as opposed to municipal law is traced. He finds little support for the theory that international arbitration is a system of compromise. He quotes Pufendorf, Klüber, Rolin-Jaequemyns, Renault, Westlake, and Martens, all to the same effect as John Bassett Moore, who says,[2] "It is important, from the practical as well as from the theoretical side of the matter, to keep in view the distinction between arbitration and mediation—a distinction either not understood or else lost sight of by many of those who have undertaken to discuss the one subject or the other. Mediation is an advisory, arbitration a judicial, function. Mediation recommends, arbitration decides." There are, of course, differences between courts of arbitration and municipal courts of law just as there are between the municipal courts of different states. For instance, arbitration courts do not consider themselves bound by the doctrine of *stare decisis*. In this respect they follow the continental system, and are none the less judicial in character. "Nevertheless," says Ralston,[3] "arbitral opinions will be continually found filled with references to the conclusions of other tribunals, as well as to the views of distinguished writers upon the subject of international law, and an arbitrator or umpire in his decisions will with hesitancy reject the solemn findings of those who have theretofore in international commissions reached definite conclusions as to controverted points. Always will he rest easier knowing that in his opinion he is supported by those of predecessors of distinction, and should his final determinations be different, he will feel the necessity of supporting them by the most careful argument." If, after a critical examination of Moore's "Digest of International Arbitrations," Mr. Ralston makes this statement, it is difficult to see what judicial characteristic they lack which can be found in the decisions of municipal courts. Moreover, this judicial character is not removed or nullified by the fact that the decisions or awards are made by judges chosen by the parties for each dispute. Even assuming

---
[1] Columbia Law Review, 15: 590-607, 662-679.
[2] History and Digest of International Arbitrations, 5:5042.
[3] International Arbitral Law and Procedure, p. iii-iv.

that each state chooses one or more of its own citizens to act as arbitrators together with one or more of neither nationality chosen jointly by them, and assuming further that the nationals are unduly biased, so that they neutralize each other, the decision may be quite as judicial as those of the United States Supreme Court rendered by a majority of one. The award must always be supported by reasoning, and this reasoning must bear the test of examination by the publicists of the world. There are, however, instances in which nationals have voted against the contentions of their own states; and the practice has been growing of selecting foreign jurists to sit for a state. In about half of the cases decided by the Permanent Court of Arbitration at the Hague no nationals of the parties to the controversy have sat as arbitrators. In considering this point, it must be remembered that the parties are sovereign states, and that, except by voluntary agreement, they are in no way obligated to submit a given question to arbitration. There is no advantage in doing this unless negotiation, or mediation, or investigation by a Commission of Inquiry has failed, and then, unless independence is at stake, law is preferable to war. It is possible also for two states by agreement to leave to a tribunal not only the task of judicial decision, but failing to come to a conclusion that will give practical satisfaction and end strife, that of mediating between extreme conflicting claims. This, however, would not be a reflection on arbitration, but a recognition beforehand that judicial decision may not end political differences, and that the sovereign states will in certain events prefer compromise. If, however, there is no agreement of this kind, it is understood that the award is binding.

It is a fact which needs explanation that the Second Hague Conference endeavored to create a Court of Arbitral Justice, while leaving the Permanent Court of Arbitration intact. The attempt failed not because such a court was thought to be useless, but on account of disagreement over the appointment of judges. In the next chapter an attempt has been made to state the advantages of a court with a permanent personnel. Here we may remark that those who distinguish between the functions of the two courts, appear to have in mind the difference between a court of equity and a court of Law, and to classify the Permanent Court of Arbitration under the former head. If so, the order of judicial development in international law is just the reverse of that in national law. Moreover, the tendency has been to abolish the distinction between law and equity, both in the United States being commonly administered by the same judges. This tends to show that in the matter of competency only one court is needed.

This brings us to the third characteristic of an arbitration tribunal. Hall[1] states that an arbitral decision may be disregarded in the following cases: "when the tribunal has clearly exceeded the powers given to it by the instrument of submission, when it is guilty of an open denial of justice, when its award is proved to have been obtained by fraud or corruption, and when the terms of the award are equivocal." These exceptions to the binding force of an award are not, it is submitted, evidences of the non-judicial character of arbitration. Remembering again that the parties are sovereign states, it is evident that the protest of one or both would be against the non-judicial character of the decisions, and that in the last resort war is the sanction for international law. The Hague Conventions provide that "recourse to arbitration implies an engagement to submit in good faith to the award," and Article 81 says that "the award, duly pronounced and notified to the agents of the parties, settles the dispute definitively and without appeal." Provision is made,[2] however, for the decision by the tribunal of disputes arising over the meaning of the award, its interpretation and execution. This clause did not appear in the Convention of 1899. Both Conventions, however, recognize the right of the parties at the time of submission of a controversy to reserve the right to demand a revision of the award on the ground of discovery of new facts calculated to exercise a decisive influence upon the award and which were unknown to the tribunal and the party demanding revision at the time of the decision. Under the Hague Conventions submission to the award rests entirely on the good faith of the

---
[1] International Law, 6th ed., p. 355.
[2] Article 82 of 1907 Convention.

parties. Under the League provision is made for enforcement, but the exact process is not defined. "In the event of any failure to carry out such an award, the Council shall propose what steps should be taken to give effect thereto" (Art. 13). There is definite agreement, however, not to go to war with a state which complies with the award.

Several important studies of international arbitration in ancient times have been made which serve to show, as Wheaton says, that the theory and practice of arbitration are as old as international relationships. It is not until the nineteenth century, however, that we find the beginning of development into a system, and until the middle of the century, the question whether arbitration should be resorted to was always left for decision until the question arose. Then the practice grew of entering into general arbitration treaties, relating not to a specific difference but to all classes of differences, with exceptions as already noted, which may arise in the future. This was the beginning of obligatory arbitration. These treaties were chiefly bipartite treaties. The tribunals were, however, to be created for each occasion. They might consist of one person, or more than one person chosen by the litigating states, or the choice of the tribunal might be delegated to a third state. If more than one person was to serve, usually an odd number was chosen, and the decision was made by majority vote. The tribunal provided its own rules of procedure unless they were given in the general arbitration treaty. The development of recent years has been in the direction of more general agreement to resort to arbitration, of determination on rules of procedure, and the creation of courts of a more or less permanent character to which recourse could be had in lieu of special tribunals.

The most recent example of *ad hoc* arbitration tribunals is contained in Articles 304 to 305 of the Treaty of Versailles. It is provided that "within three months from the date of the coming into force of the present treaty, a Mixed Arbitral Tribunal shall be established between each of the Allied and Associated Powers on the one hand and Germany on the other hand. Each such tribunal shall consist of three members." Each government chooses one member and the two governments together, the President of the Tribunal. "In case of failure to reach agreement, the President of the Tribunal and two other persons, either of whom may in case of need take his place, shall be chosen by the Council of the League of Nations, or, until this is set up, by M. Gustave Ador[1] if he is willing. These persons shall be nationals of Powers that have remained neutral during the war." Decisions are to be made by majority vote, and they are to deal with questions arising under Sections III, IV, V, and VII of Part X of the Treaty, which relate respectively to debts; property rights and interests; contracts, prescriptions and judgments; and industrial property. Questions which, under the laws of the Allied, Associated, or neutral Powers, are within the jurisdiction of the national courts are to be decided by those courts, to the exclusion of the Mixed Arbitral Tribunal. A national of an Allied or Associated Power may, however, bring the case before the Tribunal, if this is not prohibited by the laws of his country. The decisions of the Tribunal are to be final and conclusive.

By some writers it is thought that the Western Hemisphere furnished the first attempt to organize arbitration into a judicial system. Those who believe that the thirteen colonies in the act of separating from Great Britain became sovereign states, and then united in a "league of friendship," find in the Articles of Confederation (1777) provision for a true Court of Arbitration. Others see in this arrangement only the progenitor of the United States Supreme Court. Whichever view is taken, the provisions of Article 9 are interesting as a means of decision by judges chosen by the parties to a dispute. The article gave to Congress the final decision on appeal in all disputes and differences between two or more states of the Confederation "concerning boundary, jurisdiction, or any other cause whatever." Controversies over "private right of soil claimed under different grants of two or more States" were to be decided by Congress "as near as may be in the same manner." Whenever a state through its legislature, executive, or agent petitioned Congress, stating the matter in question and asking a hear-

[1] Formerly President of the Swiss Federal Council.

ing, Congress was to notify the other state and set a date for an appearance of the parties by their lawful agents, "who shall then be directed to appoint by joint consent, commissioners or judges to constitute a court for hearing and determining the matter in question." If they could not agree, then Congress was to name three persons out of each of the United States, and from this list of thirty-nine, each party was alternately to strike out one, the petitioners beginning, until the number was reduced to thirteen. From that number, not less than seven nor more than nine, as Congress directed, were to be drawn by lot. The persons thus selected or any five of them were to serve as judges "to hear and finally determine the controversy" by majority vote. If either state refused to select the judges in this manner, then the Secretary of Congress was to strike out the names from the panel in behalf of that party until the court was constituted. The judgment was in every case to be final and to be "lodged among the acts of Congress for the security of the parties concerned." The only restriction on the court was that no state should be deprived of territory for the benefit of the United States.

For an unquestioned example of a court of arbitration open to the whole world we must turn to the Permanent Court of Arbitration set up by the Hague Conference of 1899. One of the purposes of the Convention for the Pacific Settlement of International Disputes was "the permanent institution of a Court of Arbitration accessible to all, in the midst of the independent Powers." Chapter II of the Convention sets up the Court and provides rules of procedure. It has been said of this tribunal that it is neither a court nor permanent; but we have the opinion of Professor John Bassett Moore written in 1914 that the Convention establishing it "is the highest achievement of the past twenty years in the direction of an arrangement for the peaceful adjustment of international controversies."[1] The Convention was revised by the Conference of 1907, the changes being largely verbal, or concerned with procedure. The essential character of the court and its jurisdiction remain as originally provided. The features of permanent organi-

[1] International Arbitration; a survey of the present situation, p. 3.

INTERNATIONAL ARBITRATION

zation are: first, a list of judges made up of not more than four persons of known competency in questions of international law and of the highest moral reputation, chosen by each contracting state. By agreement the same person may be selected by different powers. The judges are appointed for six years and their appointments may be renewed. Second, a Permanent Administrative Council composed of the diplomatic representatives of the contracting powers accredited to The Hague and of the Netherlands Minister of Foreign Affairs who acts as President. This Council settles its rules of procedure and all other necessary regulations and decides all questions of administration with regard to the court. Nine members constitute a quorum and its decisions are by majority vote. Third, an International Bureau, under the control of the Administrative Council, which serves as registry for the Court, and as the channel for communications relative to its meetings. Fourth, the permanent seat of the Court, Administrative Council, and International Bureau is at The Hague.

The Court has no obligatory jurisdiction but is competent to decide all cases submitted to it by agreement of the contracting parties. Its jurisdiction may, within the regulations, be extended to disputes between non-contracting powers or between contracting powers and non-contracting powers, on joint petition of the parties to such disputes. It is agreed that in case of impending disputes any contracting power may, without offence, remind the parties that the Court is open to them. "Recourse to arbitration implies an engagement to submit in good faith to the award."

The decisions are not made jointly by all members of the Court. When it has been agreed to submit a case to the Court, each party must choose its arbitrators from the general list. The number may be decided upon by the parties, but if they cannot agree the Convention stipulates that each party shall choose two arbitrators from the list, only one of whom can be its national or appointee to the list, and these four arbitrators choose an umpire. If the four are equally divided, then the choice of the umpire is to be left to a third power; and if agreement cannot be reached on this third power, then each party selects a different power and the umpire is chosen by them in concert. If these two powers cannot agree within two months, then each of them presents two candidates from the list exclusive of members selected by the parties and not being nationals of either of them, and from these names the umpire is drawn by lot. The umpire acts as president.

The arbitrators having been chosen, the parties notify the International Bureau, and submit their *compromis*, that is the agreement by which the issue is defined, and any matters of special procedure set forth. The Bureau then makes the arrangement for the meeting of the Court. If the parties have not been able to agree on a *compromis*, the Court may do so at the request of both parties. In certain specified cases the Court may so act at the request of one of the parties. The *compromis* concerning disputes covered by general arbitration treaties, and over the payment of contract debts, may be settled by a commission of five chosen as are the arbitrators themselves, in which case the commission, in the absence of a contrary agreement, itself shall form the arbitration tribunal. The parties may in the *compromis* reserve the right to demand a revision of the award in case of discovery of new facts unknown at the time of the award. Concerning Article 53, the United States ratified the Convention with the following reservation: "That the United States approves this convention with the understanding that recourse to the permanent court for the settlement of differences can be had only by agreement thereto through general or special treaties of arbitration heretofore or hereafter concluded between the parties in dispute; and the United States now exercises the option contained in Article 53 of said convention, to exclude the formulation of the *compromis* by the permanent court, and hereby excludes from the competence of the permanent court the power to frame the *compromis* required by general or special treaties of arbitration concluded or hereafter to be concluded by the United States, and further expressly declares that the *compromis* required by any treaty of arbitration to which the United States may be a party shall be settled only by agreement between the contracting parties unless such treaty shall expressly provide otherwise."[1]

[1] Malloy: Treaties, 2: 2247-2248.

Pleadings are conducted by the presentation of cases, counter-cases, and replies, accompanied with papers and documents; and the arguments are developed by oral discussions. The tribunal has power to require the production of papers, and to put questions to the agents and counsel of the parties. The decision of the Court is arrived at in private by majority vote, and the proceedings remain secret. The award must give the reasons on which it is based. If there is dispute as to the interpretation and execution of the award, the questions are submitted, in absence of a contrary agreement, to the tribunal which pronounced it. The award is final unless the right of revision was reserved in the *compromis;* but it binds only the parties. If it affects third parties they may intervene in the course of the proceedings, in which case they are bound by the award. Provision is made for a simple procedure in choosing the Court and deciding cases of minor importance which admit of summary procedure.

The United States ratified the Convention with a reservation as to Article 48 which recommends that disputants be reminded of the existence of the Court. The reservation follows: "Nothing contained in this convention shall be so construed as to require the United States of America to depart from its traditional policy of not intruding upon, interfering with, or entangling itself in the political questions of policy or internal administration of any foreign state, nor shall anything contained in the said convention be construed to imply a relinquishment by the United States of its traditional attitude toward purely American questions."[1]

As pointed out by Professor Wilson in the preface to his Hague Arbitration Cases, the work of the Court has amply justified its creation. Fifteen cases have been decided relating to a variety of questions, including not only financial questions, but those of more delicate character such as the violation of territory, the right to fly the flag, the delimitation of boundaries, etc. The fact that these questions have been submitted is of great significance. Seventeen different states in all have been parties in cases before the Court. France has been a party in six cases, Great Britain in five, the

---
[1] Malloy: Treaties, 2: 2247.

United States in four, Germany and Italy in three. Europe, Asia, Africa, and North and South America have been involved.

Following is a list of the cases decided with the dates of the awards:

Mexico v. United States	Pious Fund Case	October 14, 1902
Germany, Great Britain, Italy v. Venezuela	Venezuelan Preferential Claims	February 22, 1904
France, Germany, Great Britain v Japan	Japanese House Tax Case	May 22, 1905
France v. Great Britain	Muscat Dhows Case	August 8, 1905
France v. Germany	Casablanca Case	May 22, 1909
Norway v. Sweden	Grisbadarna Case	October 23, 1909
Great Britain v. United States	North Atlantic Fisheries Case	September 7, 1910
United States v. Venezuela	Orinoco Steamship Co. Case	October 25, 1910
France v. Great Britain	Savarkar Case	February 24, 1911
Italy v. Peru	Canevaro Case	May 3, 1912
Russia v. Turkey	Russian Indemnity Case	November 11, 1912
France v. Italy	Carthage and Manouba cases	May 6, 1913
Netherlands v. Portugal	Island of Timor Case	June 25, 1914

COMMISSION OF INQUIRY CASES

Great Britain v. Russia	Dogger Bank Case	February 26, 1905
France v. Italy	Tavignano, Camouna, and Gaulois Cases	July 23, 1912

REFERENCES FOR CHAPTER XI

ARTICLES OF CONFEDERATION.
   (Thorpe, F. N. Federal and State Constitutions, 1: 9–17.)

BAKER, ERNEST. The Constitution of the League of Nations: Judicial.
(New Europe, 10: 196-203, March 13, 1919.)

BALCH. Arbitration as a Term of International Law.
(Columbia Law Review, 15: 590-607, 662-679.)

BARCLAY. New Methods of Adjusting International Disputes, 1917, p. 40-91.

HULL. The two Hague Conferences, p. 297-348.

MOORE, J. B. International Arbitration; a Survey of the Present Situation (May 27, 1914). Principles of American Diplomacy, p. 306-338. History and Digest of International Arbitrations, 6 v.

SCOTT. Hague Court Reports.

TAFT, W. H. Proposed Arbitration Treaties with Great Britain and France.
(Judicial Settlement, no. 7.)

WILSON, G. G. Hague Arbitration Cases.

CHAPTER XII

INTERNATIONAL TRIBUNALS WITH PERMANENT PERSONNEL

By Article 14 of the League Covenant, the Council is directed to "formulate and submit to the members of the League for adoption plans for the establishment of a Permanent Court of International Justice. The Court," it says, "shall be competent to hear and determine any dispute of an international character which the parties thereto submit to it. The Court may also give an advisory opinion upon any dispute or question referred to it by the Council or by the Assembly." It is significant that the Covenant does not itself erect such a court, and that while the Council must formulate and present a plan, the members of the League may or may not adopt it. If, however, a court is created, it may take jurisdiction of all classes of cases of an international character, but only when they are voluntarily submitted to it by the parties. It would have one function even though no cases were presented to it for decision; namely, to give advice, presumably of a legal character, on questions submitted to it by the Council or Assembly.[1] Since there is already in existence a Permanent Court of Arbitration at The Hague, and since, under Article 13 of the Covenant, the parties to a dispute may submit it to a court of their own choosing, it is important to inquire why any new court should be created. Is this new court to be in any way different from the existing Hague Court? It has been said of the latter that its name is misleading—that it is neither permanent nor a court. It is not permanent because there exists only a large panel from which arbitrators may be chosen by the parties to decide any particular dispute. It is not a court, because

---
[1] For the functions of the court in relation to the International Labor Organization, see Chapter XIX.

it has no continuity of personnel, and no coherent body of traditions built up by successive decisions by the same group of men. It is not bound to see that each subsequent decision is consistent in principle with preceding decisions by other men chosen from the panel. It does not uniformly render its awards according to legal principles. The parties may choose as arbitrators men appointed to the panel by themselves, and therefore compromise rather than judicial decision is to be expected. Are these criticisms justifiable? Certainly the Hague Court is not permanent if permanency requires that the same men, as long as they are members of the Court, shall sit on all cases. The members of the Court are, however, chosen for six years, and the same men could be selected for each dispute if the successive parties so desired. There is a tendency in this direction as pointed out by Professor Wilson[1] when he says, "Of the six arbitrators sitting in the cases decided in 1913 and 1914, each arbitrator had previously sat upon at least one case at The Hague and some had already appeared in several cases." Moreover, the Court has a permanent International Bureau which preserves and publishes the records and awards of the Court; and two compilations of the cases decided have been published in English. There is unquestionably a pronounced element of permanency discernible in these facts; and with few exceptions, the awards themselves show an intention to abide by precedent and the principles of international law wherever these can be agreed upon. Exceptions in this respect there are, but a similar situation exists in the decisions of national courts even in those countries where the rule of *stare decisis* is in force. On the continent, where this rule does not apply, consistency is no more required or to be found than in the awards of the Hague Court. In each case the purpose is to render substantial justice and if possible, once for all, to settle the controversy.

A fundamental difficulty encountered by the Hague Court is the absence of a positive code of international law similar to American and English statute law and the continental codes. This fact must ever be kept in mind when judging the work of international tri-

[1] Hague Arbitration Cases, p. vi.

bunals. It affects not only the character of the decisions, but the willingness of states to submit their disputes to arbitration. In order to appreciate the problems involved in the creation of a permanent Court of International Justice, we must distinguish between it and national courts. National courts are the organs of the judicial departments of state governments. Their functions are defined by the state constitutions or statutes, and their decisions are supported by the whole power of the state. They have two kinds of jurisdiction, civil and criminal. The former deals with controversies between citizens and the latter with violation of state law by a citizen. While a state may punish its subject, the subject may not sue the state without the express consent of the state. This consent is now usually given by statutes which erect special tribunals to hear such claims against the state. The consent may, however, at any time be withdrawn by state act in virtue of its sovereignty. It is a maxim of law that a state may not be sued either in its own court or in any other court without its own consent. Such consent has never been given except where the rules to be applied are well understood.

Unquestionably a state, unless its constitution forbid, may agree to submit a dispute to any international court that may be erected; but it will insist on knowing beforehand the law that is to be applied, and the extent and character of the court's jurisdiction. Except as created by the League Covenant there is nothing in the law of nations which defines crime committed by states; and breaches of the Covenant are to be dealt with, after investigation by the Council, by boycott, economic pressure, and war. A state is not compelled to submit to arbitration, but if it does not do so, it must submit to investigation.

The proposed Court of International Justice must, therefore, since no other kind of jurisdiction is provided for, be a court of arbitration—applying the same law (which as has been said has not been reduced to a code of positive law); acquiring jurisdiction in the same way (i. e., by consent of the parties); and rendering awards with the same binding effect; as does the Permanent Court of Arbitration at The Hague. Its awards will be supported by the

League organization which is more definite than that of the old Society of Nations; but the League stands also back of all arbitral awards made by tribunals chosen by the parties (Art. 13). What need, therefore, is there for a new court? In the first place, it may be convenient and proper to complete the organization of the League, as far as international law permits, by the establishment of its own court. This will aid in the centralization of records and information concerning world affairs. The court would also be at all times available, according to Article 14, for the rendition of advisory opinions upon a dispute or question referred to it by the Council or by the Assembly. It would thus serve as the expert legal department of the League, dealing with intricate and delicate matters without rendering decisions binding on the parties. This function is doubtless of extreme importance, but it could be performed by a group of legal experts not organized into a court. For further justification of its creation we are therefore forced to consider the element of permanency, and the probable number of permanent arbitrators. For this reason this chapter emphasizes permanent personnel as a characteristic of the proposed court. If eminent jurists are to devote their whole time to the court to the exclusion of all other employment, and if they are all to sit on every case, they must be fewer in number than the membership of the League. Efficiency of a permanent court requires that decisions shall be made by a comparatively small group, and therefore (1) that not all states at one and the same time shall have representatives on the court, and (2) that states agree to submit cases to a tribunal even when none of their own nationals or appointees are members of the court. These two points are illustrated in the pages that follow, in which the unsuccessful attempts to create a "Judicial Arbitration Court" and an International Prize Court, and the successful institution of a Central American Court, are described.

A small permanent court, whose members sit upon all cases, would undoubtedly be in a position to apply international law under more favorable circumstances than *ad hoc* arbitration tribunals, or the present Hague Court. There would be less temptation to be influenced by patriotism or national bias. Living continuously in a juristic atmosphere, free from politics, and with tenure of office secure, the arbitrators could devote themselves wholly and without fear to the task of applying to specific cases the principles of international law. Their successive awards might therefore contribute powerfully to the development of international law, since consistency would be sought and expected. They would have weight because backed by the whole force of the League. On the other hand, the court might find itself with few cases to decide, not because there were no disputes, but because states might prefer a court made up of arbitrators selected for each case. If a permanent arbitrator were found to possess or were suspected of possessing a bias in favor of a state or of a theory of law, states might be unwilling to submit disputes to a court in which he sat. To this objection the answer might be made that one member could not control the court which probably would decide by majority vote. Since we know nothing about the plans which will be formulated by the Council for the creation of this court, it is perhaps idle to surmise further about it; but it will be helpful to recall the experience of the past with respect to International Tribunals with permanent personnel.

Proposed Hague Judicial Arbitration Court

One successful and two unsuccessful attempts to create such a court have been made. The Second Hague Conference drew up a "Draft Convention Relative to the Creation of a Judicial Arbitration Court,"[1] and called "the attention of the signatory powers to the advisability of adopting" it, "and of bringing it into force as soon as an agreement has been reached respecting the selection of the judges and the constitution of the court." It was never adopted because these two important preliminaries were never agreed upon. It is not clear that this court would have been an improvement over the Permanent Court of Arbitration created by the First Hague Conference. The older court was not to be superseded by the new court, and the wording of the draft does not definitely distinguish the jurisdiction of the two. "With a view to

[1] See Appendix 6 (b).

promoting the cause of arbitration," reads Article 1 of the Draft, "the contracting powers agree to constitute, without altering the status of the Permanent Court of Arbitration, a Judicial Arbitration Court, of free and easy access, composed of judges representing the various juridical systems of the world, and capable of ensuring continuity in jurisprudence of arbitration."

The essential features of the proposed court may thus be summarized. The judges were to be appointed if possible from the members of the Permanent Court of Arbitration, to serve for twelve years at an annual salary of 6,000 Netherland florins, and appointments could be renewed. All were to be equal, but to rank first according to the date of their appointments, and secondly according to age. Additional compensation from their own states was prohibited. They were to enjoy diplomatic privileges and immunities. Each year the court was to nominate three judges and three substitutes to form a special delegation for the trial of cases. A judge could not sit in a case submitted by the state which appointed him, or in a case in which he had already taken some part, nor could he act as an advocate before the court. The judges might serve as members of the proposed International Prize Court. The court was to sit at The Hague on the third Wednesday in June if there was a case ready for trial. Its jurisdiction included "all cases submitted to it, in virtue either of a general undertaking to have recourse to arbitration or of a special agreement." It could act also as a Commission of Inquiry, and take summary proceedings to prepare the statement of a case in dispute. Its decisions were to be by majority vote of those present, and in case of a tie the vote of the junior judge was to be disregarded. The business of the court was to be conducted by the Administrative Council and International Bureau created by the First Hague Conference.

That the court was never created is due to the inability of the states to agree on the selection of the judges. To give every state a judge would have created a judicial assembly and not a court, and therefore the proponents of the court wished agreement either on a system of rotation, or of election. The smaller states, however, insisted on their absolute right of equality, and thus prevented the formation of the court.

INTERNATIONAL PRIZE COURT

The second attempt to establish an International Court proceeded one step farther than the one just described. The draft convention for the creation of a Judicial Arbitration Court was not only not ratified but was never signed by the delegates to the Second Hague Conference. At the same Conference was drawn up and signed a "Convention Relative to the Creation of an International Prize Court."[1] It was to have been ratified by June 30, 1909, but before that time Great Britain announced its reluctance to do so while uncertainty existed as to the interpretation of some of the principles of law which would be applied by the court. In order to clear up these doubtful questions the International Naval Conference met in London from December 4, 1908, to February 26, 1909, and concluded the Declaration of London; but as this Declaration itself was never ratified, neither it nor the Prize Court Convention ever came into force.

As stated in the Draft Convention, its purpose was to provide a means of settling "in an equitable manner the differences which sometimes arise in the course of a naval war in connection with the decisions of National Prize Courts." This, it was thought, could best be done by creating an international tribunal to which appeals could be made from national courts. The validity of captures in naval war has always been determined by the courts of the belligerent captor to whose ports, or ports under its control, prizes are brought by its prize crews. If the decision of the highest national court of appeals is adverse to a neutral or belligerent claimant no further action can be taken except through diplomatic channels. It is the theory of these courts that they apply the rules of international law, and it is by their decisions that the rules relating to naval warfare have been both crystallized and interpreted. Conflict comes, however, when the prize courts of different states interpret the rules differently. Ratification of the convention

[1] See Appendix 6 (c).

failed because the Powers were unwilling to leave to the International Court the reconciling of these differences, under Article 7. "If a question of law to be decided," it says, "is covered by a Treaty in force between the belligerent captor and a Power which is itself or whose subject or citizen is a party to the proceedings, the Court is governed by the provisions of the said Treaty. In the absence of such provisions, the Court shall apply the rules of international law. If no generally recognized rule exists, the Court shall give judgment in accordance with the general principles of justice and equity."

It is significant that neither the jurisdiction nor the constitution of the court was the cause of its failure. A prolonged contest over the right of all states to be equally represented on the bench was at last settled by giving to each of the eight Great Powers one judge to sit at all sessions; and to all of the other contracting powers jointly, seven judges to be chosen in rotation according to a plan agreed upon for six years. The Court was therefore to consist of fifteen judges, the Great Powers having a majority of one.[1] Decisions were to be made by majority vote of the judges present, and in case of a tie the vote of the junior judge was to be disregarded.

Central American Court of Justice

What the Second Hague Conference failed to accomplish was done on a smaller scale in the same year by the Central American states. We have seen (Chapter VI) that one of the features of the international organization created by the Central American Peace Conference of Washington was a Court of Justice. Unquestionably the difficulties which attended this successful attempt were immeasurably less than those encountered at the larger conference made up of the representatives of forty-four states. As has been shown, the five states have from the first considered themselves closely related in interests as they are in history and aspirations. The sixth of the Conventions[2] concluded at Washington expressed

[1] See Article 15, Appendix 6 (c), and annexed table.
[2] See Appendix 5 (d).

a desire "to promote the unification and harmony of their interests, as one of the most efficacious means to prepare for the fusion of the Central American peoples into one single nationality." Nevertheless they were and are proud little states, jealous of their sovereignty, and therefore entitled to unlimited credit for the coöperative spirit shown. Since only five states were involved, the question of equality in the choice of judges presented no difficulties. Each state could have one judge without making the Court unwieldy. All five judges or their substitutes must be present to constitute a quorum, and decisions required a majority of three. This meant of course that judges must sit in controversies in which their own states were involved, as is the case in arbitration courts. This arrangement was justified by Article 13[1] in a characteristic manner. The Court, it says, "represents the national conscience of Central America, wherefore the Justices who compose the Tribunal shall not consider themselves barred from the discharge of their duties because of the interest which the Republics, to which they owe their appointment, may have in any case or question." Nor was there contest over the rules of law to be applied. On points of fact the Court was to be "governed by its free judgment," and on points of law, "by the principles of international law" (Art. 21). Perhaps this agreement cannot be fairly contrasted with the disagreement which destroyed the International Prize Court, for none of the Central American states has a large navy or merchant marine. On the question of jurisdiction, however, the Court has set an example for the world. There are no exceptions with regard to "vital interests," or "national honor." By Article 1 of the General Treaty of Peace and Amity,[2] the states bind themselves to "decide every difference or difficulty that may arise among them, of whatsoever nature it may be, by means of the Central American Court of Justice," and by Article 1 of the Convention establishing the Court, they agree to submit to it "all controversies or questions which may arise among them, of whatsoever nature and no matter what their origin may be, in case the respective Departments of Foreign

[1] See Appendix 5 (b).
[2] See Appendix 5 (a).

Affairs should not have been able to reach an understanding." This means not only that the Court possessed jurisdiction whenever two states were in disagreement, but that both were bound to submit the case for decision and to abide by that decision without appeal. Moreover, it was required to take cognizance of questions of an international character, such as the violation of treaties, when raised by an individual of one state against another state, even when his own state did not support the claim. Under a special article the Court was empowered to settle conflicts between the legislative, executive, and judicial powers of a state; and when submitted by agreement, it had jurisdiction over cases between governments and individuals, and between a Central American government and a foreign government. In addition, it had power to fix the position in which the contending powers should remain during the pendency of a suit.

According to the terms of the Convention, the Court held its first session at Cartago, Costa Rica, on May 25, 1908, when announcement was made of a gift of $100,000 by Mr. Andrew Carnegie to construct a Peace Palace in which the Court might sit. When nearly complete, this palace was destroyed by an earthquake on May 4, 1910. After January 10, 1911, the Court sat at San José. Nine cases were decided by the Court in the ten years of its existence. When compared with the history of Central America prior to 1908, this record shows a remarkable advance toward stable conditions. Only nine times were the Foreign Offices and the national courts unable to bring controversies to a conclusion, and in those nine cases the international court took jurisdiction and rendered decisions. Three of the cases were between states, four were between individuals and states, and two were cases in which revolution was prevented in Nicaragua through mediation by the Court. The two last cases before the Court were, however, the prelude to its dissolution, and the story of these controversies illustrates the persistence of the doctrine of sovereignty and the difficulties which surround an international court even under the favorable conditions existing in Central America. By Article 27 of the Convention it was to remain in force during the term of ten years counting from the last ratification. This period ended on March 17, 1918, and Nicaragua was unwilling to renew the treaty because the decisions of the Court on September 30, 1916, and March 9, 1917, were adverse to her.

On August 5, 1914, Nicaragua and the United States concluded a treaty by which the United States, in consideration of a payment of $3,000,000 in trust to Nicaragua to be used for general education, public works, etc., acquired (1) the exclusive right to construct an interoceanic canal through Nicaragua, (2) a lease of Great and Little Corn Islands in the Caribbean Sea, and (3) the right to construct a naval station in the Gulf of Fonseca on the Pacific.[1] When the terms of this agreement became known, Costa Rica filed a complaint in the Central American Court of Justice claiming that the Treaty (Bryan-Chamorro) was in violation of the treaty rights acquired by her under the Cañas-Jerez Treaty (1858), the Cleveland Award (1888), and the Central American Treaty of Washington (1907). She took the stand that the violation of these rights made the Bryan-Chamorro Treaty void. Over the protest of Nicaragua, the Court took jurisdiction of the case, and rendered a decision in favor of Costa Rica. The essential point in the case was the fact that the San Juan River which would form part of the canal route was the boundary of the two states, and Costa Rica had full rights of commercial navigation in it. The clause in the Bryan-Chamorro Treaty relating to the Gulf of Fonseca brought Salvador into the controversy. This Gulf is a meeting place of the territories of Salvador, Honduras, and Nicaragua, and its waters were considered by the three states to be owned in common. The concession of a naval base was therefore, in the opinion of Salvador, a violation of her rights and a menace to her national security. She brought action against Nicaragua alleging violation of Articles 2 and 9 of the Treaty of Washington (1907), and was supported by the decision of the Court which declared Nicaragua to be under the obligation to "reëstablish and maintain the legal status that existed" prior to the Treaty. Throughout the proceedings in both cases, Nicaragua asserted and reasserted her sovereign right to

[1] U. S. Treaty Series, no. 624.

conclude treaties without consulting other states; and after the adverse decisions, did not move to annul the obnoxious treaty. On the other hand, the United States, which had been instrumental in forming the Court, remained silent when a treaty to which she was a party threatened the destruction of the Court. And so the Central American experiment in international judiciary came to an end.

References for Chapter XII

BAKER, ERNEST. The Constitution of the League of Nations: Judicial.
(New Europe, 10: 196-203, March 13, 1919.)

BALCH. World Court in the Light of the United States Supreme Court.

OPPENHEIM. The League of Nations and Its Problems, p. 60–74.

WHITE. Constitutionality of the Proposed International Prize Court.
(American Journal of International Law, 2: 490–506.)

CENTRAL AMERICAN LEAGUE OF NATIONS.
(World Peace Foundation. Pamphlet Series, 7: no. 1, p. 110–151.)

COSTA RICA V. NICARAGUA.
(American Journal of International Law, 11: 181–229.)

GONZALEZ, S. R. The Neutrality of Honduras and the Question of the Gulf of Fonseca.
(American Journal of International Law, 10: 509–542.)

SALVADOR V. NICARAGUA.
(American Journal of International Law, 11: 674–730.)

CHAPTER XIII

INTERNATIONAL ADMINISTRATION OF TERRITORY

THE word administration is used in several different senses and with different applications. In politics it usually designates the executive as opposed to the legislative and judicial departments of the government; but as a practical matter every executive department exercises to some extent legislative and judicial functions. The President of the United States, the Prime Minister of England, and the Premier of France are the heads of the executive departments of the respective governments and exercise both a rule-making and a discretionary power. In the United States the members of the Cabinet as heads of their respective departments are administrative officers. They also have rule-making and discretionary power. Most of their subordinates, the chiefs of divisions and their staffs, have no such power, and although members of the administrative department, exercise only ministerial functions. They merely carry out instructions.

All executives or administrators acquire their power and functions by delegation from a higher power. In the United States the delegation is made by the people themselves; in an absolute monarchy by the personal sovereign. The duties that are delegated are of a managerial character, limited usually by the constitution or other fundamental law. Yet it is possible that an active and tactful administrator may in fact acquire nearly the whole control of a government while adhering in form to a restricted sphere. He is less apt to extend his activities unduly if he is not elected or appointed for a definite period, but is a responsible minister as is the Prime Minister of England. At any moment, through a general election, his power may be taken from him.

If the above is the political meaning of administration in relation to a state, what is meant by international administration of territory? Logically and by analogy it should mean the executive department of a form of government set up by several states to govern either part or the whole of their own territory or at least some territory. Now sovereign states do not willingly consent to put their own territory under the management of other states, and so we may expect to find no examples of free and full consent to it. But we may find examples of territory whose inhabitants have to submit to management and practical control exercised by states which do not have title to that territory. It is in this sense that Article 22 of the League Covenant provides for international administration. By the Treaty of Peace with Germany (Art. 118), it is provided that "in territory outside her European frontiers as fixed by the present treaty, Germany renounces all rights, titles, and privileges whatever in or over territory which belonged to her or to her allies, and all rights, titles, and privileges, whatever their origin, *which she held as against the Allied and Associated Powers.*"[1] Thus Germany is divested of sovereignty over all lands outside her boundaries as set by the treaty. As to much of this territory in Europe, the new location of the sovereignty is definitely fixed by other parts of the treaty. But the disposition of the German colonies as provided in Article 119 raises an interesting question. "Germany renounces," it says, "*in favor of the principal Allied and Associated Powers* all her rights and titles over her overseas possessions."[2] The principal Allied and Associated Powers are the United States of America, the British Empire, France, Italy, and Japan, and the title to Germany's former colonial possessions goes to them jointly and not to any one of them singly. This has created a curious international situation in which the sovereignty of extensive territory apparently is jointly held, while the inhabitants of these territories, unless they elect to remain Germans, are deprived of nationality. They do not automatically become Americans, or Englishmen, or Frenchmen, or Italians, or Japanese, nor are they citizens of a collective state. No such state exists. Nor are

---
[1] The italics are the author's.
[2] *Ibid.*

they by virtue of the transfer under the control of a government. But a government there must be, and until or unless these colonies are made independent that government is provided for by the League Covenant. The process apparently is (1) a delegation of administration by the five Powers to the League, (2) a further delegation of actual functions to single powers to act in the name of the League. Provision for this latter step is made by Article 22 of the Covenant, in which the method is justified on the ground that the former German colonies are not yet able to govern themselves and that the well-being and development of them is a sacred trust of civilization the performance of which should be guaranteed by the League. "The best method of giving practical effect to this principle," says the Article, "is that the tutelage of such peoples should be entrusted to advanced nations who by reason of their resources, their experience, or their geographical position, can best undertake this responsibility, and who are willing to accept it, and that this tutelage should be exercised by them as Mandatories on behalf of the League." The word mandatory calls for explanation which has been given by Professor Munroe Smith (New York Times, February 9, 1919). It does not indicate a state to which a command is given, but in the Roman private law sense, one to which a commission is given to act as agent. Much of the terminology of international law comes from Roman law through the medium of continental writers. Thus it comes that to act as Mandatory on behalf of the League, means to accept a commission or authorization (i. e., mandate) to serve as agent (i. e., Mandatory) for the League. There is no suggestion in the word of power to command a state to accept such a commission, and this would have been clear without the insertion of the phrase "and who are willing to accept it." On the other hand, the mandatory system gives the people no *right* to select or be consulted in the selection of the Mandatory in whose tutelage they are to be placed. Such consultation is an act of grace and not of right. The Covenant, however, indicates the character of the mandates to be issued and the method of issuing them. They will differ, it says, "according to the stage of the development of the people, the geographical situation of the territory, its economic conditions, and other similar circumstances." In the description of general classes, it includes not only German colonies but dependencies of Germany's former allies. The first class is illustrated by "certain communities formerly belonging to the Turkish Empire" which "have reached a stage of development where their existence as independent nations can be provisionally recognized subject to the rendering of administrative advice and assistance by a Mandatory until such time as they are able to stand alone." The wishes of these communities will be considered in selecting Mandatories. The function of the Mandatories in such cases will be to render administrative advice and assistance, leaving to the communities a large measure of self-government. They, presumably, will have their own legislatures and courts, and share in appointments to executive offices.

The second class is illustrated by the Central African communities, which have never carried on their own governments and have no present possibility of doing so. These, the Covenant says, will be fully under the control of their Mandatories who are responsible to the League for guaranteeing freedom of conscience or religion as understood in civilized states, prohibition of slave trade, traffic in arms and liquor with the natives, and the limitation of their military activities to maintaining order and the public defence. A prime duty will be to secure equal opportunities of trade and commerce for members of the League. These communities will have little or no part in their own government until they have shown a capacity for it, by peaceful submission through long periods.

The third class includes territories which on account of their smallness, or sparse population, or geographical position can be administered most economically and efficiently if they are treated as though they were integral parts of the territory of their Mandatories. Such territories, according to the Covenant, are Southwest Africa and the South Pacific Islands. It is presumed that some of these communities, but for the conditions just stated, might come under the first class; but as matters now stand the laws of their Mandatories will be the laws of these territories.

To whichever class a territory may belong, its Mandatory will be responsible to the League and be obliged to render an annual report to the Council. The Council will be assisted by a Permanent Commission on Mandatories to receive and examine the annual reports and advise on all matters relating to the observance of the mandates. This is a provision for supervision of the trusts which the Mandatories have accepted. No method has been stated for protest by the subservient communities, unless it may be assumed that individual persons may communicate directly with the Secretary-General. If this is not permitted, then they would be forced to seek the intercession of some member of the League other than their own Mandatory.

"The degree of authority, control, or administration to be exercised by the Mandatory shall if not previously agreed upon by the members of the League be explicitly defined in each case by the Council."[1]

The first action under the plan for government by Mandatories was taken on May 6, 1919, by the Council of Three, consisting of President Wilson, Premier Clemenceau, and Prime Minister Lloyd George. The official statement follows:

Togoland and Kamerun.—France and Great Britain shall make a joint recommendation to the League of Nations as to their future.

German East Africa.—The mandate shall be held by Great Britain.[2]

German Southwest Africa.—The mandate shall be held by the Union of South Africa.

The German Samoan Islands.—The mandate shall be held by New Zealand.

The other German Pacific possessions south of the equator, excluding the German Samoan Islands and Nauru.—The mandate shall be held by Australia.

Nauru (Pleasant Island).—The mandate shall be given to the British Empire.

---

[1] The New York Times, August 2, 1919, reported that a commission composed of Colonel House, Lord Milner, M. Simon, and Baron Chinda had drawn up formulas for the second and third classes of Mandates.

[2] On March 15, 1920, it was announced in the British House of Commons that the mandate would be held by Great Britain and Belgium jointly.

The German Pacific islands north of the equator.—The mandate shall be held by Japan.[1]

A statement which appears to be the basis of Article 12 of the Covenant is found in the outline of a league prepared by General J. C. Smuts which was published in the Nation of February 8, 1919. General Smuts was a member of the Commission which drafted the League Covenant and therefore his statement is significant. The fact also that in his home state, South Africa, the Roman-Dutch law is in force, may account for the use of the word mandatory.

General Smuts accepts at the outset the fifth of President Wilson's famous Fourteen Points, viz., that there shall be "a free, open-minded, and absolutely impartial adjustment of all colonial claims, based upon a strict observance of the principle that in determining all such questions of sovereignty the interests of the populations concerned must have equal weight with the equitable claims of the Government whose title is to be determined." Extending this principle to all territory with which the League would have to deal, he accepts the slogan "No annexations, and the self-determination of nations." He then deals separately (1) with the territories and peoples split off from Russia, Austria, and Turkey; and (2) with the German colonies in the Pacific and Africa. The first he considers capable of some degree of self-government, either complete independence or supervised autonomy, or government chiefly by some external authority. The second class he says are wholly unable to rule themselves, because inhabited by barbarians, to whom the principle of self-determination could not now apply. Wherever an external authority must function in any degree, he then asserts that this authority must be the League of Nations as reversionary of the sovereignty formerly exercising control. The League, however, is a composite body which would find difficulty in administering any territory directly. "Joint international administration," he says, "in so far as it has been applied to territories or peoples, has been found wanting wherever it has been tried. . . . The administering personnel taken from different nations do not work

[1] Current History, 10: Pt. 1, p. 448, June, 1919.

smoothly or loyally together; the inhabitants of the territory administered are either confused, or, if they are sufficiently developed, make use of these differences by playing one set of nationals off against the other. In any case, the result is paralysis tempered by intrigue. It may be safely asserted that if the League of Nations attempts too soon to administer any people or territory directly through an international personnel, it will run a very serious risk of discrediting itself. It will have to gain much more experience in its novel functions and will have to train big staffs to look at things from a large human instead of a national point of view; it will have to train its officials taken from various nationalities to work loyally together irrespective of their national interests; it will have to do these and many other things before it could successfully undertake a task requiring fundamental unity of aims, methods, and spirit, such as the administration of an undeveloped or partly developed people." If the League, as reversionary, cannot act directly through an international personnel, what is the alternative? "The only successful administration of undeveloped or subject peoples has been carried on by states with long experience for the purpose, and staffs whose training and singleness of mind fit them for so difficult and special a task. If serious mistakes are to be prevented and the League is to avoid discrediting itself before public opinion, it will have to begin its novel administrative task by making use of the administrative organization of individual states for the purpose. That is to say, where an autonomous people or territory requires a measure of administrative assistance, advice, or control, the League should as a rule meet the case not by the direct appointment of international officials but by nominating a particular state to act for and on behalf of it in the matter, so that, subject to the supervision and ultimate control of the League, the appointment of the necessary officials and the carrying on of the necessary administration should be done by this mandatory state." He sums up his recommendations on the subject in the three following propositions:

1. That it shall be lawful for the League of Nations to delegate its authority, control, or administration in respect of any people or

territory to some other state whom it may appoint as its agent or mandatory, but that wherever possible the agent or mandatory so appointed shall be nominated or approved by the autonomous people or territory.

2. That the degree of authority, control, or administration exercised by the mandatory state shall in each case be laid down by the League in a special act or charter, which shall reserve to it complete power of ultimate control and supervision, as well as the right of appeal to it from the territory or people affected against any gross breach of the mandate by the mandatory state." It will be recalled that the latter part of this recommendation has not been specifically recognized in the Covenant.

3. That the mandatory state shall in each case be bound to maintain the policy of the open door, or equal economic opportunity for all, and shall form no military forces beyond the standard laid down by the League for purposes of internal police.

Opinions differ as to the efficacy of the mandatory scheme adopted by the League. One group claims that the plan differs essentially from the former plan of unresponsible control of undeveloped territory. Great Britain, it is claimed, since the time of Warren Hastings has administered her colonies with a view not only to their own and the Empire's good, but also for the good of the world. It is admitted, however, that the trusteeship is not complete unless there is someone to whom the trustee is responsible. Acceptance of the League as holding ultimate responsibility is therefore hailed as "the greatest single step forward ever taken toward the solution of what is undoubtedly the gravest problem which the world has to face."[1] Another group considers the plan to be either a cloak for those very annexations which had been disclaimed, or an attempt to apply the weakest form of government to territories and peoples which require the most efficient form.

It may therefore throw some light on the problem to discuss (1) the status of non-sovereign territories in international law; (2) instances of attempts at joint international administration of territory; (3) an instance of attempted application of the mandatory principle, and (4) joint administration of international rivers.

---

[1] Atticus in New Europe, 10: 78.

Non-Sovereign Territories

States, in the theory of international law, are either sovereign or not sovereign. But a distinction must be made between *de jure* states and *de facto* states. A *de facto* state needs only to be recognized by members of the family of nations to become a *de jure* state. International law therefore takes cognizance of states which may become *de jure* states and classifies them. Some of them are illogically known as half-sovereign states. States which form parts of confederations and colonies and autonomous dominions are not sovereign states in international law because they do not possess the right to make treaties directly with sovereign states, or the right of legation. They possess only an imperfect and limited independence, and do not here need to be discussed. But there are communities inhabiting territories which are said to be under the protection, or under the suzerainty, or in the sphere of influence of a state.

A protectorate is one which while having a considerable amount of political organization and development is under the protection of another power on definite conditions. Its subjects retain their nationality, and it sometimes retains the right of remaining neutral in any war in which the protecting state may engage.[1] With the latter exception, the external relations of the protectorate are in the hands of the protecting state. It is customary in general treaties, however, not to apply them to protectorates unless this effect is expressly stipulated in the treaties. In general, a protectorate retains all the powers which are not specifically resigned. It may, therefore, send and receive consuls and make other business arrangements until this right is expressly given over to the protecting state.

States under suzerainty are vassals of sovereign states. They possess only the powers that are specifically granted to them. They are nominally parts of the suzerain states, but they have obtained a degree of internal independence by the partial disruption of the suzerain state or by grace of the sovereign. Spheres of influence are regions adjacent to the possessions or protectorates of a state in

---

[1] Oppenheim: International Law, 1: 146.

which the only pretention is that as regards third states there is an inchoate priority of claim. The sphere is not considered part of the state exerting the influence, and the control by the native chieftains is not disturbed. The motive is to exclude other states from acquiring influence without taking on any obligations. Usually treaties are made with the native chiefs giving commercial and other privileges. Sometimes these arrangements are made through the agency of a trading company under the patronage of the state. The arrangements do not bind other states unless by agreement. Spheres of influence tend to merge into protectorates or vassal states, and these to merge into colonies. The latter by revolution or peaceful separation may become independent states.[1]

Except in an indefinite moral sense, unresponsible supervision by one state over non-sovereign communities is not international administration. It is not trusteeship. There are, however, historical instances of joint international administration and of delegated international administration by one state on the authority of several.

Joint Administration—Samoa

On May 6, 1919, by act of the Council of Three of the Versailles Peace Congress, the German Samoan Islands were placed under the mandate of New Zealand. Thus Germany, firmly installed since 1850, was finally eliminated from participation in the control of any part of the Samoan Islands, and British influence was restored after a period of twenty years. By a convention between Germany, Great Britain, and the United States, signed at Washington, December 2, 1899,[2] the islands had been divided between Germany and the United States, each thereafter possessing full sovereign rights over the islands allotted to them. Great Britain withdrew in consequence of the cession to her by Germany of the Tonga and other Pacific islands. This arrangement was the culmination of a

---

[1] Reference is not here made to financial spheres of influence which are often held by one state by special agreement within another sovereign state. The distinction between protectorates and states under suzerainty is vague. See Oppenheim, International Law, 1: 140-147; Hall, International Law, 6th ed., pp. 125-131; Wilson, Handbook of International Law, p. 35-39.

[2] Malloy: Treaties, 2: 1595-1597.

long series of unsuccessful experiments in joint administration. All three states were represented by commercial agents in the early fifties, when rivalry in exploitation and attempts to obtain a monopoly of trade began. In 1872 Rear-Admiral Meade, U. S. Navy, concluded an agreement with a native chief for the exclusive privilege of establishing a naval station in Pago-Pago harbor, Tutuila Island, promising in return the protection of the United States. Although this compact was disavowed by the United States, it brought the islands to the attention of the American Government and in consequence a special agent named Steinberger was sent to Samoa. He followed the unfortunate course of forming a combination with the German agent against British interests and of stirring up the natives. This led the British Government to take drastic action by seizing and deporting him on one of its war-ships. British annexation was feared, and Americans with the support of Germans raised the American flag over Apia and proclaimed an American protectorate. This action was unauthorized and subsequently disavowed by the United States, but in 1878 one of the native chiefs visited Washington and concluded an official treaty by which the United States acquired the right to erect a coaling station at Pago-Pago in return for a promise to act as mediator between Samoa and any power with which she was or might be in difficulty. A year later both Great Britain and Germany obtained similar concessions in other harbors. Now began a contest by the representatives of the three Powers, often without official authorization, to obtain control over the natives by supporting one or another of the aspirants for the throne. From time to time the three consuls would act in concert, as when in 1880 they made a compact with Malietoa Telavu to maintain him as king, while he accepted as his three advisers, an American, a German, and an Englishman. This, though unauthorized, was in fact a tripartite protectorate, in which each of the three ostensible allies was secretly plotting against the others. The German settlers were more numerous than the English or American, and had more influence with the natives. The German agent thus in 1884 forced the aged king to sign a treaty practically turning over the powers of government to him. The king protested to the British Government, and the agents of the United States and Great Britain were indignant, yet the German flag flew over the king's house. Then the American consul raised the American flag and declared Apia to be an American protectorate. War-ships were sent and disaster impended. It was averted by the United States which by virtue of the treaty of 1878 suggested a conference of the three Powers. It was held in Washington in June and July, 1887. It was proposed by the German representative that the administration of the Samoan Islands should be entrusted to a single foreign official who should be a national of that foreign power which had the largest commercial interests in the islands. This would have given to Germany a mandate under the authority of the three Powers, but this plan was not agreed to by the United States as it would not have been in conformity with the spirit of the treaty of 1878. It therefore made a counter-proposal that an international commission representing the three Powers should be formed to assist the king in administering the government. Germany objected to this on the ground that it would merely give official sanction and perpetuity to the unofficial tripartite arrangement which had worked so badly. The conference adjourned without results, and matters went from bad to worse in the islands. The German consul "declared war" on the king under a trivial pretext, and declared that joint administration was at an end. The "war" ended in success for the German consul, who became "prime minister." His administration was opposed by the American consul, Sewall, and a native aspirant for the throne, who began armed hostilities. The German gun-boats shelled the coast villages and German marines were ambushed and killed. Then there gathered in the harbor of Apia war-ships of all three interested Powers, but war was averted by the hurricane of March, 1889, which destroyed all but one of the vessels. The subsequent history up to 1899 repeats what has already been recounted. On June 14, 1889, a treaty between the three Powers was signed in Berlin. While recognizing the right of the Samoans to self-government, it stripped them of the essence of it. A chief justice was to be appointed by the three Powers, the three consuls were to have extra-territorial jurisdiction, and no legislative acts were to be valid without their joint approval. The king was to be paid $95 a month, and the foreign chief justice $500. The scheme did not work well, the natives rose in revolt, the chief justice had to take flight, and British and American ships shelled the coast. When order was restored, the three Powers sent a joint commission of investigation, which reported that the islands could not be successfully administered under a tripartite scheme, but only by a single power. The result of this report was the compromise by which in the treaty of 1899 the islands were divided.

Joint Administration—New Hebrides

The New Hebrides are a group of islands in the Pacific Ocean north of New Zealand. The native population is variously estimated at from 50,000 to 150,000 some of whom are still cannibals. The European population in 1918 numbered 630, mostly British and French. The control of these islands has been a difficult question, not easy of adjustment with two prominent European powers equally interested and with the natives incapable of self-government. French and British ships run regularly to and from Sydney, Australia, carrying timber, copra, maize, coffee, and sulphur.

In 1878, Australian newspapers agitated the annexation of the islands by Great Britain, but when France officially inquired the intentions of the Foreign Office, the plan was disclaimed. Both states gave assurance that they proposed no measures with a view to changing the "condition of independence" of the islands. The situation remained unchanged until 1887 when a convention was signed in Paris, November 16, 1887[1], in which the parties agreed to sign a declaration for the appointment of a Joint Naval Commission to maintain order, and protect the lives and property of British and French subjects. On January 26, 1888, this declaration was signed, with an annex containing regulations for the guidance of the Commission. The Commission was composed of a president and two British and two French naval officers. The presidency alternated from month to month between the commanding officers of the British and French naval forces, and meetings were called by the

[1] British and Foreign State Papers, 79: 542–550.

ADMINISTRATION OF TERRITORY

president or in his absence by the other commanding officer. Neither power could take independent action except in circumstances not admitting delay. Military force was not to be used except when indispensable, and troops which were landed must be withdrawn on order of the Commission. The Commission had no powers except those expressly delegated to it, namely to maintain order in parts of the islands where French and British subjects were settled, and protect life and property. The plan worked indifferently well.

When, in 1904, France and England were clearing up their difficulties by a series of treaties, they attempted a permanent arrangement for the New Hebrides. It was found, however, that neither was willing to relinquish its claims, and that a geographical division of the islands was particularly difficult on account of conflicting and commingling interests. The best that could be done at the time was agreement on a declaration signed at London on April 8, 1904,[1] which contained the following paragraphs:

> The two Governments agree to draw up in concert an Arrangement which, without involving any modification of the political *status quo*, shall put an end to the difficulties arising from the absence of jurisdiction over the natives of the New Hebrides.
> They agree to appoint a Commission to settle the disputes of their respective nationals in the said islands with regard to landed property. The competency of this Commission and its rules of procedure shall form the subject of a preliminary Agreement between the two Governments.

In accordance with the above a conference was held in London in February, 1906, and a draft convention prepared. It was signed on October 20, 1906, ratified on January 9, 1907,[2] and proclaimed at Vila, the chief town of the New Hebrides, on December 2, 1907. The preamble states that the two Powers are desirous of modifying the convention of November 16, 1887, in order to secure the exercise of their "paramount rights" and to assure the better protection of life and property. That convention, however, remains in force

---
[1] British and Foreign State Papers, 97: 53-55.
[2] *Ibid.*, 99: 229-252.

except where expressly modified and the Joint Naval Commission is directed to coöperate with the new government. The islands are to "form a region of joint influence" in which French and British subjects have equal rights, their nationality and that of other residents being respected. A seat of government is set up at Vila in buildings erected jointly by the two states. A French and a British High Commissioner, assisted by two Resident Commissioners, and each appointed by his own state, exercise in concert the executive power, including the issuance of local regulations. There is a police force divided into two sections, each under the control of a Resident Commissioner. All public services, such as police, post, telegraph, public health, are undertaken in common. Special New Hebrides postage stamps are issued, but either French or British money is legal tender. The High Commissioners have authority over the native chiefs, and no native may become a French or British subject. A Joint Court of three judges, with a Registrar and a Public Prosecutor, is established. Each government appoints one judge and the King of Spain the third. Except where otherwise provided in the convention the law applicable in the courts is the law of France or Great Britain and subjects of other states must choose between these two legal systems. Both the French and English languages are used. French and British national courts are also established. The treaty lays down special rules respecting land suits between natives and non-natives and between two non-natives, provides for registration of land, supervision of shipping, use of native labor, prohibits the sale or supply of arms, ammunition, and liquors to the natives, and regulates the establishment of municipalities and their administration.

Proposed Mandate—Spitzbergen

Until February 9, 1920, the Spitzbergen Islands, about 50,000 square miles in area, and situated between North Greenland and Franz Josef Land, occupied a unique political position. They were the only territory over which sovereignty had not been asserted. Discovered more than two centuries ago, and frequently visited, they had on account of their barrenness and the intense cold been

ADMINISTRATION OF TERRITORY

disregarded and allowed to remain as *terra nullius*, a no-man's-land. Their status had been the subject of negotiation between European states since their discovery, but not until 1900, when it was found that the coal deposits known to be there were of commercial value, did the matter become important. An American company found it profitable to work the veins, thus attracting citizens of other countries to a like venture. A considerable heterogeneous population thus gathered, all owing allegiance to their home states, and being bound by no local government. No state felt free at so late a date and with so patent a motive to claim sovereignty; yet some understanding was necessary in order that the rights of the various nationals might be protected. It was therefore agreed, after some diplomatic exchanges, to hold a conference of the powers interested to fix the status of the islands. The task of preparing a draft convention was delegated to Norway, Sweden, and Russia whose representatives met for this purpose at Christiania from July 19 to August 11, 1910. Their proposals after criticism and modification by other powers were put into form in 1912 and adopted as a formal recommendation. A diplomatic conference of all the interested powers met at Christiania on June 16, 1914, to consider this draft convention, but the outbreak of the European war prevented them from reaching any conclusions. Thus Spitzbergen remained unclaimed, neither independent nor possessed by any state, *terra nullius* still. What interests us at this time is the plan of government which the draft convention proposed.[1] The status of the islands was not to be changed but they were to be administered by an international commission of three of which one member each was to be appointed for six years by Norway, Sweden, and Russia. Their mandate could be renewed. The presidency was to be held in rotation by each commissioner for one year, and the commission would sit in the state of the president. Unanimity was required except when sitting as a court of appeal. The commission was to publish a Bulletin in French containing regulations as well as unofficial material. The commission was to have power to make rules and regulations and

[1] Revue Générale du Droit International Public, 20:277-297.

to act as a court of appeal from lower courts. The parties to the convention agreed to establish courts with civil and criminal jurisdiction over their own citizens. In disputes between subjects of two states the case would be tried in the court of the defendant. For specified cases, justices' courts were to be established as local international courts. The law to be applied was international private law, and the principles of justice and equity. A police force international in personnel was to keep order under a commissioner of police appointed by the commission from the nationality having most inhabitants in Spitzbergen. The treaty made regulations concerning property, labor, game, fish, and finance.

The whole situation has now been changed by a treaty signed in London, February 9, 1920, by the United States, Great Britain, Denmark, France, Italy, Japan, Norway, the Netherlands, and Sweden, which placed the islands under the sovereignty of Norway.

INTERNATIONAL RIVERS

With the exception of the open sea, and the former German colonies which have been put under the administration of Mandatories, all parts of the earth's surface belong to some state recognized in international law. Rivers which are wholly within a state belong to that state. If they form the boundary between two states then they belong to the riparian states, each owning to the centre of the main channel. This rule is sometimes modified by treaty, as in the case of the San Juan River, which separates Nicaragua from Costa Rica. In this case the sovereignty of the river, according to the Cañas-Jerez treaty of April 15, 1858, is possessed by Nicaragua. If a river in its course either traverses or divides a number of different states, then the ownership is divided among them. Thus the upper reaches of a river may belong wholly to one state; the middle portions partly to one and partly to others, according to the number of the riparian states; and the mouth wholly to one state. If the river is not navigable from the sea, this division of ownership has few consequences. If, however, it either passes through several states or separates them, and is at the same time navigable from the sea, very important rights of communication are involved. Such rivers have been called international rivers, not only because of their importance to the riparian states, but because all states having sea-going commerce are interested in them. Whether or not there is a rule of international law, as some authorities assert, that navigation on international rivers is open to all states which conform to local regulations, it is certain that such a privilege has repeatedly been recognized by treaty. The latest example is in the Treaty of Versailles, 1919, which in Articles 327-364, binds Germany to give to the Allied and Associated Powers equality of treatment in the use of her inland rivers and canals, and in Article 331, specifically declares to be international rivers the navigable portions of the Elbe, Oder,[1] Nieman, and Danube rivers, and their tributaries. It is evident that the condition of international rivers as to depth, dangerous obstacles, lighthouses, etc., and the regulations for their use laid down by the riparian states are of vital interest to all ships which navigate those rivers. The privilege or right of navigation may be practically nullified by neglect of the physical condition of the rivers or by rigorous, expensive, and vexatious regulations at various stages of the river's course. Hence arises the need either for coöperation in administration or supervision by organs created jointly by the riparian states or by them and interested non-riparian states. Such commissions to deal with European rivers have been numerous, and the activities of several were interrupted by the European war. New provision is therefore made in the peace treaties, placing the old ones that are retained and the new ones created under the supervision of the League. This supervision is to be exercised by a special tribunal appointed by the Council, and it will serve as a court of appeal to which any riparian state or any state represented on an international river commission may apply. We shall therefore have as an administrative organization for the administration of international rivers whose sovereignty rests in national states, first, the League itself; second, the tribunal appointed by the Council; third,

---

[1] The navigable portions of the Oder lie wholly within the dominion of Germany.

the various international commissions charged with the control of specified rivers. Recognition is given by Article 351 of the mandate plan, by which the maintenance of a section of a river, or the construction of new works may be entrusted to one state by the international commission.

In Articles 332-337 temporary arrangements are made for equality in navigation rights, but all these arrangements are to be superseded by a general convention to be drawn up by the Allied and Associated Powers, and approved by the League of Nations. Articles 340 and 341 provide international commissions for the Elbe and Oder; and Article 342, a commission for the Niemen, to be constituted on the request of a riparian state to the League of Nations. For the Elbe, the commission will consist of ten members, four from Germany, two from Czechoslovakia, and one each from Great Britain, France, Italy, and Belgium. Each delegation may record a vote for each delegate, even when all are not present. For the Oder, there will be a commission of nine, one representative each from Poland, Czechoslovakia, Great Britain, France, Denmark, and Sweden, and three from Prussia. The Niemen commission, if created, will have one delegate from each riparian state and three representatives of other states specified by the League. These three commissions are to meet within three months after their creation and prepare projects for the revision of existing international arrangements which shall conform to the general convention if it has already been concluded. In any case, the projects shall (1) designate the commission's headquarters, and the manner in which its president is to be nominated, (2) specify the commission's powers in regard to execution of works of maintenance, control and improvement, finance, tolls and other charges, and navigation regulations, (3) define the sections of the river or its tributaries to which the international régime shall be applied.

There still remain to be mentioned the two river systems of chief importance in Europe, the Danube and the Rhine. Both of these are considered in the treaty, and both have been under the supervision of international commissions for many years. A new commission to control that part of the Danube between Ulm and Braïla

ADMINISTRATION OF TERRITORY

which is not under the control of the existing commission is created by Articles 347 and 348. This commission will consist of representatives of two German riparian states, one from each other riparian state, and one from each non-riparian state represented in the future on the European Commission of the Danube. The latter commission, the functioning of which was interfered with by the war, reassumes all of its powers, but with a membership provisionally restricted to representatives of Great Britain, France, Italy, and Rumania. The European Danube Commission continued to meet until Rumania entered the war in 1916, although it was composed of powers already at war. It consisted of one delegate each from Austria-Hungary, France, Germany, Great Britain, Italy, Rumania, Russia, and Turkey, and its jurisdiction extended from the mouth of the river to Braïla, nearly at the head of navigation for sea-going ships. The remainder of the river's great length has now been placed under the jurisdiction of the new Danube Commission mentioned above. The old commission contained only one riparian state, in fact its whole jurisdiction is within that state, viz., Rumania. Originally there was provided a second commission made up entirely of riparian states with the duty of preparing regulations of navigation and river police, but this commission never functioned as an administrative body. The European Commission, which was not intended to be permanent, but was expected to complete improvements of the mouth of the river within a specified time, proved itself to be an efficient international organ. It meets twice a year, in April and October, but special meetings may be called by five delegates. Between sessions, the Commission is represented by an executive committee, which decides by majority vote. The Commission decides by majority vote in all except matters of principle, when unanimity is required. Notice must be given of matters to be decided in order that the respective governments may instruct their delegates. It has its own flag, and its works and establishments, as well as its personnel, are neutralized. It has power to borrow money. It appoints its own employees, maintains two hospitals, supervises lighthouses, controls all engineering works, controls lighterage, towage, and pilotage facilities, licences tugs, lighters and pilots, imposes fines for violations of regulations, hearing cases through its chief officers, the captain of the port and the inspector of navigation, with appeal to the Commission itself. It has no police power, but each state represented may maintain a guard ship at the mouth of the river. That the Commission does not, nevertheless, have sovereign powers is clearly brought out by Mr. Joseph P. Chamberlain[1] who summarizes the provision for control by the powers as follows:

In view of the remarkable powers of the Commission, it is highly important to recognize that it is in fact not an independent body, responsible only to itself, as might appear. In the first place, its members serve at the will of the powers who appoint and pay them, so that they can be removed at any time if their course of action is displeasing to their Government. It has been usual to appoint consular or diplomatic officers to these posts. In all essential matters it is furthermore under the control of the states having representatives. That is brought out clearly by the internal regulations of the Commission. The Commission is not in constant session. It meets regularly twice a year, in April and October, though special meetings may be called by five delegates.

A month before each regular meeting the matters to be brought before the meeting must be communicated in writing by the central office to each commissioner, thus giving the Governments an opportunity to instruct their commissioners in case of need. Unanimity, furthermore, is required for important legislative decisions, and the power of the majority to pass other regulations may, in fact, be limited by the requirement just mentioned and also by the provision that a proposition to raise or lower the tolls, which is within the power of the majority, may not be voted upon until the next regular meeting to that at which it is submitted. An opportunity is thus given for negotiations and for finding out the desires of the Governments.

Articles 354 to 362 of the Versailles treaty relate to the Rhine and Moselle rivers. The provisions of the Treaty of Mannheim, October 17, 1868, are to be revised by a Central Rhine Commission consisting of nineteen members, as follows: four from Germany, five from France, two each from Great Britain, Italy, Belgium,

---
[1] The Danube, p. 67-68.

the Netherlands, and Switzerland. France is to appoint the president. Each has as many votes as delegates even when all are not present. The Commission under the Treaty of Mannheim consisted of one delegate from each riparian state, so that its character is now essentially changed. Since 1804, the Rhine has been under the administration of commissions created successively by different treaties. As functioning at the beginning of 1914, under the treaty of 1868, the Commission had no power to make obligatory regulations without the approval of the signatories to the treaty, but it had extensive administrative and judicial powers. A system of inspection was maintained through local officers who reported to the Commission. The Commission's influence was felt most strongly when it acted as a court of appeals from the "Rhine Courts" which were attached to each office where duties were collected. These local courts, appointed by the local sovereigns, heard all disputes relating to the application of river regulations. From these courts appeals could be taken either to the superior local tribunals or to the Central Rhine Commission. This option served as an effective check on the local officials who might be disposed to dispense justice unevenly.

REFERENCES FOR CHAPTER XIII

MANDATORIES

DUGGAN. The League of Nations, pp. 201–217 (Chapter by E. M. Borchard).

GENERAL SMUTS'S Plan for the League of Nations.

(The Nation, 108:226–228, February 8, 1919.)

GOUDY. Mandatory government in the law of nations.

(Journal of Comparative legislation, 3d. ser. v. 1, pt. 3, p. 175–182, October, 1919.)

SMITH, MUNROE. Mandatary and Mandatory.

(New York Times, February 6, 1919.)

SNOW. The Mandatary System Under the Covenant of the League of Nations.

(Academy of Political Science. Proceedings, 8: no. 3, p. 68–79, July, 1919.)

SAMOA
    JOHNSON, W. F. America's Foreign Relations, 2: 136–159.

SPITZBERGEN
    LANSING. A Unique International Problem. (American Journal of International Law, 11:763–771, October, 1917.)
    SAYRE. Experiments in International Administration, p. 92–97.

NEW HEBRIDES
    SAYRE. *op. cit.*, p. 97–104.

INTERNATIONAL RIVERS
    DUGGAN. The League of Nations, p. 218–236 (Chapter by J. P. Chamberlain).
    KAECKENBEECK, G. International Rivers, 1918.
    OGILVIE, P. M. International Waterways, 1920.
    OPPENHEIM. International Law, 1: 239–245.
    SAYRE. *op. cit.*, p. 38–47, 131–141.
    WILSON AND TUCKER. International Law, p. 114–117.

PART III
INTERNATIONAL COÖPERATION AND THE LEAGUE

INTERNATIONAL COÖPERATION AND THE LEAGUE

XIV. INTERNATIONAL COÖPERATION DURING THE WAR
XV. DIPLOMACY AS A MEANS OF INTERNATIONAL COÖPERATION
XVI. TREATIES AND COÖPERATION
XVII. COÖPERATION IN NATIONAL LEGISLATION
XVIII. PUBLIC INTERNATIONAL UNIONS
XIX. THE INTERNATIONAL LABOR ORGANIZATION
XX. PRIVATE INTERNATIONAL CONFERENCES AND ASSOCIATIONS

CHAPTER XIV

INTERNATIONAL COÖPERATION DURING THE WAR

THE connotations of international law and international coöperation are entirely different. The first implies an obligation to act as agreed upon beforehand in the form of a set of general rules. When an event occurs, the rule of law automatically applies and a state finds itself, according to the dictates of the rule, obligated to proceed or refrain from proceeding in a given way. There may be disputes over the existence of a rule, or as to its interpretation, but if the rule and its meaning are admitted, questions of policy have no influence, unless the state is willing to become a law-breaker. In international coöperation, on the contrary, there is no legal obligation and no rule which must be followed when a contingency arises. The relationship is entirely voluntary and may be severed at will. Questions of policy enter in and profoundly affect a state's attitude. Policy may therefore counsel coöperation or its opposite, competition; and urgent necessity may compel coöperation quite as effectively as if a rule of law existed. In the normal relations of states, when they are not affected by a rule of law, we find both coöperation and competition. In earlier times, the latter was almost always in evidence. In the last century great progress has been made toward coöperation. What Macaulay said in 1857[1] is no longer unqualifiedly true. "No undertaking," said he, "which requires the hearty and long-continued coöperation of many independent states is likely to prosper. Jealousies inevitably spring up. Disputes engender disputes. Every confederate is tempted to throw on others some part of the burden which he ought himself to

[1] History of England, 5th ed., 4: 1980.

bear. Scarcely one honestly furnishes the promised contingent. Scarcely one exactly observes the appointed day." There are in existence to-day many evidences of hearty and long-continued coöperation which detract from the force of his dictum. To coöperate is to operate together for a common object or the accomplishment of a common result. It implies and is based upon a realization (1) that the end sought is of mutual benefit, and (2) that it may best be attained by concerted action. It may be expected, therefore, only between nations which have reached approximately the same stage of civilization, and even then it will be automatically applied only to two classes of objects. The first of these includes international services the absence of which has been a source of inconvenience and economic loss to several states, such as the international postal service. The second is the necessity for repelling a common danger threatening the life of several states. Between these two or commingled with them are all the other interstate relations which are not thought of as coöperation but which from time to time are consciously brought within its field. It will be the purpose in the subsequent chapters to illustrate some of the methods of coöperation already employed by states, and to show some of the influences which are at work to extend the scope of coöperation. The importance of the subject will appear if one recalls that the states are sovereign, knowing no law except that which they have agreed to, and being bound only by the logic of facts to work together. If the facts are not convincing or if they are not understood by enough states, the failure to coöperate may even overthrow the structure so recently reared in the League of Nations.

No better illustration both of the need and the efficacy of international coöperation can be found than the concerted action that was forced on the nations lately at war. Unfortunately the example was set by the Teutonic allies, who from the outset took advantage not only of unified military command, but of their geographical position, and of their combined economic resources. It was as though they had become one state, for the time, bending every effort to one end. And that end was not the destruction at one stroke of one similar huge organization, but to crush, *seriatim*, a number of states each of which was waging a separate war. Not until the close of the year 1917 did the Allies begin really to coöperate. Up to that time they were merely working for a common end, each choosing its own method. When they added to this concert of action based on an adequate interchange of information, which brought out facts from which there was no escape, the tide of battle began to turn. In this war, as has often been pointed out, victory depended not alone on military prowess and organization, but on the employment of the entire strength of the combatant states, mental, moral, spiritual, economic, agricultural, financial, commercial, industrial, as well as naval and military. And all of these could be put to nought by a failure in distribution by means of shipping and transport. Nor would the agreement of each of the Allies not to make a separate peace have been effective. As all know, events in Russia automatically cancelled her side of that compact. How much of that failure was due to a lack of coöperation cannot now be assessed; but an analysis of the figures of Allied forces in connection with Allied losses would undoubtedly have produced an argument for coöperation earlier in the war.

Strangely enough, in spite of final unity of command under Field Marshal Foch, the military and naval forces of the Allies do not furnish the best example of the efficacy of coöperation. Under the stress of immediate and pressing danger the different army units found it difficult to think of the others. But their ultimate success was made possible by a system of coöperation back of the line, and stretching in its effects to the ends of the earth. Coöperation through the ordinary diplomatic channels had not been wanting, but the process was too slow and the issues too vital. The crisis called for more intimate touch between men upon whom the weight of responsibility rested. First of all, a general plan was required, and then detailed processes of continued coöperation. It was initiated by the Inter-Allied Conference which met in Paris from November 29 to December 3, 1917, attended by representatives of seventeen states, viz., France, Great Britain, United States, Italy, Japan, Belgium, Serbia, Rumania, Greece, Portugal, Montenegro, Brazil, Cuba, Russia, Siam, China, and Liberia. The significance of this Conference lies not only in the fact that so numerous a group came together for united action, but much more in the agencies which were created for the period of the war. According to one of the participants, agreements were concluded "which mark the complete solidarity between the Allies regarding the financial, munition, transport, and supply requirements of each." There were already in existence the Commission Internationale de Ravitaillement and a Wheat Executive, but these, though coöperative enterprises, were not under international supervision. These were now included in the programme of the Conference so that the following may be considered as its product:

1. Allied Maritime Transport Council; receiving information through
    (a) Food Council, with the following Programme Committees:—
        (1) Cereals, (2) Oil seeds, (3) Sugar, (4) Meats and Fats.
    (b) Munitions Council, with the following Programme Committees:—
        (1) Nitrates, (2) Aircraft, (3) Chemicals, (4) Explosives, (5) Non-ferrous metals, (6) Mechanical Transport, (7) Steel.
    (c) Other Programme Committees.
        (1) Wool, (2) Cotton, (3) Hides and Leather, (4) Tobacco, (5) Paper, (6) Timber, (7) Petroleum, (8) Flax, Hemp, Jute, (9) Coal and Coke.
2. Inter-Allied Council on War Purchases and Finance.
3. Commission Internationale de Ravitaillement.
4. Allied Blockade Committee.
5. International Scientific Food Commission.
6. International Chartering Executive.
7. Commission for Relief in Belgium.
8. Allied Naval Conference.

Not all of these were created at one time, but they developed in accordance with plans laid by the Conference and authority given by the respective states. All of these councils, commissions, and committees were formed to provide information for the allied conduct of the war, and therefore some further organization was needed in order to put this information to its best use by making instant decisions on matters of military strategy and offence and defence. A head was needed to take advantage of the whole coöperative effort. This was developed from a body which came into existence at Rapallo, Italy, in November, 1917, just prior to the meeting of the Inter-Allied Conference in Paris. Until the end of the war it was known as the Supreme War Council. It consisted of the premiers of Great Britain, France, and Italy, and the President of the United States by his official representative; with one other representative from each of these states. It met with the Inter-Allied Conference in Paris, and after the dissolution of the Conference it became the permanent war executive of the agencies created by that Conference. It was assisted by another subordinate body, called the Permanent Central Military Committee, on which were military experts from Great Britain, France, the United States, and Italy. The purpose of this military committee was better coördination of military action on the western front. It did not supersede the general staffs and military commands of the respective allied belligerents, but, keeping daily watch of the conduct of the war, it made reports and recommendations to the Supreme War Council, which in turn submitted its own recommendations to the military representatives of all governments concerned. These recommendations were doubly valuable because based on military information on the one hand, and on the other, economic information received from the Allied Maritime Transport Council and other agencies.

The Supreme War Council met at irregular intervals, up to the signing of the Armistice. At its fifth meeting at Versailles, May 1-2, 1918, the decisive step was taken of unifying the military command in the field, under Marshal Foch. Its ninth meeting, which began on October 30, 1918, developed into an informal inter-allied conference, because of the collapse of the Teutonic resistance, and the necessity of formulating the terms of the Austro-Hungarian and German armistices.

Of chief interest are the activities and working plan of the great councils and commissions which furnished information to the Supreme War Council and which by the logic of facts made recommendations to the several states. The most pressing problem at all times was distribution of tonnage in order that the resources of the Allied and much of the neutral world might be focussed on the enemy without unnecessary hardship on the peoples of the respective states at home. The official report of the Inter-Allied Conference of Paris[1] states the problem and the solution chosen:

The special Committee for Maritime Transport and General Imports of the Inter-Allied Conference of Paris has decided by unanimous resolution of the delegates of the United States of America, Great Britain, Italy, and France, that it is necessary to arrange a form of coöperation between the Allies which will secure the following objects:

(a) To make the most economical use of tonnage under the control of all the Allies;

(b) To allot that tonnage as between the different needs of the Allies in such a way as to add most to the general war effort; and

(c) To adjust the programmes of requirements of the different Allies in such a way as to bring them within the scope of the possible carrying power of the tonnage available.

To secure these objects an International Board, with complete executive power over a common pool of tonnage, had been proposed, but has been rejected for the following reasons:

It would be difficult for any country, and particularly for America or Great Britain, to delegate absolute power to dispose of its tonnage (which is the basis of all its civilian and military requirements) to a representative on an International Board on which he might be outvoted. Such a Board, moreover, would not lead to administrative efficiency, partly because the complete control of all tonnage can scarcely be well concentrated in one place and partly because representatives upon it would tend to be at once out of touch with the actual administrative executive machinery and, at the same time, scarcely invested with sufficient authority to make reductions in the various supply programmes, munitions, food, etc.

The problem of the allocation of tonnage is largely a problem of securing that the different requirements which make demands upon tonnage should be adjusted in the fairest and best way, and these requirements can only be so restricted by the experts in each class of commodities. It is, for instance, impossible for any except the munitions experts of the different Allied countries to deal with the

[1] Here quoted from Morrow, Society of Free States, p. 104-108.

restriction of the Allied munitions programmes within specified limits.

The Allies are accordingly agreed:

(a) That America, France, Italy, and Great Britain will all tabulate and make available to each other a statement showing in detail and as nearly as possible in the same form, each class of requirements for which tonnage is needed, and, secondly, the tonnage now available and likely to be available in future through new building, etc. These requirements having been classified (showing the source of supply, etc.), and having been adjusted (1) to secure a reasonably uniform standard of adequacy both as between classes of commodities and as between countries, and (2) to bring the total within the carrying capacity of the Allies as a whole, will form the basis on which the general allocation of tonnage will be determined. The calculation will be revised at convenient intervals in the light of losses, new building, war requirements, and other factors in the problem; but it will be an essential feature of the scheme that, subject to such periodical reallocation, each nation shall manage and supervise the tonnage under its control.

(b) That the neutral and interned tonnage, obtained through any channel and by whatever country, shall be used in such a way as to increase by an equal extent the tonnage in direct war services, the extra tonnage being allotted so far as practicable to the most urgent war need of any of the Allies. The method of allocation will be worked out later, but the principle is recognized that it is urgency of war needs, and not the method by which the tonnage has been obtained, that is to be the criterion.

(c) That steps shall be taken to bring into war services all possible further tonnage, such as that in South America, etc.

(d) That control over cargoes carried shall be such as to insure that they satisfy the most urgent war needs in respect of which the tonnage has been allotted.

To carry out (a) and (b) above, allied bodies for the different main requirements for food, for munitions, and for raw materials will be formed on the model of the Wheat Executive, America being associated with these bodies.

It being necessary in order to obtain decisions by the respective governments that each country shall designate one or two Ministers —the United States one or two special delegates—who will be responsible toward their respective governments for the execution of the agreements arrived at and who will meet in conference as Allied representatives as may be necessary from time to time, whether in Paris or in London, according to the circumstances of the case, either on their own motion or at request of the executive departments, it was resolved that, for the purpose of carrying out the common policy above indicated, the appropriate Ministers in France, Italy, and Great Britain, together with representatives of America, shall take steps to secure the necessary exchange of information, and coördination of policy and effort, establishing a permanent office and staff for the purpose.

By far the most importent agency created in accordance with the above report was the Allied Maritime Transport Council. It was organized in February, 1918, and consisted of two members each from the United States, Great Britain, France, and Italy. Its members were of ministerial rank, meeting only at intervals, and intrusting the conduct of its investigations to a permanent subordinate organization, the Allied Maritime Transport Executive. The Staff of the latter was assisted by the technical shipping missions of the several states. The Transport Executive kept a systematic record of shipping available to the Allies, and charted the movements of vessels. Neither it nor the Council itself controlled these movements, which were directed by the states to which they belonged. Nor did it control the work of the various Programme Committees. Since, however, coördination of the recommendations of these Committees was required and since available tonnage was the measure of their practicability, the programmes were sent to the Transport Council in order that the programmes might be made to conform to the carrying capacity of ships. The process, as explained by Mr. Morrow, who was Adviser to the Allied Maritime Transport Council, was as follows:

The Wheat Executive, for instance, would receive from the representatives of each country a detailed statement of the needs of that country, based on rate of consumption, home-production, and sources of supply. The representatives of each country would then criticize the statements of all the others, and modifications would be made. A programme for the year grew out of the combination of these statements, which now required the assent of the respective governments. A similar process was followed in the other committees; but it is evident that without coöperation the programmes could be carried out only so far as each state had control of shipping. All of the programmes were therefore submitted to the Allied Maritime Transport Council, which possessed information on all available shipping. Its report and recommendation often necessitated the further revision of the various programmes and assent to the modifications by the states. Then came into effect the routing system required to get the greatest service out of the tonnage available. All materials were now brought from the nearest source of supply. For instance, to quote Mr. Morrow[1]:

Prior to the war wheat from India went through the Mediterranean to England, passing on the way wheat going from the United States to Italy. Under the Wheat Executive and the Programme Committees, wheat from India stopped at Italy and the corresponding amount of wheat that would have gone from America to Italy went to England or France. This was not only a saving of ships, but an avoidance of an unnecessary submarine risk in the dangerous western Mediterranean. England's oil-supply had come in very large quantity from the oil-fields of the Orient, in which her merchants had an interest, especially from Burma, Borneo, and Sumatra. American oil companies had built up a large market in China and were carrying oil from the Atlantic seaboard to China. A re-routing, which was about to go into operation when the Armistice was signed, was arranged through the Petroleum Conference, by which the American oil should go to England and the oil from the Far Eastern points should go to China.

The value of these results is self-evident; and they have led some writers to assume that they show the value of central control as opposed to coöperation. It is plain from the report of the Inter-Allied Conference that this was not the intention; for the delegation of absolute power to dispose of tonnage to a representative on an international board "on which he might be outvoted," is expressly repudiated. Moreover, it is the testimony of those who were in close touch with actual operations that the Transport Council was without final executive power; it was essentially an advisory body

[1] Society of Free States, p. 113-114.

which could only make recommendations to the executives of the respective governments or to the Supreme War Council. It was a "fact-finding" body. The facts found pointed to policies, the details of which were carried out by the states. "The Council is not concerned directly with the actual operation of ships," says one writer.[1] "It deals with general shipping policy. This distinction is important, for it has been misunderstood. Shipowners or others who object to governmental control of shipping have contended that ships are operated much less efficiently under government direction than when they are left in the practised hands of professional shipping men. In a sense, this is doubtless true. If all that was desired were to load ships rapidly to their full capacity and to send them promptly about their business there would be little justification for disturbing the ordinary course of the shipping industry; but such achievements, however desirable in themselves, are only the minor tactics of shipping operation in time of war. There remains a sort of maritime grand strategy—an ultimate military and political policy in the use of ships. This is something largely outside the experience of practical shipping men. It is something necessarily to be decided by the policy leaders of the belligerent nations. The Transport Council was designed to assist in decisions of this character. The real test of the Council's services is to be found in the character of the broad policies which it has recommended."

The necessity for coöperation did not cease with the cessation of actual hostilities. The non-continental troops had to be brought home, large groups of people in devastated regions had to be fed, and conditions in the home lands needed rectification. Certain of the coöperative councils were therefore retained, but all of them have now been discontinued. The kind of coöperation that we have been describing is so sweeping in character and far-reaching in scope that it needs back of it the driving force of overpowering necessity. Theoretically and practically it is as applicable to peace as to war. The continuance of it, or the return to it, depends on the development of internationalism in the minds of the citizens of the

---

[1] A League of Nations, 1: no. 7, p. ix.

various nationalities. Without a common understanding of the need and the ends sought coöperation on a large scale is impossible; but the essential idea has been grasped and embodied in the League of Nations Covenant, providing thus an organization for coöperation in the event of any international crisis. The world will not be content, however, until coöperation is the normal instead of the exceptional method. In order to emphasize the value of coöperation, and to provide the basis for international understanding in relation to it, the subsequent chapters treat of phases of coöperation already at work in times of peace. They are surprisingly numerous and if added to consistently will, more than any international army or navy, make for uninterrupted peace with the comfort, convenience, economy, and prosperity which are its rightful attributes.

References for Chapter XIV

ACADEMY OF POLITICAL SCIENCE. PROCEEDINGS, 8: no. 3, p.1–14.
ASTOR. Must Continue Allied Coöperation.
  (Forum, 61: 269–279, March, 1919.)
DUGGAN. The League of Nations, p. 50–63 (Chapter by J. P. Cotton and D. W. Morrow.)
FILENE, E. A. International Business Coöperation.
  (Annals of the American Academy of Political and Social Science, 82:135–421, March, 1919.)
INTERALLIED CONFERENCE AT PARIS.
  (Current History, 7: pt. 2, p. 89–91, January, 1918.)
MORROW. The Society of Free States, p. 99–118.
THE SUPREME WAR COUNCIL.
  (A League of Nations, 1: no. 7, October, 1918.)

CHAPTER XV

DIPLOMACY AS A MEANS OF INTERNATIONAL COÖPERATION

It would be easy to overlook, at this time when the efficacy of a more direct method has been so convincingly shown, the claims of diplomacy to be numbered among the means of international coöperation. Diplomacy unquestionably failed to meet the test at the outbreak of the Great War and as a means of intercourse among the Allies. It had to be supplemented by something even more intimate and personal—less formal and slow-moving. But it was supplemented and not supplanted; and it remains the normal permanent method for interchanging views and reaching agreement between states. It is the means by which states considered as persons become vocal, and gives official expression to the thought of peoples represented by their chief executives. Because a diplomat in a foreign state speaks only for his government and not in a personal capacity; because he is the representative of the head of his government; he and his family, their home and their effects, acquire an immunity and an inviolability which otherwise would attach only to the sovereign himself. This representative character must not be overlooked in considering the problems which confront the diplomatist, or in censuring his failures. He is not a free agent; he works under instructions which if unobserved may subject him to censure and recall. Yet instructions cannot cover every contingency, and even in these days of quick communications immediate advice cannot always be had. Thus the diplomat sometimes has to exercise discretion on matters of vital import requiring immediate action. His responsibility is complex. The state, although in law a separate entity from the individual persons who are subject to it, has to act through human beings. The diplomat receives his instructions from the foreign office, in the United States the Department of State, which is itself a division of the government under the control of the executive. In the United States the executive is also the head of the state, but in monarchies he is an official either responsible only to the sovereign or, as in England, responsible as a practical matter directly to the people. In carrying out his instructions the diplomat must bear in mind three systems of law, that of his own state, of the state to which he is accredited, and of international law. And back of all these stands the system of foreign policy which his government for the time being is pursuing. That policy changes with responsible government. The policy is determined not only by the Chief of State but by the Legislature through its power to control the purse. It is true that diplomatic intercourse is primarily an executive function, and that action may be taken by the executive which will bind the state; nevertheless, the exercise of this function is restrained, in the United States, for instance, not only by the necessity of obtaining the consent of the Senate to ratification of treaties, and of the House of Representatives to appropriations, where a treaty requires the expenditure of money, but also by the periodic reëlection of the president. In other states, such as Great Britain, it is restrained by a system of cabinet interpellations and the necessity of resigning to seek reëlection when the government fails to receive a vote of confidence in Parliament.

Thus, general denunciation of diplomacy is essentially a denunciation of the policy and practice of the government itself. The government is in most modern states the product of public sentiment, and to the extent that this is true, the people are responsible for mishandling of foreign affairs. The executive must therefore be responsive to public demand as far as it has been expressed, and he must also estimate and foresee the extent to which support will be given to new policies.

But perhaps the greatest difficulty in the way of giving satisfaction to all classes in the conduct of foreign affairs is the necessity for secrecy. In many instances a duty rests on the state for a time not to divulge its correspondence with another state. This is a duty to the other state, and not a duty to the people at home. Without secrecy during negotiations states would never consent to begin them. "Open covenants openly arrived at" is a phrase the limitations of which have been shown during the recent Peace Conference. Publicity of treaties is a matter altogether desirable, but publicity of negotiations can be only partially achieved. Even though all documents were immediately published, the verbal exchanges in conference remain secret until disclosed piecemeal by the participants, or in compilations of state papers long after the event. The publications of the foreign offices of all states, including our own, hold in abeyance many documents and exchanges of correspondence until long after the period of negotiations. The last volume of United States Foreign Relations, issued in 1919, contains no material later than 1912, and only a selection of documents is printed. The Senate of the United States recognizes the necessity of secrecy every time it goes into executive session for the consideration of foreign affairs; and when it calls on the Department of State for copies of correspondence it qualifies the request with the clause "if not incompatible with public interest."

All of the above emphasizes the necessity of appointing to diplomatic posts only men of the highest character and ability. Such men would, however, not accept these posts if some popular descriptions of diplomats were accurate. "How diplomats make war" is a catchy but misleading phrase. This is to place on representatives the whole burden of state policy, which as has been shown rests on the executive, the legislature, and the people for whom they are the mouthpieces.

The classic example of war made by diplomacy is the episode just prior to the Franco-Prussian war. Bismarck, authorized to make public a telegram sent to him from Ems by William I of Prussia, so condensed it without changing any words as to give it, as Moltke remarked, "a different ring." "It sounded before," said he, "like a parley; now it is like a flourish in answer to a challenge." The revised telegram, which contained the statement that William "had nothing further to communicate to the Ambassador" (Benedetti) concerning Prince Hohenzollern's renunciation of his claim to the

Spanish throne, had the effect, as Bismarck said it would, "of a red rag upon the Gallic bull," and war between France and Prussia was declared on July 19, 1870.[1] The falsifying of dispatches is no longer considered an act of statesmanship. Intrigue, trickery, false-swearing, are not characteristic of the world that has come out of the European war, and are therefore not functions of diplomatic agents. The witticism of Sir Henry Wotton, often quoted to show the evil influence of foreign representatives, should now be recalled only to deny its modern application. The story is told by Satow.[2] When Wotton was on his way to Italy to serve as British ambassador, he stayed for some days at Augsburg, Germany; and was requested by John Christopher Fleckammer to write in his album. Wotton wrote the following: "*Legatus est vir bonus peregre missus ad mentiendum Reipublicæ causa*," which he intended to mean: "An ambassador is an honest man, sent to lie abroad for the good of his country." It was a play on words not to be taken too seriously, and it did not come to public notice until eight years later when Jasper Scioppius printed it as a principle of religion professed by King James and Wotton his ambassador who was then at Venice. There it was placarded in the windows. When King James heard of it he called Wotton to account and the latter wrote an apology "so ingenious, so clear, and so choicely eloquent," says Isaak Walton, "that his Majesty (who was a pure judge of it) could not forbear, at the receit thereof, to declare publickly, that Sir Henry Wotton had commuted sufficiently for a greater offence." The spirit of the times was, however, not much misrepresented by the witticism. Walton confirms this by another incident of Wotton. He was asked by a friend about to enter the foreign service for advice as to his conduct. He replied "that, to be in safety himself, and serviceable to his country he should always, and upon all occasions, speak the truth . . . for you shall never be believed; and by this means, your truth will secure yourself, if you shall ever be called to any account; and 'twill also put your Adversaries (who will still hunt counter) to a loss in all their disquisitions and under-

---

[1] Bismarck; The Man and the Statesman, 2: 87-103.
[2] Guide to Diplomatic Practice, 1: 168-170.

takings." The function of the ambassador was, in those days of poor communications, quite as much to collect and to send home information as to conduct negotiations. The office was surrounded by an atmosphere of distrust, of finesse, and of etiquette which did not make for confidence; but this defect was not inherent in diplomacy. It was a reflection from the state of political society. The men who were chosen were fairly representative of their times. Diplomacy had not become a profession, and so they were drawn from all classes of educated men—lawyers, churchmen, soldiers, as well as men who had been in the civil service of the state. According to Bernard,[1] French missions usually included, besides a layman of high rank, a bishop and a lawyer. In England, many men who had taken Holy Orders and were learned in the canon and civil law entered the service of the state, sometimes serving abroad, and thus obtained preferment to the highest ecclesiastical honors. The attachés of missions were often chosen from young men of rank who desired to see the world and fit themselves for employment at home. They remained only for short periods and usually had no qualifications for their posts.

Gradually the need of special training became apparent, until to-day, in Europe at least, diplomacy is a profession offering a career of great dignity. In the United States, this is not yet the case, foreign agents often being appointed without previous experience abroad. Appointments are often dictated by political considerations, and the salaries are so small that only wealthy men can afford to accept them. Nevertheless, a list of American ambassadors could be compiled which would do credit to any state. Along with the many advantages of training and experience which professional diplomats possess, comes the disadvantage of being for long periods out of personal touch with conditions at home. To this aloofness have been attributed many of the evils of diplomacy. The American method meets this defect by the selection of men from all walks of life who have come to notice because of notable achievements either in politics, the professions, in business, or in literature. The professional element in American diplomacy is found in the subordi-

---
[1] Lectures on Diplomacy, p. 139.

nate offices, whose incumbents now enter the service while young men, and acquire experience in many capitals. To an increasing extent they are being advanced to the major positions. The selection of diplomats for particular posts does not, however, lie wholly in the discretion of the appointing state. Every state has the right of refusing to accept a particular agent on grounds which are summarized by the words *persona non grata*. The objection may be as to his personal character, or as to his record. For instance, in 1891, China refused to accept as United States Minister former Senator Henry W. Blair because of opinions concerning China expressed by him in the Senate.

To-day diplomacy is on a higher plane than it was when Wotton wrote or when Bismarck falsified the Ems dispatch. German diplomacy at the outset of the war was as wholly out of tune with modern feeling and practice as were their methods of making war. With the creation of the League of Nations a further advance is to be expected. If the nations involved are sincere in their declarations a new era for diplomacy has come. Diplomatic agents will be as much needed under the League as heretofore; and their opportunities for coöperation will be greater. Neither the League Assembly nor the Council will be permanently in session, and the Secretariat has no diplomatic functions. The great bulk of the agreements made at meetings of the League will have to be consummated through diplomatic means.

"Diplomacy," says Satow,[1] "is the application of intelligence and tact to the conduct of official relations between the governments of independent states, extending sometimes also to their relations with vassal states." According to another definition, diplomacy is the art and science of international business. It is not confined to negotiations, however, but includes the conduct of much routine international business in the intercourse of states. A diplomat, according to Littré, is so called because diplomas are official documents emanating from princes, and the word diploma comes from the Greek word meaning "to double", from the way in which they were folded. The word was not used in English until the year 1645.

[1] Guide to Diplomatic Practice, 1: 1.

Until the Congress of Vienna, no uniformity in titles or in gradation of rank of diplomatic agents existed. The system now generally agreed upon was adopted by that Congress on March 19, 1815, and supplemented by the Congress of Aix-la-Chapelle, 1818. There are now four classes:[1]

(1) Ambassadors, who are the personal representatives of the Heads of State, and are accredited to them. They are supposed to have the privilege of negotiating directly with the sovereign, and they therefore outrank all other agents. The first-class agents of the Holy See are called Papal Nuncios or Legates. The Pope sends agents only to states acknowledging his spiritual supremacy.

(2) Ministers Plenipotentiary and Envoys Extraordinary, and Papal Internuncios, who differ from the first class only in that they are not accredited to the Heads of State personally, and therefore do not enjoy all the special honors of ambassadors.

(3) Ministers Resident enjoy fewer honors than either of the foregoing classes. Their duties are identical, but they are usually sent by the greater to the lesser powers.

(4) Chargés d'Affaires, who are accredited from one chief of foreign office to another, and not to the state or to the Head of State. They rank lowest in diplomatic honors.

A diplomatic mission may include both an official and an unofficial suite. The latter may consist of the families of the diplomatic agents, with private chaplain, physician, secretaries, and servants. The official suite may consist of a counsel, secretaries, military and naval attachés, interpreters, clerks and accountants, couriers, a chaplain, and a physician.

Although consuls should not be confused with diplomatic agents, they should here be included among agencies for international coöperation. Their office is more ancient than that of envoys, and they were formerly intrusted with diplomatic functions. Even to-day, consuls are sometimes sent on diplomatic missions. They deal largely with commercial matters, and they also hold consular courts in states where extra-territorial rights are granted. They represent not so much the state as the interests of the citizens of the state which sends them. Their duties cover all classes of trade,

---
[1]Wilson and Tucker: International Law, p. 162–166.

under local law and commercial treaties, supervision of maritime service, assisting their fellow citizens in matters of property, contracts, the visé of passports, and the supply of information relating to commercial, economic, and political affairs, and the conditions of navigation. The consular reports printed by the various states are mines of information on matters of current international interest, which is often not elsewhere obtainable. The rank of officers in the consular service is not regulated by international agreement, but by domestic law. In the United States service the chief grades are: (1) consuls-general who ordinarily have supervisory jurisdiction over consuls in their neighborhood; (2) consuls; (3) vice-consuls; (4) consular agents; (5) consular assistants; (6) interpreters; and (7) student interpreters.

Prevention of War

The rules of international law and practice concerning the appointment, reception, duties, immunities, privileges, conduct, powers, and recall of diplomatic and consular officers are well standardized. There is already in existence a well-ordered machine for the conduct of international relations, and the scope of these relations is limited only by the desires of the states themselves. The opportunities for coöperation are unlimited. The most prominent of these is in the prevention of war. This function is recognized in practically all conventions concerning the amicable settlement of international disputes. By Articles 13 and 15 of the League Covenant members agree to submit either to arbitration or to inquiry disputes "which cannot be satisfactorily settled by diplomacy." The Hague Convention for the Pacific Settlement of International Disputes uses similar phrases. By Article 9, it is agreed that in certain circumstances disputes will be submitted to Commissions of Inquiry when the parties "have not been able to come to an agreement by means of diplomacy." Article 38 provides for arbitration as a "means of settling disputes which diplomacy has failed to settle." The Bryan treaties for the advancement of peace relate to disputes "which diplomacy shall fail to adjust," and the Convention for the Establishment of a Central American

Court of Justice gives the court jurisdiction over all controversies "in case the respective Departments of Foreign Affairs should not have been able to reach an understanding." The evolution of the functions of diplomacy has been tersely stated by Myers.[1] "The historical origin of foreign relations," he says, "as part of the business of modern government has colored their conduct. When the Italian free cities in the Middle Ages began to erect into a system the sending of diplomatic missions, they acted upon the fundamental impulse of all diplomacy, protection of the interests of the state. But the conditions of the time gave character to the innovation. Military conditions alone prevailed in Europe and the Italians found themselves incapable of withstanding the ambitious secular rulers whose policy had hardened into a habit of seizing military control of Italy in order to bring physical pressure to bear on the papacy when the Holy See periodically came to award the crown of the Holy Roman Empire. Not being able for reasons of strength to play an equal hand by force of arms in this game and being continually injured by the military incursions, the Italian city-states began fighting their defensive battles with wits rather than fists.

"When diplomacy acquired a recognized place in the scheme of governmental affairs it was considered only a part of the mechanism of war, a method of gaining results without fighting or of securing greater results from the fighting. This character was inherent in diplomacy until various phases of foreign relations originating in peace problems came to be exclusively within the jurisdiction of the foreign office. Though the old character has not entirely departed from the diplomacy of the European system, it is true that diplomatic relations now tend to displace warlike relations as the normal and primary method of international intercourse. To-day war is acknowledged as the outcome of policy and, as Clausewitz says, is simply a new phase of pursuing a political purpose. Diplomacy, the vehicle for conveying policy into realization, has thus tended to become the master of war, to which it was originally servant."

It is evident that if the policy of a state is that of peaceful co-

[1] Notes on the Control of Foreign Relations, p. 10-11.

operation, then the function of diplomacy will be not to make war but to prevent it. In the past diplomacy has been most successful when backed up by a show of force. The history of American diplomacy shows, however, that it can be effective without force. Latané[1] tells the story of the period from the announcement of the Monroe Doctrine down to 1914. The negative side of the doctrine, he says, was a declaration that the United States would not use force in support of law and justice outside of the Western Hemisphere. But this did not prevent the United States from taking diplomatic action in affairs not strictly American. In every case the attitude of the United States was clearly stated. Our delegates attended the Berlin Congress of 1884 concerning the Kongo Free State, but "on the understanding that their part should be merely deliberative, without imparting to the results any binding character so far as the United States were concerned." Delegates were sent to the Brussels Conference of 1890 concerning the suppression of the African slave trade. The United States ratified the treaty there signed, but added a resolution that there was no intention of indicating to the world "any interest whatsoever in the possessions or protectorates established or claimed" in Africa by other powers. We participated in the two Hague Conferences and in the London Naval Conference. No delegates played a more honorable or influential part than those of the United States. And finally the United States took part in the Algeciras Conference of 1906, for the purpose of adjusting a dispute between France and Germany over the status of Morocco. Here again the United States publicly announced that it had no political interest in Morocco, the declaration of the delegates being reinforced by a resolution attached to the treaty by the United States Senate. On a number of occasions the United States has protested through diplomatic means against the ill-treatment of the Jews in Russia and Rumania, and of the Armenians in Turkey. The opening of the European war marks the beginning of American diplomacy in European affairs, backed by force on a large scale. Under the League of Nations, provision is made for backing up diplomacy with the economic and military

[1] From Isolation to Leadership, p. 57-79.

force of all the members, which is a vastly different thing from that sort of entanglement which the United States has avoided throughout its history. With such an incentive for fair dealing, with a known result in case of failure to settle disputes by diplomacy, the position of the diplomat is immensely strengthened and his operations as a preventer of war should be widened in scope. In the past diplomatic intercourse has often been broken as a protest against a state's conduct. International law recognizes the right of offering to such states good offices and mediation, but in the past there was no obligation to accept them. In other words, relations once broken might not be reëstablished until after a war had ensued. Under the League (Art. 11), it is the fundamental right of each member to bring to the attention of the Assembly or Council "any circumstance whatever affecting international relations which threatens to disturb either the peace or the good understanding between nations upon which peace depends." The organs of the League then are in a position to take effective action, indirectly to reëstablish relations, and to give diplomacy a chance again to come into play.

Diplomatic Protection of Citizens Abroad

One of the most fruitful causes of misunderstandings between citizens of different states and between states is the failure of local justice to protect the interests of aliens. The intimate relations that now exist between the subjects of all states, on account of travel, temporary sojourn, permanent residence for business purposes, general commercial relations, and the consequent exchange of credits, give rise to many complications for which remedies have been provided by international law and practice. The whole subject has been exhaustively treated by Borchard[1] and only brief reference to it can be made in these pages. Broadly speaking, it is a rule that, except where extra-territorial courts are established, aliens are completely subject to local laws and to the jurisdiction of local courts and authorities. Just as this rule appears to be at first thought, it is satisfactory only where local justice

[1] Diplomatic Protection of Citizens Abroad.

is administered according to standards similar to those of the state from which the alien comes, and according to the standards of international law. The privilege of intercourse carries with it the right to fair treatment. It is not sufficient that local laws shall apply equally to aliens and nationals; there must also be equality in application and administration. The national has a political remedy by virtue of his citizenship against unjust laws and discriminative administration; the alien has no such remedy. Therefore, he must appeal to his own state for protection. This protection is provided, in the first instance, by diplomatic action, and the basis of action is not merely a claim for equality of treatment, but treatment in accordance with the rules of international law. These rules are, however, incapable in many instances of enforcement. Resort to war at each disagreement would make hostilities perpetual; the remedy would be worse than the ills to be cured. Therefore the effectiveness of diplomatic action rests chiefly on coöperation and not on a threat of war.

Many states, especially those of Latin America, have incorporated in their legislation the principle that failure of local remedies and a denial of justice must be established before diplomacy interposes; but in practice this principle is subject to many modifications which have their justification in the desire to conciliate, compromise, and coöperate. If, as a matter of fact, actual justice is not obtainable under local conditions, then the rule becomes inoperative. The cases in which a state is responsible for failure of justice to aliens are established by treaty, by practice, and by international law. The most obvious case is where officers of the government participate in the alleged wrongful act. Sometimes the injury is considered not only the basis of a claim for the benefit of a state's citizens abroad, but also an affront to the state itself. In these cases, satisfaction of the individual claim does not necessarily wipe out the collective injury. In the case of individual aliens, diplomatic protection amounts to an extraordinary legal remedy, not open to the citizens of the foreign state in relation to their own government.

When an alien is injured, under such circumstances as indicate state responsibility, and after either an attempt has been made to obtain local redress, or evidence has been shown that such redress could not satisfactorily be obtained, recourse is had to diplomacy. The injured alien makes representations to the local representative of his own state, who transmits the facts and his recommendations to the foreign office of his government. He then receives instructions how to proceed. If the home office finds that a just claim exists, its diplomatic representative is instructed to present a formal note to the Minister of Foreign Affairs in the state to which he is accredited, stating the grounds of complaint and demanding redress. From this point on, the temper of the governments, and the tact, skill, ability, and judgment of the diplomats determine whether agreement shall be reached, the claim shall stand as a continuous incentive to ill-feeling, settlement shall be reached by arbitration, or only by resort to war.

Agreement is not always reached without straining relations nearly to the breaking-point. It is an indication of a genuine desire not to be forced into hostilities that states persist in maintaining relations even when the head of a diplomatic mission finds it necessary to withdraw. In such cases the expedient is used either of leaving the embassy in the hands of a chargé, or of placing the interests of the aggrieved state in the care of the agents of a friendly third state. One example of the operation of diplomacy in the diplomatic protection of citizens abroad must suffice us here. It illustrates the difficulties as well as the accomplishments of diplomacy, but it is also an example of prevention of war.[1]

On October 15, 1890, the chief of police of New Orleans was murdered, and a number of Italians were arrested for complicity in the crime. While they were in prison, it was claimed that the Italians were mistreated by the officials, and the Italian government protested. On March 13, 1891, a jury found three of the Italians not guilty, and failed to agree as to the others. The citizens of New Orleans were greatly incensed, feeling that there had been a failure of justice, and mob violence was threatened.

---
[1] Stowell and Munro: International Cases, 1: 264–270.

The Italian consul protested to the Governor of Louisiana, asking him to send troops to protect the prisoners. He replied that he was powerless to act without the request of the Mayor, who could not be found. On March 14, 1891, a mob of about 8,000 persons broke into the jail, took out eleven prisoners and lynched them. Apparently the authorities made no attempt to restrain the mob. The Italian government now protested to the United States government and demanded satisfaction. A demand was made under the treaty of February 26, 1871,[1] between the United States and Italy which guaranteed reciprocal protection of persons and property of each state in the territory of the other state. Mr. Blaine, Secretary of State, recited this treaty to the Governor of Louisiana, and asked that all offenders against the law might be promptly brought to justice. The reply was that a Grand Jury was already investigating the case, but it was added that only two or three of the prisoners were Italian citizens. The Italian government was not satisfied with this and demanded immediate action claiming that violation of the treaty of 1871 was already established. Mr. Blaine did not admit this, but explained that investigation must first be made by the state of Louisiana under the Federal system of government. Under instructions from his foreign office, the Italian minister then left Washington, leaving the mission in charge of a subordinate. On May 5, 1891, the New Orleans Grand Jury reported that it could find no grounds for indictments. The Federal courts were found to have no jurisdiction under the United States Constitution and the matter had reached an *impasse*. The difficulty would have remained unsettled, a standing cause for disagreement, and an example of miscarriage of justice to aliens if executive action had not been taken. The incident was closed when the United States offered and Italy accepted an indemnity of 125,000 francs. The Italian minister then returned to Washington.

The third outstanding opportunity for coöperation in diplomacy is in the negotiation of treaties, which will be discussed in the next chapter.

[1] Malloy: Treaties, 1: 969–977.

References for Chapter XV

Bernard. Four Lectures on Subjects Connected with Diplomacy, p. 111–161.
Borchard. Diplomatic Protection of Citizens Abroad.
Hill. The Contemporary Development of Diplomacy.
Latané, J. H. From Isolation to Leadership, p. 57–79.
Moore, J. B. A Hundred Years of American Diplomacy. Principles of American Diplomacy.
Myers. Notes on the Control of Foreign Relations.
Neilson. How Diplomats Make War.
Satow. Guide to Diplomatic Practice.
Stowell and Munro. International Cases, 1: 264–270.

CHAPTER XVI

TREATIES AND COÖPERATION

There is only one circumstance in which a state is obliged to make a treaty; namely, the situation in which Germany found herself on June 28, 1919. She had been decisively defeated, had been stripped of her effective military and naval arms, and was cut off from commercial relations with the rest of the world. The existence of the state itself depended on compliance with the terms of the Allies. Although she signed under protest, in theory it was a voluntary act, because a choice was made of the lesser of two evils. The rule of international law that treaties are invalid without the free consent of the contracting states does not preclude the use of force in bringing a state to an understanding of conditions; but it prevents the use of threats of personal violence and placing the negotiators under constraint. All other treaties are practically as well as theoretically coöperative agreements. They are based on compromise and mutual concessions; and they are the formal expression of mutual good-will. Only so long as this good-will continues do they have their full effect.

Rules of international law govern the methods of negotiation, drafting, signing, ratification, interpretation, enforcement, and termination of treaties; but the subject matter of interstate agreement is limited only by mutual desires. A glance at the subjects listed in the index to Malloy's Treaties will show what the scope of treaty-making by the United States has been in the past. Some of the headings are: abduction, African slave trade, agriculture, Alabama claims, alliance, Amazon River, arbitration, arson, assassination, assaults on ships, asylum, balloons, bankruptcy, bigamy, blockade, boundaries, Boxer trouble, bribery, burglary, citizenship, claims, coaling stations, coasting trade, coinage, commerce and navigation, consuls, contraband goods, contract debts, copyright, corporations, counterfeiting, customs, deserters from ships, diplomatic officers, drugs, embargoes, embezzlement, emigration, extradition, extra-territoriality, fisheries, forgery, fraud, fur seals, gunpower and arms, health, house-breaking, Indians, industrial property, infanticide, judicial procedure, kidnapping, land warfare, larceny, letters of marque, liquors, manslaughter, maritime warfare, military exemptions, mining, murder, mutiny, naturalization, neutrality, parricide, patents, peace, perjury, piracy, poisoning, political offences, prize courts, property, railroads, reciprocity, religious liberty, robbery, shipwrecks, Sound dues, submarine cables, tobacco, trade-marks, visitation and search of vessels, war, weights and measures, and the white slave trade. There is, in fact, no human relationship between citizens of different states which may not become the subject of international agreement.

Attention to the foregoing list will show that there are two great classes of treaties, namely, political and non-political treaties. Political treaties are those which affect the state as a collective entity, such as treaties of alliance, of arbitration, guaranty, boundary treaties, treaties of peace, etc. Non-political treaties are engagements on behalf of the subjects of a state, such as treaties concerning copyright, patents, trade-marks, postal service, agriculture, commerce, shipping, etc. As respects the parties to agreements, they may be bipartite or multipartite. The latter involve a greater degree of coöperation than the former, because they affect at one and the same time a large group of states all of which must have reached a common understanding. Even though an equal number of states, by pairs, should conclude identical treaties, a less effective result would be obtained; for each is a separate agreement affecting only two states. Withdrawal is easier, and the coöperative system is subject to gradual disintegration. It is therefore a significant sign that conventions affecting the interests of many states have in increasing number been concluded by diplomatic conferences and congresses. Many of these are listed by Satow.[1]

Coöperation in regard to treaties is found not only in concluding

---

Diplomatic Practice, 2: 3-4, 95-96.

them, but in admitting to their benefits states which are not original parties. Many treaties provide that other states may accede to them by notification, becoming thus bound equally with the contracting parties. Even when there is no accession clause, states sometimes announce their approbation of a treaty; or they formally adhere to it, by announcing an intention to abide by its principles. By the acts of approbation and adhesion, states do not become parties to a treaty.

In the League Covenant important references are made to treaties. Emphasis is laid on the necessity of scrupulously observing all treaty obligations; on settling by arbitration disputes as to their interpretation; on the public registration of them as a prerequisite to their validity; and on the abrogation of treaties inconsistent with each other and with the Covenant. The adoption of the Covenant should therefore initiate a period of coöperative treaty-making under safeguards that are salutary and helpful. If the Secretariat in due course publishes in one series all treaties in force, and if this series is cumulative and properly indexed in detail, it will prevent much difficulty and confusion which now exist in identifying the existing obligations of states. In the past it has sometimes been difficult to ascertain whether a treaty has been ratified, or whether it was ratified with reservations. Long periods sometimes elapse between signature and ratification and many treaties are never ratified. Under the League, all treaties in force will be on file and will be published as soon as possible. Moreover, once ratified, a treaty cannot be kept secret. Heretofore most treaties have been published, and those whose terms were kept secret were usually known in substance. The treaties thus held back usually related to alliances pointed against a state or group of states. The reason for secrecy was that counter alliances might not be formed; but in practice the opposite result was produced. As soon as the alliance was suspected, other states, not knowing its exact terms, would conclude defensive treaties whose terms also were kept secret. Secret treaties thus bred other secret treaties, and an atmosphere of distrust was produced.

Eliminating from consideration secret treaties of alliance of which there should be none under the League, we find no dearth of proper subjects for coöperation in treaties. Article 23 of the Covenant and the whole of the Labor Charter provide subjects of vital interest. The abortive efforts of the Hague Conferences to conclude an acceptable prize-court convention and to create a Permanent Court of Arbitral Justice present other opportunities which now can be seized with better chance of success. As a substitute for the latter, a supreme test will come in carrying out the recommendations of the Council for the establishment of a Permanent Court of International Justice.

The remainder of this chapter is devoted to examples of coöperation in treaty-making with regard to special subjects. The illustrations both as to subject matter and difficulties encountered could be multiplied, but those chosen are typical.

Extradition

No better examples of coöperation in treaty-making can be found than those relating to extradition. "Extradition is the delivery of a prosecuted individual to the State on whose territory he has committed a crime by the State on whose territory the criminal is for the time staying."[1] Moore[2] defines it as "the delivery by a state of a person accused or convicted of a crime, to another state within whose territorial jurisdiction, actual or constructive, it was committed, and which asks for his surrender with a view to execute justice." There is no rule of international law requiring the delivery of criminals by one state to another, nor is there any such rule requiring states to enter into treaty agreements for this purpose. These matters are entirely within the competence of the several states and neither moral obligations nor custom have yet developed into a legal obligation. All civilized states, however, have a common interest in the suppression of crime, and this fact is evidenced by national legislation, by treaties and by extradition based neither on municipal law nor agreement, but on voluntary executive action. Some writers have attempted to show that a

[1] Oppenheim: International Law, 1: 403.
[2] Extradition, 1: 4.

legal duty to extradite criminals regardless of municipal law or treaties does exist, but according to Oppenheim, they merely prove that a refusal to extradite ordinary criminals is a "serious violation of the moral obligations which exist between civilized states." This is shown in the first place by the present variations in national laws concerning extradition, and in the second place by its history and present status.

In ancient times the right of asylum was generally recognized. Originally it was restricted to places to which religion had given a sacred character. Once within the walls of a monastery or a church or at a shrine, and the fugitive from justice was safe as long as he remained there. When religious asylum fell into disuse, the function of protecting fugitives was transferred to the state itself by virtue of its exclusive jurisdiction. Protection was justified on grounds of humanity, and was, moreover, an evidence of growing consciousness of national sovereignty. The right of asylum still is maintained for limited purposes on war-ships and in foreign legations. The tendency, however, is away from the right of asylum. The United States instructs its agents that "the privilege of immunity from local jurisdiction does not embrace the right of asylum for persons outside of a representative's diplomatic or personal household."[1] By some states the right of asylum is still maintained. On ships of war there are instances of asylum granted to persons fleeing from slavery, to those defeated in a political revolution, and to other political refugees in the discretion of the commander. In such cases, if a demand for surrender is made, the only recourse is through extradition proceedings. By treaty, exceptions were made in ancient times with regard to fugitives charged with political crimes. The basis of these exceptions was comity with a view to the security of states. Regicides, outlaws, heretics, and even emigrants were given up either in accordance with treaties or by voluntary action. In modern times, the practice has been reversed, political criminals ordinarily not being surrendered. Moore says that the first English treaty relating to the surrender of ordinary criminals was in 1174 when Henry II and William the Lion, of Scotland, agreed that

[1] Instructions to Diplomatic Officers, 1897, § 50.

felons fleeing to their respective domains should either be tried by the local courts or returned to England or Scotland as the case might be. Not until the eighteenth century were there extradition treaties in the modern sense. Treaties were made for the extradition of ordinary criminals besides political fugitives, conspirators, and military deserters. In 1759, France and Würtemberg agreed to surrender to each other all fugitive brigands, malefactors, robbers, incendiaries, murderers, assassins, vagabonds, as well as deserted soldiers. Vattel said in 1758 that murderers, incendiaries, and thieves were regularly given up to each other by neighboring states. Treaties of extradition were, however, looked upon with distrust, fear being felt that criminals would not receive just treatment. In the Jay Treaty of 1794, between the United States and Great Britain, Article 27 provided for the delivery up to justice of "all persons who, being charged with murder or forgery, committed within the jurisdiction of either, shall seek an asylum within any of the countries of the other, provided that this shall only be done on such evidence of criminality as, according to the laws of the place, where the fugitive or person so charged shall be found, would justify his apprehension and commitment for trial, if the offence had there been committed."[1] Restricted and guarded as this agreement was, it proved ineffective. In accordance with the provisions of the Treaty, Article 27 expired by limitation on October 28, 1807.

Even as late as the middle of the nineteenth century the distrust of extradition for ordinary criminals was so great that the conclusion of treaties did not insure their execution. The Franco-British Treaty of 1852 was not observed. From 1854 to 1858 France made seven demands under this Treaty, but none of them was acceded to. Article 10 of the Webster-Ashburton Treaty of August 9, 1842, between the United States and Great Britain contained provisions now accepted without question, but at the time they aroused violent opposition. The article is an agreement that on mutual requisitions the two states respectively will "deliver up to justice all persons who, being charged with the crime of murder,

---

[1] Malloy: Treaties, 1: 605.

or assault with intent to commit murder, or piracy, or arson, or robbery, or forgery, or the utterance of forged paper, committed within the jurisdiction of either, shall seek an asylum or shall be found within the territories of the other." Such delivery was limited by the same conditions as were stated in the Jay Treaty, with further agreement as to the manner in which warrants should be issued.[1] In the second year after it was signed, on January 30, 1844, Senator Benton presented the following in the United States Senate:

> Resolved, as the opinion of the Senate. That the President of the United States ought to give notice to the Government of Great Britain for the immediate termination of the 10th article of the treaty of 1842, being the article for the surrender of fugitive criminals.[2]

On the same day he presented a resolution calling on the President to inform the Senate concerning the refusal of Great Britain to surrender slaves who had committed crimes and had escaped to British Dominions since the ratification of the Treaty. He asked also for an explanation of the British attitude on the interpretation of the article under the above conditions.[3] A similar resolution was presented in the House of Representatives, and the reply was discussed at length by Mr. Levy, delegate from Florida, on March 5, 1844. It was contended that Lord Ashburton had used bad faith in negotiating the Treaty and that, while in New York on his journey home, he had avowed the principle that crimes committed by slaves in effecting their escape would not be covered by the Treaty, and that the "friends of the slave in England would be very watchful to see that no wrong practice took place under the treaty."[4] Such views necessarily were not well received in the slave-holding states, and when the British Government began to put them into practice, protest ensued. The legal questions of interpretation and the political reactions produced are too com-

---

[1] Malloy: Treaties, 1: 655.
[2] Senate Doc. 28th Cong., 1st Sess., v. 3, p. 125.
[3] Senate Journal, 28th Cong., 1st Sess., p. 93.
[4] Congressional Globe, v. 13, Appendix, p. 247.

plicated for discussion here. Mr. Levy went over the subject in detail from a partisan point of view, and urged that since the article operated unequally on the two sections of the United States, it should be terminated. Neither his views nor those of Mr. Benton prevailed and the article remained in force. The incident illustrates the difficulty of foreseeing all complications and of drafting extradition treaties which are applicable to countries with different standards.

Since 1850 there has been a steady increase in the number of extradition treaties and in the number of crimes included in their scope. This result naturally followed from the increase of facilities for travel whereby fugitives might be reasonably sure of escape to a near-by state or to a refuge across the ocean. "There is no civilized State in existence nowadays," says Oppenheim, "which has not concluded such treaties with the majority of the other civilized States." Malloy records treaties of extradition made by the United States with 46 states, but some of these are no longer in force. Other states have made equally rapid advances. As regards the scope of the treaties, it should be observed that whereas in the Jay Treaty of 1794 only two crimes, murder and forgery, were included, the Webster-Ashburton Treaty included seven. In the long list of subjects of treaties given at the beginning of this chapter forty-four are taken from extradition treaties. Remarkable as is this growth there is still much opportunity for improvement. It is the general rule that political crimes are not now extraditable; but there is no satisfactory definition of what political crime is. Attempts have been made[1] to distinguish between crimes committed from a political motive, those committed for a political purpose, and those committed from a political motive for a political purpose. Others restrict them to offences against the state alone, as treason and lèse-majesté. Between the clear cases lies a large group of complex crimes, where the political offence is at the same time an ordinary crime such as murder or theft. The reaction against the surrender of political fugitives came after the French Revolution. The French Constitution of 1793 granted asylum to foreigners exiled

---
[1] See Oppenheim: International Law, 1: 415.

"for the cause of liberty." A state which owed its existence to revolution naturally would be lenient toward political fugitives from other states. Thus Belgium, lately freed by revolt from the Netherlands, in 1834 agreed with France to give asylum to political fugitives. In fact, it is generally true that this principle has been adopted in most states where individual liberty is the basis of political life. Since the exemption was open to abuse, some states have specified particular crimes which though political in nature are to be extraditable. Belgium in 1856 stipulated that murder of the head of a foreign government should not be considered a political crime; and Switzerland in 1892 passed a law for the extradition of political criminals in case the chief feature of the offence wears more the aspect of an ordinary than of a political crime, leaving the decision on this point to the highest Swiss Court. The whole question of the definition of political crime is one which ought to be cleared up by international agreement.

In the next chapter attention is given to the need for coöperation in national legislation relating to extradition; but this would not be fully effective without coöperation in treaty-making. Much has already been accomplished by the multiplication of bipartite treaties, but these vary so much in detail and are subject to so many exceptions that they need unification in a general treaty to which many states are parties. At the Second Pan-American Conference of 1902 a treaty was drawn up and signed by twelve states, but it was not ratified. The Central American Peace Conference of 1907 drew up an extradition treaty which was signed by representatives of Costa Rica, Guatemala, Honduras, Nicaragua, and Salvador. It remains in force until one year after notification of a desire to terminate it, and even then continues in force between the states which have not renounced it. This treaty is unusual in that it does not indicate by name crimes which are extraditable.[1] Article 1 provides for the delivery of persons who "have been condemned as authors, accomplices, or abettors of a crime, to a penalty of not less than two years of deprivation of their liberty," or who have been indicted for a crime which carries an equal or greater penalty.

[1] Malloy: Treaties, 2: 2406–10.

Article 2 gives the exceptions to Article 1. Extradition shall not be granted (1) when the evidence of criminality would not justify his apprehension in the state where he is found, (2) when the offence is of a political nature, or connected with one, (3) when under the laws of the demanding country or of that of asylum, the action or the penalty has been barred, (4) if he has already been tried and sentenced for the same act in the state where he resides, (5) if in that state his alleged act is not considered a crime, (6) when the penalty would be death, unless the demanding government agrees to apply the next lower penalty. Article 3 declares that an "attempt against the life of the head of the Government or anarchistical attempts shall not be considered a political crime, provided that the law of the demanding country and of the country of which extradition is requested shall have fixed a penalty for said acts. In that case extradition shall be granted, even when the crime in question shall carry a penalty of less than two years of imprisonment." In this connection Article 10 of the General Treaty of Peace and Amity[1] concluded on the same date as the above extradition treaty has interest. It provides that "the Governments of the contracting Republics bind themselves to respect the inviolability of the right of asylum aboard the merchant vessels of whatsoever nationality anchored in their ports. Therefore, only persons accused of common crimes can be taken from them after due legal procedure and by order of the competent judge. Those prosecuted on account of political crimes or common crimes in connection with political ones can only be taken therefrom in case they have embarked in a port of the State which claims them, during their stay in its jurisdictional waters, and after the requirements hereinbefore set forth in the case of common crimes have been fulfilled."

Labor Treaties

The Labor Charter incorporated in the Treaty of Versailles is up to the present the most conspicuous example of coöperation in the making of labor treaties. Various aspects of that Charter will be discussed in later chapters. The point for notice in this place is

---
[1] See Appendix 5 (a).

that the Charter merely lays the foundations for future action. The purpose is the improvement of conditions of labor "by the regulation of the hours of work, including the establishment of a maximum working day and week, the regulation of the labor supply, the prevention of unemployment, the provision of an adequate living wage, the protection of the worker against sickness, disease, and injury arising out of his employment, the protection of children, young persons and women, provision for old age and injury, protection of the interests of workers when employed in countries other than their own, recognition of the principle of freedom of association, the organization of vocational and technical education and other measures."[1] The Charter creates an organization to carry out these purposes. One of the means to be employed is the drafting of international labor conventions for ratification by the states which are members of the League of Nations. When such a convention has been drafted it is to be deposited with the Secretary-General of the League who will communicate a copy to each of the members. "Each of the members undertakes that it will, within the period of one year at most from the closing of the session of the conference, or if it is impossible owing to exceptional circumstances to do so within the period of one year, then at the earliest practicable moment and in no case later than eighteen months from the closing of the conference, bring the . . . draft convention before the authority or authorities within whose competence the matter lies, for . . . action" (Art. 405). If, however, no action is taken, or if the draft is disapproved, "no further obligation shall rest upon the member." In other words, the ratification of proposed treaties is expressly recognized as a voluntary act depending on local conditions and the desire to coöperate. The difficulties that exist are taken into consideration when it is provided that draft conventions shall "have due regard to those countries in which climatic conditions, the imperfect development of industrial organization, or other special circumstances make the industrial conditions substantially different" (Art. 405).

The Labor Charter is the highest point to which the interna-

[1] Preamble, Part XIII of the Treaty.

tional labor movement has reached. It began in 1818 when Robert Owen, a Scotchman, presented a petition to the Conference of Aix-la-Chapelle in which he urged the assembling of a conference in London to consider labor questions. His suggestion was not adopted. In 1840 Daniel Legrand, a Frenchman, began to address memorials to the different governments urging that labor conditions could be improved only by international action. The idea was first taken up by Switzerland, in 1855, and it was fostered by international conferences, public, private, and national associations, hereafter to be mentioned. Although the states were officially represented in many of these conferences, in only three of them did the delegates have power to sign treaties, and in only one were conventions actually signed in final form for ratification. The Berlin Conference of 1890 adopted a protocol, but no international convention resulted. The Berne Conference of 1905 was composed of official delegates from fifteen states, who had the option of concluding conventions on the spot, for subsequent ratification, or of drafting conventions for examination and later signature at another conference. They chose the latter option. The purpose of the Conference was to outline international conventions (1) to prohibit the use of white phosphorus in the manufacture of matches, and (2) to interdict the night work of women. In the next year, on the proposal of the Swiss Federal Council, an international diplomatic conference met at Berne from September 17 to 26. It revised the two draft conventions and they were signed and subsequently ratified. The first, relating to white phosphorus matches, was ratified by forty-three states, and the second, relating to night work of women, by twenty-three states. The United States is not a party to either treaty. At this conference Great Britain advocated the creation of an International Commission to supervise the operation of the treaties; but so many states objected on the ground that this would be an infringement of their sovereignty, that the project was abandoned. A conference was held in Berne, September 15 to 25, 1913, attended by delegates of fifteen states, which drew up several draft labor treaties. These were to have been further considered at a diplomatic conference at Berne to meet on September 3, 1914, but the outbreak of war prevented it from convening.

This is not the sum total of coöperation in labor treaty-making. Numerous bipartite treaties have been concluded for the protection of labor. The first of these was signed April 15, 1904, between Italy and France. Its two general purposes were (1) to grant to nationals of either country laboring in territory of the other reciprocal banking accommodations and advantages of social insurance, (2) to guarantee the mutual maintenance of protective labor measures, and coöperation in the advancement of labor legislation. Twenty-two such treaties, including many relating specifically to accident insurance, are described by Lowe.[1] The latest was the agreement of May 12–21 between Italy and Germany made just before Austria and Italy declared war. It contained the following clause: "The subjects of either of the two States shall continue to enjoy the benefits provided in the laws in force in the other country in the matter of social insurance. The power to take advantage of the rights in question shall not be restricted in any manner."

Maritime Treaties

In Chapter VII reference was made to ancient codes of sea laws as one of the sources of international law. As soon as maritime commerce began to develop, rules applicable between the merchants of the several countries grew up and were accepted as customary laws. Since the length of voyages was not great, these rules had what now would be called only local application. In different centuries different codes were recognized for portions of the Mediterranean Sea, for Southern Europe, for Western Europe, for the Baltic states, and for the Hanse towns. In modern maritime law many remains of these codes can be found; but the growth of nationalism, emphasis on the right of independent legislation, and the unlimited expansion of commerce due to the use of steam, steel ships, the telegraph, and the dependence of modern states on the products of other states, brought about a situation that needed rectification.

[1] International Aspects of the Labor Problem.

Conflict of laws in relation to shipping, navigation, and credit, was not only inconvenient but expensive; and so, about the middle of the last century, an attempt was made to obtain universal acceptance of a code that had been prepared by a body of jurists. The attempt failed because the code was based more on legalistic conceptions than on actual experience of traders and shipowners. It is only within the last twenty-five years that genuine progress has been made toward unification of practice. It is due largely to the efforts of the International Maritime Committee which was organized in 1898. The Committee is the central organ of seventeen national associations, and has a permanent office in Antwerp where it publishes a bulletin. Its objects are (1) to further by conferences, publications, and other methods, the unification of maritime law, (2) to encourage the creation of national associations for the same purpose, (3) to maintain between these associations regular communication and united action. Through its influence two international conventions have been signed. They relate to maritime salvage, and collisions at sea. The method employed, as described by Woolf,[1] was to send a questionnaire to each national association relating to each topic on which an international convention was proposed. The replies when tabulated brought out the variations in national laws, and the central committee then formulated proposals for unification based on a general principle acceptable to all the associations. These were discussed in general conferences, and draft conventions were then drawn up. The next step was to prevail on the states to assemble a diplomatic conference. Three of these conferences were held in 1905, 1909, and 1910 resulting in the signing of the two conventions above mentioned. Two other draft conventions relating to maritime mortgages and the limitation of shipowners' liability were examined but not accepted as satisfactory. Before the two conventions which were signed could be agreed to, either the Continental or the Anglo-American practice had to be abandoned. There was a great difference in practice as to the apportionment of liability in case of damages to ships, persons, and property, and as to what courts ought to have jurisdiction

[1] International Government, p. 269–285.

TREATIES AND COÖPERATION

in collision cases. In these instances the Continental gave way to the Anglo-American system. In the preparation of later draft conventions, notably the Freight Code, the British practice was set aside for the Continental. As Mr. Woolf points out, this spirit of practical compromise was displayed because it was to the interest of the great shipowners and operators to have a uniform law; and they in turn through their national associations were able, as practical men, to convince their respective governments that the national interests were best served by official international coöperation in the form of treaties.

REFERENCES FOR CHAPTER XVI

EXTRADITION

BIRON AND CHALMERS. Extradition. London, 1903.
CLARKE, ED. Law of Extradition. London, 1903.
INSTITUTE OF INTERNATIONAL LAW, 1880 (Annuaire V, p. 117).
MOORE, J. B. The Difficulties of Extradition.
  (Academy of Political Science. Publications, 1: 625–634, 1911.)
  Principles of American Diplomacy, p. 424–425. Treatise on Extradition and Interstate Rendition, 1891. 2 v.
OPPENHEIM. International Law, 1: 403–422.
STOWELL AND MUNRO. International Cases, 1: 403–422.

LABOR

ACADEMY OF POLITICAL SCIENCE. Proceedings, 8: no. 3, p. 90–99.
LOWE. International Aspects of the Labor Problem.
REINSCH. Public International Unions, p. 42-49.
TEAD. The People's Part in Peace, p. 74–90.
WOOLF. International Government, p. 285–304.

MARITIME TREATIES

WOOLF. International Government, p. 269–285.

CHAPTER XVII

COÖPERATION IN NATIONAL LEGISLATION

EVERY person who has travelled from one country to another, especially if he has sojourned in a foreign state, could give instances of laws different from those under which he lives at home. Without leaving the United States, in the passage from New York to New Jersey, for instance, he may observe evidences of differences in legislation. If he carries on business outside of New York, he will need expert advice on matters which would be simple if confined to New York. There is then, even in the United States, a disagreement on the rules applicable to the same act or transaction depending on the jurisdiction where the rule is to be applied. This disagreement has sometimes been termed conflict of laws. In order to remove some of the inconveniences of this disagreement, a movement has been on foot for some years for uniformity of legislation on a selected group of subjects. Since 1892 the National Conference of Commissioners on Uniform State Laws has met annually. It is made up of commissioners appointed by the various states for the promotion of uniformity of legislation, and is therefore a conference of officials representing the various state governments. Between meetings the Conference carries on its work through standing committees which attempt to draft acts which may be acceptable to all state governments. For instance, the drafting of a bill on divorce would be assigned to a committee which would report at the next annual meeting. It would continue its labors from year to year until the Conference was able to approve the draft as suitable for adoption in all states. The formal adoption would carry with it a recommendation to the several states, each by its own legislature to enact the statute into law, in order by coöperation to bring uniformity out of conflict in the law of divorce in the United States. No sort of obligation rests on the states to follow the recommendation, and in fact no bill drafted by the Conference has been accepted by all of the states. Even within one national state and in relation to subjects of common interest, the several independent law-making bodies have not been able to agree; but considerable progress has been made. Uniform acts have been drafted and recommended for adoption relating to negotiable instruments, sales, warehouse receipts, divorce, bills of lading, stock transfers, family desertion, probate of foreign wills, marriage licenses, child labor, marriage evasion, acknowledgments, partnership, cold storage, and workmen's compensation. In 1915, the Conference reported that no act had been adopted in all jurisdictions of the United States, and no state had adopted every act recommended.

The efforts above described attempt to unify in certain subjects the law in the several jurisdictions of one sovereign state, the United States. A much more imposing task is that of unifying law in the respective sovereign states of the world. The need is almost, if not quite, as great as it is in the United States. Because the jurisdictions are independent states, this subject of disagreement of national laws, this conflict of laws, has sometimes been called international private law. It is international, because sovereign states are involved, and private because it deals with the relations between persons of different states rather than between the different states as is the case with public international law. In the United States there is a Federal constitution which has a unifying influence and in some respects prohibits conflict of laws. Among independent states there is no such supreme constitution, and the law of nations takes no note of private law. Any uniformity that comes must be the result of voluntary coöperation either by treaty, by national legislation, or by administration. Agreements by treaty on matters of private law often need national legislation to make them effective; and their effect is further modified and influenced by the decisions of national courts and the discretion exercised by administrative officers. The Hague Conventions relating to peace and war have received so much attention, and war has been so much in the foreground in recent years, that another series of Hague Conventions has been well-nigh overlooked. Conferences on private law have met at The Hague intermittently since 1893, resulting in the conclusion of seven Conventions which, according to Mr. Baty, "have substantially unified the rules of Private International Law for the central part of the continent of Europe." They relate to marriage law, divorce, effects of marriage, guardianship of minors, interdiction, civil procedure, and bills of exchange. None of them have been ratified by all states, and two important states, Great Britain and the United States, are parties to none of them. The Convention on Bills of Exchange has been signed by twenty-seven states but no ratifications have yet been exchanged.

There is an important difference between the first six and the seventh of these Conventions. The former are not drafts of acts in the form of treaties to become law in each of the signatory states, but they are agreements as to how the states will procede in cases of conflict of law. For instance, the fourth Convention begins[1] "Guardianship is governed by the law of the minor's nationality. If the law of his nationality makes no provision for the administration within its territory of the guardianship of minors whose habitual residence is situated abroad, the diplomatic or consular representative, duly authorized in that behalf, of the State whose subject the minor is, may provide for such administration in accordance with the law of that State, provided that the State where the minor habitually resides offers no objection." This is an illustration of private international law considered as the science of selecting the law which is applicable to foreigners. Mr. Baty entitles his book on private international law, Polarized Law, because neither Conflict of Law, nor Interlocking Law, nor Harmonizations of Law, nor The Correlations of Law express for him the real content of the subject. "The analogy of the mathematical conception of polarity," he says, "according to which a single element may have constantly varying moments, according as it is referred to one 'pole' or another, appears to be very applicable to

---
[1] Baty: Polarized Law, p. 187.

the system in which one relation may have an indefinite number of jural reflections, according as it is referred to one or another body of law."[1] Later he says that polarized or private international law "means simply the set of rules that a given nation adopts for the occasional application of foreign law instead of its own, in peculiar circumstances." The Hague Conventions, except the last, for the most part are agreements on rules for the application of foreign law, without attempting to change that law.

The Convention on Bills of Exchange is of an entirely different character. It is a genuine attempt to unify the law on that subject throughout the world. The signatories to the Convention, says Professor Lorenzen,[2] "have assumed the obligation to adopt the Uniform Law textually without any derogations, except so far as they may be expressly authorized by the convention itself. As long as the convention is in force in a given country, its provisions are to supplant wholly the former national law." The Uniform Law referred to is annexed to the treaty. In the following pages, illustrations are given of the need for coöperation in national legislation in relation to (1) extradition, (2) nationality, naturalization and expatriation, and (3) labor.

Extradition Laws

In the last chapter a survey was made of progress in coöperative treaty-making with regard to extradition. Not all statesmen agree that this is the best way to handle the matter. In England, Lords Campbell and Brougham believed that bordering states at least should each provide by general law for the surrender of fugitives from justice, and in the United States Senator Morrill, on December 13, 1875, introduced a resolution (which, however, produced no result) "that the Committee on Foreign Relations be instructed to inquire into the expediency of providing, by general law, for the extradition of fugitives from justice upon the proper application and proof by the governments from whence they may have escaped, and also as to the propriety of refusing asylum to

---
[1] Baty, p. vi.
[2] Conflict of Laws Relating to Bills and Notes, p. 18.

fugitive criminals, and removing them from the country."[1] In 1889 Canada passed a general extradition law referring to many specified crimes, which were to be extraditable regardless of any treaty. The act became operative with respect to a particular state only on the proclamation of the Governor-General.

There are serious objections to general extradition laws which take effect with regard to all states unconditionally. Systems of jurisprudence and standards of humanity differ so much between states, especially between the East and the West, that an unrestricted surrender might in a given case mean unnecessary cruelty, and the application of penalties unsuited to the crime. Moreover, the arrangement by treaty, or by general law to apply only on proclamation, provides for reciprocity which is essential to suppression of crime on the one hand and to progress toward humane ideals on the other. "The objects of extradition treaties," says Moore,[2] "are: (1) to render the obligation to surrender certain; (2) to insure reciprocity; (3) to adapt the list of extraditable offences to the relative social and political conditions of the two countries; (4) to regulate procedure." In the United States, since treaties are the supreme law of the land, extradition treaties supersede all municipal law inconsistent with them, and have a sanction additional to the general sanction of international law.

There is much need of coöperation in national legislation concerning the power to make extradition treaties and concerning the means of executing them. In the United States, the President, by and with the advice of the Senate, may negotiate extradition treaties like all other treaties. The French President has unrestricted power in this respect. In some states, however, the power is limited by municipal law which restricts the possibility of reciprocity. Belgium, Great Britain, Holland, Luxemburg, Argentina, Peru, and Switzerland have such laws. General agreement in this respect would further the cause of coöperation. France, for instance, never surrenders her own citizens, while Great Britain and the United States regularly do so. This dis-

---
[1] Moore: Extradition, 1: 79–80.
[2] Extradition, 1: 82.

NATIONAL LEGISLATION

agreement sometimes produces a conflict between municipal law and treaties. For example, Italy and the United States in 1868[1] made an extradition treaty without exempting nationals. Italy does not extradite her own citizens, and so in 1888 she refused to surrender Salvatore Paladini, charged with passing counterfeit money. The United States therefore no longer asks for the surrender of Italian citizens, although she still considers herself bound by the treaty to give up her own subjects. An important example of the situation produced is found in the Charlton case.[2] Porter Charlton, an American citizen, murdered his wife at Moltrasio, Italy, and after his escape to New Jersey confessed the crime. Extradition proceedings were begun by Italy, he was arrested, and the magistrate committed him to await a warrant of extradition from the Secretary of State. Before the warrant could be executed, *habeas corpus* proceedings were begun. The petition for the writ was dismissed and appeal was taken to the United States Supreme Court. Two points made by Charlton's attorneys were (1) that under the treaty neither party is bound to deliver up its own citizens, and (2) that since Italy refuses to give up her own citizens, the treaty lacked mutuality, and, as regards the Charlton case, had been abrogated. Neither argument was effective with the court, which held (1) that the word "persons" used in the treaty includes citizens, in spite of the municipal laws of Italy, and (2) that the absence of mutuality made the treaty voidable and not void. The Secretary of State had already stated that "it would seem entirely sound to consider ourselves as bound to surrender our citizens to Italy, even though Italy should not, by reason of the provision of her municipal law, be able to surrender its citizens to us," the United States preferring this line of action rather than to abandon its interpretation of the word "persons." Charlton eventually was surrendered, tried, and convicted of murder.

There is much divergence in national legislation concerning the administration and execution of extradition under treaties. This is a serious deterrent to coöperation under them. In most treaties

[1] Malloy: Treaties, 1: 966-968.
[2] Stowell and Munro: International Cases, 1: 408-411; 229 U. S. 447-476.

there is a condition that a fugitive shall be surrendered only on such proof of guilt as would justify his commitment for trial in the country in which he was found, if the crime had been there committed. How shall it be determined whether the proof submitted is sufficient, and what are the results of too cumbersome a system? On the Continent, the power of decision is largely an administrative function. In the United States and Great Britain it is partly judicial and partly administrative. Professor Moore [1] has recounted the development under this system in the United States. He shows that serious obstacles to extradition have been raised by the failure of the Executive to issue warrants after "probable cause" has been found by a magistrate; and by the prolongation of litigation through the entertainment of technical objections by the court. This increases the cost of extradition proceedings so much as almost to make it prohibitive. The expense often runs from $5,000 to $50,000. "Now, the point which I specially desire to make," says Professor Moore, "is, can any one give even a plausible reason for the existence of such a state of things? Let us analyze the subject into its elements. We have for years had upon our statute books laws by which we have repelled or expelled from our shores alien immigrants by the thousand without the slightest compunction. The grounds of exclusion have repeatedly been enlarged, till the prohibited classes embrace idiots, epileptics, and persons afflicted with a loathsome or with a dangerous contagious disease; insane persons, and persons who have been insane within the five preceding years or who have had two or more attacks of insanity at any time; paupers, professional beggars, or persons likely to become a public charge, of which likelihood the possession of less than fifty dollars is considered as proof; polygamists; persons convicted of a non-political crime or misdemeanor involving moral turpitude, whether they have or have not served their sentence; prostitutes or procurers; anarchists, or persons who believe in or advocate the violent overthrow of the United States government or of all governments or all forms of law, or the assassination of public officials; and persons under contract to labor, with the exception of persons

[1] Academy of Political Science, 1: 625-634.

belonging to the professional classes, persons employed strictly as personal or domestic servants, and skilled laborers of a class in which none unemployed can be found in the United States.

"Instead of obstructing the execution of these laws, we make a general demand for their rigorous enforcement. Let an alien come to our shores who is guilty of the omission to have fifty dollars, and we send him back without hesitation to the country from which he came. Let him come with the guilt resting upon him of murder, burglary, arson, or other crime, and we cover him with the mantle of our protection and extend to him the sympathy due to a hero and a martyr. In other words, call our statute an immigration law, its enforcement is commended and arouses no suspicion; call it an extradition law, and large opportunities are afforded to evade and defeat it." To remedy these conditions he recommends three things, (1) that every nation should have a general law authorizing the Executive or administrative authorities to deliver up fugitives from justice, specifying the cases in which this may be done and regulating the procedure, conditioned partly on reciprocity; (2) make a distinction between citizens and aliens; and (3) a distinction between persons charged with crime and those convicted of crime. He does not recommend letting down the bars as far as political offenders are concerned.

NATIONALITY, NATURALIZATION, AND EXPATRIATION

Closely connected with the idea of extradition are conflicting municipal laws concerning nationality, naturalization, and expatriation. If it were generally agreed that states would distinguish between citizens and aliens in the administration of their extradition laws, there would still remain the fundamental question: Who are citizens? There is no international law on this subject, and there is much conflict in national laws. It is still possible for a person to be claimed as a citizen by two states, so that while in the first he is, according to its law, a citizen of that state, and while in the second, a citizen of it. He may thus have what has been called dual nationality, and he may in fact even be without nationality, a man without a country. In time of peace, or in the absence of any unusual incident, this circumstance may cause little real inconvenience, although it often affects property rights, suffrage, the status of married women and children, and the obligation to undergo military training. When actual military service is required, in time of war, a more critical situation arises; and the lack of certainty as to nationality creates many international complications when a person whose status is in doubt seeks the diplomatic protection of a state in which he claims nationality.

Nationality is the status of an individual as subject or citizen in relation to a particular sovereign state. It involves the reciprocal relations of allegiance on the part of the person and protection on the part of the state. It may be acquired by birth, or marriage, or election on reaching the age of majority, or by transfer of territory from one sovereignty to another. These, and other means, involve no change of domicile. Nationality throws its mantle over the person without any physical act of his own. But nationality may be acquired by removal from one sovereign jurisdiction to another coupled with compliance with the naturalization laws of the second state. This involves two conceptions: first, expatriation, or the casting off of obligations to the state of which one is a national, and, second, the assumption of the duty of allegiance to the state in which nationality is sought. On nearly all of these means of acquiring nationality and on the right to relinquish it, and especially on the procedure involved, there is great disagreement among states. Perhaps the only instance of absolute agreement is that children born to subjects of a state while within the territory, actual or constructive, of that state are *ipso facto* citizens or subjects. But when a child is born abroad, his status depends on municipal law. There are two opposing doctrines on this point. Some states follow one, some the other, and some combine the two. The first doctrine is that a child, wherever born, inherits the nationality of his father according to the *jus sanguinis*, which applies, for instance, in Austria, Germany, Sweden, and Switzerland. The second is that a child, according to the *jus soli*, whatever its parentage, is a national of the state in which it is born. Most South American states follow this rule. The United States and Great

Britain combine the two rules, holding not only that children of their subjects born abroad become their subjects, but that children of aliens born on their territory also are subjects.[1] In other states different variations of the two chief rules have been adopted, thus increasing the confusion. There are some states which still hold to the rule, once a national always a national. Russia and Turkey absolutely deny the right of voluntary expatriation. The various modifications of this extreme rule as applied in various countries are summarized by Borchard.[2] In most countries the rule is that expatriation is admitted and citizenship ceases upon naturalization abroad; in other states—for example, France—expatriation is permitted provided all military service has been performed; in Switzerland, representing another class, expatriation is allowed, if citizenship has been renounced in accordance with Swiss law; another group, illustrated by Venezuela, admits expatriation and recognizes foreign naturalization, but the rights of citizenship revert upon return to the native country; and finally, in some states, expatriation is assumed from various acts such as long-continued residence abroad, unauthorized performance of military service on behalf of a foreign government, and the unauthorized acceptance of public office abroad. Expatriation is the voluntary renunciation or abandonment of citizenship and allegiance. It is recognized by all except a few states as either a personal right or a privilege which may be exercised under the conditions listed above, but these conditions are sufficiently diverse to cause conflict. Moreover, the administrative regulations, the periods of time involved, and the varying interpretations of the national laws by courts produce further complications. It is only within the past fifty years that the doctrine of indissoluble or perpetual allegiance has been generally abandoned; but uniformity of rules under the present doctrine has not yet been developed.

Add to difficulties caused by lack of uniform rules as to nationality of origin and expatriation those which come from divergent naturalization laws, and it becomes evident beyond a doubt that

[1] U. S. Revised Statutes, 1992–1993; U. S. Constitution, 14th Amendment.
[2] Diplomatic Protection of Citizens Abroad, p. 684.

coöperation in national legislation is needed. Naturalization is an act of state by which a foreigner is admitted to citizenship. The conditions under which it is permitted, the time within which it takes effect, the status of the person during the probationary period, his liabilities, duties, and immunities, are all determined by the state in which he seeks citizenship. On the other hand, his right to divest himself of his original nationality, the question whether he has fulfilled all duties prerequisite to expatriation, his status in case he should return to the country of origin before completing naturalization, are matters over which the second state can assert no jurisdiction. If he should visit a third state during the probationary period and there become involved in controversy, a three-cornered international disagreement might result. "Naturalization is the act of adopting a foreigner and clothing him with the privileges of a citizen."[1] But a state cannot confer citizenship on an alien against his will, or without some express manifestation of a desire to change his nationality. A few states in South America have attempted to force citizenship on alien residents who purchased real property or had children born in those countries; but these attempts have never been allowed to succeed where United States citizens are concerned. If expatriation and naturalization always took place simultaneously, one cause of conflict would be removed, but this would not be possible without uniformity of expatriation rules, a result difficult to attain unless military conscription is altogether abolished. We do not yet know what effect the recommendations of the Council of the League of Nations relating to reduction of national armaments may have on conscription and compulsory military training. If these are everywhere abolished, one serious obstacle to the universal acceptance of unrestricted expatriation will be removed, thus removing the conflict between expatriation and naturalization. Another method would be for all states to permit naturalization only to persons who can show documentary evidence of expatriation issued by the state of their original nationality. This would require efforts on the part of aliens which would themselves indicate a genuine desire to change

---

[1] Van Dyne, Naturalization, p. 5.

allegiance, and would perhaps remove some causes of international disagreement. Naturalization would be a more difficult process than it now is, but this would be in conformity with the views of many in states directly involved in the recent war. To show this, we need only quote the opening paragraph of Mr. Odgers's book on Nationality and Naturalization. "During the first six or eight months of the Great War," he says, "nothing—except the War itself—attracted so much public attention in Great Britain as questions concerning naturalization and its kindred subject, nationality. On every hand one heard the fiercest denunciation of ex-Germans who had become naturalized British subjects. This state of feeling—in many cases quite unjustifiable—was aroused partly by a campaign in a section of our Press and partly by our appreciation at the eleventh hour of the value and thoroughness of the German system of espionage. It was suddenly borne in upon the man in the street that naturalization does not and cannot change a man, heart and soul—least of all an ex-German, in whom there is an inborn love of his Kaiser and his Fatherland, and whose whole life and training have been based upon the theory that where the Fatherland is concerned the end justifies the means, however repulsive they may be; in short, that a German naturalized here remains a German at heart. Fair-minded people no doubt admitted that if they had become naturalized in Germany they would still have remained English at heart, and would have wished to help England in every way they could. But, whatever view was taken, the main question raised was simply this: Do we too readily admit aliens into our midst and grant them naturalization on too-lenient terms?" Chapter IV of Mr. Odgers's book suggests changes in the British law by which naturalization would be safeguarded from fraud.

The whole question of naturalization is of importance to countries from which or to which there is any considerable movement of foreign people. Up until the early fifties, the United States held the view that expatriation was not a voluntary right, but dependent entirely on the will of the state. It was not until immigration to the United States assumed large proportions that the inconsistency of this position was seen. Foreigners were being admitted to citizenship, while the country of their origin continued to deny the right of expatriation. After the Fenian agitation, during the course of which naturalized American citizens of British origin were arrested and held in Ireland as British subjects, Congress passed an act in which it was declared that "the right of expatriation is a natural and inherent right of all people." In this direction the national legislation of states has tended, and attempts to come to further agreements by treaty have been made. For the most part they have been unsuccessful; and the only practicable mode of procedure for the future would seem to be (1) at a general diplomatic congress, or meetings of the Assembly of the League of Nations, to lay down principles which if followed would remove conflict, and (2) to urge the states themselves to coöperate in the revision of national laws.

Labor Legislation

The Labor Charter of the Treaty of Versailles distinguishes clearly between national labor legislation and treaties (Art. 405). In either case the International Labor Conference merely recommends the legislation or the draft convention to the several states, and the same limitations as to the nature of the recommendations as affected by natural and economic conditions apply to legislation as to treaties. There is no obligation to adopt either. But political conditions also enter in. In some states, the constitution interferes with the ratification of labor treaties or the passage of general labor laws. In the United States, for instance, the power to regulate labor resides in the constituent states, and the Federal government is therefore without power to enact general labor laws or to override state laws by treaty agreements.[1] Therefore the following clause was included in the Labor Charter: "In the case of a federal state, the power of which to enter into conventions on labor matters is subject to limitations, it shall be in the discretion of that Government to treat a draft convention to which such limitations apply as a recommendation (for legislation) only, and the

---
[1] For the practice in regulation of trades and occupations, see Tiedeman, State and Federal Control of Persons and Property, 1: 233-612.

provisions of this article with respect to recommendations shall apply in such case" (Art. 405). The constitutional difficulty in the United States explains why we have seldom been represented officially at international labor conferences, and why the Treaty of Versailles is the first labor treaty to which the United States has been a party. In only one instance has the Federal government been able to take direct action to conform to international labor proposals. Not being a party to the Berne treaty prohibiting the use of white phosphorus in the manufacture of matches, and not being competent to pass a general law on the subject, much the same result was accomplished in 1912 by placing a prohibitive tax on the manufacture of such matches and prohibiting their importation and exportation. The states themselves have passed numerous laws relating to all phases of labor including workmen's compensation and industrial insurance.[1]

References for Chapter XVII

BATY. Polarized Law.
BEALE. Treatise on the Conflict of Laws.
LORENZEN. Conflict of Laws Relating to Bills and Notes.
WOOLF. International Government, p. 266–310.

EXTRADITION

STOWELL AND MUNRO. International Cases, 1: 408–411.

POLICE POWER IN THE UNITED STATES

TIEDEMAN. State and Federal Control of Persons and Property.

EXPATRIATION AND NATURALIZATION

MOORE, J. B. Principles of American Diplomacy, p. 270–304.
BORCHARD. Diplomatic Protection of Citizens Abroad, p. 528–592, 674–712.
STOWELL AND MUNRO. International Cases, 1: 311–325.
WILSON AND TUCKER. International Law, p. 130–138.
ODGERS. Nationality and Naturalization, p. 1–40.

---
[1] See Labor Laws of the United States, Washington, 1914, 2 v.

CHAPTER XVIII

PUBLIC INTERNATIONAL UNIONS

A MEANING of the word administration somewhat different from that discussed in Chapter XIII is that which applies it to the management of business enterprises, or the conduct of an office or bureau. In this sense the word has no political significance. For instance, there is an administrative officer for every corporation, society, or institution. The organization may be for profit or for pleasure, or for the purpose of accomplishing some great end for the benefit of humanity. It may be for economy or for convenience. Such organizations may be international as well as national in scope. We are here concerned not with international enterprises for personal profit, but with those that are professedly international not only in scope but in personnel. For instance, the Standard Oil Company and the National City Bank are organizations which do an international business and have offices throughout the world. Their scope is thus international, but their control is confined to the citizens of one state. Moreover, the purpose is the personal profit of the organizers. Opposed to this class of international organization and administration are those in which the personnel and control are international and which are not for the profit of individuals. These may be of two kinds, public and private. Public international organizations are those in which two or more states in their political capacity are concerned. Private international organizations are those in which the citizens of two or more states are concerned, the states having no official or directive connection with them. Since the former are organizations created by states, they must owe their existence to international agreements. The latter, on the contrary, are created by agreement between the citizens of different states. An example of the first is the Universal Postal

Union, and of the second, the Interparliamentary Union. Both are the result of voluntary coöperation, and both function partly through administrative offices or bureaus. In this chapter we are concerned only with permanent public coöperative international organizations, those which owe their existence to private initiative and effort being reserved for Chapter XX.

The League Covenant pays attention to these public organizations in Article 24. It provides that "all international bureaus already established by general treaties" shall with the parties' consent be placed under the direction of the League. It is agreed that all new international bureaus and "all commissions for the regulation of matters of international interest" shall automatically come under its care; and where no bureau or commission is created to execute the regulations of general conventions relating to matters of international interest, the Secretariat of the League, with the consent of the Council and of the parties to the treaties, shall act as a bureau of information and "render any other assistance which may be necessary or desirable."

If the members of the League agree to turn over to it all existing public international bureaus, and if, as is required, all permanent bureaus hereafter created are placed under its direction, this function of the Secretariat will be no mean task.

It is necessary, therefore, to examine the Secretariat itself as a type of administrative organ and to compare it with others already in existence. We will in this case be dealing with administration in the narrowest sense of the word, meaning a department of a larger organization with specific duties, largely ministerial.

The Secretariat is referred to in the Covenant in Articles 1, 2, 6, 7, 11, 15, 18, 24, and Annex 2. Summarizing these, we find the Secretariat to be one of the permanent instrumentalities through which the action of the League is effected. Its office is at Geneva, the seat of the League, and it consists of a "Secretary-General and such secretaries and staff as may be required." The latter are appointed by the Secretary-General with the approval of the Council. The first Secretary-General, named in Annex 2, is Sir James Eric Drummond, and subsequent incumbents are to be appointed by the Council with the approval of the majority of the Assembly. While acting officially, the Secretary-General enjoys diplomatic privileges and immunities. Appointments under him are open to women as well as men. His first duty was the establishment of temporary headquarters, and in conjunction with a special commission sitting in London, to arrange for the first meeting of the League. Article 1 indicates the first ministerial duty after the adoption of the Covenant. All states, not original members and named in Annex 1, which wish to join, must deposit with the Secretariat within two months of the coming into force of the Covenant a declaration of accession without reservations. Notice of these accessions shall then be sent to all members of the League by the Secretary-General. Among the functions of the Secretariat specifically mentioned are the following: On request of any member of the League, in case of threat of war, to summon a meeting of the Council; to receive communications from members of the League concerning impending international disputes and arrange for investigation by the Council in case the disputes are not submitted to arbitration; to receive and register all conventions and international engagements hereafter entered into by members of the League, and to publish these treaties and engagements as soon as possible; to collect and distribute all relevant information and render any other assistance necessary or desirable, with the consent of the Council, in connection with matters of international interest regulated by general conventions which are not placed under the control of an international bureau or commission; to serve as a central office for all international bureaus and commissions which come under the direction of the League. The expenses of any such bureau or commission may, by the Council, be included in the expenses of the Secretariat, which in turn "shall be borne by the members of the League in accordance with the apportionment of the expenses of the International Bureau of the Universal Postal Union" (Art. 6). As this method of distributing expenses of international bureaus has been often adopted, the details of the plan may well be explained at this point. They are found in Article 38 of the Rules of the Universal Postal Union.[1]

[1]Annuaire de la Vie Internationale, 1908–9, p. 260–261.

PUBLIC INTERNATIONAL UNIONS

The states which are members of the Union are divided into seven classes each contributing in proportion to a certain number of assigned units, as follows:

Classes	Units
1	25
2	20
3	15
4	10
5	5
6	3
7	1

The classification of the members of the Union in 1909 was:

1st Class—Germany, Austria, United States, France, Great Britain, Hungary, British India, Australian Commonwealth, Canada, British colonies and protectorates in South Africa, all other British colonies and protectorates collectively, Italy, Japan, Russia, Turkey.

2nd Class—Spain.

3rd Class—Belgium, Brazil, Egypt, Netherlands, Rumania, Sweden, Switzerland, Algeria, French colonies and protectorates in Indo-China, all other French colonies collectively, all insular possessions of the United States collectively, Dutch East Indies.

4th Class—Denmark, Norway, Portugal, Portuguese colonies in Africa, all other Portuguese colonies collectively.

5th Class—Argentina, Bosnia-Herzegovina, Bulgaria, Chili, Colombia, Greece, Mexico, Peru, Serbia, Tunis.

6th Class—Bolivia, Costa Rica, Cuba, Dominican Republic, Ecuador, Guatemala, Haiti, Honduras, Luxemburg, Nicaragua, Panama, Paraguay, Persia, Salvador, Siam, Uruguay, Venezuela, German protectorates in Africa, German protectorates in Asia and Australasia, Danish colonies, Curaçao, Surinam.

7th Class—Kongo Free State, Korea, Crete, Spanish establishments in the Gulf of Guinea, all Italian colonies collectively, Liberia, Montenegro.

It is evident that the above classification cannot be applied to the world of to-day without revision. One of the first duties of the League must be a new grouping of old states and of states newly created in order that the expenses of the Bureau may be apportioned.

There are only two existing international administrative organs comparable to the Secretariat of the League. These are the International Bureau of the Permanent Court of Arbitration at The Hague, and the International Central American Bureau. The former was created by Article 22 of the Hague Convention for the Pacific Settlement of International Disputes, 1899, and continued by Article 43 of the convention of the same name concluded by the Second Hague Conference. It is mentioned in Articles 15, 16, 43, 44, 46, 47, 48, 49, 50, and 63 of this convention. The Bureau is directly under the control of the Permanent Administrative Council, created by Article 49, composed of the diplomatic representatives of the contracting powers accredited to The Hague and of the Netherlands Foreign Minister who is president of the Council. The Council appoints, suspends, and dismisses the officials and employés of the Bureau, fixes salaries, and controls expenditures. It adopts regulations for the Bureau, and makes an annual report to the powers concerning its labors and the work of the Permanent Court of Arbitration. At its meetings, an attendance of nine members makes a quorum, and decisions are taken by majority vote. It holds in relation to the Bureau a position similar to that of the Council of the League in relation to the Secretariat. The Bureau itself is purely a ministerial body. It has charge of the archives of the Permanent Court of Arbitration and of all international commissions for which it acts. It is the registry for the Court of Arbitration in all its activities, and serves as the channel for communications relative to the meetings of the Court. It receives and preserves all "laws, regulations, and documents showing the execution of the awards given by the Court." In case of threatened disputes, it receives the offer of either or both of the parties to submit the matter to arbitration. The expenses of the Bureau are distributed among the contracting powers in the proportion fixed for the International Bureau of the Universal Postal Union.

The International Central American Bureau was created by a special Convention signed in Washington, December 20, 1907, by the five Central American States.[1] It is still in existence, since the

---
[1] See Appendix 5 (c).

life of the Convention is fifteen years. Its seat is at Guatemala. It consists of one delegate from each state, the presidency being held alternately by each. Its general purpose is "to develop the interests common to Central America," which interests are the peaceful reorganization of Central America; improvement of education and its development along common lines; development of commerce; of agriculture and industries; procurement of uniformity in civil, commercial, and criminal legislation; in customs laws; monetary systems; sanitation; weights and measures; and the definition of "real property." It has all functions necessary to carry out these purposes, and makes a semi-annual report to each state. Its expenses are equally divided among the states. The most important work of the Bureau has been the preparation of the programmes for the six Central American Conferences held from 1907 to 1914.

Of public international bureaus, which in all probability will come under the direction of the League, there are at least thirty already in existence, while others are now in process of formation. In discussing these, we will not confine ourselves to the executive organs, but examine the whole organization of which the bureaus are parts. They are all coöperative international institutions, set up by joint state action, and strictly limited in their powers and functions by the treaties to which they owe their existence. Their voluntary character is recognized in Article 24 of the League Covenant which places their bureaus under the direction of the League only if the parties to them consent. Signature to the Covenant is itself consent in the case of new organizations which have bureaus or commissions; but it should be noted that new organizations which do not have such bureaus do not automatically come under the League, and that the Secretariat cannot act for them without the consent of the Council and the members of the organizations. The fact should therefore be emphasized that it is the bureaus, namely the organs having chiefly ministerial power, which the League is to direct, leaving the unions to function as formerly.

Public international unions are created by general treaties and conventions, and not by accumulation of bilateral agreements to the same effect. Both are evidences of coöperation, and the general agreements come usually after prolonged attempts to deal with matters intrinsically international by means of single treaties. The subjects to which these general agreements relate are classified by Reinsch[1] as (1) communications, (2) economic interests, (3) sanitation and prison reform, (4) police powers, (5) scientific purposes, (6) special and local purposes. Woolf[2] groups the organs created into four classes, those with (1) permanent deliberative or legislative organs working in conjunction with administrative organs, (2) periodic conferences in conjunction with permanent international bureaus or offices, (3) conferences and conventions with the object of unifying national laws or administrations, (4) special international organs of a permanent character. Sayre[3] divides all international administrative organs, including those which have to do with the control of territory, into three groups which he denominates (1) international organs with little or no power, (2) international organs with power of control over local situations, and (3) international organs with power of control over the member states. Any classification is bound to be imperfect because each organization is the result of evolution under different conditions and to accomplish specific ends. The best that can be done is to indicate methods of organization that recur and tend to become standards, not forgetting that the types overlap and fade into each other.

It is a general principle, subject to but few minor exceptions, that the organizations can take no action binding on the states which are members without their specific consent. The acts of the general assemblies are therefore really recommendations rather than legislation, and these recommendations become effective only by subsequent formal agreement through the medium of treaties. It is true that the permanent governing bodies often have power to make rules and regulations which have far-reaching results, but

---

[1] Public International Unions.
[2] International Government, p. 159-161.
[3] Experiments in International Administration.

these are supposed to deal only with the efficient execution of policies already agreed upon.

The unions already in existence have either two or three organs through which they function. They all have a general assembly which meets periodically or on call attended by delegates officially appointed by the states. Sometimes this assembly is called a congress and sometimes a conference. It is the medium for discussion, debate, and mutual understanding. It may revise regulations, and often prepares "draft" conventions which the states are asked to adopt through diplomatic conferences. When the subject for decision has been notified to the states before the meeting, the delegates are sometimes authorized to serve in a diplomatic capacity and conclude conventions, which must, however, be subsequently ratified by the governments of the states. It is a general rule that decisions and recommendations of the Congress must be taken by unanimous vote, but there is a tendency to depart from this rule, especially in matters which do not essentially affect the policy of the organization or place any new duty on the member states. Regulations may in many unions be changed by majority vote.

The permanent organ of the unions is the Bureau or Office; but it is often subject to direction by a third organ called the Commission, which acts as a governing body or board of directors between meetings of the Congress. They often appoint the officials and staff of the Bureau, prepare its budget, and direct its expenditures. The Commission is of comparatively recent development, the older unions intrusting its functions to the government in whose territory the Bureau is situated. We have seen that the Hague Bureau is under the direction of an Administrative Council made up of the diplomatic representatives accredited at The Hague under the presidency of the Netherlands Minister of Foreign Affairs. Among the unions which have Commissions are the Pan-American Union, the Sugar Union, the International Institute of Agriculture, the Seismological Union, the Geodetic Union, and the Metrical Union. Whereas all of the member states are represented in the Congress, it is usual to have a smaller number in the Commissions either elected by the Congress, or specified in the original treaty of organization. In the Commission, the decisions often do not depend on unanimity, a majority vote being sufficient. The International Bureaus, though clothed with least power, and theoretically only ministerial in function, have great value because of their permanent character. Even the Commission is not permanently in session. Without the Bureau the whole organization would be ineffective. It acts as the channel of intercourse between the governments, carries out the specific administrative behests of the regulations, collects information, preserves the archives, issues reports, and arranges for the meetings of the Commissions and Congresses. Its value does not depend on the possession of power, in fact, the possession of power by the Bureaus is a positive danger to the whole international organization. Bureaus are essentially non-political in character, operating best and accomplishing most when they carry out instructions and place before the member states facts which may serve as a basis for coöperative action.

Universal Postal Union

The organization of the Universal Postal Union has often been described, but since it is referred to in the League Covenant, and is an example of a union which has undoubtedly been successful, its essential features may be given here. It owes its existence in its present form to the Universal Postal Convention signed at Rome, May 26, 1906.[1] This Convention laid down principles for the handling of international mail matter, and detailed regulations and coöperative agreements to be followed in all states which are parties to the treaty. It thus combined into one postal territory many states under different sovereignties, each of which gives unrestricted right of transit at standardized charges, reckoned according to weight of material and mileage covered. For the administration of this system three organs are provided: a Permanent International Bureau, a Conference, and a Congress. The Confer-

---

[1] Hertslet's Commercial Treaties, 25: 430-501. For the character of this convention, see Four Packages of Cut Diamonds v. United States, 256 Federal Reporter, 305, where it is said that universal postal conventions are not treaties because not made by and with the advice and consent of the Senate, and they are not laws because not enacted by Congress.

ence has never met under the present Convention and may therefore be eliminated from consideration. It was intended to meet at intervals for the decision of purely administrative matters. Its functions are carried on by the Swiss Postal Department which by the Convention is given surveillance of the Bureau. The Congress is composed of one or more delegates from each member, but each government has only one vote. New states are admitted on request, and protectorates, colonies, and dominions are entitled to membership as though they were sovereign states. The Congress meets every five years in a place fixed by the preceding Congress. It may be called at any time when demanded by two-thirds of the governments. Its delegates have diplomatic powers, authorizing them to make alterations in the original Convention and in the regulations. When acting as a diplomatic congress, the rule of unanimity applies. Changes in the Convention must be ratified by the states after signature. In the interval between meetings changes may be made in the Convention by a different method which gives to the members ample opportunity for deliberation. When three states propose a change, the Bureau notifies the members, which have six months in which to examine the proposals and to criticize them. The proposed changes are brought together by the Bureau and the members then vote on the definite revised proposition. Unanimity is required for alterations in important articles, a two-thirds vote in less important matters, and a bare majority when the interpretation of the Convention is concerned. As has been explained, the expenses of the Union are borne in unequal amounts by the members. This does not, however, affect their voting power, each member having an equal voice. As a matter of fact, in any question of great importance the preponderance of power would lie with the Great Powers having possessions which are members. There are instances, however, of autonomous dominions voting against the parent state. The International Bureau of the Union is located at Berne, under the supervision of the Swiss government. Its duties are to gather, coördinate, publish, and distribute information of all kinds relative to the international postal service; to give advice, on request of the parties interested, on controversial questions; to give form to propositions for modifying the acts of the Congress; to announce the changes made; and in general do such work and make such investigations as will promote the purposes of the Union. It publishes a monthly journal in French, German, and English.

INTERNATIONAL INSTITUTE OF AGRICULTURE

The International Institute of Agriculture, having restricted functions which in no way bind the states, and being precluded from consideration of "all questions concerning the economic interests, the legislation, and the administration of a particular nation" presents some interesting features of organization. It was created by a Convention signed at Rome, June 7, 1905.[1] Confining its operations within an international sphere, its purpose is to collect, study, and publish statistical, technical, and economic information concerning farming, commerce in agricultural products, prices, wages of farm labor, vegetable diseases, agricultural cooperation, insurance, and credit, and to submit for the approval of the governments measures for the protection of the common interests of farmers and for the improvement of their condition. It has two organs: a General Assembly and a Permanent Committee with offices at Rome. Each state, or colony if admitted on the "request of the nations to which they belong," may have as many delegates as it chooses, but the voting is regulated by a special scheme. It elects its own president and vice-presidents and fixes the date for its next meeting. Its deliberations are invalid unless attended by representatives of two-thirds of the members.

The Permanent Committee carries out the decisions of the General Assembly. Each state has one representative, but a delegate from one member may serve also for another, provided the actual representation is not less than fifteen. The delegates are chosen by the member states; and the method of voting is the same as in the General Assembly. It elects for three years its own president and general secretary, the latter serving in a like capacity for the General Assembly. For the purpose of voting as well as for the

[1] Malloy: Treaties, 2: 2140–2144.

distribution of the expenses, the members are grouped into five classes to which are assigned voting units and different assessment units as follows:

Group	Number of Votes	Units of Assessment
1	5	16
2	4	8
3	3	4
4	2	2
5	1	1

The members themselves choose the group to which they shall belong.

INTERNATIONAL SUGAR COMMISSION

Another variety of international unions is found in the International Sugar Commission, created by a Convention signed at Brussels, March 5, 1902, and supplemented by an Additional Act of August 28, 1907.[1] The purpose of the Convention was the suppression of direct and indirect sugar bounties which during the preceding quarter century had artificially cheapened that commodity and flooded the markets of the world. The signatories agreed to comply with specified regulations concerning the manufacture and care of sugar in their own territory, to provide rigid methods of inspection, to abolish by legislation any bounties, drawbacks, or exemptions from taxation; to limit their import duties on sugar not supported by bounties; and to impose countervailing duties on imports of sugar supported by bounties. In other words, the states agreed to coöperate by national legislation in neutralizing the effects of bounties, so that the natural laws of competition might operate. They agreed to transmit to the Belgian government, for use at the seat of the Commission in Brussels, copies of all laws, orders, and regulations made by them concerning the taxation of sugar. The organs created by the Convention are the Commission itself and the Permanent Bureau, which acts under the direction

---

[1] Hertslet's Commercial Treaties, 23: 579–588; 25: 547–550; reprinted in Sayre, Experiments in International Administration, p. 189–201.

of the Belgian government through which it receives and sends all its communications. The Commission is composed of one delegate from each member; it elects its own president, and meets when summoned by him. Its action is taken by majority vote, with opportunity for reconsideration, after which it becomes final. All votes have equal weight. Although the duty of the Commission is limited to findings and investigations, when made in due form some of them impose duties on the states in conformity with the Convention, and thus take away the power of independent contrary action. The duties of the delegates are (a) to establish the fact that in the contracting states no direct or indirect bounty is granted; (b) to determine whether the contracting states, which are not exporters, continue in that special condition; (c) to pronounce whether bounties exist in non-signatory states, and to estimate the amounts; (d) to give advisory decisions on contested questions; (e) to prepare for consideration requests for admission to the Union, and (f) to authorize the increase of the sugar tariff in exceptional cases by certain states (Final Protocol). In case (f) action by a state is dependent on the permission of the Commission, and in cases (b) and (c) state legislation must be passed as a result of the findings. As stated by Reinsch,[1] "the Sugar Commission is the only international organ which has a right, through its determinations and decisions, to cause a direct modification of the laws existing in the individual treaty states, within the dispositions of the Convention. Though not given direct legislative power, it makes determinations of fact upon which changes in the laws of the individual states become obligatory under the treaty. Its function may be compared to that intrusted to the President of the United States in the reciprocity provisions of the McKinley and Dingley tariff laws." The Commission has a Permanent Bureau with specified administrative functions. Its expenses are divided among the states by the Commission.

Unquestionably we have here an international union endowed with power, and unquestionably it accomplished its purpose of suppressing, at least for a time, all sugar bounties. Its history,

[1] Public International Unions, p. 51.

however, illustrates the danger of placing power over member states in the hands of a central commission which acts by majority vote, with no right of appeal. Its very success was the cause of complaint by its most influential member, Great Britain. When the price of sugar rose, and the members who were unequally affected placed retaliatory duties on other articles than sugar, applications began to come in for exemptions from the provisions of the Convention. Exceptions were made in favor of Brazil, Mexico, Cuba, Venezuela, Switzerland, Russia, and Great Britain, in some instances amounting for a particular state to a nullification of the purpose of the Convention. Finally, because of a refusal to allow a further exemption to Russia, Great Britain—herself at liberty to admit bounty-supported sugar—withdrew, carrying Italy with her. The Convention after a life of seventeen years is still in force, but with reduced membership and effectiveness. In this case, at least, the impossibility of binding a powerful state contrary to its interests was exemplified.

References for Chapter XVIII

REINSCH. Public International Unions, 2d ed.

SAYRE, F. B. Experiments in International Administration, p. 19–26, 117–131.

WOOLF. International Government, p. 153–265.

INTERNATIONAL LABOR PROGRAMME.

(Current History, 10: pt. 1, p. 516–525, June, 1919.)

CHAPTER XIX

THE INTERNATIONAL LABOR ORGANIZATION

WITH the foregoing summaries, illustrations, and comments in mind, we may now examine more intelligently the latest attempt at the formation of an effective public international union. This is the International Labor Organization created by the Versailles Peace Treaty, and in accordance with Article 23 of the League of Nations Covenant. In that article the members of the League pledge themselves to "endeavor to secure and maintain fair and humane conditions of labor for men, women, and children, both in their own countries and in all countries to which their commercial and industrial relations extend, and for that purpose will establish and maintain the necessary international organizations." One of the important commissions of the Peace Conference was that on International Labor Legislation engaged, contemporaneously with the sessions of the League of Nations Commission, in giving life to the pledge just quoted from the Covenant. It drew up a draft of an international labor convention which was presented to the Peace Conference on April 11, 1919, and subsequently adopted by it as part of the Peace Treaty. It now is Part XIII of that treaty, and is in fact a league of nations covenant as remarkable as the Covenant of the League of Nations itself.[1] By it a close connection is established between the League and the new International Labor Organization. According to the preamble, the ultimate aim of the Labor Organization, as of the League Covenant, is the establishment of universal peace, because "such a peace can be established only if it is based upon social justice." It then enumerates some of the conditions of labor that should be remedied, ending with the statement that "the failure of any nation

[1] See Appendix 1.

to adopt humane conditions of labor is an obstacle in the way of other nations which desire to improve the conditions in their own countries." Wherefore agreement is made on general principles to be followed in the future, and on the detailed organization of an international body with rules for its government and procedure. A permanent organization is set up by Articles 387 to 399. The original members of the League of Nations are by that fact members of the Labor Organization, and a state cannot become a member of the former without joining also the latter. The permanent organization consists of (1) a General Conference of representatives of the members, (2) a Governing Body, and (3) an International Labor Office.

The General Conference consists of delegates appointed by the members. Each government appoints four delegates, two of whom are "Government delegates", and the two others representative respectively of "the employers and the workpeople of each of the members." The two latter, the member states agree to appoint when chosen "in agreement with the industrial organizations, if such organizations exist, which are most representative of employers or workpeople, as the case may be, in their respective countries."

Each delegate may be accompanied by advisers chosen in like manner, but the advisers may not vote or speak except when formally acting as deputies of their delegates. At other times they may not vote, and may speak only on the request of the delegates whom they accompany, with permission of the President. The Conference may by a two-thirds vote refuse to admit any delegate or adviser whom it deems not to have been properly nominated. Women may serve as advisers on questions affecting women.

Meetings shall be held at least once a year and at other times as occasion may require. Each delegate is entitled to vote individually, so that the attitude of the governments, the employers, and the workers may be truly represented by the votes. This plan differs from all of the others which have been described. In both the Universal Postal Union and the International Sugar Commission each government has only one vote, but in the former they may have more than one delegate. In the International Institute of

Agriculture the governments each have one delegate but their votes have weight according to the number of units assigned to them. Except where otherwise specified, the decisions in the Labor Conference are taken by simple majority vote; but the exceptions are very important. They are five in number: (1) when a programme for a coming conference has been prepared and sent to the members, if any of their governments objects to the inclusion of one of the agenda, it may not be considered at the Conference unless two-thirds of the delegates present vote in favor of its inclusion. The Conference may by a two-thirds vote decide on the agenda to be considered at its next meeting (Art. 402); (2) when the Conference has decided on the adoption of proposals with regard to an item on the agenda, it will rest with the Conference to determine whether they shall take the form (a) of a recommendation to be submitted to the members for consideration with a view to effect being given to it by national legislation or otherwise, or (b) of a draft convention for ratification by the members. In either case a two-thirds majority of the delegates present is required (Art. 405); (3) the Conference may by a two-thirds vote exclude any delegate or adviser whom it deems not to have been properly nominated (Art. 389); (4) a two-thirds vote is required to change the meeting place of the Labor Organization (Art. 391); (5) amendments to the Labor Covenant may be made only by a two-thirds majority of the delegates present at the Conference, and they do not take effect until ratified by the states whose representatives compose the Council of the League of Nations and by three-fourths of the members (Art. 422). The last is the only instance in which any action of the Labor Organization may result in an obligation by a state to accept a change in a treaty without its own consent, and this result is only brought about after ratification by the states represented on the League of Nations Council, and by three-fourths of the members of the League, the membership in the League and in the Labor Organization being identical.

The International Labor Office is to be located at Geneva, the seat of the League of Nations. It has a Director who is responsible for the conduct of the Office and who in person or by deputy must attend all meetings of the Governing Body. He is secretary of the Conference. He appoints his own staff, selecting them as far as possible from different nationalities. Some of the appointees must be women. The functions of the Labor Office include the collection and distribution of information on all subjects relating to the international adjustment of conditions of industrial life and labor and particularly of subjects which it is proposed to bring before the Conference with a view to the conclusion of international conventions, and the conduct of such special investigations as may be ordered by the Conference; the preparation of programmes for meetings of the Conference; and the publication of an international labor periodical in several languages. The Director carries on correspondence with the members through their representatives on the Governing Body or through some other official appointed by the respective governments. He is entitled to the assistance of the Secretary-General of the League of Nations and is responsible to him for the expenditure of his office budget.

The Governing Body consists of twenty-four persons, twelve representing the governments; six, the employers; and six, the workers. Of the twelve persons representing the governments, eight are nominated by the members "which are of the chief industrial importance" (to be decided in case of dispute by the Council of the League of Nations), and four by the members selected for the purpose by the government delegates, excluding the delegates of the eight members above. Members of the Governing Body serve for three years. It elects its own chairman, regulates its own procedure, and fixes the time for regular meetings. Special meetings may be called on the written request of ten of its members. The International Labor Office is under the control of the Governing Body which appoints its Director.

The Governing Body decides upon the agenda for all meetings of the Conference, giving consideration to suggestions made by governments or by organizations representing employers and workpeople. The agenda are sent to the members by the Director so as to reach them four months before the meeting of the Conference. Objections may then be made and passed upon by the

Conference as stated above. When members have become parties to conventions, and subsequently representations are made to the Labor Office by an industrial association of employers or workers that a member has failed to observe the terms of the convention "the Governing Body may communicate this representation to the Government against which it is made, and may invite that Government to make such statement on the subject as it may think fit" (Art. 409). If no statement or an unsatisfactory one is received the Governing Body may then publish the representation and the statement. A similar process is followed on the complaint of a member or on the initiative of the Governing Body; but in this case the Governing Body may apply for the appointment of a Commission of Inquiry to consider the complaint and report on it. When the above matters are under consideration, a government not represented on the Governing Body is entitled to temporary representation.

Detailed provision is made for Commissions of Inquiry to which investigations are referred (Art. 412-420). They are to consist of three persons chosen as follows: each member is to nominate within six months after the peace treaty comes into force three persons of industrial experience of whom one represents the employers, one the workers, and of whom one is "of independent standing," who together form a panel. Persons deemed unfit may be rejected by a two-thirds vote of the Governing Body. Upon its request, the Secretary-General of the League nominates from this panel three persons, one from each of its sections, who constitute the Commission of Inquiry for a particular matter. None of the three may be a panel nominee of an interested state. The Secretary-General of the League of Nations designates the President of the Commission. The members agree to furnish to the Commission all pertinent information. The report of the Commission embodies all findings of fact and recommendations for meeting the complaint, with the time within which the steps should be taken. It indicates also "the measures, if any, of an economic character against a defaulting Government which it considers to be appropriate, and which it considers Governments would be justified in adopting" (Art. 414). The Secretary-General of the League of Nations then communicates the report to each of the governments concerned in the complaint, and publishes it. Within one month, each of these governments agrees to inform him whether or not it "accepts the recommendations," and if not whether it proposes to refer the complaint to the Permanent Court of International Justice of the League of Nations.

Recourse to the League Court of International Justice is recognized as a regular procedure under the Labor Covenant (Art. 416). If any member fails to take action with regard to a recommendation or a draft convention, any other member may refer the matter to the Court. Its decisions are final. It may affirm, vary, or reverse the findings and recommendations of a Commission of Inquiry and, to quote again for emphasis, "indicate the measures, if any, of an economic character which it considers to be appropriate, and which other Governments would be justified in adopting against a defaulting Government." It is agreed that failure to follow the recommendations either of the Court or of a Commission of Inquiry within the time fixed justifies any other member in taking the economic measures indicated. These measures will be discontinued when the recommendations are complied with. Compliance is to be notified to the Secretary-General, who may be requested to constitute a Commission of Inquiry to verify the claimed compliance. By Article 423, any dispute relating to the interpretation of the Labor Covenant or any subsequent labor treaty must be referred to the Court for decision. This provision limits as to labor matters the means of settling disputes. Under the League the reference may be to any arbitration tribunal chosen by the parties. The Labor Covenant, however, provides that pending the creation of the Permanent Court, disputes shall be referred to a tribunal of three appointed by the League Council.

The obligations which the members assume are therefore of great importance because it is expected that through publicity, or moral or economic pressure, they will be enforced. It will be observed, however, that members are under no compulsion to accept recommendations or to ratify draft conventions. In order to make this clear, I quote from the official introduction which was issued with the draft of the Labor Covenant. It says:[1]

Article 19[2] treats of the obligations of the States concerned in regard to the adoption and ratification of draft conventions agreed upon by the International Conference.

The original draft proposed that any draft convention adopted by the conference by a two-thirds majority must be ratified by every State participating, unless within one year the national Legislature should have expressed its disapproval of the draft convention.

This implies an obligation on every State to submit any draft convention approved by the conference to its national Legislature within one year, whether its own Government representatives had voted in favor of its adoption or not.

This provision was inspired by the belief that although the time had not yet come when anything in the nature of an international Legislature whose decisions should be binding on the different States was possible, yet it was essential for the progress of international labor legislation to require the Governments to give their national Legislatures the opportunity of expressing their opinion on the measures favored by a two-thirds majority of the Labor Conference.

The French and Italian delegations, on the other hand, desired that States should be under an obligation to ratify conventions so adopted, whether their legislative authorities approved them or not, subject to a right of appeal to the Executive Council of the League of Nations. The council might invite the conference to reconsider its decision, and in the event of its being reaffirmed there would be no further right of appeal.

Other delegations, though not unsympathetic to the hope . . . that in course of time the Labor Conference might, through the growth of a spirit of internationality, acquire the powers of a truly legislative international assembly, felt that the time for such a development was not ripe.

If an attempt were made at this stage to deprive States of a large measure of their sovereignty in regard to labor legislation, the result would be that a considerable number of States would either refuse to accept the present convention altogether or, if they accepted it, would subsequently denounce it, and might even prefer to re-

---
[1]Current History, v. 10, pt. 1, p. 517–518, June, 1919.
[2]Now Article 405 of the Peace Treaty, see Appendix 1.

INTERNATIONAL LABOR ORGANIZATION

sign their membership in the League of Nations rather than jeopardize their national economic position by being obliged to carry out the decision of the International Labor Conference.

The majority of the commission therefore decided in favor of making ratification of a convention subject to the approval of the national legislatures or other competent authorities.

The American delegation, however, found themselves unable to accept the obligations implied in the British draft on account of the limitations imposed on the central executive and legislative powers by the Constitution of certain Federal States, and notably of the United States themselves. They pointed out that the Federal Government could not accept the obligation to ratify conventions dealing with matters within the competence of the forty-eight States of the Union, with which the power of labor legislation for the most part rested.

Further, the Federal Government could not guarantee that the constituent States, even if they passed the necessary legislation to give effect to a convention, would put it into effective operation, nor could it provide against the possibility of such legislation being declared unconstitutional by the supreme judicial authorities.

The Government could not, therefore, engage to do something which was not within its power to perform and the non-performance of which would render them liable to complaint.

The commission felt that they were here faced by a serious dilemma, which threatened to make the establishment of any real system of international labor legislation impossible.

The commission spent a considerable amount of time in attempting to devise a way out of this dilemma. Article 19,[1] as now drafted, represents a solution found by a sub-commission consisting of representatives of the American, British, and Belgian delegations specially appointed to consider the question.

It provides that the decisions of the Labor Conference may take the form either of recommendations or of draft conventions. Either must be deposited with the Secretary-General of the League of Nations and each State undertakes to bring it within one year before its competent authorities for the enactment of legislation or other action. If no legislation or other action to make a recommendation effective follows, or if a draft convention fails to obtain the consent of the competent authorities concerned, no further obligation will rest on the State in question.

In the case of a Federal State, however, whose power to enter into conventions on labor matters is subject to limitations, its

[1] Now 405.

Government may treat a draft convention to which such limitations apply as are commendation only.

Subjects will probably come before the conference which, owing to their complexity and the wide differences in the circumstances of different countries, will be incapable of being reduced to any universal and uniform mode of application. In such cases a convention might prove impossible, but a recommendation of principles in more or less detail which left the individual States freedom to apply them in the manner best suited to their conditions would undoubtedly have considerable value.

The exception in the case of Federal States is of greater importance. It places the United States and States which are in a similar position under a less degree of obligation than other States in regard to draft conventions. But it will be observed that the exception extends only to those Federal States which are subject to limitations in respect of their treaty-making powers on labor matters and that it extends only in so far as those limitations apply in any particular case.

In time the Labor Organization hopes to establish a general fund for its support, but until then, expenses are to be born in accordance with the apportionment employed in the Universal Postal Union. The funds are to be deposited with the Secretary-General of the League of Nations who will disburse them through the agency of the Director of the Labor Office.

Conforming to the Annex to Article 426, an organizing committee was appointed, and the first meeting of the International Labor Conference was called by President Wilson. It met in the Conference Room, Pan American Union, Washington, D.C., and held twenty-five sessions, October 29 to November 29, 1919, attended by delegates from thirty-four states.[1] The United States was not officially represented, but Hon. W. B. Wilson, Secretary of Labor, was elected president during the period of organization. The agenda for the meeting were provided by the Annex to Article 426, and the Conference adopted six draft conventions. The Conference

---

[1] Argentina, Belgium, Brazil, Canada, Czechoslovakia, Cuba, Denmark, Ecuador, Finland, France, Great Britain, Greece, Guatemala, India, Italy, Japan, Netherlands, Nicaragua, Norway, Paraguay, Persia, Peru, Poland, Portugal, Rumania, Salvador, Siam, Serbs-Croats-Slovenes, South Africa, Spain, Sweden, Switzerland, Uruguay, and Venezuela.

published a daily bulletin in French and English. On November 25, the Governing Body was organized with Arthur Fontaine (France) as permanent chairman. Albert Thomas (France) was provisionally selected as Director-General of the International Labor Office, which has its seat temporarily in London.

From January 26 to 28, 1920, the Governing Body met in Paris, where it confirmed the appointment of M. Thomas, and formally adopted the draft conventions and recommendations passed by the Washington Conference. They were referred to the Secretary-General of the League of Nations to be transmitted to the various governments for ratification.

References for Chapter XIX

ACADEMY OF POLITICAL SCIENCE. Proceedings, 8: No. 3, p. 80-102.

REPORT OF THE COMMISSION ON INTERNATIONAL LABOR LEGISLATION OF THE PEACE CONFERENCE.
(International Conciliation. No. 140, July, 1919.)

CHAPTER XX

PRIVATE INTERNATIONAL CONFERENCES AND ASSOCIATIONS

PRACTICALLY all public international unions owe their origin to private initiative; and when they are organized they prosper or are allowed to lapse according as they are suited to the needs of citizens of the various states. States make agreements concerning their relations as separate collective entities, but people are drawn together into international organizations because they have common problems and needs. This is a method of coöperation more vital than official coöperation. It is the result of popular movements, independent of governmental action, social in character, and prompted by a realization of the solidarity of economic life. The process is usually the simultaneous and spontaneous formation of groups of private persons in a few states in which some need requires unity of action. When it is seen that the project is not limited by national boundaries, a private international conference is held, which discusses a prepared programme and adopts resolutions. Often no international organization is created until several conferences have been held. Then a bureau, with permanent offices and staff, and some kind of a governing body or council, are created. The functions of the central bureau are usually to promote the organization of new national associations, to serve as a channel of communication between them, and to prepare the programmes for the international conferences. An essential feature of organization is permanent committees to prepare detailed reports and recommendations to be presented to the conferences.

It sometimes happens that the programmes are of direct interest to the respective governments, in which case, with the permission of the private associations, official delegates are sent, thus giving the conferences a semi-public character. In other cases the governments show their interest by financial subventions, and by instructing their officers to coöperate with the national associations. Sometimes the private international unions eventually become public by being taken over by the governments, or by the creation of an official union which makes the private organization no longer necessary. The private unions and national associations sometimes are nevertheless continued as a means of maintaining connection with the people most concerned. There is a distinct advantage in the presence of governmental delegates in private international conferences because the purpose of most international organizations is to move governments to action either by legislation or treaty making. The closest connection possible is seen in the Interparliamentary Union, which is composed of national associations made up of members and ex-members of parliaments, but who belong in a private capacity without appointment by or responsibility to their governments.

The subjects to which international private conferences have devoted themselves are almost as numerous as human group interests. The conferences and associations that had been held or were in existence up to 1907 were listed under subject divisions by Mr. Simeon E. Baldwin.[1] The subjects are significant enough to be worth repeating. They include agriculture and botany, aeronautics, American interests, commerce, corporations, crime and prisons, education, economics, electricity and its applications, fisheries, geography, industrial arts, intoxicating liquors, labor, languages, law, literature and the fine arts, medicine, surgery and physiology, money, navigation, peace and arbitration, philanthropy, police, politics, the press, races, religion, science, socialism, sociology and social science, women, and zoölogy. In commenting on these conferences and their effects Mr. Baldwin[2] remarks that "in one respect the unofficial congress tends, even more strongly than the official congress, to promote the solidarity of the world. Its members come together as servants of no master. They meet

[1] American Journal of International Law, 1: 818-829.
[2] Ibid., 1: 573-576.

on a common footing. They are responsible only to themselves. As scientific investigators, or men of similar business pursuits, or perhaps humanitarians, they are drawn together by natural tendencies. . . . The public congress is naturally under the domination of more particularistic influences. . . . It is the business of a nation to be selfish. Altruism is for individuals. It must ever be prompted by the voice of conscience or sentiment; not by that of law. This is intrinsically necessary. A government represents all and speaks for all who owe it allegiance. It can rightfully compel them all to promote its welfare. It cannot rightfully compel them all to promote the good of other nations, except so far as it may gain something from this for itself. . . . It is not the duty of a nation to love any other nation. It is its duty to deal fairly with other nations and respect their rights. Policy may lead to closer relations with some of them; but it will always, at root, be a selfish policy. A selfish policy may dictate, and often has dictated, coöperation between nations in the interests of humanity and civilization. But when it does, we shall commonly find that the initiative has been found in individual action, prompted by considerations sometimes commercial, sometimes scientific or philosophic, sometimes altruistic. So, and for similar reasons, it has often been found that the public congress of moment to the world has been the immediate consequence of a private congress."

Men gathered in private international conferences, unhampered by governmental restraints and instructions, often find by discussion of concrete problems and a comparison of difficulties that in their particular field their interests are far more international than national. This is particularly true of navigation, shipping, and foreign trade generally. Anything in national laws, customs, and traditions which hampers the conduct of business is examined with an impartial eye, and when this is done by practical men from many states the idea of compromise inevitably suggests itself. This has been illustrated in the conferences of the International Maritime Committee. The results of compromise and coöperation prompted by business interests have been duplicated in results attained by associations purely altruistic in character, or based on the fundamentally sound conception that the good of all is the good of each. This type of organization is illustrated by the numerous Peace Societies and the Interparliamentary Union.

Red Cross Societies

The history of an association which has rendered such signal service in the late war and to which has been devoted a separate Article in the League of Nations Covenant is worth telling for its own sake, but it is here briefly related because it is an example of a great enterprise for the benefit of humanity initiated, organized, maintained, and still existing as the result of private international coöperation. The Red Cross Society had its inception in the desire to alleviate the suffering of the sick and wounded on the field of battle. Throughout the ages, societies have existed for this purpose, usually under religious auspices. The idea is not unconnected with that of asylum which had its origin in protection given by holy places to the victims of private wars. It was not, however, until the Red Cross Society exerted its influence that succor of the wounded was placed on an international basis. The Society owes its origin to the presence of M. Henri Dunant at the Battle of Solferino, Italy, in 1859. After a battle which lasted fifteen hours, 16,000 French and Sardinian soldiers and 20,000 Austrians lay on the field either dead or wounded. The sanitary and medical corps were utterly incapable of caring for the living, and the dead could not be buried. M. Dunant told of the horror of the situation in his "Souvenir of Solferino," and he lectured before the Society of Public Utility of Geneva on the need for more humane and extensive means of aiding wounded soldiers. The Society under the presidency of Gustav Moynier took up the suggestion, and held a special meeting on February 9, 1863, to consider "a proposition relative to the formation of permanent societies for the relief of wounded soldiers." A committee was intrusted with power to formulate plans for such societies, and it, after presenting the project to the International Statistical Congress, which was in session at Berlin in September, 1863, decided to call an international conference to meet in Geneva on October 26, 1863. It was attended by thirty-six delegates, of whom eighteen were official representatives of fourteen governments, six were delegates from private associations, seven unaccredited visitors, and five, members of the Geneva Committee. The Conference lasted four days, and after considering the *Projet de Concordat* presented by the Geneva Committee, adopted a set of resolutions, which recommended (1) that in each country there should be a committee whose duty would be to coöperate in time of war with the sanitary service of the army; (2) that in time of peace these committees should prepare themselves to be useful in war; (3) that they should be prepared on the demand or with the consent of the military authorities to send volunteer nurses to the battlefields; (4) that such nurses should wear a red cross, as a distinctive and uniform badge; (5) that the committees from each country should meet in international conferences, "in order to communicate to each other the results of their experience, and to decide on the measures to be adopted for the advancement of the work"; and (6) that the medium of communication between the committees of the different nations should be the Geneva Committee. It expressed the wish also that the respective governments would grant protection to the national committees, and that in war-time the belligerents might consider as neutral all field and stationary hospitals, their officials, volunteer nurses, and all who assist the wounded, and the wounded themselves.

Since Red Cross work was to be done on the battlefield, and since agreement to spare hospitals and relief workers would have to be international, the next step was to induce the states to meet in a diplomatic conference. This was done on the initiative of Switzerland, resulting in the signing on August 22, 1864, of the Geneva Convention for the "amelioration of the condition of the wounded in time of war."[1] It was in the main based on the resolutions of the first Conference of Geneva, and was a success beyond the hopes of the originators of the plan. In 1868, additional articles were adopted extending the application of the Convention of 1864 to naval warfare, but they never went into effect. The

[1] Malloy: Treaties, 2: 1903–1906.

First Hague Conference concluded a Convention adapting to naval war the Convention of 1864.

These Conventions, eventually signed by most states, remained in force without change until 1906. At the Hague Conference of 1899 the wish had been unanimously expressed that a conference might soon be held for the revision of the Convention of 1864. The Conference met in Geneva on June 11, 1906, and concluded a Convention signed by thirty-five states.[1] In the following year the Second Hague Conference adopted a "Convention for the Adaptation to Naval War of the Principles of the Geneva Convention."[2]

Meanwhile the national Red Cross Societies had multiplied, and had held periodic international conferences arranged by the Permanent International Red Cross Committee of Geneva. In every war since 1864, the Red Cross organization has played a prominent part, but in none so great as in the European war of 1914. Its activities are not, however, confined to war, although its first and chief aim has been the care of the wounded in battle. The various national societies choose for themselves a policy concerning peace activities. The American Society has helped at home and abroad during famine, flood, plague, and disaster. All of the associations are unofficial, but to a limited extent under the protection of their own governments. The degree of support and encouragement given has varied greatly in different states. Article 25 of the League of Nations Covenant recognizes that it is a duty of states to uphold the efforts of Red Cross Societies, and that their voluntary character should be continued, but that, since war is to be made less frequent, support should be given chiefly to societies engaging in peace activities. "The members of the League agree," says the Covenant, "to encourage and promote the establishment and coöperation of duly-authorized voluntary National Red Cross organizations having as purposes the improvement of health, the prevention of disease, and the mitigation of suffering throughout the world."

---

[1] Malloy: Treaties, 2: 2183–2205.
[2] *Ibid.*, 2: 2326–2340.

Almost as soon as this clause in the Covenant was made public, announcement was made of a plan for the adjustment of the Red Cross organizations of the world to the large duties implied in the Article.

Articles of association of a League of Red Cross Societies were signed in Paris on May 5 by authorized representatives of the Red Cross Societies of America, Great Britain, France, Italy, and Japan, and these representatives form the present Board of Governors. The Board will consist eventually of not more than fifteen members. The control of the League is by a General Council, composed of representatives of all members, and meeting at designated periods.

The objects of the League as formally set forth in its articles of association are: 1. To encourage and promote in every country in the world a duly-authorized voluntary National Red Cross organization, having as purposes the improvement of health, prevention of disease, and mitigation of suffering throughout the world, and to secure the coöperation of such organizations for these purposes. 2. To promote the welfare of mankind by furnishing a medium for bringing within reach of all peoples the benefits to be derived from present known facts, and new contributions to science and medical knowledge, and their application. 3. To furnish a medium for coördinating relief work in case of great national or international disasters.

The first meeting of the General Council was held at Geneva, March 2 to 9, 1920, attended by representatives of twenty-eight Red Cross Societies.

Labor Conferences and Associations

Space has already been devoted to the subject of labor, as illustrating coöperation in treaty-making, in national legislation, and in the administration of international enterprises. It is, however, a topic of so much importance that it requires further consideration in order to emphasize the fact that the whole movement was started and fostered by private enterprise. Like the idea of the Red Cross, its international aspects were conceived by an individual, Robert Owen, and were emphasized by another advocate, Daniel Legrand.[1] The first international labor congress met in 1866 in Geneva on the call of the International Workingmen's Association, which had been founded in London in 1864. It was attended by unofficial delegates of trades unions from several states. By this time national organizations of workers in the various states had become numerous, but they devoted themselves largely to domestic problems. In some countries the cause of labor was taken up as a political question, and by various organizations advocating one social theory or another. The need for international factory legislation was discussed in the Swiss National Council in 1880-1881, and the Federal Council took up the question of an international conference with a number of states. Private international congresses on labor were held at Frankfort, in 1882, and in Paris in 1883, the deliberations of the latter receiving attention in the following two years in the French Parliament. In several countries works were published on the projects for international protection of labor, and the idea received unfavorable criticism from Bismarck. An important private international labor congress was held in Paris in 1886, and in 1889 the Swiss Federal Council began to test sentiment of the powers on the question of calling an official international congress to meet at Berne. The plan would have been carried through had not the German Emperor intervened to ask that the conference be held in Berlin. This congress, held from March 15 to 29, 1890, was official in character. In April, 1897, was held the first international congress at which the United States was represented. It was held at Zurich on the call of the Swiss Workingmen's Society and was attended by delegates from fourteen states, but it had no official character. It urged the Swiss government to continue its attempts to induce the governments to agree on international labor conventions, and advocated the establishment of an international labor office. The next important congress was of a semi-public character since some states sent official delegates. It was called the Congress for International Labor Legislation and was held at

[1] See Chapter XVI.

Brussels in September, 1897. It was unable to decide whether an official or an unofficial international labor office would be preferable, and the results of its other discussions were indefinite. At its close an unauthorized committee was formed which drafted plans for an international labor association. French, Belgian, and German students of labor became interested, and the French labor group summoned an unofficial congress to meet at Paris, July 25 to 29, 1900, during the Paris Exposition. This congress is notable because at it was created the International Association for the Legal Protection of Labor, with a permanent International Labor office at Basle, Switzerland. The Association is governed by a Central Committee composed of delegates elected by the national sections which make up the Association. Meetings are held every two years, seven having been held from 1901 to 1912. A review of labor legislation is published in three languages. The purpose of the Association as shown by its constitution is (1) to serve as a bond of union to all who believe in the necessity for the internationalization of labor legislation; (2) to organize an International Labor Office; (3) to facilitate the study of labor legislation in all countries, and to provide information on the subject; (4) to promote international agreements on questions relating to conditions of labor; (5) to organize international congresses on labor legislation.

It is a notable fact that at the meetings of delegates of the Association there are present representatives of states as well as of national associations, thus establishing a connection between governments and private labor interests. The procedure at these meetings is to assign the investigation of various subjects to committees which work between meetings and report to the constituent assembly. When the Association is agreed on a programme, the national associations seek to have its principles recognized in national legislation, and the Central Committee in conjunction with the national associations urges the various governments to meet in non-diplomatic conferences to agree on draft conventions. The next step is to hold diplomatic conferences for the signature of these conventions. The treaties thus agreed to as a result of the work of the International Association have been described in Chapter XVI. A number of non-diplomatic conferences have been held which did not produce draft conventions; but the work of the Association and its national sections has borne fruit in many treaties entered into by two states at a time.

By the creation of an official International Labor Organization, with direct relations to the League of Nations, the voluntary association would appear to have lost most of its functions. The need for its continuance is lessened because as described in Chapter XIX representation of private labor interests is insured. Indeed the new organization brings into the group the third element needed for coöperation in improving conditions of labor. Not only the workers and the governments but the employers have representation in the General Conference and Governing Body of the organization. Moreover, there is provision for expressing by vote the opinions of each delegate, just as there was in the voluntary association. The beneficial effects of the organization of individual persons into national associations, and of the latter into an international association, which finally brings about an official international association in which private interests are safeguarded, are clearly illustrated in the history of the international labor movement. Nevertheless, there assembled in Amsterdam on July 26, 1919, an International Trades Union Congress at which a new international federation of labor was formed. The Congress adjourned on August 2, after having adopted several resolutions concerning the relation of the League of Nations to labor.

Interparliamentary Union

"The Interparliamentary Union has for its aim," says its revised constitution of 1912, "the uniting in common action the Members of all parliaments constituted in National Groups in order to bring about the acceptance in their respective countries, either by legislation or by international treaties, of the principle that differences between nations should be settled by arbitration or in other ways either amicable or judicial. It likewise has for its aim the study of other questions of international law and in general of all problems relating to the development of peaceful relations between nations." Some account of an organization whose purposes are so similar to that of the League of Nations has a place in this book; but it is noteworthy also as a private voluntary international organization, whose members while officials of their respective governments have banded themselves together as individuals. Although it is now partly supported by government subventions, this gives the governments no control over it, either as to its organization or membership, or as to the subjects which it shall take up. The official aid comes as a recognition of the value of attempts made on private initiative to solve problems which are of importance to the entire world.

A brief sketch of its history will show how it arrived at the status which existed at the outbreak of the European war which, although interrupting its programme, emphasized the importance of the measures which it advocated.[1] In 1887, Sir William R. Cremer initiated in England a movement in favor of arbitration treaties between the principal states. It met with no immediate success, but resulted in the formation of the Interparliamentary Union. Cremer with the coöperation of Frédéric Passy, on October 31, 1888, succeeded in calling together in Paris twenty-five French and nine British members of the respective legislatures for the purpose of formulating plans for arbitration treaties between France and the United States and Great Britain and the United States. This was an informal meeting, but a second was called for the following year, which met at Paris on June 29-30, 1889, attended by members of nine different parliaments to the number of ninety-six, including one member from the United States. The reason for international conferences of members of parliaments was set forth in one of the resolutions of that Conference as follows: "The conduct of governments tending to become more and more the expression only of ideas and sentiments voiced by the body of citizens, it is for the electors to lead the policy of their country in the direction of justice, of right, and of the brotherhood of

---

[1] The facts are digested from the Hand Book of the American Group of the Interparliamentary Union, published in 1914.

nations." Without any formal permanent organization, the conferences came together four times from 1889 to 1892, but their members were invited to form Interparliamentary Committees in each country, which are the basis of the present system of national groups. At the Berne Conference of 1892 an Interparliamentary Bureau was instituted with offices in Switzerland, under the control of a Permanent Committee. From 1892 to 1912, fourteen conferences were held, that of 1904 being in St. Louis, Missouri. In 1899, the Permanent Committee was superseded by an Interparliamentary Council, composed of two members from each national Group. Further reorganization was made in 1908, at Berlin, and the present organization as shown by the constitution of 1912 consists of (1) Interparliamentary Conferences; (2) a Council; (3) a Bureau; and (4) an Executive Committee.

In 1915, twenty-four states had Interparliamentary Groups whose membership is drawn from (1) members of parliaments; (2) ex-members of the Interparliamentary Council; and (3) ex-members of parliaments admitted by vote of the Council. The British Group consists of the members of the House of Lords and the House of Commons who have signed the following declaration:

"The undersigned, regarding with satisfaction the success which has attended the Interparliamentary Conferences at Paris (twice), London (twice), Rome, Berne, The Hague (twice), Brussels (four times), Buda-Pesth, Christiania, Vienna, St. Louis, U.S., Berlin, and Geneva, and in the belief that the meeting together from year to year of Members of various Parliaments is a practical step in the direction of international peace, gives his adhesion to the movement, and promises to assist in its development."

There are now 3,300 members drawn from the twenty-four Groups. All members of the Union may attend conferences, but many Groups have adopted the practice of designating delegates.

The Council is composed of two members appointed from each national Group to serve from one Conference to the next. The Council summons the Conferences, decides on the resolutions to be submitted to it, organizes Commissions of Study, nominates officers and members of the Executive Committee, and controls the finances and budget. The Interparliamentary Bureau, with offices at Brussels, is under the direction of a paid secretary appointed by the Council. Its duties are to record the condition and encourage the formation of national Groups, and serve as a means of communication between them; to prepare questions to be submitted to the Council and Conferences; to see that decisions are put into force; to preserve the archives of the Union; and collect documents on subjects in which it is interested. The Bureau is controlled by the Executive Committee of five members representing different Groups. One Group which is to have a representative on the Executive Committee is chosen annually by the Council, and each year one Group ceases to have representation.

During the life of the Union, the cause to which it is devoted has made remarkable progress. It has concentrated its efforts on international arbitration and questions relating to international law. National political questions and economic problems have been avoided. In 1895, it approved a draft convention on a Permanent International Court, many of the provisions of which were adopted by the First Hague Conference. In 1904, it urged President Roosevelt to call a Second Hague Conference and received his promise to do so, a promise which he redeemed, although he later withdrew out of courtesy to the Russian Czar. It drew up a model arbitration treaty which was presented by the Portuguese delegation to the Hague Conference of 1907. In its organization, it bears a remarkable likeness to public international unions, but it has preserved its private attributes, using the parliamentary character of its membership only to influence national legislatures to a favorable consideration of projects for world peace. It is thus a genuine example of coöperation through a private international association devoted to international purposes, and meeting in international conferences which discuss programmes prepared by a permanent international bureau.

REFERENCES FOR CHAPTER XX

AMERICAN JOURNAL OF INTERNATIONAL LAW, 1: 565–578, July, 1907; 1: 808–829, October, 1907.

RED CROSS

BARTON, CLARA. The Red Cross, p. 23–76.
FERGUSON, J. H. The International Conference of the Hague, p. 54–97, The Geneva Convention applied to Naval Warfare.
THE RED CROSS MAGAZINE.

LABOR

LOWE. International Aspects of the Labor Problem.
WOOLF. International Government, p. 285–304.

INTERPARLIAMENTARY UNION

THE INTERPARLIAMENTARY UNION, its Work and Its Present Organization. Brussels, 1910.
THE INTERPARLIAMENTARY UNION. Handbook of the American Group. Washington, 1914.

PART IV
APPENDICES

APPENDICES

1. TREATY OF PEACE WITH GERMANY
   (a) The Covenant of the League of Nations
   (b) Selected Articles from the Treaty
   (c) Labor Organization
2. THE TRIPLE ALLIANCE
   (a) Dual Alliance, October 7, 1879
   (b) Triple Alliance, May, 1882
3. RUSSO-FRENCH ALLIANCE
   (a) Projet de Convention Militaire, December, 1893
   (b) Convention Navale, July 16, 1912
4. THE HOLY ALLIANCE ACT
5. CENTRAL AMERICAN TREATIES, December 20, 1907
   (a) General Treaty of Peace and Amity
   (b) Convention for the Establishment of a Central American Court of Justice
   (c) Convention for the Establishment of an International Central American Bureau
   (d) Convention Concerning Future Central American Conferences
6. HAGUE CONVENTIONS AND DRAFTS, 1907
   (a) Convention for the Pacific Settlement of International Disputes
   (b) Draft Convention Relative to the Creation of a Judicial Arbitration Court
   (c) Convention Relative to the Creation of an International Prize Court
7. TREATY FOR THE ADVANCEMENT OF PEACE BETWEEN THE UNITED STATES OF AMERICA AND GUATEMALA, September 20, 1913
8. BIBLIOGRAPHY
   INDEX

APPENDIX 1

TREATY OF PEACE WITH GERMANY

THE UNITED STATES OF AMERICA, THE BRITISH EMPIRE, FRANCE, ITALY, and JAPAN,

These Powers being described in the present Treaty as the Principal Allied and Associated Powers,

BELGIUM, BOLIVIA, BRAZIL, CHINA, CUBA, ECUADOR, GREECE, GUATEMALA, HAITI, THE HEDJAZ, HONDURAS, LIBERIA, NICARAGUA, PANAMA, PERU, POLAND, PORTUGAL, ROUMANIA, THE SERB-CROAT-SLOVENE STATE, SIAM, CZECHO-SLOVAKIA and URUGUAY,

These Powers constituting with the Principal Powers mentioned above the Allied and Associated Powers,

of the one part;

And GERMANY,

of the other part;

Bearing in mind that on the request of the Imperial German Government an Armistice was granted on November 11, 1918, to Germany by the Principal Allied and Associated Powers in order that a Treaty of Peace might be concluded with her, and

The Allied and Associated Powers, being equally desirous that the war in which they were successively involved directly or indirectly and which originated in the declaration of war by Austria-Hungary on July 28, 1914, against Serbia, the declaration of war by Germany against Russia on August 1, 1914, and against France on August 3, 1914, and in the invasion of Belgium, should be replaced by a firm, just, and durable Peace,

For this purpose the HIGH CONTRACTING PARTIES represented as follows:

THE PRESIDENT OF THE UNITED STATES OF AMERICA, by:

> The Honourable Woodrow WILSON, PRESIDENT OF THE UNITED STATES, acting in his own name and by his own proper authority;
>
> The Honourable Robert LANSING, Secretary of State;
>
> The Honourable Henry WHITE, formerly Ambassador Extraordinary and Plenipotentiary of the United States at Rome and Paris;
>
> The Honourable Edward M. HOUSE;
>
> General Tasker H. BLISS, Military Representative of the United States on the Supreme War Council;

HIS MAJESTY THE KING OF THE UNITED KINGDOM OF GREAT BRITAIN AND IRELAND AND OF THE BRITISH DOMINIONS BEYOND THE SEAS, EMPEROR OF INDIA, by:

> The Right Honourable David LLOYD GEORGE, M. P., First Lord of His Treasury and Prime Minister;
>
> The Right Honourable Andrew BONAR LAW, M. P., His Lord Privy Seal;
>
> The Right Honourable Viscount MILNER, G.C.B., G.C.M.G., His Secretary of State for the Colonies;
>
> The Right Honourable Arthur James BALFOUR, O.M., M.P., His Secrertary of State for Foreign Affairs;
>
> The Right Honourable George Nicoll BARNES, M.P., Minister without portfolio;

And

for the DOMINION of CANADA, by:

> The Honourable Charles Joseph DOHERTY, Minister of Justice;
>
> The Honourable Arthur Lewis SIFTON, Minister of Customs;

for the COMMONWEALTH of AUSTRALIA, by:

> The Right Honourable William Morris HUGHES, Attorney General and Prime Minister;
>
> The Right Honourable Sir Joseph COOK, G.C.M.G., Minister for the Navy;

TREATY OF PEACE WITH GERMANY

for the UNION of SOUTH AFRICA, by:

> General the Right Honourable Louis BOTHA, Minister of Native Affairs and Prime Minister;
>
> Lieutenant-General the Right Honourable Jan Christiaan SMUTS, K.C., Minister of Defence;

for the DOMINION of NEW ZEALAND, by:

> The Right Honourable William Ferguson MASSEY, Minister of Labour and Prime Minister;

for INDIA, by:

> The Right Honourable Edwin Samuel MONTAGU, M.P., His Secretary of State for India;
>
> Major-General His Highness Maharaja Sir Ganga Singh Bahadur, Maharaja of BIKANER, G.C.S.I., G.C.I.E., G.C.V.O., K.C.B., A.D.C.;

THE PRESIDENT OF THE FRENCH REPUBLIC, by:

> Mr. Georges CLEMENCEAU, President of the Council, Minister of War;
>
> Mr. Stephen PICHON, Minister for Foreign Affairs;
>
> Mr. Louis-Lucien KLOTZ, Minister of Finance;
>
> Mr. André TARDIEU, Commissary General for Franco-American Military Affairs;
>
> Mr. Jules CAMBON, Ambassador of France;

HIS MAJESTY THE KING OF ITALY, by:

> Baron S. SONNINO, Deputy;
>
> Marquis G. IMPERIALI, Senator, Ambassador of His Majesty the King of Italy at London;
>
> Mr. S. CRESPI, Deputy;

HIS MAJESTY THE EMPEROR OF JAPAN, by:

> Marquis SAÏONZI, formerly President of the Council of Ministers;
>
> Baron MAKINO, formerly Minister for Foreign Affairs, Member of the Diplomatic Council;
>
> Viscount CHINDA, Ambassador Extraordinary and Plenipotentiary of H. M. the Emperor of Japan at London;
>
> Mr. K. MATSUI, Ambassador Extraordinary and Plenipotentiary of H. M. the Emperor of Japan at Paris;

Mr. H. Ijuin, Ambassador Extraordinary and Plenipotentiary of H. M. the Emperor of Japan at Rome;

HIS MAJESTY THE KING OF THE BELGIANS, by:

Mr. Paul Hymans, Minister for Foreign Affairs, Minister of State;

Mr. Jules van den Heuvel, Envoy Extraordinary and Minister Plenipotentiary, Minister of State;

Mr. Emile Vandervelde, Minister of Justice, Minister of State;

THE PRESIDENT OF THE REPUBLIC OF BOLIVIA, by:

Mr. Ismael Montes, Envoy Extraordinary and Minister Plenipotentiary of Bolivia at Paris;

THE PRESIDENT OF THE REPUBLIC OF BRAZIL, by:

Mr. João Pandiá Calogeras, Deputy, formerly Minister of Finance;

Mr. Raul Fernandes, Deputy;

Mr. Rodrigo Octavio de L. Menezes, Professor of International Law of Rio de Janeiro;

THE PRESIDENT OF THE CHINESE REPUBLIC, by:

Mr. Lou Tseng-Tsiang, Minister for Foreign Affairs:

Mr. Chengting Thomas Wang, formerly Minister of Agriculture and Commerce;

THE PRESIDENT OF THE CUBAN REPUBLIC, by:

Mr. Antonio Sánchez de Bustamante, Dean of the Faculty of Law in the University of Havana, President of the Cuban Society of International Law;

THE PRESIDENT OF THE REPUBLIC OF ECUADOR, by:

Mr Enrique Dorn y de Alsúa, Envoy Extraordinary and Minister Plenipotentiary of Ecuador at Paris:

HIS MAJESTY THE KING OF THE HELLENES, by:

Mr. Eleftherios K. Venisélos, President of the Council of Ministers;

Mr. Nicolas Politis, Minister for Foreign Affairs;

THE PRESIDENT OF THE REPUBLIC OF GUATEMALA, by:

Mr. Joaquin Méndez, formerly Minister of State for Public

Works and Public Instruction, Envoy Extraordinary and Minister Plenipotentiary of Guatemala at Washington, Envoy Extraordinary and Minister Plenipotentiary on special mission at Paris;

THE PRESIDENT OF THE REPUBLIC OF HAITI, by:

Mr. Tertullien GUILBAUD, Envoy Extraordinary and Minister Plenipotentiary of Haiti at Paris;

HIS MAJESTY THE KING OF THE HEDJAZ, by:

Mr. Rustem HAÏDAR;

Mr. Abdul Hadi AOUNI;

THE PRESIDENT OF THE REPUBLIC OF HONDURAS, by:

Dr. Policarpo BONILLA, on special mission to Washington, formerly President of the Republic of Honduras, Envoy Extraordinary and Minister Plenipotentiary;

THE PRESIDENT OF THE REPUBLIC OF LIBERIA, by:

The Honourable Charles Dunbar Burgess KING, Secretary of State;

THE PRESIDENT OF THE REPUBLIC OF NICARAGUA, by:

Mr. Salvador CHAMORRO, President of the Chamber of Deputies;

THE PRESIDENT OF THE REPUBLIC OF PANAMA, by:

Mr. Antonio BURGOS, Envoy Extraordinary and Minister Plenipotentiary of Panama at Madrid;

THE PRESIDENT OF THE REPUBLIC OF PERU, by:

Mr. Carlos G. CANDAMO, Envoy Extraordinary and Minister Plenipotentiary of Peru at Paris:

THE PRESIDENT OF THE POLISH REPUBLIC, by:

Mr. Ignace J. PADEREWSKI, President of the Council of Ministers, Minister for Foreign Affairs;

Mr. Roman DMOWSKI, President of the Polish National Committee;

THE PRESIDENT OF THE PORTUGUESE REPUBLIC, by:

Dr. Affonso Augusto DA COSTA, formerly President of the Council of Ministers;

Dr. Augusto Luiz Vìeira SOARES, formerly Minister for Foreign Affairs;

HIS MAJESTY THE KING OF ROUMANIA, by:

Mr. Ion I. C. BRATIANO, President of the Council of Ministers, Minister for Foreign Affairs;

General Constantin COANDA, Corps Commander, A.D.C. to the King, formerly President of the Council of Ministers;

HIS MAJESTY THE KING OF THE SERBS, THE CROATS, AND THE SLOVENES, by:

Mr. Nicolas P. PACHITCH, formerly President of the Council of Ministers;

Mr. Ante TRUMBIC, Minister for Foreign Affairs;

Mr. Milenko VESNITCH, Envoy Extraordinary and Minister Plenipotentiary of H. M. the King of the Serbs, the Croats and the Slovenes at Paris:

HIS MAJESTY THE KING OF SIAM, by:

His Highness Prince CHAROON, Envoy Extraordinary and Minister Plenipotentiary of H. M. the King of Siam at Paris;

His Serene Highness Prince Traidos PRABANDHU, Under Secretary of State for Foreign Affairs;

THE PRESIDENT OF THE CZECHO-SLOVAK REPUBLIC, by:

Mr. Karel KRAMÁŘ, President of the Council of Ministers;

Mr. Eduard BENEŠ, Minister for Foreign Affairs;

THE PRESIDENT OF THE REPUBLIC OF URUGUAY, by:

Mr. Juan Antonio BUERO, Minister for Foreign Affairs, formerly Minister of Industry;

GERMANY, by:

Mr. Hermann MÜLLER, Minister for Foreign Affairs of the Empire;

Dr. BELL, Minister of the Empire;

Acting in the name of the German Empire and of each and every component State,

WHO having communicated their full powers found in good and due form have AGREED AS FOLLOWS:

From the coming into force of the present Treaty the state of war will terminate. From that moment and subject to the provisions of this Treaty official relations with Germany, and with any of the German States, will be resumed by the Allied and Associated Powers.

PART I.

THE COVENANT OF THE LEAGUE OF NATIONS

The High Contracting Parties,

In order to promote international co-operation and to achieve international peace and security

>by the acceptance of obligations not to resort to war,
>
>by the prescription of open, just and honourable relations between nations,
>
>by the firm establishment of the understandings of international law as the actual rule of conduct among Governments, and
>
>by the maintenance of justice and a scrupulous respect for all treaty obligations in the dealings of organised peoples with one another,

Agree to this Covenant of the League of Nations.

Art. 1. The original Members of the League of Nations shall be those of the Signatories which are named in the Annex to this Covenant and also such of those other States named in the Annex as shall accede without reservation to this Covenant. Such accession shall be effected by a Declaration deposited with the Secretariat within two months of the coming into force of the Covenant. Notice thereof shall be sent to all other Members of the League.

Any fully self-governing State, Dominion or Colony not named in the Annex may become a Member of the League if its admission is agreed to by two thirds of the Assembly, provided that it shall give effective guarantees of its sincere intention to observe its international obligations, and shall accept such regulations as may be prescribed by the League in regard to its military, naval, and air forces and armaments.

APPENDIX

Any Member of the League may, after two years' notice of its intention so to do, withdraw from the League, provided that all its international obligations and all its obligations under this Covenant shall have been fulfilled at the time of its withdrawal.

ART. 2. The action of the League under this Covenant shall be effected through the instrumentality of an Assembly and of a Council, with a permanent Secretariat.

ART. 3. The Assembly shall consist of Representatives of the Members of the League.

The Assembly shall meet at stated intervals and from time to time as occasion may require at the Seat of the League or at such other place as may be decided upon.

The Assembly may deal at its meetings with any matter within the sphere of action of the League or affecting the peace of the world.

At meetings of the Assembly each Member of the League shall have one vote, and may have not more than three Representatives.

ART. 4. The Council shall consist of Representatives of the Principal Allied and Associated Powers, together with Representatives of four other Members of the League. These four Members of the League shall be selected by the Assembly from time to time in its discretion. Until the appointment of the Representatives of the four Members of the League first selected by the Assembly, Representatives of Belgium, Brazil, Spain, and Greece shall be members of the Council.

With the approval of the majority of the Assembly, the Council may name additional Members of the League whose Representatives shall always be members of the Council; the Council with like approval may increase the number of members of the League to be selected by the Assembly for representation on the Council.

The Council shall meet from time to time as occasion may require, and at least once a year, at the Seat of the League, or at such other place as may be decided upon.

The Council may deal at its meetings with any matter within the sphere of action of the League or affecting the peace of the world.

Any Member of the League not represented on the Council shall

TREATY OF PEACE WITH GERMANY

be invited to send a Representative to sit as a member at any meeting of the Council during the consideration of matters specially affecting the interests of that Member of the League.

At meetings of the Council, each Member of the League represented on the Council shall have one vote, and may have not more than one Representative.

ART. 5. Except where otherwise expressly provided in this Covenant or by the terms of the present Treaty, decisions at any meeting of the Assembly or of the Council shall require the agreement of all the Members of the League represented at the meeting.

All matters of procedure at meetings of the Assembly or of the Council, including the appointment of Committees to investigate particular matters, shall be regulated by the Assembly or by the Council and may be decided by a majority of the Members of the League represented at the meeting.

The first meeting of the Assembly and the first meeting of the Council shall be summoned by the President of the United States of America.

ART. 6. The permanent Secretariat shall be established at the Seat of the League. The Secretariat shall comprise a Secretary General and such secretaries and staff as may be required.

The first Secretary General shall be the person named in the Annex; thereafter the Secretary General shall be appointed by the Council with the approval of the majority of the Assembly.

The secretaries and staff of the Secretariat shall be appointed by the Secretary General with the approval of the Council.

The Secretary General shall act in that capacity at all meetings of the Assembly and of the Council.

The expenses of the Secretariat shall be borne by the Members of the League in accordance with the apportionment of the expenses of the International Bureau of the Universal Postal Union.

ART. 7. The Seat of the League is established at Geneva.

The Council may at any time decide that the Seat of the League shall be established elsewhere.

All positions under or in connection with the League, including the Secretariat, shall be open equally to men and women.

Representatives of the Members of the League and officials of the League when engaged on the business of the League shall enjoy diplomatic privileges and immunities.

The buildings and other property occupied by the League or its officials or by Representatives attending its meetings shall be inviolable.

ART. 8. The Members of the League recognize that the maintenance of peace requires the reduction of national armaments to the lowest point consistent with national safety and the enforcement by common action of international obligations.

The Council, taking account of the geographical situation and circumstances of each State, shall formulate plans for such reduction for the consideration and action of the several Governments.

Such plans shall be subject to reconsideration and revision at least every ten years.

After these plans shall have been adopted by the several Governments, the limits of armaments therein fixed shall not be exceeded without the concurrence of the Council.

The Members of the League agree that the manufacture by private enterprise of munitions and implements of war is open to grave objections. The Council shall advise how the evil effects attendant upon such manufacture can be prevented, due regard being had to the necessities of those Members of the League which are not able to manufacture the munitions and implements of war necessary for their safety.

The Members of the League undertake to interchange full and frank information as to the scale of their armaments, their military, naval and air programmes and the condition of such of their industries as are adaptable to war-like purposes.

ART. 9. A permanent Commission shall be constituted to advise the Council on the execution of the provisions of Articles 1 and 8 and on military, naval and air questions generally.

ART. 10. The Members of the League undertake to respect and preserve as against external aggression the territorial integrity and existing political independence of all Members of the League. In case of any such aggression or in case of any threat or danger of such aggression the Council shall advise upon the means by which this obligation shall be fulfilled.

Art. 11. Any war or threat of war, whether immediately affecting any of the Members of the League or not, is hereby declared a matter of concern to the whole League, and the League shall take any action that may be deemed wise and effectual to safeguard the peace of nations. In case any such emergency should arise the Secretary General shall on the request of any Member of the League forthwith summon a meeting of the Council.

It is also declared to be the friendly right of each Member of the League to bring to the attention of the Assembly or of the Council any circumstance whatever affecting international relations which threatens to disturb international peace or the good understanding between nations upon which peace depends.

Art. 12. The Members of the League agree that if there should arise between them any dispute likely to lead to a rupture, they will submit the matter either to arbitration or to inquiry by the Council, and they agree in no case to resort to war until three months after the award by the arbitrators or the report by the Council.

In any case under this Article the award of the arbitrators shall be made within a reasonable time, and the report of the Council shall be made within six months after the submission of the dispute.

Art. 13. The Members of the League agree that whenever any dispute shall arise between them which they recognise to be suitable for submission to arbitration and which cannot be satisfactorily settled by diplomacy, they will submit the whole subject-matter to arbitration.

Disputes as to the interpretation of a treaty, as to any question of international law, as to the existence of any fact which if established would constitute a breach of any international obligation, or as to the extent and nature of the reparation to be made for any such breach, are declared to be among those which are generally suitable for submission to arbitration.

For the consideration of any such dispute the court of arbitration to which the case is referred shall be the Court agreed on by the parties to the dispute or stipulated in any convention existing between them.

The Members of the League agree that they will carry out in full good faith any award that may be rendered, and that they will not resort to war against a Member of the League which complies therewith. In the event of any failure to carry out such an award, the Council shall propose what steps should be taken to give effect thereto.

ART. 14. The Council shall formulate and submit to the Members of the League for adoption plans for the establishment of a Permanent Court of International Justice. The Court shall be competent to hear and determine any dispute of an international character which the parties thereto submit to it. The Court may also give an advisory opinion upon any dispute or question referred to it by the Council or by the Assembly.

ART. 15. If there should arise between Members of the League any dispute likely to lead to a rupture, which is not submitted to arbitration in accordance with Article 13, the Members of the League agree that they will submit the matter to the Council. Any party to the dispute may effect such submission by giving notice of the existence of the dispute to the Secretary General, who will make all necessary arrangements for a full investigation and consideration thereof.

For this purpose the parties to the dispute will communicate to the Secretary General, as promptly as possible, statements of their case with all the relevant facts and papers, and the Council may forthwith direct the publication thereof.

The Council shall endeavour to effect a settlement of the dispute, and if such efforts are successful, a statement shall be made public giving such facts and explanations regarding the dispute and the terms of settlement thereof as the Council may deem appropriate.

If the dispute is not thus settled, the Council either unanimously or by a majority vote shall make and publish a report containing a statement of the facts of the dispute and the recommendations which are deemed just and proper in regard thereto.

Any Member of the League represented on the Council may make public a statement of the facts of the dispute and of its conclusions regarding the same.

If a report by the Council is unanimously agreed to by the members thereof other than the Representatives of one or more of the parties to the dispute, the Members of the League agree that they will not go to war with any party to the dispute which complies with the recommendations of the report.

If the Council fails to reach a report which is unanimously agreed to by the members thereof, other than the Representatives of one or more of the parties to the dispute, the Members of the League reserve to themselves the right to take such action as they shall consider necessary for the maintenance of right and justice.

If the dispute between the parties is claimed by one of them, and is found by the Council, to arise out of a matter which by international law is solely within the domestic jurisdiction of that party, the Council shall so report, and shall make no recommendation as to its settlement.

The Council may in any case under this Article refer the dispute to the Assembly. The dispute shall be so referred at the request of either party to the dispute, provided that such request be made within fourteen days after the submission of the dispute to the Council.

In any case referred to the Assembly, all the provisions of this Article and of Article 12 relating to the action and powers of the Council shall apply to the action and powers of the Assembly, provided that a report made by the Assembly, if concurred in by the Representatives of those Members of the League represented on the Council and of a majority of the other Members of the League, exclusive in each case of the Representatives of the parties to the dispute, shall have the same force as a report by the Council concurred in by all the members thereof other than the Representatives of one or more of the parties to the dispute.

ART. 16. Should any Member of the League resort to war in disregard of its covenants under Articles 12, 13 or 15, it shall *ipso facto* be deemed to have committed an act of war against all other Members of the League, which hereby undertake immediately to subject it to the severance of all trade or financial relations, the prohibition of all intercourse between their nationals and the nationals of the covenant-breaking State, and the prevention of all financial, commercial or personal intercourse between the nationals of the covenant-breaking State and the nationals of any other State, whether a Member of the League or not.

It shall be the duty of the Council in such case to recommend to the several Governments concerned what effective military, naval or air force the Members of the League shall severally contribute to the armed forces to be used to protect the covenants of the League.

The Members of the League agree, further, that they will mutually support one another in the financial and economic measures which are taken under this Article, in order to minimise the loss and inconvenience resulting from the above measures, and that they will mutually support one another in resisting any special measures aimed at one of their number by the covenant-breaking State, and that they will take the necessary steps to afford passage through their territory to the forces of any of the Members of the League which are co-operating to protect the covenants of the League.

Any Member of the League which has violated any covenant of the League may be declared to be no longer a Member of the League by a vote of the Council concurred in by the Representatives of all the other Members of the League represented thereon.

ART. 17. In the event of a dispute between a Member of the League and a State which is not a Member of the League, or between States not Members of the League, the State or States not Members of the League shall be invited to accept the obligations of membership in the League for the purposes of such dispute, upon such conditions as the Council may deem just. If such invitation is accepted, the provisions of Articles 12 to 16 inclusive shall be applied with such modifications as may be deemed necessary by the Council.

Upon such invitation being given the Council shall immediately institute an inquiry into the circumstances of the dispute, and recommend such action as may seem best and most effectual in the circumstances.

If a State so invited shall refuse to accept the obligations of

TREATY OF PEACE WITH GERMANY

membership in the League for the purposes of such dispute, and shall resort to war against a Member of the League, the provisions of Article 16 shall be applicable as against the State taking such action.

If both parties to the dispute when so invited refuse to accept the obligations of membership in the League for the purposes of such dispute, the Council may take such measures and make such recommendations as will prevent hostilities and will result in the settlement of the dispute.

ART. 18. Every treaty or international engagement entered into hereafter by any Member of the League shall be forthwith registered with the Secretariat and shall as soon as possible be published by it. No such treaty or international engagement shall be binding until so registered.

ART. 19. The Assembly may from time to time advise the reconsideration by Members of the League of treaties which have become inapplicable and the consideration of international conditions whose continuance might endanger the peace of the world.

ART. 20. The Members of the League severally agree that this Covenant is accepted as abrogating all obligations or understandings *inter se* which are inconsistent with the terms thereof, and solemnly undertake that they will not hereafter enter into any engagements inconsistent with the terms thereof.

In case any Member of the League shall, before becoming a Member of the League, have undertaken any obligations inconsistent with the terms of this Covenant, it shall be the duty of such Member to take immediate steps to procure its release from such obligations.

ART. 21. Nothing in this Covenant shall be deemed to affect the validity of international engagements, such as treaties of arbitration or regional understandings like the Monroe doctrine, for securing the maintenance of peace.

ART. 22. To those colonies and territories which as a consequence of the late war have ceased to be under the sovereignty of the States which formerly governed them and which are inhabited by peoples not yet able to stand by themselves under the strenuous conditions of the modern world, there should be applied the principle that the well-being and development of such peoples form a sacred trust of civilisation and that securities for the performance of this trust should be embodied in this Covenant.

The best method of giving practical effect to this principle is that the tutelage of such peoples should be entrusted to advanced nations who by reason of their resources, their experience or their geographical position can best undertake this responsibility, and who are willing to accept it, and that this tutelage should be exercised by them as Mandatories on behalf of the League.

The character of the mandate must differ according to the stage of the development of the people, the geographical situation of the territory, its economic conditions and other similar circumstances.

Certain communities formerly belonging to the Turkish Empire have reached a stage of development where their existence as independent nations can be provisionally recognized subject to the rendering of administrative advice and assistance by a Mandatory until such time as they are able to stand alone. The wishes of these communities must be a principal consideration in the selection of the Mandatory.

Other peoples, especially those of Central Africa, are at such a stage that the Mandatory must be responsible for the administration of the territory under conditions which will guarantee freedom of conscience and religion, subject only to the maintenance of public order and morals, the prohibition of abuses such as the slave trade, the arms traffic and the liquor traffic, and the prevention of the establishment of fortifications or military and naval bases and of military training of the natives for other than police purposes and the defence of territory, and will also secure equal opportunities for the trade and commerce of other Members of the League.

There are territories, such as South-West Africa and certain of the South Pacific Islands, which, owing to the sparseness of their population, or their small size, or their remoteness from the centres of civilisation, or their geographical contiguity to the territory of the Mandatory, and other circumstances, can be best administered under the laws of the Mandatory as integral portions of its territory, subject to the safeguards above mentioned in the interests of the indigenous population.

In every case of mandate, the Mandatory shall render to the Council an annual report in reference to the territory committed to its charge.

The degree of authority, control, or administration to be exercised by the Mandatory shall, if not previously agreed upon by the Members of the League, be explicitly defined in each case by the Council.

A permanent Commission shall be constituted to receive and examine the annual reports of the Mandatories and to advise the Council on all matters relating to the observance of the mandates.

ART. 23. Subject to and in accordance with the provisions of international conventions existing or hereafter to be agreed upon, the Members of the League:

(a) will endeavour to secure and maintain fair and humane conditions of labour for men, women, and children, both in their own countries and in all countries to which their commercial and industrial relations extend, and for that purpose will establish and maintain the necessary international organisations;

(b) undertake to secure just treatment of the native inhabitants of territories under their control;

(c) will entrust the League with the general supervision over the execution of agreements with regard to the traffic in women and children, and the traffic in opium and other dangerous drugs;

(d) will entrust the League with the general supervision of the trade in arms and ammunition with the countries in which the control of this traffic is necessary in the common interest;

(e) will make provision to secure and maintain freedom of communications and of transit and equitable treatment for the commerce of all Members of the League. In this connection, the special necessities of the regions devastated during the war of 1914-1918 shall be borne in mind;

(f) will endeavour to take steps in matters of international concern for the prevention and control of disease.

APPENDIX

ART. 24. There shall be placed under the direction of the League all international bureaux already established by general treaties if the parties to such treaties consent. All such international bureaux and all commissions for the regulation of matters of international interest hereafter constituted shall be placed under the direction of the League.

In all matters of international interest which are regulated by general conventions but which are not placed under the control of international bureaux or commissions, the Secretariat of the League shall, subject to the consent of the Council and if desired by the parties, collect and distribute all relevant information and shall render any other assistance which may be necessary or desirable.

The Council may include as part of the expenses of the Secretariat the expenses of any bureau or commission which is placed under the direction of the League.

ART. 25. The members of the League agree to encourage and promote the establishment and co-operation of duly authorized voluntary national Red Cross organizations having as purposes the improvement of health, the prevention of disease and the mitigation of suffering throughout the world.

ART. 26. Amendments to the Covenant will take effect when ratified by the Members of the League whose Representatives compose the Council and by a majority of the Members of the League whose Representatives compose the Assembly.

No such amendment shall bind any Member of the League which signifies its dissent therefrom, but in that case it shall cease to be a Member of the League.

ANNEX.

I. ORIGINAL MEMBERS OF THE LEAGUE OF NATIONS SIGNATORIES OF THE TREATY OF PEACE.

UNITED STATES OF AMERICA.
BELGIUM.
BOLIVIA.
BRAZIL.
HAITI.
HEDJAZ.
HONDURAS.
ITALY.

BRITISH EMPIRE.	JAPAN.
CANADA.	LIBERIA.
AUSTRALIA.	NICARAGUA.
SOUTH AFRICA.	PANAMA.
NEW ZEALAND.	PERU.
INDIA.	POLAND.
CHINA.	PORTUGAL.
CUBA.	ROUMANIA.
ECUADOR.	SERB-CROAT-SLOVENE STATE.
FRANCE.	SIAM.
GREECE.	CZECHO-SLOVAKIA.
GUATEMALA.	URUGUAY.

STATES INVITED TO ACCEDE TO THE COVENANT.

ARGENTINE REPUBLIC.	PERSIA.
CHILI.	SALVADOR.
COLOMBIA.	SPAIN.
DENMARK.	SWEDEN.
NETHERLANDS.	SWITZERLAND.
NORWAY.	VENEZUELA.
PARAGUAY.	

II. FIRST SECRETARY GENERAL OF THE LEAGUE OF NATIONS.

The Honourable Sir James Eric DRUMMOND, K.C.M.G., C.B.

PART II.

BOUNDARIES OF GERMANY.

ART. 27-29.

ART. 30. In the case of boundaries which are defined by a waterway, the terms "course" and "channel" used in the present Treaty signify: in the case of non-navigable rivers, the median line of the waterway or of its principal arm, and, in the case of navigable rivers, the median line of the principal channel of navigation. It will rest with the Boundary Commissions provided by the present Treaty to specify in each case whether the frontier line shall follow

APPENDIX

any changes of the course or channel which may take place or whether it shall be definitely fixed by the position of the course or channel at the time when the present Treaty comes into force.

PART III.

POLITICAL CLAUSES FOR EUROPE.

SECTION I.

BELGIUM.

ART. 31-33.

ART. 34. Germany renounces in favour of Belgium all rights and title over the territory comprising the whole of the *Kreise* of Eupen and of Malmédy.

During the six months after the coming into force of this Treaty, registers will be opened by the Belgian authority at Eupen and Malmédy in which the inhabitants of the above territory will be entitled to record in writing a desire to see the whole or part of it remain under German sovereignty.

The results of this public expression of opinion will be communicated by the Belgian Government to the League of Nations, and Belgium undertakes to accept the decision of the League.

ART. 35-39.

SECTION II.

LUXEMBURG.

ART. 40-41.

SECTION III.

LEFT BANK OF THE RHINE.

ART. 42-44.

SECTION IV.

SAAR BASIN.

ART. 45-47.

ART. 48. . . . A Commission composed of five members, one appointed by France, one by Germany, and three by the Council of the League of Nations, which will select nationals of other Powers, will be constituted within fifteen days from the coming into force of the present Treaty, to trace on the spot the frontier line described above.

In those parts of the preceding line which do not coincide with administrative boundaries, the Commission will endeavour to keep to the line indicated, while taking into consideration, so far as is possible, local economic interests and existing communal boundaries.

The decisions of this Commission will be taken by a majority, and will be binding on the parties concerned.

ART. 49. Germany renounces in favour of the League of Nations, in the capacity of trustee, the government of the territory defined above.

At the end of fifteen years from the coming into force of the present Treaty the inhabitants of the said territory shall be called upon to indicate the sovereignty under which they desire to be placed.

ART. 50. and ANNEX.

CHAPTER I.

CESSION AND EXPLOITATION OF MINING PROPERTY.

1–15.

CHAPTER II.

GOVERNMENT OF THE TERRITORY OF THE SAAR BASIN.

16. The Government of the territory of the Saar Basin shall be entrusted to a Commission representing the League of Nations. This Commission shall sit in the territory of the Saar Basin.

17. The Governing Commission provided for by paragraph 16 shall consist of five members chosen by the Council of the League of Nations, and will include one citizen of France, one native inhabitant of the Saar Basin, not a citizen of France, and three members belonging to three countries other than France or Germany.

The members of the Governing Commission shall be appointed for one year and may be re-appointed. They can be removed by the Council of the League of Nations, which will provide for their replacement.

The members of the Governing Commission will be entitled to a salary which will be fixed by the Council of the League of Nations, and charged on the local revenues.

18. The Chairman of the Governing Commission shall be appointed for one year from among the members of the Commission by the Council of the League of Nations and may be re-appointed.

The Chairman will act as the executive of the Commission.

19. Within the territory of the Saar Basin the Governing Commission shall have all the powers of government hitherto belonging to the German Empire, Prussia, or Bavaria, including the appointment and dismissal of officials, and the creation of such administrative and representative bodies as it may deem necessary.

It shall have full powers to administer and operate the railways, canals and the different public services.

Its decisions shall be taken by a majority.

20-33.

Chapter III.

PLEBISCITE.

34. At the termination of a period of fifteen years from the coming into force of the present Treaty, the population of the territory of the Saar Basin will be called upon to indicate their desires in the following manner:

A vote will take place by communes or districts, on the three following alternatives: (a) maintenance of the régime established by the present Treaty and by this Annex; (b) union with France; (c) union with Germany.

All persons without distinction of sex, more than twenty years old at the date of the voting, resident in the territory at the date of the signature of the present Treaty, will have the right to vote.

The other conditions, methods and the date of the voting shall be fixed by the Council of the League of Nations in such a way as to secure the freedom, secrecy and trustworthiness of the voting.

35. The League of Nations shall decide on the sovereignty under which the territory is to be placed, taking into account the wishes of the inhabitants as expressed by the voting:

(*a*) If, for the whole or part of the territory, the League of Nations decides in favour of the maintenance of the régime established by the present Treaty and this Annex, Germany hereby agrees to make such renunciation of her sovereignty in favour of the League of Nations as the latter shall deem necessary. It will be the duty of the League of Nations to take appropriate steps to adapt the régime definitively adopted to the permanent welfare of the territory and the general interest;

(*b*) If, for the whole or part of the territory, the League of Nations decides in favour of union with France, Germany hereby agrees to cede to France in accordance with the decision of the League of Nations all rights and title over the territory specified by the League;

(*c*) If, for the whole or part of the territory, the League of Nations decides in favour of union with Germany, it will be the duty of the League of Nations to cause the German Government to be reestablished in the government of the territory specified by the League.

36. If the League of Nations decides in favour of the union of the whole or part of the territory of the Saar Basin with Germany, France's rights of ownership in the mines situated in such part of the territory will be repurchased by Germany in their entirety at a price payable in gold. The price to be paid will be fixed by three experts, one nominated by Germany, one by France, and one, who shall be neither a Frenchman nor a German, by the Council of the League of Nations; the decision of the experts will be given by a majority.

The obligation of Germany to make such payment shall be taken into account by the Reparation Commission, and for the purpose of this payment Germany may create a prior charge upon her assets or revenues upon such detailed terms as shall be agreed to by the Reparation Commission.

If, nevertheless, Germany after a period of one year from the date on which the payment becomes due shall not have effected the said payment, the Reparation Commission shall do so in accordance with such instructions as may be given by the League of Nations, and, if necessary, by liquidating that part of the mines which is in question.

37. If, in consequence of the repurchase provided for in paragraph 36, the ownership of the mines or any part of them is transferred to Germany, the French State and French nationals shall have the right to purchase such amount of coal of the Saar Basin as their industrial and domestic needs are found at that time to require. An equitable arrangement regarding amounts of coal, duration of contract, and prices will be fixed in due time by the Council of the League of Nations.

38. It is understood that France and Germany may, by special agreements concluded before the time fixed for the payment of the price for the repurchase of the mines, modify the provisions of paragraphs 36 and 37.

39. The Council of the League of Nations shall make such provisions as may be necessary for the establishment of the régime which is to take effect after the decisions of the League of Nations mentioned in paragraph 35 have become operative, including an equitable apportionment of any obligations of the Government of the territory of the Saar Basin arising from loans raised by the Commission or from other causes.

From the coming into force of the new régime, the powers of the Governing Commission will terminate, except in the case provided for in paragraph 35 (*a*).

40. In all matters dealt with in the present Annex, the decisions of the Council of the League of Nations will be taken by a majority.

Section V.

ALSACE-LORRAINE.

The High Contracting Parties, recognizing the moral obligation to redress the wrong done by Germany in 1871 both to the rights of France and to the wishes of the population of Alsace and Lorraine, which were separated from their country in spite of the solemn protest of their representatives at the Assembly of Bordeaux,

Agree upon the following Articles:

ART. 51–79.

Section VI.
AUSTRIA.

ART. 80. Germany acknowledges and will respect strictly the independence of Austria, within the frontiers which may be fixed in a Treaty between that State and the Principal Allied and Associated Powers; she agrees that this independence shall be inalienable, except with the consent of the Council of the League of Nations.

Section VII.
CZECHO-SLOVAK STATE.

ART. 81–86.

Section VIII.
POLAND.

ART. 87–93.

Section IX.
EAST PRUSSIA.

ART. 94–97.

ART. 98. Germany and Poland undertake, within one year of the coming into force of this Treaty, to enter into conventions of which the terms, in case of difference, shall be settled by the Council of the League of Nations, with the object of securing, on the one hand to Germany full and adequate railroad, telegraphic and telephonic facilities for communication between the rest of Germany and East Prussia over the intervening Polish territory, and on the other hand to Poland full and adequate railroad, telegraphic and telephonic facilities for communication between Poland and the Free City of Danzig over any German territory that may, on the right bank of the Vistula, intervene between Poland and the Free City of Danzig.

APPENDIX

Section X.
MEMEL.

ART. 99.

Section XI.
FREE CITY OF DANZIG.

ART. 100–101.

ART. 102. The Principal Allied and Associated Powers undertake to establish the town of Danzig, together with the rest of the territory described in Article 100, as a Free City. It will be placed under the protection of the League of Nations.

ART. 103. A constitution for the Free City of Danzig shall be drawn up by the duly appointed representatives of the Free City in agreement with a High Commissioner to be appointed by the League of Nations. This constitution shall be placed under the guarantee of the League of Nations.

The High Commissioner will also be entrusted with the duty of dealing in the first instance with all differences arising between Poland and the Free City of Danzig in regard to this Treaty or any arrangements or agreements made thereunder.

The High Commissioner shall reside at Danzig.

ART. 104–108.

Section XII.
SCHLESWIG.

ART. 109–114.

Section XIII.
HELIGOLAND.

ART. 115.

Section XIV.
RUSSIA AND RUSSIAN STATES.

ART. 116–117.

PART IV.

GERMAN RIGHTS AND INTERESTS OUTSIDE GERMANY.

Art. 118. In territory outside her European frontiers as fixed by the present Treaty, Germany renounces all rights, titles and privileges whatever in or over territory which belonged to her or to her allies, and all rights, titles and privileges whatever their origin which she held as against the Allied and Associated Powers.

Germany hereby undertakes to recognize and to conform to the measures which may be taken now or in the future by the Principal Allied and Associated Powers, in agreement where necessary with third Powers, in order to carry the above stipulation into effect.

In particular Germany declares her acceptance of the following Articles relating to certain special subjects.

Section I.
GERMAN COLONIES.

Art. 119. Germany renounces in favour of the Principal Allied and Associated Powers all her rights and titles over her oversea possessions.

Art. 120–127.

Section II.
CHINA.

Art. 128–134.

Section III.
SIAM.

Art. 135–137.

Section IV.
LIBERIA.

Art. 138–140.

Section V.
MOROCCO.

ART. 141. Germany renounces all rights, titles and privileges conferred on her by the General Act of Algeciras of April 7, 1906, and by the Franco-German Agreements of February 9, 1909, and November 4, 1911. All treaties, agreements, arrangements and contracts concluded by her with the Sherifian Empire are regarded as abrogated as from August 3, 1914.

In no case can Germany take advantage of these instruments and she undertakes not to intervene in any way in negotiations relating to Morocco which may take place between France and the other Powers.

ART. 142-146.

Section VI.
EGYPT.

ART. 147-154.

Section VII.
TURKEY AND BULGARIA.

ART. 155. Germany undertakes to recognize and accept all arrangements which the Allied and Associated Powers may make with Turkey and Bulgaria with reference to any rights, interests and privileges whatever which might be claimed by Germany or her nationals in Turkey and Bulgaria and which are not dealt with in the provisions of the present Treaty.

Section VIII.
SHANTUNG.

ART. 156. Germany renounces, in favour of Japan, all her rights, title and privileges—particularly those concerning the territory of Kiaochow, railways, mines and submarine cables—which she acquired in virtue of the Treaty concluded by her with China on March 6, 1898, and of all other arrangements relative to the Province of Shantung.

All German rights in the Tsingtao-Tsinanfu Railway, including its branch lines, together with its subsidiary property of all kinds, stations, shops, fixed and rolling stock, mines, plant and material for the exploitation of the mines, are and remain acquired by Japan, together with all rights and privileges attaching thereto.

The German state submarine cables from Tsingtao to Shanghai and from Tsingtao to Chefoo, with all the rights, privileges and properties attaching thereto, are similarly acquired by Japan, free and clear of all charges and encumbrances.

ART. 157. The movable and immovable property owned by the German State in the territory of Kiaochow, as well as all the rights which Germany might claim in consequence of the works or improvements made or of the expenses incurred by her, directly or indirectly, in connection with this territory, are and remain acquired by Japan, free and clear of all charges and encumbrances.

ART. 158. Germany shall hand over to Japan within three months from the coming into force of the present Treaty the archives, registers, plans, title-deeds and documents of every kind, wherever they may be, relating to the administration, whether civil, military, financial, judicial or other, of the territory of Kiaochow.

Within the same period Germany shall give particulars to Japan of all treaties, arrangements or agreements relating to the rights, title or privileges referred to in the two preceding Articles.

PART V.

MILITARY, NAVAL AND AIR CLAUSES.

SECTION I.
MILITARY CLAUSES.

CHAPTER I.

EFFECTIVES AND CADRES OF THE GERMAN ARMY.

ART. 159–163.

Chapter II.

ARMAMENT, MUNITIONS AND MATERIAL.

ART. 164. Up till the time at which Germany is admitted as a member of the League of Nations the German Army must not possess an armament greater than the amounts fixed in Table No. II annexed to this Section, with the exception of an optional increase not exceeding one-twentyfifth part for small arms and one-fiftieth part for guns, which shall be exclusively used to provide for such eventual replacements as may be necessary.

Germany agrees that after she has become a member of the League of Nations the armaments fixed in the said Table shall remain in force until they are modified by the Council of the League. Furthermore she hereby agrees strictly to observe the decisions of the Council of the League on this subject.

ART. 165–172.

Chapter III.

RECRUITING AND MILITARY TRAINING.

ART. 173–179.

Chapter IV.

FORTIFICATIONS.

ART. 180.

Section II.

NAVAL CLAUSES.

ART. 181–197.

Section III.

AIR CLAUSES.

ART. 198–202.

Section IV.

INTER-ALLIED COMMISSIONS OF CONTROL.

ART. 203. All the military, naval and air clauses contained in the present Treaty, for the execution of which a time-limit is prescribed, shall be executed by Germany under the control of Inter-Allied Commissions specially appointed for this purpose by the Principal Allied and Associated Powers.

ART. 204. The Inter-Allied Commissions of Control will be specially charged with the duty of seeing to the complete execution of the delivery, destruction, demolition and rendering things useless to be carried out at the expense of the German Government in accordance with the present Treaty.

They will communicate to the German authorities the decisions which the Principal Allied and Associated Powers have reserved the right to take, or which the execution of the military, naval and air clauses may necessitate.

ART. 205. The Inter-Allied Commissions of Control may establish their organisations at the seat of the central German Government.

They shall be entitled as often as they think desirable to proceed to any point whatever in German territory, or to send sub-commissions, or to authorize one or more of their members to go, to any such point.

ART. 206. The German Government must give all necessary facilities for the accomplishment of their missions to the Inter-Allied Commissions of Control and to their members.

It shall attach a qualified representative to each Inter-Allied Commission of Control for the purpose of receiving the communications which the Commission may have to address to the German Government and of supplying or procuring for the Commission all information or documents which may be required.

The German Government must in all cases furnish at its own cost all labour and material required to effect the deliveries and the works of destruction, dismantling, demolition, and of rendering things useless, provided for in the present Treaty.

ART. 207. The upkeep and cost of the Commissions of Control and the expenses involved by their work shall be borne by Germany.

ART. 208. The Military Inter-Allied Commission of Control will represent the Governments of the Principal Allied and Associated Powers in dealing with the German Government in all matters concerning the execution of the military clauses.

In particular it will be its duty to receive from the German Government the notifications relating to the location of the stocks and depots of munitions, the armament of the fortified works, fortresses and forts which Germany is allowed to retain, and the location of the works or factories for the production of arms, munitions and war material and their operations.

It will take delivery of the arms, munitions and war material, will select the points where such delivery is to be effected, and will supervise the works of destruction, demolition, and of rendering things useless, which are to be carried out in accordance with the present Treaty.

The German Government must furnish to the Military Inter-Allied Commission of Control all such information and documents as the latter may deem necessary to ensure the complete execution of the military clauses, and in particular all legislative and administrative documents and regulations.

ART. 209. The Naval Inter-Allied Commission of Control will represent the Governments of the Principal Allied and Associated Powers in dealing with the German Government in all matters concerning the execution of the naval clauses.

In particular it will be its duty to proceed to the building yards and to supervise the breaking-up of the ships which are under construction there, to take delivery of all surface ships or submarines, salvage ships, docks and the tubular docks, and to supervise the destruction and breaking-up provided for.

The German Government must furnish to the Naval Inter-Allied Commission of Control all such information and documents as the Commission may deem necessary to ensure the complete execution of the naval clauses, in particular the designs of the warships, the composition of their armaments, the details and models of the guns, munitions, torpedoes, mines, explosives, wireless telegraphic apparatus and, in general, everything relating to naval war material, as well as all legislative or administrative documents or regulations.

ART. 210. The Aeronautical Inter-Allied Commission of Control will represent the Governments of the Principal Allied and Associated Powers in dealing with the German Government in all matters concerning the execution of the air clauses.

In particular it will be its duty to make an inventory of the aeronautical material existing in German territory, to inspect aeroplane, balloon and motor manufactories, and factories producing arms, munitions and explosives capable of being used by aircraft, to visit all aerodromes, sheds, landing grounds, parks and depots, to authorise, where necessary, a removal of material and to take delivery of such material.

The German Government must furnish to the Aeronautical Inter-Allied Commission of Control all such information and legislative, administrative or other documents which the Commission may consider necessary to ensure the complete execution of the air clauses, and in particular a list of the personnel belonging to all the German Air Services, and of the existing material, as well as of that in process of manufacture or on order, and a list of all establishments working for aviation, of their positions, and of all sheds and landing grounds.

Section V.
GENERAL ARTICLES.

ART. 211–212.

ART. 213. So long as the present Treaty remains in force, Germany undertakes to give every facility for any investigation which the Council of the League of Nations, acting if need be by a majority vote, may consider necessary.

PART VI.
PRISONERS OF WAR AND GRAVES.

Section I.
PRISONERS OF WAR.

ART. 214–224.

Section II.
GRAVES.

Art. 225–226.

PART VII.
PENALTIES.

Art. 227–230.

PART VIII.
REPARATION.

Section I.
GENERAL PROVISIONS.

Art. 231. The Allied and Associated Governments affirm and Germany accepts the responsibility of Germany and her allies for causing all the loss and damage to which the Allied and Associated Governments and their nationals have been subjected as a consequence of the war imposed upon them by the aggression of Germany and her allies.

Art. 232. The Allied and Associated Governments recognize that the resources of Germany are not adequate, after taking into account permanent diminutions of such resources which will result from other provisions of the present Treaty, to make complete reparation for all such loss and damage.

The Allied and Associated Governments, however, require, and Germany undertakes, that she will make compensation for all damage done to the civilian population of the Allied and Associated Powers and to their property during the period of the belligerency of each as an Allied or Associated Power against Germany by such aggression by land, by sea and from the air, and in general all damage as defined in Annex I hereto.

In accordance with Germany's pledges, already given, as to complete restoration for Belgium, Germany undertakes, in addition to the compensation for damage elsewhere in this Part provided for, as a consequence of the violation of the Treaty of 1839, to make reimbursement of all sums which Belgium has borrowed from the Allied and Associated Governments up to November 11, 1918, together with interest at the rate of five per cent. (5%) per annum on such sums. This amount shall be determined by the Reparation Commission, and the German Government undertakes thereupon forthwith to make a special issue of bearer bonds to an equivalent amount payable in marks gold, on May 1, 1926, or, at the option of the German Government, on the 1st of May in any year up to 1926. Subject to the foregoing, the form of such bonds shall be determined by the Reparation Commission. Such bonds shall be handed over to the Reparation Commission, which has authority to take and acknowledge receipt thereof on behalf of Belgium.

ART. 233. The amount of the above damage for which compensation is to be made by Germany shall be determined by an Inter-Allied Commission, to be called the *Reparation Commission* and constituted in the form and with the powers set forth hereunder and in Annexes II to VII inclusive hereto.

This Commission shall consider the claims and give to the German Government a just opportunity to be heard.

The findings of the Commission as to the amount of damage defined as above shall be concluded and notified to the German Government on or before May 1, 1921, as representing the extent of that Government's obligations.

The Commission shall concurrently draw up a schedule of payments prescribing the time and manner for securing and discharging the entire obligation within a period of thirty years from May 1, 1921. If, however, within the period mentioned, Germany fails to discharge her obligations, any balance remaining unpaid may, within the discretion of the Commission, be postponed for settlement in subsequent years, or may be handled otherwise in such manner as the Allied and Associated Governments, acting in accordance with the procedure laid down in this Part of the present Treaty, shall determine.

ART. 234-244.

ANNEX II.

1. The Commission referred to in Article 233 shall be called "The Reparation Commission" and is hereinafter referred to as "the Commission".

2. Delegates to this Commission shall be nominated by the United States of America, Great Britain, France, Italy, Japan, Belgium and the Serb-Croat-Slovene State. Each of these Powers will appoint one Delegate and also one Assistant Delegate, who will take his place in case of illness or necessary absence, but at other times will only have the right to be present at proceedings without taking any part therein.

On no occasion shall the Delegates of more than five of the above Powers have the right to take part in the proceedings of the Commission and to record their votes. The Delegates of the United States, Great Britain, France and Italy shall have this right on all occasions. The Delegate of Belgium shall have this right on all occasions other than those referred to below. The Delegate of Japan shall have this right on occasions when questions relating to damage at sea, and questions arising under Article 260 of Part IX (Financial Clauses) in which Japanese interests are concerned, are under consideration. The Delegate of the Serb-Croat-Slovene State shall have this right when questions relating to Austria, Hungary or Bulgaria are under consideration.

Each Government represented on the Commission shall have the right to withdraw therefrom upon twelve months notice filed with the Commission and confirmed in the course of the sixth month after the date of the original notice.

3. Such of the other Allied and Associated Powers as may be interested shall have the right to appoint a Delegate to be present and act as Assessor only while their respective claims and interests are under examination or discussion, but without the right to vote.

4. In case of the death, resignation or recall of any Delegate, Assistant Delegate or Assessor, a successor to him shall be nominated as soon as possible.

TREATY OF PEACE WITH GERMANY

5. The Commission will have its principal permanent Bureau in Paris and will hold its first meeting in Paris as soon as practicable after the coming into force of the present Treaty, and thereafter will meet in such place or places and at such time as it may deem convenient and as may be necessary for the most expeditious discharge of its duties.

6. At its first meeting the Commission shall elect, from among the Delegates referred to above, a Chairman and a Vice-Chairman, who shall hold office for one year and shall be eligible for re-election. If a vacancy in the Chairmanship or Vice-Chairmanship should occur during the annual period, the Commission shall proceed to a new election for the remainder of the said period.

7. The Commission is authorized to appoint all necessary officers, agents and employees who may be required for the execution of its functions, and to fix their remuneration; to constitute committees, whose members need not necessarily be members of the Commission, and to take all executive steps necessary for the purpose of discharging its duties; and to delegate authority and discretion to officers, agents and committees.

8. All proceedings of the Commission shall be private, unless, on particular occasions, the Commission shall otherwise determine for special reasons.

9. The Commission shall be required, if the German Government so desire, to hear, within a period which it will fix from time to time, evidence and arguments on the part of Germany on any question connected with her capacity to pay.

10. The Commission shall consider the claims and give to the German Government a just opportunity to be heard, but not to take any part whatever in the decisions of the Commission. The Commission shall afford a similar opportunity to the allies of Germany, when it shall consider that their interests are in question.

11. The Commission shall not be bound by any particular code or rules of law or by any particular rule of evidence or of procedure, but shall be guided by justice, equity and good faith. Its decisions must follow the same principles and rules in all cases where they are

applicable. It will establish rules relating to methods of proof of claims. It may act on any trustworthy modes of computation.

12–23.

Section II.
SPECIAL PROVISIONS.

Art. 245–247.

PART IX.

FINANCIAL CLAUSES.

Art. 248–253.

Art. 254. The Powers to which German territory is ceded shall, subject to the qualifications made in Article 255, undertake to pay:

(1) A portion of the debt of the German Empire as it stood on August 1, 1914, calculated on the basis of the ratio between the average for the three financial years 1911, 1912, 1913, of such revenues of the ceded territory, and the average for the same years of such revenues of the whole German Empire as in the judgment of the Reparation Commission are best calculated to represent the relative ability of the respective territories to make payment;

(2) A portion of the debt as it stood on August 1, 1914, of the German State to which the ceded territory belonged, to be determined in accordance with the principle stated above.

Such portions shall be determined by the Reparation Commission.

The method of discharging the obligation, both in respect of capital and of interest, so assumed shall be fixed by the Reparation Commission. Such method may take the form, *inter alia*, of the assumption by the Power to which the territory is ceded of Germany's liability for the German debt held by her nationals. But in the event of the method adopted involving any payments to the German Government, such payments shall be transferred to the Reparation Commission on account of the sums due for reparation so long as any balance in respect of such sums remains unpaid.

ART. 255. (1) As an exception to the above provision and inasmuch as in 1871 Germany refused to undertake any portion of the burden of the French debt, France shall be, in respect of Alsace-Lorraine, exempt from any payment under Article 254.

(2) In the case of Poland that portion of the debt which, in the opinion of the Reparation Commission, is attributable to the measures taken by the German and Prussian Governments for the German colonisation of Poland shall be excluded from the apportionment to be made under Article 254.

(3) In the case of all ceded territories other than Alsace-Lorraine, that portion of the debt of the German Empire or German States which, in the opinion of the Reparation Commission, represents expenditure by the Governments of the German Empire or States upon the Government properties referred to in Article 256 shall be excluded from the apportionment to be made under Article 254.

ART. 256. Powers to which German territory is ceded shall acquire all property and possessions situated therein belonging to the German Empire or to the German States, and the value of such acquisitions shall be fixed by the Reparation Commission, and paid by the State acquiring the territory to the Reparation Commission for the credit of the German Government on account of the sums due for reparation.

For the purpose of this Article the property and possessions of the German Empire and States shall be deemed to include all the property of the Crown, the Empire or the States, and the private property of the former German Emperor and other Royal personages.

In view of the terms on which Alsace-Lorraine was ceded to Germany in 1871, France shall be exempt in respect thereof from making any payment or credit under this Article for any property or possessions of the German Empire or States situated therein.

Belgium also shall be exempt from making any payment or any credit under this Article for any property or possessions of the German Empire or States situated in German territory ceded to Belgium under the present Treaty.

ART. 257. In the case of the former German territories, including colonies, protectorates or dependencies, administered by a Mandatory under Article 22 of Part I (League of Nations) of the present Treaty, neither the territory nor the Mandatory Power shall be charged with any portion of the debt of the German Empire or States.

All property and possessions belonging to the German Empire or to the German States situated in such territories shall be transferred with the territories to the Mandatory Power in its capacity as such and no payment shall be made nor any credit given to those Governments in consideration of this transfer.

For the purposes of this Article the property and possessions of the German Empire and of the German States shall be deemed to include all the property of the Crown, the Empire or the States and the private property of the former German Emperor and other Royal personages.

ART. 258–263.

PART X.

ECONOMIC CLAUSES.

Section I.

COMMERCIAL RELATIONS.

Chapter I.

CUSTOMS REGULATIONS, DUTIES AND RESTRICTIONS.

ART. 264–270.

Chapter II.

SHIPPING.

ART. 271. As regards sea fishing, maritime coasting trade, and maritime towage, vessels of the Allied and Associated Powers shall enjoy, in German territorial waters, the treatment accorded to vessels of the most favoured nation.

ART. 272. Germany agrees that, notwithstanding any stipulation to the contrary contained in the Conventions relating to the North Sea fisheries and liquor traffic, all rights of inspection and police shall, in the case of fishing-boats of the Allied Powers, be exercised solely by ships belonging to those Powers.

ART. 273.

CHAPTER III.

UNFAIR COMPETITION.

ART. 274-275.

CHAPTER IV.

TREATMENT OF NATIONALS OF ALLIED AND ASSOCIATED POWERS.

ART. 276-279.

CHAPTER V.

GENERAL ARTICLES.

ART. 280. The obligations imposed on Germany by Chapter I and by Articles 271 and 272 of Chapter II above shall cease to have effect five years from the date of the coming into force of the present Treaty, unless otherwise provided in the text, or unless the Council of the League of Nations shall, at least twelve months before the expiration of that period, decide that these obligations shall be maintained for a further period with or without amendment.

Article 276 of Chapter IV shall remain in operation, with or without amendment, after the period of five years for such further period, if any, not exceeding five years, as may be determined by a majority of the Council of the League of Nations.

ART. 281. If the German Government engages in international trade, it shall not in respect thereof have or be deemed to have any rights, privileges or immunities of sovereignty.

SECTION II.

TREATIES.

ART. 282. From the coming into force of the present Treaty and subject to the provisions thereof the multilateral treaties, conventions and agreements of an economic or technical character enumerated below and in the subsequent Articles shall alone be applied as between Germany and those of the Allied and Associated Powers party thereto:

(1) Conventions of March 14, 1884, December 1, 1886, and March 23, 1887, and Final Protocol of July 7, 1887, regarding the protection of submarine cables.

(2) Convention of October 11, 1909, regarding the international circulation of motor-cars.

(3) Agreement of May 15, 1886, regarding the sealing of railway trucks subject to customs inspection, and Protocol of May 18, 1907.

(4) Agreement of May 15, 1886, regarding the technical standardisation of railways.

(5) Convention of July 5, 1890, regarding the publication of customs tariffs and the organisation of an International Union for the publication of customs tariffs.

(6) Convention of December 31, 1913, regarding the unification of commercial statistics.

(7) Convention of April 25, 1907, regarding the raising of the Turkish customs tariff.

(8) Convention of March 14, 1857, for the redemption of toll dues on the Sound and Belts.

(9) Convention of June 22, 1861, for the redemption of the Stade Toll on the Elbe.

(10) Convention of July 16, 1863, for the redemption of the toll dues on the Scheldt.

(11) Convention of October 29, 1888, regarding the establishment of a definite arrangement guaranteeing the free use of the Suez Canal.

(12) Conventions of September 23, 1910, respecting the unification of certain regulations regarding collisions and salvage at sea.

(13) Convention of December 21, 1904, regarding the exemption of hospital ships from dues and charges in ports.

(14) Convention of February 4, 1898, regarding the tonnage measurement of vessels for inland navigation.

(15) Convention of September 26, 1906, for the suppression of nightwork for women.

(16) Convention of September 26, 1906, for the suppression of the use of white phosphorus in the manufacture of matches.

(17) Conventions of May 18, 1904, and May 4, 1910, regarding the suppression of the White Slave Traffic.

(18) Convention of May 4, 1910, regarding the suppression of obscene publications.

(19) Sanitary Conventions of January 30, 1892, April 15, 1893, April 3, 1894, March 19, 1897, and December 3, 1903.

(20) Convention of May 20, 1875, regarding the unification and improvement of the metric system.

(21) Convention of November 29, 1906, regarding the unification of pharmacopœial formulæ for potent drugs.

(22) Convention of November 16 and 19, 1885, regarding the establishment of a concert pitch.

(23) Convention of June 7, 1905, regarding the creation of an International Agricultural Institute at Rome.

(24) Conventions of November 3, 1881, and April 15, 1889, regarding precautionary measures against phylloxera.

(25) Convention of March 19, 1902, regarding the protection of birds useful to agriculture.

(26) Convention of June 12, 1902, as to the protection of minors.

ART. 283. From the coming into force of the present Treaty the High Contracting Parties shall apply the conventions and agreements hereinafter mentioned, in so far as concerns them, on condition that the special stipulations contained in this Article are fulfilled by Germany.

Postal Conventions:

Conventions and agreements of the Universal Postal Union concluded at Vienna, July 4, 1891.

Conventions and agreements of the Postal Union signed at Washington, June 15, 1897.

Conventions and agreements of the Postal Union signed at Rome, May 26, 1906.

Telegraphic Conventions:

International Telegraphic Conventions signed at St. Petersburg July 10/22, 1875.

Regulations and Tariffs drawn up by the International Telegraphic Conference, Lisbon, June 11, 1908.

Germany undertakes not to refuse her assent to the conclusion by the new States of the special arrangements referred to in the conventions and agreements relating to the Universal Postal Union and to the International Telegraphic Union, to which the said new States have adhered or may adhere.

ART. 284. From the coming into force of the present Treaty the High Contracting Parties shall apply, in so far as concerns them, the International Radio-Telegraphic Convention of July 5, 1912, on condition that Germany fulfils the provisional regulations which will be indicated to her by the Allied and Associated Powers.

If within five years after the coming into force of the present Treaty a new convention regulating international radio-telegraphic communications should have been concluded to take the place of the Convention of July 5, 1912, this new convention shall bind Germany, even if Germany should refuse either to take part in drawing up the convention, or to subscribe thereto.

This new convention will likewise replace the provisional regulations in force.

ART. 285. From the coming into force of the present Treaty, the High Contracting Parties shall apply in so far as concerns them and under the conditions stipulated in Article 272, the conventions hereinafter mentioned:

(1) The Conventions of May 6, 1882, and February 1, 1889, regulating the fisheries in the North Sea outside territorial waters.

(2) The Conventions and Protocols of November 16, 1887, February 14, 1893, and April 11, 1894, regarding the North Sea liquor traffic.

ART. 286. The International Convention of Paris of March 20, 1883, for the protection of industrial property, revised at Washington on June 2, 1911; and the International Convention of Berne of September 9, 1886, for the protection of literary and artistic works, revised at Berlin on November 13, 1908, and completed by the additional Protocol signed at Berne on March 20, 1914, will again come into effect as from the coming into force of the present Treaty, in so far as they are not affected or modified by the exceptions and restrictions resulting therefrom.

ART. 287. From the coming into force of the present Treaty the High Contracting Parties shall apply, in so far as concerns them, the convention of The Hague of July 17, 1905, relating to civil procedure. This renewal, however, will not apply to France, Portugal and Roumania.

ART. 288. The special rights and privileges granted to Germany by Article 3 of the Convention of December 2, 1899, relating to Samoa shall be considered to have terminated on August 4, 1914.

ART. 289. Each of the Allied or Associated Powers, being guided by the general principles or special provisions of the present Treaty, shall notify to Germany the bilateral treaties or conventions which such Allied or Associated Power wishes to revive with Germany.

The notification referred to in the present Article shall be made either directly or through the intermediary of another Power. Receipt thereof shall be acknowledged in writing by Germany. The date of the revival shall be that of the notification.

The Allied and Associated Powers undertake among themselves not to revive with Germany any conventions or treaties which are not in accordance with the terms of the present Treaty.

The notification shall mention any provisions of the said conventions and treaties which, not being in accordance with the terms of the present Treaty, shall not be considered as revived.

In case of any difference of opinion, the League of Nations will be called on to decide.

A period of six months from the coming into force of the present Treaty is allowed to the Allied and Associated Powers within which to make the notification.

Only those bilateral treaties and conventions which have been the subject of such a notification shall be revived between the Allied and

Associated Powers and Germany; all the others are and shall remain abrogated.

The above regulations apply to all bilateral treaties or conventions existing between all the Allied and Associated Powers signatories to the present Treaty and Germany, even if the said Allied and Associated Powers have not been in a state of war with Germany.

ART. 290-294.

ART. 295. Those of the High Contracting Parties who have not yet signed, or who have signed but not yet ratified, the Opium Convention signed at The Hague on January 23, 1912, agree to bring the said Convention into force, and for this purpose to enact the necessary legislation without delay and in any case within a period of twelve months from the coming into force of the present Treaty.

Furthermore, they agree that ratification of the present Treaty should in the case of Powers which have not yet ratified the Opium Convention be deemed in all respects equivalent to the ratification of that Convention and to the signature of the Special Protocol which was opened at The Hague in accordance with the resolutions adopted by the Third Opium Conference in 1914 for bringing the said Convention into force.

For this purpose the Government of the French Republic will communicate to the Government of the Netherlands a certified copy of the protocol of the deposit of ratifications of the present Treaty, and will invite the Government of the Netherlands to accept and deposit the said certified copy as if it were a deposit of ratifications of the Opium Convention and a signature of the Additional Protocol of 1914.

SECTION III.

DEBTS.

ART. 296.

SECTION IV.

PROPERTY, RIGHTS AND INTERESTS.

ART. 297–298.

Section V.
CONTRACTS, PRESCRIPTIONS, JUDGMENTS.
Art. 299–303.

Section VI.
MIXED ARBITRAL TRIBUNAL.

Art. 304. (a) Within three months from the date of the coming into force of the present Treaty, a Mixed Arbitral Tribunal shall be established between each of the Allied and Associated Powers on the one hand and Germany on the other hand. Each such Tribunal shall consist of three members. Each of the Governments concerned shall appoint one of these members. The President shall be chosen by agreement between the two Governments concerned.

In case of failure to reach agreement, the President of the Tribunal and two other persons either of whom may in case of need take his place, shall be chosen by the Council of the League of Nations, or, until this is set up, by M. Gustave Ador if he is willing. These persons shall be nationals of Powers that have remained neutral during the war.

If any Government does not proceed within a period of one month in case there is a vacancy to appoint a member of the Tribunal, such member shall be chosen by the other Government from the two persons mentioned above other than the President.

The decision of the majority of the members of the Tribunal shall be the decision of the Tribunal.

(b) The Mixed Arbitral Tribunals established pursuant to paragraph (a), shall decide all questions within their competence under Sections III, IV, V and VII.

In addition, all questions, whatsoever their nature, relating to contracts concluded before the coming into force of the present Treaty between nationals of the Allied and Associated Powers and German nationals shall be decided by the Mixed Arbitral Tribunal, always excepting questions which, under the laws of the Allied,

Associated or Neutral Powers, are within the jurisdiction of the National Courts of those Powers. Such questions shall be decided by the National Courts in question, to the exclusion of the Mixed Arbitral Tribunal. The party who is a national of an Allied or Associated Power may nevertheless bring the case before the Mixed Arbitral Tribunal if this is not prohibited by the laws of his country.

(c) If the number of cases justifies it, additional members shall be appointed and each Mixed Arbitral Tribunal shall sit in divisions. Each of these divisions will be constituted as above.

(d) Each Mixed Arbitral Tribunal will settle its own procedure except in so far as it is provided in the following Annex, and is empowered to award the sums to be paid by the loser in respect of the costs and expenses of the proceedings.

(e) Each Government will pay the remuneration of the member of the Mixed Arbitral Tribunal appointed by it and of any agent whom it may appoint to represent it before the Tribunal. The remuneration of the President will be determined by special agreement between the Governments concerned; and this remuneration and the joint expenses of each Tribunal will be paid by the two Governments in equal moieties.

(f) The High Contracting Parties agree that their courts and authorities shall render to the Mixed Arbitral Tribunals direct all the assistance in their power, particularly as regards transmitting notices and collecting evidence.

(g) The High Contracting Parties agree to regard the decisions of the Mixed Arbitral Tribunal as final and conclusive, and to render them binding upon their nationals.

ART. 305. Whenever a competent court has given or gives a decision in a case covered by Sections III, IV, V or VII, and such decision is inconsistent with the provisions of such Sections, the party who is prejudiced by the decision shall be entitled to obtain redress which shall be fixed by the Mixed Arbitral Tribunal. At the request of the national of an Allied or Associated Power, the redress may, whenever possible, be effected by the Mixed Arbitral Tribunal directing the replacement of the parties in the position occupied by them before the judgment was given by the German court.

Section VII.
INDUSTRIAL PROPERTY.
Art. 306–311.

Section VIII.
SOCIAL AND STATE INSURANCE IN CEDED TERRITORY.

Art. 312. Without prejudice to the provisions contained in other Articles of the present Treaty, the German Government undertakes to transfer to any Power to which German territory in Europe is ceded, and to any Power administering former German territory as a mandatory under Article 22 of Part I (League of Nations), such portion of the reserves accumulated by the Government of the German Empire or of German States, or by public or private organisations under their control, as is attributable to the carrying on of Social or State Insurance in such territory.

The Powers to which these funds are transferred must apply them to the performance of the obligations arising from such insurances.

The conditions of the transfer will be determined by special conventions to be concluded between the German Government and the Governments concerned.

In case these special conventions are not concluded in accordance with the above paragraph within three months after the coming into force of the present Treaty, the conditions of transfer shall in each case be referred to a Commission of five members, one of whom shall be appointed by the German Government, one by the other interested Government and three by the Governing Body of the International Labour Office from the nationals of other States. This Commission shall by majority vote within three months after appointment adopt recommendations for submission to the Council of the League of Nations, and the decisions of the Council shall forthwith be accepted as final by Germany and the other Government concerned

PART XI.

AERIAL NAVIGATION.

ART. 313. The aircraft of the Allied and Associated Powers shall have full liberty of passage and landing over and in the territory and territorial waters of Germany, and shall enjoy the same privileges as German aircraft, particularly in case of distress by land or sea.

ART. 314. The aircraft of the Allied and Associated Powers shall, while in transit to any foreign country whatever, enjoy the right of flying over the territory and territorial waters of Germany without landing, subject always to any regulations which may be made by Germany, and which shall be applicable equally to the aircraft of Germany and to those of the Allied and Associated countries.

ART. 315. All aerodromes in Germany open to national public traffic shall be open for the aircraft of the Allied and Associated Powers, and in any such aerodrome such aircraft shall be treated on a footing of equality with German aircraft as regards charges of every description, including charges for landing and accommodation.

ART. 316. Subject to the present provisions, the rights of passage, transit and landing, provided for in Articles 313, 314 and 315, are subject to the observance of such regulations as Germany may consider it necessary to enact, but such regulations shall be applied without distinction to German aircraft and to those of the Allied and Associated countries.

ART. 317–319.

ART. 320. The obligations imposed by the preceding provisions shall remain in force until January 1, 1923, unless before that date Germany shall have been admitted into the League of Nations or shall have been authorised, by consent of the Allied and Associated Powers, to adhere to the Convention relative to Aerial Navigation concluded between those Powers.

PART XII.

PORTS, WATERWAYS AND RAILWAYS.

Section I.
GENERAL PROVISIONS.

Art. 321. Germany undertakes to grant freedom of transit through her territories on the routes most convenient for international transit, either by rail, navigable waterway, or canal, to persons, goods, vessels, carriages, wagons and mails coming from or going to the territories of any of the Allied and Associated Powers (whether contiguous or not); for this purpose the crossing of territorial waters shall be allowed. Such persons, goods, vessels, carriages, wagons and mails shall not be subjected to any transit duty or to any undue delays or restrictions, and shall be entitled in Germany to national treatment as regards charges, facilities, and all other matters.

Goods in transit shall be exempt from all Customs or other similar duties.

All charges imposed on transport in transit shall be reasonable, having regard to the conditions of the traffic. No charge, facility or restriction shall depend directly or indirectly on the ownership or on the nationality of the ship or other means of transport on which any part of the through journey has been, or is to be, accomplished.

Art. 322. Germany undertakes neither to impose nor to maintain any control over transmigration traffic through her territories beyond measures necessary to ensure that passengers are *bonâ fide* in transit; nor to allow any shipping company or any other private body, corporation or person interested in the traffic to take any part whatever in, or to exercise any direct or indirect influence over, any administrative service that may be necessary for this purpose.

Art. 323. Germany undertakes to make no discrimination or preference, direct or indirect, in the duties, charges and prohibitions relating to importations into or exportations from her territories, or, subject to the special engagements contained in the present Treaty, in the charges and conditions of transport of goods or persons entering or leaving her territories, based on the frontier crossed; or on the kind, ownership or flag of the means of transport (including aircraft) employed; or on the original or immediate place of departure of the vessel, wagon or aircraft or other means of transport employed, or its ultimate or intermediate destination; or on the route of or places of trans-shipment on the journey; or on whether any port through which the goods are imported or exported is a German port or a port belonging to any foreign country or on whether the goods are imported or exported by sea, by land or by air.

Germany particularly undertakes not to establish against the ports and vessels of any of the Allied and Associated Powers any surtax or any direct or indirect bounty for export or import by German ports or vessels, or by those of another Power, for example by means of combined tariffs. She further undertakes that persons or goods passing through a port or using a vessel of any of the Allied and Associated Powers shall not be subjected to any formality or delay whatever to which such persons or goods would not be subjected if they passed through a German port or a port of any other Power, or used a German vessel or a vessel of any other Power.

ART. 324. All necessary administrative and technical measures shall be taken to shorten, as much as possible, the transmission of goods across the German frontiers and to ensure their forwarding and transport from such frontiers, irrespective of whether such goods are coming from or going to the territories of the Allied and Associated Powers or are in transit from or to those territories, under the same material conditions in such matters as rapidity of carriage and care *en route* as are enjoyed by other goods of the same kind carried on German territory under similar conditions of transport.

In particular, the transport of perishable goods shall be promptly and regularly carried out, and the customs formalities shall be effected in such a way as to allow the goods to be carried straight through by trains which make connection.

ART. 325. The seaports of the Allied and Associated Powers are entitled to all favours and to all reduced tariffs granted on German railways or navigable waterways for the benefit of German ports or of any port of another Power.

ART. 326. Germany may not refuse to participate in the tariffs or combinations of tariffs intended to secure for ports of any of the Allied and Associated Powers advantages similar to those granted by Germany to her own ports or the ports of any other Power.

Section II.
NAVIGATION.

Chapter I.
Freedom of Navigation.

ART. 327. The nationals of any of the Allied and Associated Powers as well as their vessels and property shall enjoy in all German ports and on the inland navigation routes of Germany the same treatment in all respects as German nationals, vessels and property.

In particular the vessels of any one of the Allied or Associated Powers shall be entitled to transport goods of any description, and passengers, to or from any ports or places in German territory to which German vessels may have access, under conditions which shall not be more onerous than those applied in the case of national vessels; they shall be treated on a footing of equality with national vessels as regards port and harbour facilities and charges of every description, including facilities for stationing, loading and unloading, and duties and charges of tonnage, harbour, pilotage, lighthouse, quarantine, and all analogous duties and charges of whatsoever nature, levied in the name of or for the profit of the Government, public functionaries, private individuals, corporations or establishments of any kind.

In the event of Germany granting a preferential régime to any of the Allied or Associated Powers or to any other foreign Power, this régime shall be extended immediately and unconditionally to all the Allied and Associated Powers.

There shall be no impediment to the movement of persons or vessels other than those arising from prescriptions concerning customs, police, sanitation, emigration and immigration, and those relating to the import and export of prohibited goods. Such regulations must be reasonable and uniform and must not impede traffic unnecessarily.

Chapter II.

FREE ZONES IN PORTS.

Art. 328–330.

Chapter III.

CLAUSES RELATING TO THE ELBE, THE ODER, THE NIEMEN (RUSSSTROMMEMEL-NIEMEN) AND THE DANUBE.

(1)—*General Clauses.*

Art. 331. The following rivers are declared international:

the Elbe (*Labe*) from its confluence with the Vltava (*Moldau*), and the Vltava (*Moldau*) from Prague;

the Oder (*Odra*) from its confluence with the Oppa;

the Nieman (*Russstrom-Memel-Niemen*) from Grodno;

the Danube from Ulm;

and all navigable parts of these river systems which naturally provide more than one State with access to the sea, with or without transshipment from one vessel to another; together with lateral canals and channels constructed either to duplicate or to improve naturally navigable sections of the specified systems, or to connect two naturally navigable sections of the same river.

The same shall apply to the Rhine-Danube navigable waterway, should such a waterway be constructed under the conditions laid down in Article 353.

Art. 332. On the waterways declared to be international in the preceding Article, the nationals, property and flags of all Powers shall be treated on a footing of perfect equality, no distinction being made to the detriment of the nationals, property or flag of any

Power between them and the nationals, property or flag of the riparian State itself or of the most favoured nation.

Nevertheless, German vessels shall not be entitled to carry passengers or goods by regular services between the ports of any Allied or Associated Power, without special authority from such Power.

ART. 333. Where such charges are not precluded by any existing conventions, charges varying on different sections of a river may be levied on vessels using the navigable channels or their approaches, provided that they are intended solely to cover equitably the cost of maintaining in a navigable condition, or of improving, the river and its approaches, or to meet expenditure incurred in the interests of navigation. The schedule of such charges shall be calculated on the basis of such expenditure and shall be posted up in the ports. These charges shall be levied in such a manner as to render any detailed examination of cargoes unnecessary, except in cases of suspected fraud or contravention.

ART. 334. The transit of vessels, passengers and goods on these waterways shall be effected in accordance with the general conditions prescribed for transit in Section I above.

When the two banks of an international river are within the same State goods in transit may be placed under seal or in the custody of customs agents. When the river forms a frontier goods and passengers in transit shall be exempt from all customs formalities; the loading and unloading of goods, and the embarkation and disembarkation of passengers, shall only take place in the ports specified by the riparian State.

ART. 335. No dues of any kind other than those provided for in the present Part shall be levied along the course or at the mouth of these rivers.

This provision shall not prevent the fixing by the riparian States of customs, local octroi or consumption duties, or the creation of reasonable and uniform charges levied in the ports, in accordance with public tariffs, for the use of cranes, elevators, quays, warehouses, etc.

ART. 336. In default of any special organisation for carrying out the works connected with the upkeep and improvement of the international portion of a navigable system, each riparian State shall be bound to take suitable measures to remove any obstacle or danger to navigation and to ensure the maintenance of good conditions of navigation.

If a State neglects to comply with this obligation any riparian State, or any State represented on the International Commission, if there is one, may appeal to the tribunal instituted for this purpose by the League of Nations.

ART. 337. The same procedure shall be followed in the case of a riparian State undertaking any works of a nature to impede navigation in the international section. The tribunal mentioned in the preceding Article shall be entitled to enforce the suspension or suppression of such works, making due allowance in its decisions for all rights in connection with irrigation, water-power, fisheries, and other national interests, which, with the consent of all the riparian States or of all the States represented on the International Commission, if there is one, shall be given priority over the requirements of navigation.

Appeal to the tribunal of the League of Nations does not require the suspension of the works.

ART. 338. The régime set out in Articles 332 to 337 above shall be superseded by one to be laid down in a General Convention drawn up by the Allied and Associated Powers, and approved by the League of Nations, relating to the waterways recognised in such Convention as having an international character. This Convention shall apply in particular to the whole or part of the above-mentioned river systems of the Elbe (*Labe*), the Oder (*Odra*), the Niemen (*Russstrom-Memel-Niemen*), and the Danube, and such other parts of these river systems as may be covered by a general definition.

Germany undertakes, in accordance with the provisions of Article 379, to adhere to the said General Convention as well as to all projects prepared in accordance with Article 343 below for the revision of existing international agreements and regulations.

ART. 339. Germany shall cede to the Allied and Associated

Powers concerned, within a maximum period of three months from the date on which notification shall be given her, a proportion of the tugs and vessels remaining registered in the ports of the river systems referred to in Article 331 after the deduction of those surrendered by way of restitution or reparation. Germany shall in the same way cede material of all kinds necessary to the Allied and Associated Powers concerned for the utilisation of those river systems.

The number of the tugs and boats, and the amount of the material so ceded, and their distribution, shall be determined by an arbitrator or arbitrators nominated by the United States of America, due regard being had to the legitimate needs of the parties concerned, and particularly to the shipping traffic during the five years preceding the war.

All craft so ceded shall be provided with their fittings and gear, shall be in a good state of repair and in condition to carry goods, and shall be selected from among those most recently built.

The cessions provided for in the present Article shall entail a credit of which the total amount, settled in a lump sum by the arbitrator or arbitrators, shall not in any case exceed the value of the capital expended in the initial establishment of the material ceded, and shall be set off against the total sums due from Germany; in consequence, the indemnification of the proprietors shall be a matter for Germany to deal with.

(2) *Special Clauses relating to the Elbe, the Oder and the Niemen (Russstrom-Memel-Niemen).*

ART. 340. The Elbe (*Labe*) shall be placed under the administration of an International Commission which shall comprise:

4 representatives of the German States bordering on the river;
2 representatives of the Czecho-Slovak State;
1 representative of Great Britain;
1 representative of France;
1 representative of Italy;
1 representative of Belgium.

Whatever be the number of members present, each delegation shall have the right to record a number of votes equal to the number of representatives allotted to it.

If certain of these representatives cannot be appointed at the time of the coming into force of the present Treaty, the decisions of the Commission shall nevertheless be valid.

ART. 341. The Oder (*Odra*) shall be placed under the administration of an International Commission, which shall comprise:

1 representative of Poland;
3 representatives of Prussia;
1 representative of the Czecho-Slovak State;
1 representative of Great Britain;
1 representative of France;
1 representative of Denmark;
1 representative of Sweden.

If certain of these representatives cannot be appointed at the time of the coming into force of the present Treaty, the decisions of the Commission shall nevertheless be valid.

ART. 342. On a request being made to the League of Nations by any riparian State, the Niemen (*Russstrom-Memel-Niemen*) shall be placed under the administration of an International Commission, which shall comprise one representative of each riparian State, and three representatives of other States specified by the League of Nations.

ART. 343. The International Commissions referred to in Articles 340 and 341 shall meet within three months of the date of the coming into force of the present Treaty. The International Commission referred to in Article 342 shall meet within three months from the date of the request made by a riparian State. Each of these Commissions shall proceed immediately to prepare a project for the revision of the existing international agreements and regulations, drawn up in conformity with the General Convention referred to in Article 338, should such Convention have been already concluded. In the absence of such Convention, the project for revision shall be in conformity with the principles of Articles 332 to 337 above.

Art. 344. The projects referred to in the preceding Article shall, *inter alia*:

(a) designate the headquarters of the International Commission, and prescribe the manner in which its President is to be nominated;

(b) specify the extent of the Commission's powers, particularly in regard to the execution of works of maintenance, control, and improvement on the river system, the financial régime, the fixing and collection of charges, and regulations for navigation;

(c) define the sections of the river or its tributaries to which the international régime shall be applied.

Art. 345. The international agreements and regulations at present governing the navigation of the Elbe (*Labe*), the Oder (*Odra*), and the Niemen (*Russstrom-Memel-Niemen*) shall be provisionally maintained in force until the ratification of the above-mentioned projects. Nevertheless, in all cases where such agreements and regulations in force are in conflict with the provisions of Articles 332 to 337 above, or of the General Convention to be concluded, the latter provisions shall prevail.

(3) *Special Clauses relating to the Danube.*

Art. 346. The European Commission of the Danube reassumes the powers it possessed before the war. Nevertheless, as a provisional measure, only representatives of Great Britain, France, Italy and Roumania shall constitute this Commission.

Art. 347. From the point where the competence of the European Commission ceases, the Danube system referred to in Article 331 shall be placed under the administration of an International Commission composed as follows:

2 representatives of German riparian States;

1 representative of each other riparian State;

1 representative of each non-riparian State represented in the future on the European Commission of the Danube.

If certain of these representatives cannot be appointed at the time of the coming into force of the present Treaty, the decisions of the Commission shall nevertheless be valid.

ART. 348. The International Commission provided for in the preceding Article shall meet as soon as possible after the coming into force of the present Treaty, and shall undertake provisionally the administration of the river in conformity with the provisions of Articles 332 to 337, until such time as a definitive statute regarding the Danube is concluded by the Powers nominated by the Allied and Associated Powers.

ART. 349. Germany agrees to accept the régime which shall be laid down for the Danube by a Conference of the Powers nominated by the Allied and Associated Powers, which shall meet within one year after the coming into force of the present Treaty, and at which German representatives may be present.

ART. 350. The Mandate given by Article 57 of the Treaty of Berlin of July 13, 1878, to Austria-Hungary, and transferred by her to Hungary, to carry out works at the Iron Gates, is abrogated. The Commission entrusted with the administration of this part of the river shall lay down provisions for the settlement of accounts subject to the financial provisions of the present Treaty. Charges which may be necessary shall in no case be levied by Hungary.

ART. 351. Should the Czecho-Slovak State, the Serb-Croat-Slovene State or Roumania, with the authorisation of or under mandate from the International Commission, undertake maintenance, improvement, weir, or other works on a part of the river system which forms a frontier, these States shall enjoy on the opposite bank, and also on the part of the bed which is outside their territory, all necessary facilities for the survey, execution and maintenance of such works.

ART. 352. Germany shall be obliged to make to the European Commission of the Danube all restitutions, reparations and indemnities for damages inflicted on the Commission during the war.

ART. 353. Should a deep-draught Rhine-Danube navigable waterway be constructed, Germany undertakes to apply thereto the régime prescribed in Articles 332 to 338.

Chapter IV.

CLAUSES RELATING TO THE RHINE AND THE MOSELLE.

ART. 354. As from the coming into force of the present Treaty, the Convention of Mannheim of October 17, 1868, together with the Final Protocol thereof, shall continue to govern navigation on the Rhine, subject to the conditions hereinafter laid down.

In the event of any provisions of the said Convention being in conflict with those laid down by the General Convention referred to in Article 338 (which shall apply to the Rhine) the provisions of the General Convention shall prevail.

Within a maximum period of six months from the coming into force of the present Treaty, the Central Commission referred to in Article 355 shall meet to draw up a project of revision of the Convention of Mannheim. This project shall be drawn up in harmony with the provisions of the General Convention referred to above, should this have been concluded by that time, and shall be submitted to the Powers represented on the Central Commission. Germany hereby agrees to adhere to the project so drawn up.

Further, the modifications set out in the following Articles shall immediately be made in the Convention of Mannheim.

The Allied and Associated Powers reserve to themselves the right to arrive at an understanding in this connection with Holland, and Germany hereby agrees to accede if required to any such understanding.

ART. 355. The Central Commission provided for in the Convention of Mannheim shall consist of nineteen members, viz.:

2 representatives of the Netherlands;
2 representatives of Switzerland;
4 representatives of German riparian States;
4 representatives of France, which in addition shall appoint the President of the Commission;
2 representatives of Great Britain;
2 representatives of Italy;
2 representatives of Belgium.

The headquarters of the Central Commission shall be at Strassburg.

Whatever be the number of members present, each Delegation shall have the right to record a number of votes equal to the number of representatives allotted to it.

If certain of these representatives cannot be appointed at the time of the coming into force of the present Treaty, the decisions of the Commission shall nevertheless be valid.

ART. 356. Vessels of all nations, and their cargoes, shall have the same rights and privileges as those which are granted to vessels belonging to the Rhine navigation, and to their cargoes.

None of the provisions contained in Articles 15 to 20 and 26 of the above-mentioned Convention of Mannheim, in Article 4 of the Final Protocol thereof, or in later Conventions, shall impede the free navigation of vessels and crews of all nations on the Rhine and on waterways to which such Conventions apply, subject to compliance with the regulations concerning pilotage and other police measures drawn up by the Central Commission.

The provisions of Article 22 of the Convention of Mannheim and of Article 5 of the Final Protocol thereof shall be applied only to vessels registered on the Rhine. The Central Commission shall decide on the steps to be taken to ensure that other vessels satisfy the conditions of the general regulations applying to navigation on the Rhine.

ART. 357. Within a maximum period of three months from the date on which notification shall be given, Germany shall cede to France tugs and vessels, from among those remaining registered in German Rhine ports after the deduction of those surrendered by way of restitution or reparation, or shares in German Rhine navigation companies.

When vessels and tugs are ceded, such vessels and tugs, together with their fittings and gear, shall be in good state of repair, shall be in condition to carry on commercial traffic on the Rhine, and shall be selected from among those most recently built.

The same procedure shall be followed in the matter of the cession by Germany to France of:

(1) the installations, berthing and anchorage accommodation, platforms, docks, warehouses, plant, etc., which German subjects or German companies owned on August 1, 1914, in the port of Rotterdam, and

(2) the shares or interests which Germany or German nationals possessed in such installations at the same date.

The amount and specifications of such cessions shall be determined within one year of the coming into force of the present Treaty by an arbitrator or arbitrators appointed by the United States of America, due regard being had to the legitimate needs of the parties concerned.

The cessions provided for in the present Article shall entail a credit of which the total amount, settled in a lump sum by the arbitrator or arbitrators mentioned above, shall not in any case exceed the value of the capital expended in the initial establishment of the ceded material and installations, and shall be set off against the total sums due from Germany; in consequence, the indemnification of the proprietors shall be a matter for Germany to deal with.

ART. 358. Subject to the obligation to comply with the provisions of the Convention of Mannheim or of the Convention which may be substituted therefor, and to the stipulations of the present Treaty, France shall have on the whole course of the Rhine included between the two extreme points of the French frontiers:

(a) the right to take water from the Rhine to feed navigation and irrigation canals (constructed or to be constructed) or for any other purpose, and to execute on the German bank all works necessary for the exercise of this right;

(b) the exclusive right to the power derived from works of regulation on the river, subject to the payment to Germany of the value of half the power actually produced, this payment, which will take into account the cost of the works necessary for producing the power, being made either in money or in power and in default of agreement being determined by arbitration. For this purpose France alone shall have the right to carry out in this part of the river all works of regulation (weirs or other works) which she may consider necessary for the production of power. Similarly, the right of taking water from the Rhine is accorded to Belgium to feed the Rhine-Meuse navigable waterway provided for below.

The exercise of the rights mentioned under (*a*) and (*b*) of the present Article shall not inferfere with navigability nor reduce the facilities for navigation, either in the bed of the Rhine or in the derivations which may be substituted therefor, nor shall it involve any increase in the tolls formerly levied under the Convention in force. All proposed schemes shall be laid before the Central Commission in order that that Commission may assure itself that these conditions are complied with.

To ensure the proper and faithful execution of the provisions contained in (*a*) and (*b*) above, Germany:

(1) binds herself not to undertake or to allow the construction of any lateral canal or any derivation on the right bank of the river opposite the French frontiers;

(2) recognises the possession by France of the right of support on and the right of way over all lands situated on the right bank which may be required in order to survey, to build, and to operate weirs which France, with the consent of the Central Commission, may subsequently decide to establish. In accordance with such consent, France shall be entitled to decide upon and fix the limits of the necessary sites, and she shall be permitted to occupy such lands after a period of two months after simple notification, subject to the payment by her to Germany of indemnities of which the total amount shall be fixed by the Central Commission. Germany shall make it her business to indemnify the proprietors whose property will be burdened with such servitudes or permanently occupied by the works.

Should Switzerland so demand, and if the Central Commission approves, the same rights shall be accorded to Switzerland for the part of the river forming her frontier with other riparian States;

(3) shall hand over to the French Government, during the month following the coming into force of the present Treaty, all projects,

designs, drafts of concessions and of specifications concerning the regulation of the Rhine for any purpose whatever which have been drawn up or received by the Governments of Alsace-Lorraine or of the Grand Duchy of Baden.

ART. 359. Subject to the preceding provisions, no works shall be carried out in the bed or on either bank of the Rhine where it forms the boundary of France and Germany without the previous approval of the Central Commission or of its agents.

ART. 360. France reserves the option of substituting herself as regards the rights and obligations resulting from agreements arrived at between the Government of Alsace-Lorraine and the Grand Duchy of Baden concerning the works to be carried out on the Rhine; she may also denounce such agreements within a term of five years dating from the coming into force of the present Treaty.

France shall also have the option of causing works to be carried out which may be recognized as necessary by the Central Commission for the upkeep or improvement of the navigability of the Rhine above Mannheim.

ART. 361. Should Belgium within a period of 25 years from the coming into force of the present Treaty decide to create a deep-draught Rhine-Meuse navigable waterway, in the region of Ruhrort, Germany shall be bound to construct, in accordance with plans to be communicated to her by the Belgian Government, after agreement with the Central Commission, the portion of this navigable waterway situated within her territory.

The Belgian Government shall, for this purpose, have the right to carry out on the ground all necessary surveys.

Should Germany fail to carry out all or part of these works, the Central Commission shall be entitled to carry them out instead; and, for this purpose, the Commission may decide upon and fix the limits of the necessary sites and occupy the ground after a period of two months after simple notification, subject to the payment of indemnities to be fixed by it and paid by Germany.

This navigable waterway shall be placed under the same

administrative régime as the Rhine itself, and the division of the cost of initial construction, including the above indemnities, among the States crossed thereby shall be made by the Central Commission.

ART. 362. Germany hereby agrees to offer no objection to any proposals of the Central Rhine Commission for extending its jurisdiction:

(1) to the Moselle below the Franco-Luxemburg frontier down to the Rhine, subject to the consent of Luxemburg;

(2) to the Rhine above Basle up to the Lake of Constance, subject to the consent of Switzerland;

(3) to the lateral canals and channels which may be established either to duplicate or to improve naturally navigable sections of the Rhine or the Moselle, or to connect two naturally navigable sections of these rivers, and also any other parts of the Rhine river system which may be covered by the General Convention provided for in Article 338 above.

Chapter V.

Clauses giving to the Czecho-Slovak State the use of Northern ports.

ART. 363. In the ports of Hamburg and Stettin Germany shall lease to the Czecho-Slovak State, for a period of 99 years, areas which shall be placed under the general régime of free zones and shall be used for the direct transit of goods coming from or going to that State.

ART. 364. The delimitation of these areas, and their equipment, their exploitation, and in general all conditions for their utilisation, including the amount of the rental, shall be decided by a Commission consisting of one delegate of Germany, one delegate of the Czecho-Slovak State and one delegate of Great Britain. These conditions shall be susceptible of revision every ten years in the same manner.

Germany declares in advance that she will adhere to the decisions so taken.

Section III.

RAILWAYS.

Chapter I.

CLAUSES RELATING TO INTERNATIONAL TRANSPORT.

Art. 365-369.

Chapter II.

ROLLING-STOCK.

Art. 370.

Chapter III.

CESSIONS OF RAILWAY LINES.

Art. 371.

Chapter IV.

PROVISIONS RELATING TO CERTAIN RAILWAY LINES.

Art. 372-374.

Chapter V.

TRANSITORY PROVISIONS

Art. 375.

Section IV.

DISPUTES.

AND REVISION OF PERMANENT CLAUSES.

Art. 376. Disputes which may arise between interested Powers with regard to the interpretation and application of the preceding Articles shall be settled as provided by the League of Nations.

Art. 377. At any time the League of Nations may recommend the revision of such of these Articles as relate to a permanent administrative régime.

APPENDIX

ART. 378. The stipulations in Articles 321 to 330, 332, 365, and 367 to 369 shall be subject to revision by the Council of the League of Nations at any time after five years from the coming into force of the present Treaty.

Failing such revision, no Allied or Associated Power can claim after the expiration of the above period of five years the benefit of any of the stipulations in the Articles enumerated above on behalf of any portion of its territories in which reciprocity is not accorded in respect of such stipulations. The period of five years during which reciprocity cannot be demanded may be prolonged by the Council of the League of Nations.

Section V.

SPECIAL PROVISION.

ART. 379. Without prejudice to the special obligations imposed on her by the present Treaty for the benefit of the Allied and Associated Powers, Germany undertakes to adhere to any General Conventions regarding the international régime of transit, waterways, ports or railways which may be concluded by the Allied and Associated Powers, with the approval of the League of Nations, within five years of the coming into force of the present Treaty.

Section VI.

CAUSES RELATING TO THE KIEL CANAL.

ART. 380. The Kiel Canal and its approaches shall be maintained free and open to the vessels of commerce and of war of all nations at peace with Germany on terms of entire equality.

ART. 381. The nationals, property and vessels of all Powers shall, in respect of charges, facilities, and in all other respects, be treated on a footing of perfect equality in the use of the Canal, no distinction being made to the detriment of nationals, property and vessels of any Power between them and the nationals, property and vessels of Germany or of the most favoured nation.

No impediment shall be placed on the movement of persons or

vessels other than those arising out of police, customs, sanitary, emigration or immigration regulations and those relating to the import or export of prohibited goods. Such regulations must be reasonable and uniform and must not unnecessarily impede traffic.

ART. 382. Only such charges may be levied on vessels using the Canal or its approaches as are intended to cover in an equitable manner the cost of maintaining in a navigable condition, or of improving, the Canal or its approaches, or to meet expenses incurred in the interests of navigation. The schedule of such charges shall be calculated on the basis of such expenses, and shall be posted up in the ports.

These charges shall be levied in such a manner as to render any detailed examination of cargoes unnecessary, except in the case of suspected fraud or contravention.

ART. 383. Goods in transit may be placed under seal or in the custody of customs agents; the loading and unloading of goods, and the embarkation and disembarkation of passengers, shall only take place in the ports specified by Germany.

ART. 384. No charges of any kind other than those provided for in the present Treaty shall be levied along the course or at the approaches of the Kiel Canal.

ART. 385. Germany shall be bound to take suitable measures to remove any obstacle or danger to navigation, and to ensure the maintenance of good conditions of navigation. She shall not undertake any works of a nature to impede navigation on the Canal or its approaches.

ART. 386. In the event of violation of any of the conditions of Articles 380 to 386, or of disputes as to the interpretation of these Articles, any interested Power can appeal to the jurisdiction instituted for the purpose by the League of Nations.

In order to avoid reference of small questions to the League of Nations, Germany will establish a local authority at Kiel qualified to deal with disputes in the first instance and to give satisfaction so far as possible to complaints which may be presented through the consular representatives of the interested Powers.

PART XIII.

LABOUR

SECTION I.

ORGANISATION OF LABOUR.

Whereas the League of Nations has for its object the establishment of universal peace, and such a peace can be established only if it is based upon social justice;

And whereas conditions of labour exist involving such injustice, hardship and privation to large numbers of people as to produce unrest so great that the peace and harmony of the world are imperilled; and an improvement of those conditions is urgently required: as, for example, by the regulation of the hours of work, including the establishment of a maximum working day and week, the regulation of the labour supply, the prevention of unemployment, the provision of an adequate living wage, the protection of the worker against sickness, disease and injury arising out of his employment, the protection of children, young persons and women, provision for old age and injury, protection of the interests of workers when employed in countries other than their own, recognition of the principle of freedom of association, the organisation of vocational and technical education and other measures;

Whereas also the failure of any nation to adopt humane conditions of labour is an obstacle in the way of other nations which desire to improve the conditions in their own countries;

The HIGH CONTRACTING PARTIES, moved by sentiments of justice and humanity as well as by the desire to secure the permanent peace of the world, agree to the following:

CHAPTER I.

ORGANISATION.

ART. 387. A permanent organisation is hereby established for the promotion of the objects set forth in the Preamble.

The original Members of the League of Nations shall be the

original Members of this organisation, and hereafter membership of the League of Nations shall carry with it membership of the said organisation.

ART. 388. The permanent organisation shall consist of:

(1) a General Conference of Representatives of the Members and,

(2) an International Labour Office controlled by the Governing Body described in Article 393.

ART. 389. The meetings of the General Conference of Representatives of the Members shall be held from time to time as occasion may require, and at least once in every year. It shall be composed of four Representatives of each of the Members, of whom two shall be Government Delegates and the two others shall be Delegates representing respectively the employers and the workpeople of each of the Members.

Each Delegate may be accompanied by advisers, who shall not exceed two in number for each item on the agenda of the meeting. When questions specially affecting women are to be considered by the Conference, one at least of the advisers should be a woman.

The Members undertake to nominate non-Government Delegates and advisers chosen in agreement with the industrial organisations, if such organisations exist, which are most representative of employers or workpeople, as the case may be, in their respective countries.

Advisers shall not speak except on a request made by the Delegate whom they accompany and by the special authorization of the President of the Conference, and may not vote.

A Delegate may by notice in writing addressed to the President appoint one of his advisers to act as his deputy, and the adviser, while so acting, shall be allowed to speak and vote.

The names of the Delegates and their advisers will be communicated to the International Labour Office by the Government of each of the Members.

The credentials of Delegates and their advisers shall be subject to scrutiny by the Conference, which may, by two-thirds of the votes cast by the Delegates present, refuse to admit any Delegate or adviser whom it deems not to have been nominated in accordance with this Article.

ART. 390. Every Delegate shall be entitled to vote individually on all matters which are taken into consideration by the Conference.

If one of the Members fails to nominate one of the non-Government Delegates whom it is entitled to nominate, the other non-Government Delegate shall be allowed to sit and speak at the Conference, but not to vote.

If in accordance with Article 389 the Conference refuses admission to a Delegate of one of the Members, the provisions of the present Article shall apply as if that Delegate had not been nominated.

ART. 391. The meetings of the Conference shall be held at the seat of the League of Nations, or at such other place as may be decided by the Conference at a previous meeting by two-thirds of the votes cast by the Delegates present.

ART. 392. The International Labour Office shall be established at the seat of the League of Nations as part of the organisation of the League.

ART. 393. The International Labour Office shall be under the control of a Governing Body consisting of twenty-four persons, appointed in accordance with the following provisions:

The Governing Body of the International Labour Office shall be constituted as follows:

Twelve persons representing the Governments;

Six persons elected by the Delegates to the Conference representing the employers;

Six persons elected by the Delegates to the Conference representing the workers.

Of the twelve persons representing the Governments eight shall be nominated by the Members which are of the chief industrial importance, and four shall be nominated by the Members selected for the purpose by the Government Delegates to the Conference, excluding the Delegates of the eight Members mentioned above.

Any question as to which are the Members of the chief industrial importance shall be decided by the Council of the League of Nations.

The period of office of the Members of the Governing Body will be three years. The method of filling vacancies and other similar questions may be determined by the Governing Body subject to the approval of the Conference.

The Governing Body shall, from time to time, elect one of its members to act as its Chairman, shall regulate its own procedure and shall fix its own times of meeting. A special meeting shall be held if a written request to that effect is made by at least ten members of the Governing Body.

ART. 394. There shall be a Director of the International Labour Office, who shall be appointed by the Governing Body, and, subject to the instructions of the Governing Body, shall be responsible for the efficient conduct of the International Labour Office and for such other duties as may be assigned to him.

The Director or his deputy shall attend all meetings of the Governing Body.

ART. 395. The staff of the International Labour Office shall be appointed by the Director, who shall, so far as is possible with due regard to the efficiency of the work of the Office, select persons of different nationalities. A certain number of these persons shall be women.

ART. 396. The functions of the International Labour Office shall include the collection and distribution of information on all subjects relating to the international adjustment of conditions of industrial life and labour, and particularly the examination of subjects which it is proposed to bring before the Conference with a view to the conclusion of international conventions, and the conduct of such special investigations as may be ordered by the Conference. It will prepare the agenda for the meetings of the Conference.

It will carry out the duties required of it by the provisions of this Part of the present Treaty in connection with international disputes.

It will edit and publish in French and English, and in such other languages as the Governing Body may think desirable, a periodical paper dealing with problems of industry and employment of international interest.

Generally, in addition to the functions set out in this Article, it shall have such other powers and duties as may be assigned to it by the Conference.

ART. 397. The Government Departments of any of the Members which deal with questions of industry and employment may communicate directly with the Director through the Representative of their Government on the Governing Body of the International Labour Office, or failing any such Representative, through such other qualified official as the Government may nominate for the purpose.

ART. 398. The International Labour Office shall be entitled to the assistance of the Secretary-General of the League of Nations in any matter in which it can be given.

ART. 399. Each of the Members will pay the travelling and subsistence expenses of its Delegates and their advisers and of its Representatives attending the meetings of the Conference or Governing Body, as the case may be.

All the other expenses of the International Labour Office and of the meetings of the Conference or Governing Body shall be paid to the Director by the Secretary-General of the League of Nations out of the general funds of the League.

The Director shall be responsible to the Secretary-General of the League for the proper expenditure of all moneys paid to him in pursuance of this Article.

CHAPTER II.

PROCEDURE.

ART. 400. The agenda for all meetings of the Conference will be settled by the Governing Body, who shall consider any suggestion as to the agenda that may be made by the Government of any of the Members or by any representative organisation recognised for the purpose of Article 389.

ART. 401. The Director shall act as the Secretary of the Conference, and shall transmit the agenda so as to reach the Members four months before the meeting of the Conference, and, through them, the non-Government Delegates when appointed.

ART. 402. Any of the Governments of the Members may formally object to the inclusion of any item or items in the agenda. The grounds for such objection shall be set forth in a reasoned statement addressed to the Director, who shall circulate it to all the Members of the Permanent Organisation.

Items to which such objection has been made shall not, however, be excluded from the agenda, if at the Conference a majority of two-thirds of the votes cast by the Delegates present is in favour of considering them.

If the Conference decides (otherwise than under the preceding paragraph) by two-thirds of the votes cast by the Delegates present that any subject shall be considered by the Conference, that subject shall be included in the agenda for the following meeting.

ART. 403. The Conference shall regulate its own procedure, shall elect its own President, and may appoint committees to consider and report on any matter.

Except as otherwise expressly provided in this Part of the present Treaty, all matters shall be decided by a simple majority of the votes cast by the Delegates present.

The voting is void unless the total number of votes cast is equal to half the number of the Delegates attending the Conference.

ART. 404. The Conference may add to any committees which it appoints technical experts, who shall be assessors without power to vote.

ART. 405. When the Conference has decided on the adoption of proposals with regard to an item in the agenda, it will rest with the Conference to determine whether these proposals should take the form: (*a*) of a recommendation to be submitted to the Members for consideration with a view to effect being given to it by national legislation or otherwise, or (*b*) of a draft international convention for ratification by the Members.

In either case a majority of two-thirds of the votes cast by the Delegates present shall be necessary on the final vote for the adoption of the recommendation or draft convention, as the case may be, by the Conference.

In framing any recommendation or draft convention of general application the Conference shall have due regard to those countries in which climatic conditions, the imperfect development of industrial organisation or other special circumstances make the industrial conditions substantially different and shall suggest the modifications, if any, which it considers may be required to meet the case of such countries.

A copy of the recommendation or draft convention shall be authenticated by the signature of the President of the Conference and of the Director and shall be deposited with the Secretary-General of the League of Nations. The Secretary-General will communicate a certified copy of the recommendation or draft convention to each of the Members.

Each of the Members undertakes that it will, within the period of one year at most from the closing of the session of the Conference, or if it is impossible owing to exceptional circumstances to do so within the period of one year, then at the earliest practicable moment and in no case later than eighteen months from the closing of the session of the Conference, bring the recommendation or draft convention before the authority or authorities within whose competence the matter lies, for the enactment of legislation or other action.

In the case of a recommendation, the Members will inform the Secretary-General of the action taken.

In the case of a draft convention, the Member will, if it obtains the consent of the authority or authorities within whose competence the matter lies, communicate the formal ratification of the convention to the Secretary-General and will take such action as may be necessary to make effective the provisions of such convention.

If on a recommendation no legislative or other action is taken to make a recommendation effective, or if the draft convention fails to obtain the consent of the authority or authorities within whose competence the matter lies, no further obligation shall rest upon the Member.

In the case of a federal State, the power of which to enter into conventions on labour matters is subject to limitations, it shall be in the discretion of that Government to treat a draft convention to which such limitations apply as a recommendation only, and the provisions of this Article with respect to recommendations shall apply in such case.

The above Article shall be interpreted in accordance with the following principle:

In no case shall any Member be asked or required, as a result of the adoption of any recommendation or draft convention by the Conference, to lessen the protection afforded by its existing legislation to the workers concerned.

ART. 406. Any convention so ratified shall be registered by the Secretary-General of the League of Nations, but shall only be binding upon the Members which ratify it.

ART. 407. If any convention coming before the Conference for final consideration fails to secure the support of two-thirds of the votes cast by the Delegates present, it shall nevertheless be within the right of any of the Members of the Permanent Organisation to agree to such convention among themselves.

Any convention so agreed to shall be communicated by the Governments concerned to the Secretary-General of the League of Nations, who shall register it.

ART. 408. Each of the Members agrees to make an annual report to the International Labour Office on the measures which it has taken to give effect to the provisions of conventions to which it is a party. These reports shall be made in such form and shall contain such particulars as the Governing Body may request. The Director shall lay a summary of these reports before the next meeting of the Conference.

ART. 409. In the event of any representation being made to the International Labour Office by an industrial association of employers or of workers that any of the Members has failed to secure in any respect the effective observance within its jurisdiction of any convention to which it is a party, the Governing Body may communicate this representation to the Government against which it is made and may invite that Government to make such statement on the subject as it may think fit.

ART. 410. If no statement is received within a reasonable time from the Government in question, or if the statement when received is not deemed to be satisfactory by the Governing Body, the latter shall have the right to publish the representation and the statement, if any, made in reply to it.

ART. 411. Any of the Members shall have the right to file a complaint with the International Labour Office if it is not satisfied that any other Member is securing the effective observance of any convention which both have ratified in accordance with the foregoing Articles.

The Governing Body may, if it thinks fit, before referring such a complaint to a Commission of Enquiry, as hereinafter provided for, communicate with the Government in question in the manner described in Article 409.

If the Governing Body does not think it necessary to communicate the complaint to the Government in question, or if, when they have made such communication, no statement in reply has been received within a reasonable time which the Governing Body considers to be satisfactory, the Governing Body may apply for the appointment of a Commission of Enquiry to consider the complaint and to report thereon.

The Governing Body may adopt the same procedure either of its own motion or on receipt of a complaint from a Delegate to the Conference.

When any matter arising out of Articles 410 or 411 is being considered by the Governing Body, the Government in question shall, if not already represented thereon, be entitled to send a representative to take part in the proceedings of the Governing Body while the matter is under consideration. Adequate notice of the date on which the matter will be considered shall be given to the Government in question.

ART. 412. The Commission of Enquiry shall be constituted in accordance with the following provisions:

Each of the Members agrees to nominate within six months of the date on which the present Treaty comes into force three persons of industrial experience, of whom one shall be a representative of employers, one a representative of workers, and one a person of independent standing, who shall together form a panel from which the Members of the Commission of Enquiry shall be drawn.

The qualifications of the persons so nominated shall be subject to scrutiny by the Governing Body, which may by two-thirds of the votes cast by the representatives present refuse to accept the nomination of any person whose qualifications do not in its opinion comply with the requirements of the present Article.

Upon the application of the Governing Body, the Secretary-General of the League of Nations shall nominate three persons, one from each section of this panel, to constitute the Commission of Enquiry, and shall designate one of them as the President of the Commission. None of these three persons shall be a person nominated to the panel by any Member directly concerned in the complaint.

ART. 413. The Members agree that, in the event of the reference of a complaint to a Commission of Enquiry under Article 411, they will each, whether directly concerned in the complaint or not, place at the disposal of the Commission all the information in their possession which bears upon the subject-matter of the complaint.

ART. 414. When the Commission of Enquiry has fully considered the complaint, it shall prepare a report embodying its findings on all questions of fact relevant to determining the issue between the parties and containing such recommendations as it may think proper as to the steps which should be taken to meet the complaint and the time within which they should be taken.

It shall also indicate in this report the measures, if any, of an economic character against a defaulting Government which it considers to be appropriate, and which it considers other Governments would be justified in adopting.

ART. 415. The Secretary-General of the League of Nations shall communicate the report of the Commission of Enquiry to each of the Governments concerned in the complaint, and shall cause it to be published.

Each of these Governments shall within one month inform the Secretary-General of the League of Nations whether or not it accepts the recommendations contained in the report of the Commission; and if not, whether it proposes to refer the complaint to the Permanent Court of International Justice of the League of Nations.

ART. 416. In the event of any Member failing to take the action required by Article 405, with regard to a recommendation or draft Convention, any other Member shall be entitled to refer the matter to the Permanent Court of International Justice.

ART. 417. The decision of the Permanent Court of International Justice in regard to a complaint or matter which has been referred to it in pursuance of Article 415 or Article 416 shall be final.

ART. 418. The Permanent Court of International Justice may affirm, vary or reverse any of the findings or recommendations of the Commission of Enquiry, if any, and shall in its decision indicate the measures, if any, of an economic character which it considers to be appropriate, and which other Governments would be justified in adopting against a defaulting Government.

ART. 419. In the event of any Member failing to carry out within the time specified the recommendations, if any, contained in the report of the Commission of Enquiry, or in the decision of the Permanent Court of International Justice, as the case may be, any other Member may take against that Member the measures of an economic character indicated in the report of the Commission or in the decision of the Court as appropriate to the case.

ART. 420. The defaulting Government may at any time inform the Governing Body that it has taken the steps necessary to comply with the recommendations of the Commission of Enquiry or with those in the decision of the Permanent Court of International Justice, as the case may be, and may request it to apply to the Secretary-General of the League to constitute a Commission of Enquiry to verify its contention. In this case the provisions of Articles 412, 413, 414, 415, 417 and 418 shall apply, and if the report of the Commission of Enquiry or the decision of the Permanent Court of International Justice is in favour of the defaulting Government, the other Governments shall forthwith discontinue the measures of an economic character that they have taken against the defaulting Government.

Chapter III.

GENERAL.

Art. 421. The Members engage to apply conventions which they have ratified in accordance with the provisions of this Part of the present Treaty to their colonies, protectorates and possessions which are not fully self-governing:

(1) Except where owing to the local conditions the Convention is inapplicable, or

(2) Subject to such modifications as may be necessary to adapt the Convention to local conditions.

And each of the Members shall notify to the International Labour Office the action taken in respect of each of its colonies, protectorates and possessions which are not fully self-governing.

Art. 422. Amendments to this Part of the present Treaty which are adopted by the Conference by a majority of two-thirds of the votes cast by the Delegates present shall take effect when ratified by the States whose representatives compose the Council of the League of Nations and by three-fourths of the Members.

Art. 423. Any question or dispute relating to the interpretation of this Part of the present Treaty or of any subsequent convention concluded by the Members in pursuance of the provisions of this Part of the present Treaty shall be referred for decision to the Permanent Court of International Justice.

Chapter IV.

TRANSITORY PROVISIONS.

Art. 424. The first meeting of the Conference shall take place in October, 1919. The place and agenda for this meeting shall be as specified in the Annex hereto.

Arrangements for the convening and the organisation of the first meeting of the Conference will be made by the Government designated for the purpose in the said Annex. That Government shall be assisted in the preparation of the documents for submission to the Conference by an International Committee constituted as provided in the said Annex.

The expenses of the first meeting and of all subsequent meetings held before the League of Nations has been able to establish a general fund, other than the expenses of Delegates and their advisers, will be borne by the Members in accordance with the apportionment of the expenses of the International Bureau of the Universal Postal Union.

ART. 425. Until the League of Nations has been constituted all communications which under the provisions of the foregoing Articles should be addressed to the Secretary-General of the League will be preserved by the Director of the International Labour Office, who will transmit them to the Secretary-General of the League.

ART. 426. Pending the creation of a Permanent Court of International Justice disputes which in accordance with this Part of the present Treaty would be submitted to it for decision will be referred to a tribunal of three persons appointed by the Council of the League of Nations.

ANNEX.

FIRST MEETING OF ANNUAL LABOUR CONFERENCE, 1919.

The place of meeting will be Washington.

The Government of the United States of America is requested to convene the Conference.

The International Organising Committee will consist of seven Members, appointed by the United States of America, Great Britain, France, Italy, Japan, Belgium and Switzerland. The Committee may, if it thinks necessary, invite other Members to appoint representatives.

Agenda:

(1) Application of principle of the 8-hours day or of the 48-hours week.

(2) Question of preventing or providing against unemployment.

(3) Women's employment:
- (a) Before and after child-birth, including the question of maternity benefit;
- (b) During the night;
- (c) In unhealthy processes.

(4) Employment of children:
- (a) Minimum age of employment;
- (b) During the night;
- (c) In unhealthy processes.

(5) Extension and application of the International Conventions adopted at Berne in 1906 on the prohibition of night work for women employed in industry and the prohibition of the use of white phosphorus in the manufacture of matches.

Section II.

GENERAL PRINCIPLES.

ART. 427. The High Contracting Parties, recognising that the well-being, physical, moral and intellectual, of industrial wage-earners is of supreme international importance, have framed, in order to further this great end, the permanent machinery provided for in Section 1 and associated with that of the League of Nations.

They recognise that differences of climate, habits and customs, of economic opportunity and industrial tradition, make strict uniformity in the conditions of labour difficult of immediate attainment. But, holding as they do, that labour should not be regarded merely as an article of commerce, they think that there are methods and principles for regulating labour conditions which all industrial communities should endeavour to apply, so far as their special circumstances will permit.

Among these methods and principles, the following seem to the High Contracting Parties to be of special and urgent importance:

First.—The guiding principle above enunciated that labour should not be regarded merely as a commodity or article of commerce.

Second.—The right of association for all lawful purposes by the employed as well as by the employers.

Third.—The payment to the employed of a wage adequate to maintain a reasonable standard of life as this is understood in their time and country.

Fourth.—The adoption of an eight-hours day or a forty-eight hours week as the standard to be aimed at where it has not already been attained.

Fifth.—The adoption of a weekly rest of at least twenty-four hours, which should include Sunday wherever practicable.

Sixth.—The abolition of child labour and the imposition of such limitations on the labour of young persons as shall permit the continuation of their education and assure their proper physical development.

Seventh.—The principle that men and women should receive equal remuneration for work of equal value.

Eighth.—The standard set by law in each country with respect to the conditions of labour should have due regard to the equitable economic treatment of all workers lawfully resident therein.

Ninth.—Each State should make provision for a system of inspection in which women should take part, in order to ensure the enforcement of the laws and regulations for the protection of the employed.

Without claiming that these methods and principles are either complete or final, the High Contracting Parties are of opinion that they are well fitted to guide the policy of the League of Nations; and that if adopted by the industrial communities who are members of the League, and safeguarded in practice by an adequate system of such inspection, they will confer lasting benefits upon the wage-earners of the world.

PART XIV.

GUARANTEES.

Section I.

WESTERN EUROPE.

Art. 428–432.

Section II.

EASTERN EUROPE.

Art. 433.

PART XV.

MISCELLANEOUS PROVISIONS.

Art. 434–436.

Art. 437. The High Contracting Parties agree that, in the absence of a subsequent agreement to the contrary, the Chairman of any Commission established by the present Treaty shall in the event of any equality of votes be entitled to a second vote.

Art. 438–440.

THE PRESENT TREATY, of which the French and English texts are both authentic, shall be ratified.

The deposit of ratifications shall be made at Paris as soon as possible.

Powers of which the seat of the Government is outside Europe will be entitled merely to inform the Government of the French Republic through their diplomatic representative at Paris that their ratification has been given; in that case they must transmit the instrument of ratification as soon as possible.

A first procès-verbal of the deposit of ratifications will be drawn up as soon as the Treaty has been ratified by Germany on the one hand, and by three of the Principal Allied and Associated Powers on the other hand.

From the date of this first procès-verbal the Treaty will come into force between the High Contracting Parties who have ratified it. For the determination of all periods of time provided for in the present Treaty this date will be the date of the coming into force of the Treaty.

In all other respects the Treaty will enter into force for each Power at the date of the deposit of its ratification.

The French Government will transmit to all the signatory Powers a certified copy of the procès-verbaux of the deposit of ratifications.

IN FAITH WHEREOF the above-named Plenipotentiaries have signed the present Treaty.

Done at Versailles, the twenty-eighth day of June, one thousand nine hundred and nineteen, in a single copy which will remain deposited in the archives of the French Republic, and of which authenticated copies will be transmitted to each of the Signatory Powers.

APPENDIX 2 (a)

Treaty of Alliance Between Germany and Austria. Vienna, October 7, 1879.[1]

Considering that Their Majesties the German Emperor, King of Prussia, and the Emperor of Austria, King of Hungary, must esteem it as their incontestable duty as sovereigns to take care in all circumstances for the security of their empires and for the tranquillity of their peoples;

Considering that the two monarchs as in the previously existing confederation will be in a position, by a firm alliance of the two empires, to fulfil this duty more easily and more efficaciously;

Considering, finally, that an intimate accord between Germany and Austria-Hungary can menace nobody, but is, on the contrary, qualified to consolidate the peace of Europe created by the stipulations of the Treaty of Berlin;

Their Majesties the German Emperor and the Emperor of Austria, King of Hungary, promising one another never to give any aggressive tendency in any direction to their purely defensive agreement, have resolved to conclude an alliance of peace and reciprocal protection.

With this object Their Majesties have named as their plenipotentiaries:

For His Majesty the German Emperor, his Ambassador and Plenipotentiary Extraordinary, Lieutenant-General Prince Henry VII of Reuss, etc., etc.

For His Majesty the Emperor of Austria, King of Hungary, his Privy Counsellor the Minister of the Imperial Household and of

---

[1] Translation from Oakes and Mowat, Great European Treaties, p. 372–374. A different translation is in British and Foreign State Papers, 73: 270.

Foreign Affairs, Field-Marshal-Lieutenant Julius, Count Andrassy, etc.

Who have come together to-day, at Vienna, and after having exchanged their powers duly recognized as good and sufficient, have concluded what follows:

ART. I. If, contrary to expectation and against the sincere desire of both the High Contracting Parties, one of the two Empires shall be attacked on the part of Russia, the High Contracting Parties are bound to assist each other with the whole of the military power of their Empire, and consequently only to conclude peace conjointly and by agreement.

ART. II. Should one of the High Contracting Parties be attacked by another Power, the other High Contracting Party hereby engages not only not to assist the aggressor against his High Ally, but at the least to observe a benevolent neutral attitude with regard to the High Contracting Party.

If, however, in such a case the attacking Power should be supported on the part of Russia, whether by way of active co-operation, or by military measures which menace the attacked Power, then the obligation of reciprocal assistance with full military power, which is stipulated in the first article of this Treaty, will in this case enter immediately into effect, and the conduct of war of both the High Contracting Parties shall be then also in common until the joint conclusion of Peace.

ART. III. This Treaty, in conformity with its pacific character and to prevent any misconstruction, shall be kept secret by both High Contracting Parties, and it will be communicated to a Third Power only with the consent of both Parties, and strictly according to a special agreement.

Both High Contracting Parties, in view of the sentiments expressed by the Emperor Alexander at the interview at Alexandrowo, hope that the preparations of Russia will not prove in reality to be a menace to them, and for this reason they have for the present no occasion for a communication. But if, contrary to expectation, this hope should prove a vain one, the two High Contracting Parties will recognize it as a loyal obligation, to inform the Emperor

Alexander at least confidentially that they must consider an attack against one of them as directed against both.

In witness whereof the Plenipotentiaries have signed this treaty with their own hand, and have affixed their seals.

Done at Vienna, the 7th October, 1879.

H. VII. P. REUSS. ANDRASSY.

APPENDIX 2 (b)

THE TRIPLE ALLIANCE. MAY, 1882.[1]
THE PUBLISHED SECTIONS OF THE TRIPLE ALLIANCE TREATY BETWEEN AUSTRIA AND ITALY (AS RENEWED IN 1887, 1891, 1902 AND 1912)

CLAUSE III. In case one or two of the High Contracting Parties, without direct provocation on their part, should be attacked by one or more Great Powers not signatory of the present Treaty and should become involved in a war with them, the *casus fœderis* would arise simultaneously for all the High Contracting Parties.

CLAUSE IV. In case a Great Power not signatory of the present Treaty should threaten the State security of one of the High Contracting Parties, and in case the threatened party should thereby be compelled to declare war against that Great Power, the two other contracting parties engage themselves to maintain benevolent neutrality towards their Ally. Each of them reserves its right, in this case, to take part in the war if it thinks fit in order to make common cause with its Ally.

CLAUSE VII. Austria-Hungary and Italy, who have solely in view the maintenance, as far as possible, of the territorial *status quo* in the East, engage themselves to use their influence to prevent all territorial changes which might be disadvantageous to the one or the other of the Powers signatory of the present Treaty. To this end they will give reciprocally all information calculated to enlighten each other concerning their own intentions and those of other Powers. Should, however, the case arise that, in the course of events, the maintenance of the *status quo* in the territory of the Balkans or of the Ottoman coasts and islands in the Adriatic or the Aegean Sea becomes impossible, and that, either in conse-

---
[1] Oakes and Mowat. Great European Treaties, p. 374-375.

quence of the action of a third Power or for any other reason, Austria-Hungary or Italy should be obliged to change the *status quo* on their part by a temporary or permanent occupation, such occupation would only take place after previous agreement between the two Powers, which would have to be based upon the principle of a reciprocal compensation for all territorial or other advantages that either of them might acquire over and above the existing *status quo*, and would have to satisfy the interests and rightful claims of both parties.

APPENDIX 3 (a)

PROJET DE CONVENTION MILITAIRE.[1] RUSSO-FRENCH ALLIANCE

La France et la Russie, étant animées d'un égal désir de conserver la paix, et n'ayant d'autre but que de parer aux nécessités d'une guerre défensive, provoquée par une attaque des forces de la Triple Alliance contre l'une ou l'autre d'entre elles, sont convenues des dispositions suivantes:

1. Si la France est attaquée par l'Allemagne, ou par l'Italie soutenue par l'Allemagne, la Russie emploiera toutes ses forces disponibles pour attaquer l'Allemagne.

Si la Russie est attaquée par l'Allemagne, ou par l'Autriche soutenue par l'Allemagne, la France emploiera toutes ses forces disponibles pour combattre l'Allemagne.

2. Dans le cas où les forces de la Triple Alliance, ou d'une des Puissances qui en font partie, viendraient à se mobiliser, la France et la Russie, à la première annonce de l'événement, et sans qu'il soit besoin d'un concert préalable, mobiliseront immédiatement et simultanément la totalité de leurs forces, et les porteront le plus près possible de leurs frontières.

3. Les forces disponibles qui doivent être employées contre l'Allemagne seront, du côté de la France, de 1,300,000 hommes, du côté de la Russie, de 700,000 à 800,000 hommes.

Ces forces s'engageront à fond, en toute diligence, de manière que l'Allemagne ait à lutter, à la fois, à l'Est et à l'Ouest.

---

[1] "Ce document est conservé dans une enveloppe portant cette annotation autographe: 'La convention militaire est acceptée par la lettre de M. de Giers à M. de Montebello donnant force de traité à cette Convention.—(Signé) FÉLIX FAURE, 15 octobre.'" On December 30, 1893, the formal ratification by the Russian Emperor was announced in a letter from the French Ambassador at St. Petersburg to the French Minister of Foreign Affairs.—Documents Diplomatiques, Paris, 1918. p. 92 and 127.

4. Les États-Majors des Armées des deux pays se concerteront en tout temps pour préparer et faciliter l'exécution des mesures prévues ci-dessus.

Ils se communiquéront, dès le temps de paix, tous les renseignements relatifs aux armées de la Triple Alliance qui sont ou parviendront à leur connaissance.

Les voies et moyens de correspondre en temps de guerre seront étudiés et prévus d'avance.

5. La France et la Russie ne concluront pas la paix séparément.

6. La présente Convention aura la même durée que la Triple Alliance.

7. Toutes les clauses énumérées ci-dessus seront tenues rigoureusement secrètes.

Signature du Ministre:

Signature du Ministre:

L'Aide de Camp général, Chef de l'État-Major général, Signé: OBROUTCHEFF.

Le Général de Division, Conseiller d'État, Sous-Chef d'État-Major de l'Armée, Signé: BOISDEFFRE

APPENDIX 3 (b)

Convention pour l'échange de Renseignements entre la Marine Russe et la Marine Française[1]

A la suite d'un échange de vues survenu dans le courant du mois de juillet 1912, entre M. le Vice-Amiral, Prince Lieven, Chef d'État-Major général de la Marine impériale russe, et M. le Vice-Amiral Aubert, Chef d'État-Major général de la Marine française, les décisions de principe qui suivent ont été arrêtées entre les deux conférents:

1. A partir du 1/14 septembre 1912, le Chef d'État-Major général de la Marine impériale russe et le Chef d'État-Major général de la Marine française échangeront tous renseignements sur leurs marines respectives et, régulièrement tous les mois, par écrit, les renseignements que ces deux pays pourront se procurer; le télégraphe chiffré pourra être employé en certains cas urgents;

2. Pour éviter toute indiscrétion ou toute divulgation relative á ces renseignements, il est indispensable d'adopter le procédé de transmission suivant:

Toute demande de renseignements sur la Marine française, intéressant la Marine russe, sera adressée par l'Attaché naval russe à Paris au Chef d'État-Major général de la Marine française; et, réciproquement, toute demande de renseignements sur la Marine russe, intéressant la Marine française, sera adressée par l'Attaché naval français à Saint-Pétersbourg au Chef d'État-Major général de la Marine russe.

Ce procédé sera exclusif de tout autre: on ne pourra donc pas, en principe, demander directement aux Attachés navals des renseignements sur leur propre Marine.

Paris, le 16 juillet 1912.

Le Chef d'État-Major général de la Marine française,	Le Chef d'État-Major général de la Marine russe,
Signé: Aubert.	Signé: Prince Lieven.

[1] "L' original de ce document est au Ministère de la Marine." Documents Diplomatiques, Paris, 1918, p. 136–137.

APPENDIX 4

The Act of the Holy Alliance,[1] Paris September 14/26, 1815.

In the name of the Most Holy and Indivisible Trinity.

Their Majesties the Emperor of Austria, the King of Prussia, and the Emperor of Russia, having, in consequence of the great events which have marked the course of the three last years in Europe, and especially of the blessings which it has pleased Divine Providence to shower down upon those States which place their confidence and their hope in it alone, acquired the intimate conviction of the necessity of settling the steps to be observed by the Powers, in their reciprocal relations, upon the sublime truths which the holy religion of our Saviour teaches;

They solemnly declare that the present Act has no other object than to publish, in the face of the whole world, their fixed resolution, both in the administration of their respective States, and in their political relations with every other Government, to take for their sole guide the precepts of that Holy Religion, namely, the precepts of Justice, Christian Charity and Peace, which, far from being applicable only to private concerns, must have an immediate influence upon the counsels of Princes, and guide all their steps as being the only means of consolidating human institutions and remedying their imperfections. In consequence, their Majesties have agreed on the following articles:

Art. I. Conformably to the words of the Holy Scriptures which command all men to consider each other as brethren, the Three contracting Monarchs will remain united by the bonds of a true and indissoluble fraternity, and, considering each other as fellow-countrymen, they will, on all occasions and in all places, lend each

---

[1]Phillips: Confederation of Europe, p. 301-302. The French text is in British and Foreign State Papers, 3: 211-212.

other aid and assistance; and, regarding themselves towards their subjects and armies as fathers of families, they will lend them, in the same spirit of fraternity with which they are animated, to protect Religion, Peace, and Justice.

ART. II. In consequence, the sole principle of force, whether between the said Governments or between their subjects, shall be that of doing each other reciprocal service, and of testifying by unalterable goodwill the mutual affection with which they ought to be animated, to consider themselves all as members of one and the same Christian nation; the three allied Princes, looking on themselves as merely delegated by Providence to govern three branches of the One family, namely, Austria, Prussia, and Russia, thus confessing that the Christian world, of which they and their people form a part has in reality no other Sovereign than Him to whom alone power really belongs, because in Him alone are found all the treasures of love, science and infinite wisdom, that is to say, God, our Divine Saviour, the Word of the Most High, the Word of Life. Their Majesties consequently recommend to their people with the most tender solicitude, as the sole means of enjoying that Peace which alone is durable, to strengthen themselves every day more and more in the principles and exercise of the duties which the Divine Saviour has taught to mankind.

ART. III. All the Powers who shall choose solemnly to avow the sacred principles which have dictated the present Act, and shall acknowledge how important it is for the happiness of nations, too long agitated, that these truths should henceforth exercise over the destinies of mankind all the influence which belongs to them, will be received with equal ardour and affection into this Holy Alliance.

FRANÇOIS.
Frederic-GUILLAUME.
ALEXANDRE.

APPENDIX 5 (a)

GENERAL TREATY OF PEACE AND AMITY,[1] CONCLUDED AT THE CENTRAL AMERICAN PEACE CONFERENCE, DECEMBER 20, 1907.

The Governments of the Republics of Costa Rica, Guatemala, Honduras, Nicaragua, and Salvador, being desirous of establishing the foundations which fix the general relations of said countries, have seen fit to conclude a General Treaty of Peace and Amity which will attain said end, and for that purpose have named as Delegates:

[Names of Delegates.]

By virtue of the invitation sent in accordance with Article II of the Protocol signed at Washington on September 17, 1907, by the Plenipotentiary Representatives of the five Central American Republics, their excellencies, the Representative of the Government of the United Mexican States, Ambassador Don Enrique C. Creel, and the Representative of the Government of the United States of America, Mr. William I. Buchanan, were present at all the deliberations.

The Delegates, assembled in the Central American Peace Conference at Washington, after having communicated to one another their respective full powers, which they found to be in due form, have agreed to carry out the said purpose in the following manner:

ART. I.—The Republics of Central America consider as one of their first duties, in their mutual relations, the maintenance of peace; and they bind themselves always to observe the most complete harmony, and decide every difference or difficulty that may arise among them, of whatsoever nature it may be, by means of the Central American Court of Justice, created by the Convention which they have concluded for that purpose on this date.

---
[1] Malloy: Treaties, 2: 2392-2398.

Art. II.—Desiring to secure in the Republics of Central America the benefits which are derived from the maintenance of their institutions, and to contribute at the same time to maintaining their stability and the prestige with which they ought to be surrounded, it is declared that every disposition or measure which may tend to alter the constitutional organization in any of them is to be deemed a menace to the peace of said Republics.

Art. III.—Taking into account the central geographical position of Honduras and the facilities which owing to this circumstance have made its territory most often the theatre of Central American conflicts, Honduras declares from now on its absolute neutrality in event of any conflict between the other Republics; and the latter, in their turn provided such neutrality be observed, bind themselves to respect it and in no case to violate the Honduranean territory.

Art. IV.—Bearing in mind the advantages which must be gained from the creation of Central American institutions for the development of their most vital interests, besides the Pedagogical Institute and the International Central American Bureau which are to be established according to the Conventions concluded to that end by this Conference, the creation of a practical Agricultural School in the Republic of Salvador, one of Mines and Mechanics in that of Honduras, and another of Arts and Trades in that of Nicaragua, is especially recommended to the Governments.

Art. V.—In order to cultivate the relations between the States, the contracting Parties obligate themselves each to accredit to the others a permanent Legation.

Art. VI.—The citizens of one of the contracting Parties, residing in the territory of any of the others, shall enjoy the same civil rights as are enjoyed by nationals, and shall be considered as citizens in the country of their residence if they fulfill the conditions which the respective constituent laws provide. Those that are not naturalized shall be exempt from obligatory military service, either on sea or land, and from every forced loan or military requisition, and they shall not be obliged on any account to pay greater contributions or ordinary or extraordinary imposts than those which natives pay.

ART. VII.—The individuals who have acquired a professional degree in any of the contracting Republics, may, without special exaction, practice their professions, in accordance with the respective laws, in any one of the others, without other requirements than those of presenting the respective degree or diploma properly authenticated and of proving, in case of necessity, their personal identity and of obtaining a permit from the Executive Power where the law so requires.

In like manner shall validity attach to the scientific studies pursued in the universities, professional schools, and the schools of higher education of any one of the contracting countries, provided the documents which evidence such studies have been authenticated, and the identity of the person proved.

ART. VIII.—Citizens of the signatory countries who reside in the territory of the others shall enjoy the right of literary, artistic or industrial property in the same manner and subject to the same requirements as natives.

ART. IX.—The merchant ships of the signatory countries shall be considered upon the sea, along the coasts, and in the ports of said countries as national vessels; they shall enjoy the same exemptions, immunities and concessions as the latter, and shall not pay other dues nor be subject to further taxes than those imposed upon and paid by the vessels of the country.

ART. X.—The Governments of the contracting Republics bind themselves to respect the inviolability of the right of asylum aboard the merchant vessels of whatsoever nationality anchored in their ports. Therefore, only persons accused of common crimes can be taken from them after due legal procedure and by order of the competent judge. Those prosecuted on account of political crimes or common crimes in connection with political ones, can only be taken therefrom in case they have embarked in a port of the State which claims them, during their stay in its jurisdictional waters, and after the requirements hereinbefore set forth in the case of common crimes have been fulfilled.

ART. XI.—The Diplomatic and Consular Agents of the contracting Republics in foreign cities, towns and ports shall afford to the persons, vessels and other property of the citizens of any one of them, the same protection as to the persons, ships and other properties of their compatriots, without demanding for their services other or higher charges than those usually made with respect to their nationals.

ART. XII.—In the desire of promoting commerce between the contracting Republics, their respective Governments shall agree upon the establishment of national merchant marines engaged in coastwise commerce and the arrangements to be made with and the subsidies to be granted to steamship companies engaged in the trade between national and foreign ports.

ART. XIII.—There shall be a complete and regular exchange of every class of official publications between the contracting Parties.

ART. XIV.—Public instruments executed in one of the contracting Republics shall be valid in the others, provided they shall have been properly authenticated and in their execution the laws of the Republic whence they issue shall have been observed.

ART. XV.—The judicial authorities of the contracting Republics shall carry out the judicial commissions and warrants in civil, commercial or criminal matters, with regard to citations, interrogatories and other acts of procedure or judicial function.

Other judicial acts, in civil or commercial matters, arising out of a personal suit, shall have in the territory of any one of the contracting Parties equal force with those of the local tribunals and shall be executed in the same manner, provided always that they shall first have been declared executory by the Supreme Tribunal of the Republic wherein they are to be executed, which shall be done if they meet the essential requirements of their respective legislation and they shall be carried out in accordance with the laws enacted in each country for the execution of judgments.

ART. XVI.—Desiring to prevent one of the most frequent causes of disturbances in the Republics, the contracting Governments shall not permit the leaders or principal chiefs of political refugees, nor their agents, to reside in the departments bordering on the countries whose peace they might disturb.

Those who may have established their permanent residence in a frontier department may remain in the place of their residence under the immediate surveillance of the Government affording them an asylum, but from the moment when they become a menace to public order they shall be included in the rule of the preceding paragraph.

ART. XVII.—Every person, no matter what his nationality, who, within the territory of one of the contracting Parties, shall initiate or foster revolutionary movements against any of the others, shall be immediately brought to the capital of the Republic, where he shall be submitted to trial according to law.

ART. XVIII.—With respect to the Bureau of Central American Republics which shall be established in Guatemala, and with respect to the Pedagogical Institute which is to be created in Costa Rica, the Conventions celebrated to that end shall be observed, and those that refer to Extradition, Communications, and Annual Conferences, shall remain in full force for the unification of Central American interests.

ART. XIX.—The present Treaty shall remain in force for the term of ten years counted from the day of the exchange of ratifications. Nevertheless, if one year before the expiration of said term none of the contracting Parties shall have given special notice to the others concerning its intention to terminate it, it shall remain in force until one year after such notification shall have been made.

ART. XX.—The stipulation of the Treaties heretofore concluded among the contracting Countries, being comprised or suitably modified in this, it is declared that all stipulations remain void and revoked by the present, after final approval and exchange of ratifications.

ART. XXI.—The exchange of ratifications of the present Treaty, as well as that of the other Conventions of this date, shall be made by means of communications which are to be addressed by the Governments to that of Costa Rica, in order that the latter shall notify the other contracting States. The Government of Costa Rica shall also communicate its ratification if it effects it.

Signed at the city of Washington on the twentieth day of December, one thousand nine hundred and seven.

LUIS ANDERSON	E. CONSTANTINO FIALLOS
J. B. CALVO	JOSÉ MADRIZ
ANTONIO BATRES JÁUREGUI	LUIS F. COREA
LUIS TOLEDO HERRARTE	SALVADOR GALLEGOS
VICTOR SÁNCHEZ O.	SALVADOR RODRÍGUEZ G.
POLICARPO BONILLA	F. MEJÍA
ANGEL UGARTE	

ADDITIONAL TREATY, CONCLUDED DECEMBER 20, 1907.

ART. I.—The Governments of the High Contracting Parties shall not recognize any other Government which may come into power in any of the five Republics as a consequence of a *coup d'état* or of a revolution against the recognized Government, so long as the freely elected representatives of the people thereof have not constitutionally re-organized the country.

ART. II.—No Government of Central America shall in case of civil war intervene in favor of or against the Government of the country where the struggle takes place.

ART. III.—The Governments of Central America, in the first place, are recommended to endeavor to bring about, by the means at their command, a constitutional reform in the sense of prohibiting the re-election of the President of a Republic, where such prohibition does not exist, secondly to adopt all measures necessary to effect a complete guarantee of the principle of alternation in power.

Signed at the city of Washington on the twentieth day of December, one thousand nine hundred and seven.

APPENDIX 5 (b).

Convention for the Establishment of a Central American Court of Justice,[1] Concluded December 20, 1907.

The Governments of the Republics of Costa Rica, Guatemala, Honduras, Nicaragua and Salvador, for the purpose of efficaciously guaranteeing their rights and maintaining peace and harmony inalterably in their relations, without being obliged to resort in any case to the employment of force, have agreed to conclude a Convention for the constitution of a Court of Justice charged with accomplishing such high aims, and, to that end, have named as Delegates:

[Names of Delegates.]

The Delegates, assembled in the Central American Peace Conference at Washington, after having communicated to one another their respective full powers, which they found to be in due form, have agreed to carry out the said purpose in the following manner:

Art. I.—The High Contracting Parties agree by the present Convention to constitute and maintain a permanent tribunal which shall be called the "Central American Court of Justice," to which they bind themselves to submit all controversies or questions which may arise among them, of whatsoever nature and no matter what their origin may be, in case the respective Departments of Foreign Affairs should not have been able to reach an understanding.

Art. II.—This Court shall also take cognizance of the questions which individuals of one Central American country may raise against any of the other contracting Governments, because of the violation of treaties or conventions, and other cases of an international character; no matter whether their own Government supports said claim or not; and provided that the remedies which the

---
[1] Malloy: Treaties, 2: 2399-2406.

laws of the respective country provide against such violation shall have been exhausted or that denial of justice shall have been shown.

ART. III[1].—It shall also take cognizance of the cases which by common accord the contracting Governments may submit to it, no matter whether they arise between two or more of them or between one of said Governments and individuals.

ART. IV.—The Court can likewise take cognizance of the international questions which by special agreement any one of the Central American Governments and a foreign Government may have determined to submit to it.

ART. V.—The Central American Court of Justice shall sit at the City of Cartago in the Republic of Costa Rica, but it may temporarily transfer its residence to another point in Central America whenever it deems it expedient for reasons of health, or in order to insure the exercise of its functions, or for the personal safety of its members.

ART. VI.—The Central American Court of Justice shall consist of five Justices, one being appointed by each Republic and selected from among the jurists who possess the qualifications which the laws of each country prescribe for the exercise of high judicial office, and who enjoy the highest consideration, both because of their moral character and their professional ability.

Vacancies shall be filled by substitute Justices, named at the same time and in the same manner as the regular Justices and who shall unite the same qualifications as the latter.

The attendance of the five Justices who constitute the Tribunal is indispensable in order to make a legal quorum in the decisions of the Court.

ART. VII.—The Legislative Power of each one of the five contracting Republics shall appoint their respective Justices, one regular and two substitutes.

---

[1]An additional protocol, signed at Washington, December 20, 1907, corrects this article to read as follows:

"It shall also have jurisdiction over cases arising between any of the contracting Governments and individuals, when by common accord they are submitted to it."

The salary of each Justice shall be eight thousand dollars, gold, per annum, which shall be paid them by the Treasury of the Court. The salary of the Justice of the country where the Court resides shall be fixed by the Government thereof. Furthermore, each State shall contribute two thousand dollars, gold, annually toward the ordinary and extraordinary expenses of the Tribunal. The Governments of the contracting Republics bind themselves to include their respective contributions in their estimates of expenses and to remit quarterly in advance to the Treasury of the Court the share they may have to bear on account of such services.

Art. VIII.—The regular and substitute Justices shall be appointed for a term of five years, which shall be counted from the day on which they assume the duties of their office, and they may be re-elected.

In case of death, resignation or permanent incapacity of any of them, the vacancy shall be filled by the respective Legislature, and the Justice elected shall complete the term of his predecessor.

Art. IX.—The regular and substitute Justices shall take oath or make affirmation prescribed by law before the authority that may have appointed them, and from that moment they shall enjoy the immunities and prerogatives which the present Convention confers upon them. The regular Justices shall likewise enjoy thenceforth the salary fixed in Article VII.

Art. X.—While they remain in the country of their appointment the regular and substitute Justices shall enjoy the personal immunity which the respective laws grant to the magistrates of the Supreme Court of Justice, and in the other contracting Republics they shall have the privileges and immunities of Diplomatic Agents.

Art. XI.—The office of Justice while held is incompatible with the exercise of his profession, and with the holding of public office. The same incompatibility applies to the substitute Justices so long as they may actually perform their duties.

Art. XII.—At its first annual session the Court shall elect from among its own members a President and Vice-President; it shall organize the personnel of its office by designating a Clerk, a Treasurer, and such other subordinate employees as it may deem necessary, and it shall draw up the estimate of its expenses.

ART. XIII.—The Central American Court of Justice represents the national conscience of Central America, wherefore the Justices who compose the Tribunal shall not consider themselves barred from the discharge of their duties because of the interest which the Republics, to which they owe their appointment, may have in any case or question. With regard to allegations of personal interest, the rules of procedure which the Court may fix shall make proper provision.

ART. XIV.—When differences or questions subject to the jurisdiction of the Tribunal arise, the interested party shall present a complaint which shall comprise all the points of fact and law relative to the matter, and all pertinent evidence. The Tribunal shall communicate without loss of time a copy of the complaint to the Governments or individuals interested, and shall invite them to furnish their allegations and evidence within the term that it may designate to them, which, in no case, shall exceed sixty days counted from the date of notice of the complaint.

ART. XV.—If the term designated shall have expired without answer having been made to the complaint, the Court shall require the defendant or defendants to do so within a further term not to exceed twenty days, after the expiration of which and in view of the evidence presented and of such evidence as it may *ex officio* have seen fit to obtain, the Tribunal shall render its decision in the case, which decision shall be final.

ART. XVI.—If the Government, Governments or individuals sued shall have appeared in time before the Court, presenting their allegations and evidence, the Court shall decide the matter within thirty days following, without further process or proceedings; but if a new term for the presentation of evidence be solicited, the Court shall decide whether or not there is occasion to grant it; and, if this is granted, it shall fix therefor a reasonable time. Upon the expiration of such term, the Court shall pronounce its final judgment within thirty days.

ART. XVII.—Each one of the Governments or individuals

directly concerned in the questions to be considered by the Court has the right to be represented before it by a trustworthy person or persons, who shall present evidence, formulate arguments, and shall, within the terms fixed by this Convention and by the rules of the Court of Justice, do everything that in their judgment shall be beneficial to the defense of the rights they represent.

ART. XVIII.—From the moment in which any suit is instituted against any one or more governments up to that in which a final decision has been pronounced, the Court may at the solicitation of any one of the parties fix the situation in which the contending parties must remain, to the end that the difficulty shall not be aggravated and that things shall be conserved in *status quo* pending a final decision.

ART. XIX.—For all the effects of this Convention, the Central American Court of Justice may address itself to the Governments or tribunals of justice of the contracting States, through the medium of the Ministry of Foreign Relations or the office of the Clerk of the Supreme Court of Justice of the respective country, according to the nature of the requisite proceeding, in order to have the measures that it may dictate within the scope of its jurisdiction carried out.

ART. XX.—It may also appoint special commissioners to carry out the formalities above referred to, when it deems it expedient for their better fulfilment. In such case, it shall ask of the Government where the proceeding is to be had, its co-operation and assistance, in order that the Commissioner may fulfill his mission. The contracting Governments formally bind themselves to obey and to enforce the orders of the Court, furnishing all the assistance that may be necessary for their best and most expeditious fulfilment.

ART. XXI.—In deciding points of fact that may be raised before it, the Central American Court of Justice shall be governed by its free judgment, and, with respect to points of law, by the principles of international law. The final judgment shall cover each one of the points in litigation.

ART. XXII.—The Court is competent to determine its jurisdiction, interpreting the Treaties and Conventions germane to the matter in dispute and applying the principles of international law.

ART. XXIII.—Every final or interlocutory decision shall be rendered with the concurrence of at least three of the Justices of the Court. In case of disagreement, one of the substitute Justices shall be chosen by lot, and if still a majority of three be not thus obtained other Justices shall be successively chosen by lot until three uniform votes shall have been obtained.

ART. XXIV.—The decisions must be in writing and shall contain a statement of the reasons upon which they are based. They must be signed by all the Justices of the Court and countersigned by the Clerk. Once they have been notified they can not be altered on any account; but, at the request of any of the parties, the Tribunal may declare the interpretation which must be given to its judgments.

ART. XXV.—The judgments of the Court shall be communicated to the five Governments of the contracting Republics. The interested parties solemnly bind themselves to submit to said judgments, and all agree to lend all moral support that may be necessary in order that they may be properly fulfilled, thereby constituting a real and positive guaranty of respect for this Convention and for the Central American Court of Justice.

ART. XXVI.—The Court is empowered to make its rules, to formulate the rules of procedure which may be necessary, and to determine the forms and terms not prescribed in the present Convention. All the decisions which may be rendered in this respect shall be communicated immediately to the High Contracting Parties.

ART. XXVII.—The High Contracting Parties solemnly declare that on no ground nor in any case will they consider the present Convention as void; and that, therefore, they will consider it as being always in force during the term of ten years counted from the last ratification. In the event of the change or alteration of the political status of one or more of the Contracting Republics, the functions of the Central American Court of Justice created by this Convention shall be suspended *ipso facto;* and a conference to adjust the constitution of said Court to the new order of things shall be forthwith convoked by the respective Governments; in case they do not unanimously agree the present Convention shall be considered as rescinded.

ART. XXVIII.—The exchange of ratifications of the present Convention shall be made in accordance with Article XXI of the General Treaty of Peace and Amity concluded on this date.

Provisional Article.—As recommended by the five Delegations an Article is annexed which contains an amplification of the jurisdiction of the Central American Court of Justice, in order that the Legislatures may, if they see fit, include it in this Convention upon ratifying it.

Annexed Article.—The Central American Court of Justice shall also have jurisdiction over the conflicts which may arise between the Legislative, Executive and Judicial Powers, and when as a matter of fact the judicial decisions and resolutions of the National Congress are not respected.

Signed at the city of Washington on the twentieth day of December, one thousand nine hundred and seven.

APPENDIX 5 (c)

CONVENTION FOR THE ESTABLISHMENT OF AN INTERNATIONAL CENTRAL AMERICAN BUREAU,[1] CONCLUDED AT THE CENTRAL AMERICAN PEACE CONFERENCE, DECEMBER 20, 1907.

The Governments of the Republics of Costa Rica, Guatemala, Honduras, Nicaragua, and Salvador being desirous to develop the interests common to Central America, have agreed to establish an International Bureau that shall take charge of the supervision and care of such interests, and, in order to attain so important an end, have seen fit to conclude a special Convention, and for that purpose have named as Delegates:

[Names of Delegates].

ART. I. The following Central American interests are recognized as being those to which special attention should be paid.

1. To combine every effort toward the peaceful reorganization of their mother country, Central America.

2. To impress upon public education an essentially Central American character, in a uniform sense, making it as broad, practical, and complete as possible, in accordance with the modern pedagogical tendency.

3. The development of Central American Commerce and of all that may tend to make it more active and profitable, and its expansion with other nations.

4. The advancement of agriculture and industries that can be developed to advantage in its different sections.

5. The uniformity of civil, commercial, and criminal legislation, recognizing as a fundamental principle the inviolability of life, respect for property, and the most absolute sacredness of the personal rights of man; uniformity in the system of custom-houses; in the

---
[1] Malloy: Treaties, 2: 2411-2413.

monetary system, in such manner as to secure a fixed rate of exchange; general sanitation, and especially that of the Central American ports; confidence in the Central American credit; uniformity in the system of weights and measures; the definition of what constitutes real property, in such a firm and unquestionable manner as will serve as a solid foundation for credit and permit the establishment of mortgage banks.

ART. II. For the purpose hereinbefore mentioned the signatory Governments bind themselves to establish an International Central American Bureau, composed of one delegate from each one of them.

ART. III. The Presidency of the Bureau shall be exercised alternatively by the members that compose it, the alphabetical order of the contracting States being followed for that purpose.

ART. IV. The functions of the Bureau shall be all those considered necessary and expedient to achieve the objects placed in its care by the present agreement, and to that end the office shall enumerate them in the rules that it may establish, being empowered to make all provisions of internal regulation that may be conducive to the proper fulfillment of the mission of maintaining and developing the Central American interests that may be placed under its care and supervision.

In order to attain this end the contracting Governments bind themselves to lend to the Bureau all the support and protection necessary for the proper fulfillment of its object.

ART. V. The Bureau shall every six months send to each of the signatory Governments a detailed report of the work accomplished in the preceding half-year.

ART. VI. The Bureau shall be located in the city of Guatemala, and effort shall be made to install it at the latest on September 15 of the coming year 1908.

ART. VII. The diplomatic and consular agents of the contracting Governments shall lend all the assistance that the Bureau may ask of them, furnishing it with all the needed data, reports, and information and shall fulfill the commissions and requests that it may see fit to entrust to them.

ART. VIII. The expenses incident to the maintenance of the Bureau shall be paid in equal parts by the signatory Powers.

ART. IX. The Bureau shall have an organ of publicity in connection with its work, and shall endeavor to maintain intercourse with other offices of a like nature, particularly with the International Bureau of the American Republics established in Washington.

ART. X. The Bureau shall be a medium of intelligence among the signatory countries and shall send the respective governments the communications, information, and reports that it may deem necessary for the development of the relations and interests with which it is entrusted.

ART. XI. The present Convention shall remain in force for fifteen years, and may be extended at the will of the High Contracting Parties.

APPENDIX 5 (d)

CONVENTION CONCERNING FUTURE CENTRAL AMERICAN CONFERENCES,[1] CONCLUDED DECEMBER 20, 1907.

The Governments of the Republics of Costa Rica, Guatemala, Honduras, Nicaragua, and Salvador, desiring to promote the unification and harmony of their interests, as one of the most efficacious means to prepare for the fusion of the Central American peoples into one single nationality, have agreed to conclude a Convention for the naming of Commissions and for the meeting of Central American Conferences, which shall agree upon the most efficacious and proper means to the end of bringing uniformity into their economical and fiscal interests; and to that end have named as Delegates:

[Names of Delegates].

ART. I. Each one of the contracting Governments obligates itself to name within one month, counted from the last ratification of this agreement, one or more Commissions, which shall occupy themselves preferably with the study of all that concerns the monetary system of their respective countries, especially in relation to those of the other States, and interchange amongst them; and, besides, the study of everything relating to the custom-house systems, the system of weights and measures, and other matters of an economic and fiscal nature which it may be deemed expedient to make uniform in Central America.

ART. II. The Commissions shall present a report within six months after their appointment, and each Government shall communicate such report to the others, inviting them to designate forthwith one or more delegates, in order that they may attend a Central American Conference, which shall be inaugurated on the first of the following January, and shall have for its object the con-

---

[1] Malloy: Treaties, 2: 2416-2418.

clusion of a Convention for the purpose of defining the means tending to the accomplishment of the ends to which Article 1 relates, giving preference to what relates to the monetary system of the five Republics and endeavoring to establish therein a fixed rate of exchange with regard to gold.

Art. III. Conferences shall be held annually thereafter, which shall open on the first day of January, in order to treat the questions comprised in Article 1 of this Convention which have not been settled at the previous Conference; and all the other matters which the Governments may see fit to submit to said Conferences.

Art. IV. The first Conference shall meet at the city of Tegucigalpa on the date indicated in Article 11, and when its sessions are over it shall designate the place in which the next Conference shall meet, and so on successively.

Art. V. The present Convention shall remain in force for five years, but if at the expiration of that term none of the signatory Governments shall have denounced it, it shall continue in force until six months after one of the High Contracting Parties shall have notified the others of its determination to withdraw from it.

APPENDIX 6 (a)

CONVENTION (1) FOR THE PACIFIC SETTLEMENT OF INTERNATIONAL DISPUTES.[1]—SIGNED AT THE HAGUE, OCTOBER 18, 1907.

His Majesty the German Emperor, King of Prussia; [etc.]:

Animated by the sincere desire to work for the maintenance of general peace;

Resolved to promote by all the efforts in their power the friendly settlement of international disputes;

Recognizing the solidarity uniting the members of the society of civilized nations;

Desirous of extending the empire of law and of strengthening the appreciation of international justice;

Convinced that the permanent institution of a tribunal of arbitration, accessible to all, in the midst of independent Powers will contribute effectively to this result;

Having regard to the advantages attending the general and regular organization of the procedure of arbitration;

Sharing the opinion of the august initiator of the International Peace Conference that it is expedient to record in an international agreement the principles of equity and right on which are based the security of States and the welfare of peoples;

Being desirous, with this object, of insuring the better working in practice of commissions of inquiry and tribunals of arbitration, and of facilitating recourse to arbitration in cases which allow of a summary procedure;

Have deemed it necessary to revise in certain particulars and to complete the work of the First Peace Conference for the pacific settlement of international disputes;

The high contracting Parties have resolved to conclude a new

[1] Malloy: Treaties, 2: 2220–2248.

Convention for this purpose, and have appointed the following as their plenipotentiaries:

[Names of plenipotentiaries.]

Who, after having deposited their full powers, found in good and due form, have agreed upon the following:

PART I.—THE MAINTENANCE OF GENERAL PEACE

ART. 1. With a view to obviating as far as possible recourse to force in the relations between States, the contracting Powers agree to use their best efforts to insure the pacific settlement of international differences.

PART II.—GOOD OFFICES AND MEDIATION

ART. 2. In case of serious disagreement or dispute, before an appeal to arms, the contracting Powers agree to have recourse, as far as circumstances allow, to the good offices or mediation of one or more friendly Powers.

ART. 3. Independently of this recourse, the contracting Powers deem it expedient and desirable that one or more Powers, strangers to the dispute, should, on their own initiative and as far as circumstances may allow, offer their good offices or mediation to the States at variance.

Powers strangers to the dispute have the right to offer good offices or mediation even during the course of hostilities.

The exercise of this right can never be regarded by either of the parties in dispute as an unfriendly act.

ART. 4. The part of the mediator consists in reconciling the opposing claims and appeasing the feelings of resentment which may have arisen between the States at variance.

ART. 5. The functions of the mediator are at an end when once it is declared, either by one of the parties to the dispute or by the mediator himself, that the means of reconciliation proposed by him are not accepted.

ART. 6. Good offices and mediation undertaken either at the request of the parties in dispute or on the initiative of Powers strangers to the dispute have exclusively the character of advice, and never have binding force.

ART. 7. The acceptance of mediation can not, unless there be an agreement to the contrary, have the effect of interrupting, delaying, or hindering mobilization or other measures of preparation for war.

If it takes place after the commencement of hostilities, the military operations in progress are not interrupted in the absence of an agreement to the contrary.

ART. 8. The contracting Powers are agreed in recommending the application, when circumstances allow, of special mediation in the following form:

In case of a serious difference endangering peace, the States at variance choose respectively a Power, to which they intrust the mission of entering into direct communication with the Power chosen on the other side, with the object of preventing the rupture of pacific relations.

For the period of this mandate, the term of which, unless otherwise stipulated, can not exceed thirty days, the States in dispute cease from all direct communication on the subject of the dispute, which is regarded as referred exclusively to the mediating Powers, which must use their best efforts to settle it.

In case of a definite rupture of pacific relations, these Powers are charged with the joint task of taking advantage of any opportunity to restore peace.

PART III.—INTERNATIONAL COMMISSIONS OF INQUIRY

ART. 9. In disputes of an international nature involving neither honor nor vital interests, and arising from a difference of opinion on points of fact, the contracting Powers deem it expedient and desirable that the parties who have not been able to come to an agreement by means of diplomacy, should, as far as circumstances allow, institute an international commission of inquiry, to facilitate a solution of these disputes by elucidating the facts by means of an impartial and conscientious investigation.

ART. 10. International commissions of inquiry are constituted by special agreement between the parties in dispute.

The inquiry convention defines the facts to be examined; it determines the mode and time in which the commission is to be formed and the extent of the powers of the commissioners.

It also determines, if there is need, where the commission is to sit, and whether it may remove to another place, the language the commission shall use and the languages the use of which shall be authorized before it, as well as the date on which each party must deposit its statement of facts, and, generally speaking, all the conditions upon which the parties have agreed.

If the parties consider it necessary to appoint assessors, the convention of inquiry shall determine the mode of their selection and the extent of their powers.

ART. 11. If the inquiry convention has not determined where the commission is to sit, it will sit at The Hague.

The place of meeting, once fixed, can not be altered by the commission except with the assent of the parties.

If the inquiry convention has not determined what languages are to be employed, the question shall be decided by the commission.

ART. 12. Unless an undertaking is made to the contrary, commissions of inquiry shall be formed in the manner determined by Articles 45 and 57 of the present Convention.

ART. 13. Should one of the commissioners or one of the assessors, should there be any, either die, or resign, or be unable for any reason whatever to discharge his functions, the same procedure is followed for filling the vacancy as was followed for appointing him.

ART. 14. The parties are entitled to appoint special agents to attend the commission of inquiry, whose duty it is to represent them and to act as intermediaries between them and the commission.

They are further authorized to engage counsel or advocates, appointed by themselves, to state their case and uphold their interests before the commission.

ART. 15. The International Bureau of the Permanent Court of Arbitration acts as registry for the commissions which sit at The Hague, and shall place its offices and staff at the disposal of the contracting Powers for the use of the commission of inquiry.

ART. 16. If the commission meets elsewhere than at The Hague, it appoints a secretary general, whose office serves as registry.

It is the function of the registry, under the control of the president, to make the necessary arrangements for the sittings of the commission, the preparation of the minutes, and, while the inquiry lasts, for the charge of the archives, which shall subsequently be transferred to the International Bureau at The Hague.

ART. 17. In order to facilitate the constitution and working of commissions of inquiry, the contracting Powers recommend the following rules, which shall be applicable to the inquiry procedure in so far as the parties do not adopt other rules.

ART. 18. The commission shall settle the details of the procedure not covered by the special inquiry convention or the present Convention, and shall arrange all the formalities required for dealing with the evidence.

ART. 19. On the inquiry both sides must be heard.

At the dates fixed, each party communicates to the commission and to the other party the statements of facts, if any, and, in all cases, the instruments, papers, and documents which it considers useful for ascertaining the truth, as well as the list of witnesses and experts whose evidence it wishes to be heard.

ART. 20. The commission is entitled, with the assent of the Powers, to move temporarily to any place where it considers it may be useful to have recourse to this means of inquiry or to send one or more of its members. Permission must be obtained from the State on whose territory it is proposed to hold the inquiry.

ART. 21. Every investigation, and every examination of a locality, must be made in the presence of the agents and counsel of the parties or after they have been duly summoned.

ART. 22. The commission is entitled to ask from either party for such explanations and information as it considers necessary.

ART. 23. The parties undertake to supply the commission of inquiry, as fully as they may think possible, with all means and facilities necessary to enable it to become completely acquainted with, and to accurately understand, the facts in question.

They undertake to make use of the means at their disposal, under their municipal law, to insure the appearance of the witnesses or experts who are in their territory and have been summoned before the commission.

If the witnesses or experts are unable to appear before the commission, the parties will arrange for their evidence to be taken before the qualified officials of their own country.

ART. 24. For all notices to be served by the commission in the territory of a third contracting Power, the commission shall apply direct to the Government of the said Power. The same rule applies in the case of steps being taken on the spot to procure evidence.

The requests for this purpose are to be executed so far as the means at the disposal of the Power applied to under its municipal law allow. They can not be rejected unless the Power in question considers they are calculated to impair its sovereign rights or its safety.

The commission will equally be always entitled to act through the Power on whose territory it sits.

ART. 25. The witnesses and experts are summoned on the request of the parties or by the commission of its own motion, and, in every case, through the Government of the State in whose territory they are.

The witnesses are heard in succession and separately, in the presence of the agents and counsel, and in the order fixed by the commission.

ART. 26. The examination of witnesses is conducted by the president.

The members of the commission may however put to each witness questions which they consider likely to throw light on and complete his evidence, or get information on any point concerning the witness within the limits of what is necessary in order to get at the truth.

The agents and counsel of the parties may not interrupt the witness when he is making his statement, nor put any direct question to him, but they may ask the president to put such additional questions to the witness as they think expedient.

ART. 27. The witness must give his evidence without being allowed to read any written draft. He may, however, be permitted by the president to consult notes or documents if the nature of the facts referred to necessitates their employment.

Art. 28. A minute of the evidence of the witness is drawn up forthwith and read to the witness. The latter may make such alterations and additions as he thinks necessary, which will be recorded at the end of his statement.

When the whole of his statement has been read to the witness, he is asked to sign it.

Art. 29. The agents are authorized, in the course of or at the close of the inquiry, to present in writing to the commission and to the other party such statements, requisitions, or summaries of the facts as they consider useful for ascertaining the truth.

Art. 30. The commission considers its decisions in private and the proceedings are secret.

All questions are decided by a majority of the members of the commission.

If a member declines to vote, the fact must be recorded in the minutes.

Art. 31. The sittings of the commission are not public, nor the minutes and documents connected with the inquiry published except in virtue of a decision of the commission taken with the consent of the parties.

Art. 32. After the parties have presented all the explanations and evidence, and the witnesses have all been heard, the president declares the inquiry terminated, and the commission adjourns to deliberate and to draw up its report.

Art. 33. The report is signed by all the members of the commission.

If one of the members refuses to sign, the fact is mentioned; but the validity of the report is not affected.

Art. 34. The report of the commission is read at a public sitting, the agents and counsel of the parties being present or duly summoned.

A copy of the report is given to each party.

Art. 35. The report of the commission is limited to a statement of facts, and has in no way the character of an award. It leaves to the parties entire freedom as to the effect to be given to the statement.

ART. 36. Each party pays its own expenses and an equal share of the expenses incurred by the commission.

PART IV.—INTERNATIONAL ARBITRATION

CHAPTER I.—*The System of Arbitration*

ART. 37. International arbitration has for its object the settlement of disputes between States by judges of their own choice and on the basis of respect for law.

Recourse to arbitration implies an engagement to submit in good faith to the award.

ART. 38. In questions of a legal nature, and especially in the interpretation or application of international conventions, arbitration is recognized by the contracting Powers as the most effective, and, at the same time, the most equitable means of settling disputes which diplomacy has failed to settle.

Consequently, it would be desirable that, in disputes about the above-mentioned questions, the contracting Powers should, if the case arose, have recourse to arbitration, in so far as circumstances permit.

ART. 39. The arbitration convention is concluded for questions already existing or for questions which may arise eventually.

It may embrace any dispute or only disputes of a certain category.

ART. 40. Independently of general or private treaties expressly stipulating recourse to arbitration as obligatory on the contracting Powers, the said Powers reserve to themselves the right of concluding new agreements, general or particular, with a view to extending compulsory arbitration to all cases which they may consider it possible to submit to it.

CHAPTER II.—*The Permanent Court of Arbitration*

ART. 41. With the object of facilitating an immediate recourse to arbitration for international differences, which it has not been possible to settle by diplomacy, the contracting Powers undertake to maintain the Permanent Court of Arbitration, as established by the First Peace Conference, accessible at all times, and operating, unless otherwise stipulated by the parties, in accordance with the rules of procedure inserted in the present Convention.

Art. 42. The Permanent Court is competent for all arbitration cases, unless the parties agree to institute a special tribunal.

Art. 43. The Permanent Court sits at The Hague.

An International Bureau serves as registry for the Court. It is the channel for communications relative to the meetings of the Court; it has charge of the archives and conducts all the administrative business.

The contracting Powers undertake to communicate to the Bureau, as soon as possible, a certified copy of any conditions of arbitration arrived at between them and of any award concerning them delivered by a special tribunal.

They likewise undertake to communicate to the Bureau the laws, regulations, and documents eventually showing the execution of the awards given by the Court.

Art. 44. Each contracting Power selects four persons at the most, of known competency in questions of international law, of the highest moral reputation, and disposed to accept the duties of arbitrator.

The persons thus selected are inscribed, as members of the Court, in a list which shall be notified to all the contracting Powers by the Bureau.

Any alteration in the list of arbitrators is brought by the Bureau to the knowledge of the contracting Powers.

Two or more Powers may agree on the selection in common of one or more members.

The same person can be selected by different Powers.

The members of the Court are appointed for a term of six years. These appointments are renewable.

Should a member of the Court die or resign, the same procedure is followed for filling the vacancy as was followed for appointing him. In this case the appointment is made for a fresh period of six years.

ART. 45. When the contracting Powers wish to have recourse to the Permanent Court for the settlement of a difference which has arisen between them, the arbitrators called upon to form the tribunal with jurisdiction to decide this difference must be chosen from the general list of members of the Court.

Failing the direct agreement of the parties on the composition of the arbitration tribunal, the following course shall be pursued:

Each party appoints two arbitrators, of whom one only can be its national or chosen from among the persons selected by it as members of the Permanent Court. These arbitrators together choose an umpire.

If the votes are equally divided, the choice of the umpire is intrusted to a third Power, selected by the parties by common accord.

If an agreement is not arrived at on this subject each party selects a different Power, and the choice of the umpire is made in concert by the Powers thus selected.

If, within two months' time, these two Powers can not come to an agreement, each of them presents two candidates taken from the list of members of the Permanent Court, exclusive of the members selected by the parties and not being nationals of either of them. Drawing lots determines which of the candidates thus presented shall be umpire.

ART. 46. The tribunal being thus composed, the parties notify to the Bureau their determination to have recourse to the Court, the text of their compromis, and the names of the arbitrators.

The Bureau communicates without delay to each arbitrator the compromis, and the names of the other members of the tribunal.

The tribunal assembles at the date fixed by the parties. The Bureau makes the necessary arrangements for the meeting.

The members of the tribunal, in the exercise of their duties and out of their own country, enjoy diplomatic privileges and immunities.

ART. 47. The Bureau is authorized to place its offices and staff at the disposal of the contracting Powers for the use of any special board of arbitration.

The jurisdiction of the Permanent Court may, within the conditions laid down in the regulations, be extended to disputes between non-contracting Powers or between contracting Powers and non-contracting Powers, if the parties are agreed on recourse to this tribunal.

ART. 48. The contracting Powers consider it their duty, if a serious dispute threatens to break out between two or more of them, to remind these latter that the Permanent Court is open to them.

Consequently, they declare that the fact of reminding the parties at variance of the provisions of the present Convention, and the advice given to them, in the highest interests of peace, to have recourse to the Permanent Court, can only be regarded as friendly actions.

In case of dispute between two Powers, one of them can always address to the International Bureau a note containing a declaration that it would be ready to submit the dispute to arbitration.

The Bureau must at once inform the other Power of the declaration.

ART. 49. The Permanent Administrative Council composed of the diplomatic representatives of the contracting Powers accredited to The Hague and of the Netherlands Minister for Foreign Affairs, who will act as president, is charged with the direction and control of the International Bureau.

The Council settles its rules of procedure and all other necessary regulations.

It decides all questions of administration which may arise with regard to the operations of the Court.

It has entire control over the appointment, suspension, or dismissal of the officials and employes of the Bureau.

It fixes the payments and salaries, and controls the general expenditure.

At meetings duly summoned the presence of nine members is sufficient to render valid the discussions of the Council. The decisions are taken by a majority of votes.

The Council communicates to the contracting Powers without delay the regulations adopted by it. It furnishes them with an annual report on the labors of the Court, the working of the administration, and the expenditure. The report likewise contains a résumé of what is important in the documents communicated to the Bureau by the Powers in virtue of Article 43, paragraphs 3 and 4.

ART. 50. The expenses of the Bureau shall be borne by the contracting Powers in the proportion fixed for the International Bureau of the Universal Postal Union.

The expenses to be charged to the adhering Powers shall be reckoned from the date on which their adhesion comes into force.

CHAPTER III.—*Arbitration Procedure*

ART. 51. With a view to encouraging the development of arbitration, the contracting Powers have agreed on the following rules, which are applicable to arbitration procedure, unless other rules have been agreed on by the parties.

ART. 52. The Powers which have recourse to arbitration sign a compromis, in which the subject of the dispute is clearly defined, the time allowed for appointing arbitrators, the form, order, and time in which the communication referred to in Article 63 must be made, and the amount of the sum which each party must deposit in advance to defray the expenses.

The compromis likewise defines, if there is occasion, the manner of appointing arbitrators, any special powers which may eventually belong to the tribunal, where it shall meet, the language it shall use, and the languages the employment of which shall be authorized before it, and, generally speaking, all the conditions on which the parties are agreed.

ART. 53. The Permanent Court is competent to settle the compromis, if the parties are agreed to have recourse to it for the purpose.

It is similarly competent, even if the request is only made by one of the parties, when all attempts to reach an understanding through the diplomatic channel have failed, in the case of—

1. A dispute covered by a general treaty of arbitration concluded or renewed after the present Convention has come into

force, and providing for a compromise in all disputes and not either explicitly or implicitly excluding the settlement of the compromise from the competence of the Court. Recourse can not, however, be had to the Court if the other party declares that in its opinion the dispute does not belong to the category of disputes which can be submitted to compulsory arbitration, unless the treaty of arbitration confers upon the arbitration tribunal the power of deciding this preliminary question.

2. A dispute arising from contract debts claimed from one Power by another Power as due to its nationals, and for the settlement of which the offer of arbitration has been accepted. This arrangement is not applicable if acceptance is subject to the condition that the compromis should be settled in some other way.

Art. 54. In the cases contemplated in the preceding article, the compromis shall be settled by a commission consisting of five members selected in the manner arranged for in Article 45, paragraphs 3 to 6.

The fifth member is president of the commission ex officio.

Art. 55. The duties of arbitrator may be conferred on one arbitrator alone or on several arbitrators selected by the parties as they please, or chosen by them from the members of the Permanent Court of Arbitration established by the present Convention.

Failing the constitution of the tribunal by direct agreement between the parties, the course referred to in Article 45, paragraphs 3 to 6, is followed.

Art. 56. When a sovereign or the chief of a State is chosen as arbitrator, the arbitration procedure is settled by him.

Art. 57. The umpire is president of the tribunal ex officio.

When the tribunal does not include an umpire, it appoints its own president.

Art. 58. When the compromis is settled by a commission, as contemplated in Article 54, and in the absence of an agreement to the contrary, the commission itself shall form the arbitration tribunal.

Art. 59. Should one of the arbitrators either die, retire, or be unable for any reason whatever to discharge his functions, the same procedure is followed for filling the vacancy as was followed for appointing him.

ART. 60. The tribunal sits at The Hague, unless some other place is selected by the parties.

The tribunal can only sit in the territory of a third Power with the latter's consent.

The place of meeting once fixed can not be altered by the tribunal, except with the consent of the parties.

ART. 61. If the question as to what languages are to be used has not been settled by the compromis, it shall be decided by the tribunal.

ART. 62. The parties are entitled to appoint special agents to attend the tribunal to act as intermediaries between themselves and the tribunal.

They are further authorized to retain for the defense of their rights and interests before the tribunal counsel or advocates appointed by themselves for this purpose.

The members of the Permanent Court may not act as agents, counsel, or advocates except on behalf of the Power which appointed them members of the Court.

ART. 63. As a general rule arbitration procedure comprises two distinct phases: pleadings and oral discussions.

The pleadings consist in the communication by the respective agents to the members of the tribunal and the opposite party of cases, counter-cases, and, if necessary, of replies; the parties annex thereto all papers and documents called for in the case. This communication shall be made either directly or through the intermediary of the International Bureau, in the order and within the time fixed by the compromis.

The time fixed by the compromis may be extended by mutual agreement by the parties, or by the tribunal when the latter considers it necessary for the purpose of reaching a just decision.

The discussions consist in the oral development before the tribunal of the arguments of the parties.

ART. 64. A certified copy of every document produced by one party must be communicated to the other party.

ART. 65. Unless special circumstances arise, the tribunal does not meet until the pleadings are closed.

ART. 66. The discussions are under the control of the president.

They are only public if it be so decided by the tribunal, with the assent of the parties.

They are recorded in minutes drawn up by the secretaries appointed by the president. These minutes are signed by the president and by one of the secretaries and alone have an authentic character.

ART. 67. After the close of the pleadings, the tribunal is entitled to refuse discussion of all new papers or documents which one of the parties may wish to submit to it without the consent of the other party.

ART. 68. The tribunal is free to take into consideration new papers or documents to which its attention may be drawn by the agents or counsel of the parties.

In this case, the tribunal has the right to require the production of these papers or documents, but is obliged to make them known to the opposite party.

ART. 69. The tribunal can, besides, require from the agents of the parties the production of all papers, and can demand all necessary explanations. In case of refusal the tribunal takes note of it.

ART. 70. The agents and the counsel of the parties are authorized to present orally to the tribunal all the arguments they may consider expedient in defense of their case.

ART. 71. They are entitled to raise objections and points. The decisions of the tribunal on these points are final and can not form the subject of any subsequent discussion.

ART. 72. The members of the tribunal are entitled to put questions to the agents and counsel of the parties, and to ask them for explanations on doubtful points.

Neither the questions put, nor the remarks made by members of the tribunal in the course of the discussions, can be regarded as an expression of opinion by the tribunal in general or by its members in particular.

ART. 73. The tribunal is authorized to declare its competence in interpreting the compromis, as well as the other papers and documents which may be invoked and in applying the principles of law.

ART. 74. The tribunal is entitled to issue rules of procedure for the conduct of the case, to decide the forms, order, and time in which each party must conclude its arguments, and to arrange all the formalities required for dealing with the evidence.

ART. 75. The parties undertake to supply the tribunal, as fully as they consider possible, with all the information required for deciding the case.

ART. 76. For all notices which the tribunal has to serve in the territory of a third contracting Power, the tribunal shall apply direct to the Government of that Power. The same rule applies in the case of steps being taken to procure evidence on the spot.

The requests for this purpose are to be executed as far as the means at the disposal of the Power applied to under its municipal law allow. They can not be rejected unless the Power in question considers them calculated to impair its own sovereign rights or its safety.

The Court will equally be always entitled to act through the Power on whose territory it sits.

ART. 77. When the agents and counsel of the parties have submitted all the explanations and evidence in support of their case the president shall declare the discussion closed.

ART. 78. The tribunal considers its decisions in private and the proceedings remain secret.

All questions are decided by a majority of the members of the tribunal.

ART. 79. The award must give the reasons on which it is based. It contains the names of the arbitrators; it is signed by the president and registrar or by the secretary acting as registrar.

ART. 80. The award is read out in public sitting, the agents and counsel of the parties being present or duly summoned to attend.

ART. 81. The award, duly pronounced and notified to the agents of the parties, settles the dispute definitively and without appeal.

ART. 82. Any dispute arising between the parties as to the interpretation and execution of the award shall, in the absence of an agreement to the contrary, be submitted to the tribunal which pronounced it.

ART. 83. The parties can reserve in the compromis the right to demand the revision of the award.

In this case and unless there be an agreement to the contrary, the demand must be addressed to the tribunal which pronounced the award. It can only be made on the ground of the discovery of some new fact calculated to exercise a decisive influence upon the award and which was unknown to the tribunal and to the party which demanded the revision at the time the discussion was closed.

Proceedings for revision can only be instituted by a decision of the tribunal expressly recording the existence of the new fact, recognizing in it the character described in the preceding paragraph, and declaring the demand admissible on this ground.

The compromis fixes the period within which the demand for revision must be made.

ART. 84. The award is not binding except on the parties in dispute.

When it concerns the interpretation of a Convention to which Powers other than those in dispute are parties, they shall inform all the signatory Powers in good time. Each of these Powers is entitled to intervene in the case. If one or more avail themselves of this right, the interpretation contained in the award is equally binding on them.

ART. 85. Each party pays its own expenses and an equal share of the expenses of the tribunal.

CHAPTER IV.—*Arbitration by Summary Procedure*

ART. 86. With a view to facilitating the working of the system of arbitration in disputes admitting of a summary procedure, the contracting Powers adopt the following rules, which shall be observed in the absence of other arrangements and subject to the reservation that the provisions of Chaper III apply so far as may be.

ART. 87. Each of the parties in dispute appoints an arbitrator. The two arbitrators thus selected choose an umpire. If they do not agree on this point, each of them proposes two candidates taken from the general list of the members of the Permanent Court exclusive of the members appointed by either of the parties and not being nationals of either of them; which of the candidates thus proposed shall be the umpire is determined by lot.

The umpire presides over the tribunal, which gives its decisions by a majority of votes.

ART. 88. In the absence of any previous agreement the tribunal, as soon as it is formed, settles the time within which the two parties must submit their respective cases to it.

ART. 89. Each party is represented before the tribunal by an agent, who serves as intermediary between the tribunal and the Government who appointed him.

ART. 90. The proceedings are conducted exclusively in writing. Each party, however, is entitled to ask that witnesses and experts should be called. The tribunal has, for its part, the right to demand oral explanations from the agents of the two parties, as well as from the experts and witnesses whose appearance in Court it may consider useful.

PART V.—FINAL PROVISIONS

ART. 91. The present Convention, duly ratified, shall replace, as between the contracting Powers, the Convention for the pacific settlement of international disputes of the 29th July, 1899.

ART. 92. The present Convention shall be ratified as soon as possible.

The ratifications shall be deposited at The Hague.

The first deposit of ratifications shall be recorded in a procès-verbal signed by the representatives of the Powers which take part therein and by the Netherlands Minister for Foreign Affairs.

The subsequent deposits of ratifications shall be made by means of a written notification, addressed to the Netherlands Government and accompanied by the instrument of ratification.

A duly certified copy of the procès-verbal relative to the first deposit of ratifications, of the notifications mentioned in the preceding paragraph, and of the instruments of ratification, shall be immediately sent by the Netherlands Government, through the diplomatic channel, to the Powers invited to the Second Peace Conference, as well as to those Powers which have adhered to the convention. In the cases contemplated in the preceding paragraph, the said Government shall at the same time inform the Powers of the date on which it received the notification.

ART. 93. Non-signatory Powers which have been invited to the Second Peace Conference may adhere to the present Convention.

The Power which desires to adhere notifies its intention in writing to the Netherlands Government, forwarding to it the act of adhesion, which shall be deposited in the archives of the said Government.

This Government shall immediately forward to all the other Powers invited to the Second Peace Conference a duly certified copy of the notification as well as of the act of adhesion, mentioning the date on which it received the notification.

ART. 94. The conditions on which the Powers which have not been invited to the Second Peace Conference may adhere to the present Convention shall form the subject of a subsequent agreement between the contracting Powers.

ART. 95. The present Convention shall take effect, in the case of the Powers which were not a party to the first deposit of ratifications, sixty days after the date of the procès-verbal of this deposit, and, in the case of the Powers which ratify subsequently or which adhere, sixty days after the notification of their ratification or of their adhesion has been received by the Netherlands Government.

ART. 96. In the event of one of the contracting Powers wishing to denounce the present Convention, the denunciation shall be notified in writing to the Netherlands Government, which shall immediately communicate a duly certified copy of the notification to all the other Powers informing them of the date on which it was received.

The denunciation shall only have effect in regard to the notifying Power, and one year after the notification has reached the Netherlands Government.

ART. 97. A register kept by the Netherlands Minister for Foreign Affairs shall give the date of the deposit of ratifications effected in virtue of Article 92, paragraphs 3 and 4, as well as the date on which the notifications of adhesion (Article 93, paragraph 2) or of denunciation (Article 96, paragraph 1) have been received.

Each contracting Power is entitled to have access to this register and to be supplied with duly certified extracts from it.

In faith whereof the plenipotentiaries have appended their signatures to the present Convention.

Done at The Hague, the 18th October, 1907, in a single copy, which shall remain deposited in the archives of the Netherlands Government, and duly certified copies of which shall be sent, through the diplomatic channel, to the contracting Powers.

[Here follow signatures.]

APPENDIX 6 (b)

DRAFT CONVENTION RELATIVE TO THE CREATION OF A JUDICIAL ARBITRATION COURT[1]

PART I.—CONSTITUTION OF THE JUDICIAL ARBITRATION COURT

ART. 1. With a view to promoting the cause of arbitration, the contracting Powers agree to constitute, without altering the status of the Permanent Court of Arbitration, a Judicial Arbitration Court, of free and easy access, composed of judges representing the various juridical systems of the world, and capable of insuring continuity in jurisprudence of arbitration.

ART. 2. The Judicial Arbitration Court is composed of judges and deputy judges chosen from persons of the highest moral reputation, and all fulfilling conditions qualifying them, in their respective countries, to occupy high legal posts, or be jurists of recognized competence in matters of international law.

The judges and deputy judges of the Court are appointed, as far as possible, from the members of the Permanent Court of Arbitration. The appointment shall be made within the six months following the ratification of the present Convention.

ART. 3. The judges and deputy judges are appointed for a period of twelve years, counting from the date on which the appointment is notified to the Administrative Council created by the Convention for the pacific settlement of international disputes. Their appointments can be renewed.

Should a judge or deputy judge die or retire, the vacancy is filled in the manner in which his appointment was made. In this case, the appointment is made for a fresh period of twelve years.

ART. 4. The judges of the Judicial Arbitration Court are equal and rank according to the date on which their appointment was

[1] Malloy: Treaties, 1: 2380–2385.

notified. The judge who is senior in point of age takes precedence when the date of notification is the same.

The deputy judges are assimilated, in the exercise of their functions, with the judges. They rank, however, below the latter.

ART. 5. The judges enjoy diplomatic privileges and immunities in the exercise of their functions, outside their own country.

Before taking their seat, the judges and deputy judges must swear, before the Administrative Council, or make a solemn affirmation to exercise their functions impartially and conscientiously.

ART. 6. The Court annually nominates three judges to form a special delegation and three more to replace them should the necessity arise. They may be reëlected. They are balloted for. The persons who secure the largest number of votes are considered elected. The delegation itself elects its president, who, in default of a majority, is appointed by lot.

A member of the delegation can not exercise his duties when the Power which appointed him or of which he is a national, is one of the parties.

The members of the delegation are to conclude all matters submitted to them, even if the period for which they have been appointed judges has expired.

ART. 7. A judge may not exercise his judicial functions in any case in which he has, in any way whatever, taken part in the decision of a national tribunal, of a tribunal of arbitration, or of a commission of inquiry, or has figured in the suit as counsel or advocate for one of the parties.

A judge can not act as agent or advocate before the Judicial Arbitration Court or the Permanent Court of Arbitration, before a special tribunal of arbitration or a commission of inquiry, nor act for one of the parties in any capacity whatsoever so long as his appointment lasts.

ART. 8. The Court elects its president and vice-president by an absolute majority of the votes cast. After two ballots, the election is made by a bare majority and, in case the votes are even, by lot.

Art. 9. The judges of the Judicial Arbitration Court receive an annual salary of 6,000 Netherlands florins. This salary is paid at the end of each half-year, reckoned from the date on which the Court meets for the first time.

In the exercise of their duties during the sessions or in the special cases covered by the present Convention, they receive the sum of 100 florins per diem. They are further entitled to receive a traveling allowance fixed in accordance with regulations existing in their own country. The provisions of the present paragraph are applicable also to a deputy judge when acting for a judge.

These emoluments are included in the general expenses of the Court dealt with in Article 31, and are paid through the International Bureau created by the Convention for the pacific settlement of international disputes.

Art. 10. The judges may not accept from their own Government or from that of any other Power any remuneration for services connected with their duties in their capacity of members of the Court.

Art. 11. The seat of the Judicial Court of Arbitration is at The Hague, and can not be transferred, unless absolutely obliged by circumstances, elsewhere.

The delegation may choose, with the assent of the parties concerned, another site for its meetings, if special circumstances render such a step necessary.

Art. 12. The Administrative Council fulfils with regard to the Judicial Court of Arbitration the same functions as to the Permanent Court of Arbitration.

Art. 13. The International Bureau acts as registry to the Judicial Court of Arbitration, and must place its offices and staff at the disposal of the Court. It has charge of the archives and carries out the administrative work.

The secretary general of the Bureau discharges the functions of registrar.

The necessary secretaries to assist the registrar, translators and shorthand writers are appointed and sworn in by the Court.

Art. 14. The Court meets in session once a year. The

session opens the third Wednesday in June and lasts until all the business on the agenda has been transacted.

The Court does not meet in session if the delegation considers that such meeting is unnecessary. However, when a Power is party in a case actually pending before the Court, the pleadings in which are closed, or about to be closed, it may insist that the session should be held.

When necessary, the delegation may summon the Court in extraordinary session.

ART. 15. A report of the doings of the Court shall be drawn up every year by the delegation. This report shall be forwarded to the contracting Powers through the International Bureau. It shall also be communicated to the judges and deputy judges of the Court.

ART. 16. The judges and deputy judges, members of the Judicial Arbitration Court, can also exercise the functions of judge and deputy judge in the International Prize Court.

PART II.—COMPETENCY AND PROCEDURE

ART. 17. The Judicial Court of Arbitration is competent to deal with all cases submitted to it, in virtue either of a general undertaking to have recourse to arbitration or of a special agreement.

ART. 18. The delegation is competent—

1. To decide the arbitrations referred to in the preceding article, if the parties concerned are agreed that the summary procedure, laid down in Part IV, Chapter IV, of the Convention for the pacific settlement of international disputes is to be applied;

2. To hold an inquiry under and in accordance with Part III of the said Convention, in so far as the delegation is intrusted with such inquiry by the parties acting in common agreement. With the assent of the parties concerned, and as an exception to Article 7, paragraph 1, the members of the delegation who have taken part in the inquiry may sit as judges, if the case in dispute is submitted to the arbitration of the Court or of the delegation itself.

Art. 19. The delegation is also competent to settle the compromis referred to in Article 52 of the Convention for the pacific settlement of international disputes if the parties are agreed to leave it to the Court.

It is equally competent to do so, even when the request is only made by one of the parties concerned, if all attempts have failed to reach an understanding through the diplomatic channel in the case of—

1. A dispute covered by a general treaty of arbitration concluded or renewed after the present Convention has come into force, providing for a compromis in all disputes, and not either explicitly or implicitly excluding the settlement of the compromis from the competence of the delegation. Recourse can not, however, be had to the Court if the other party declares that in its opinion the dispute does not belong to the category of questions to be submitted to compulsory arbitration, unless the treaty of arbitration confers upon the arbitration tribunal the power of deciding this preliminary question.

2. A dispute arising from contract debts claimed from one Power by another Power as due to its nationals, and for the settlement of which the offer of arbitration has been accepted. This arrangement is not applicable if acceptance is subject to the condition that the compromis should be settled in some other way.

Art. 20. Each of the parties concerned may nominate a judge of the Court to take part, with power to vote, in the examination of the case submitted to the delegation.

If the delegation acts as a commission of inquiry, this task may be intrusted to persons other than the judges of the Court. The traveling expenses and remuneration to be given to the said persons are fixed and borne by the Powers appointing them.

Art. 21. The contracting Powers only may have access to the Judicial Arbitration Court set up by the present Convention.

Art. 22. The Judicial Court of Arbitration follows the rules of procedure laid down in the Convention for the pacific settlement of international disputes, except in so far as the procedure is laid down in the present Convention.

ART. 23. The Court determines what language it will itself use and what languages may be used before it.

ART. 24. The International Bureau serves as channel for all communications to be made to the judges during the interchange of pleadings provided for in Article 63, paragraph 2, of the Convention for the pacific settlement of international disputes.

ART. 25. For all notices to be served, in particular on the parties, witnesses, or experts, the Court may apply direct to the Government of the State on whose territory the service is to be carried out. The same rule applies in the case of steps being taken to procure evidence.

The requests addressed for this purpose can only be rejected when the Power applied to considers them likely to impair its sovereign rights or its safety. If the request is complied with, the fees charged must only comprise the expenses actually incurred.

The Court is equally entitled to act through the Power on whose territory it sits.

Notices to be given to parties in the place where the Court sits may be served through the International Bureau.

ART. 26. The discussions are under the control of the president or vice-president, or, in case they are absent or can not act, of the senior judge present.

The judge appointed by one of the parties can not preside.

ART. 27. The Court considers its decisions in private, and the proceedings are secret.

All decisions are arrived at by a majority of the judges present. If the number of judges is even and equally divided, the vote of the junior judge, in the order of precedence laid down in Article 4, paragraph 1, is not counted.

ART. 28. The judgment of the Court must give the reasons on which it is based. It contains the names of the judges taking part in it; it is signed by the president and registrar.

ART. 29. Each party pays its own costs and an equal share of the costs of the trial.

ART. 30. The provisions of Articles 21 to 29 are applicable by analogy to the procedure before the delegation.

When the right of attaching a member to the delegation has been exercised by one of the parties only, the vote of the member attached is not recorded if the votes are evenly divided.

ART. 31. The general expenses of the Court are borne by the contracting Powers.

The Administrative Council applies to the Powers to obtain the funds requisite for the working of the Court.

ART. 32. The Court itself draws up its own rules of procedure, which must be communicated to the contracting Powers.

After the ratification of the present Convention the Court shall meet as early as possible in order to elaborate these rules, elect the president and vice-president, and appoint the members of the delegation.

ART. 33. The Court may propose modifications in the provisions of the present Convention concerning procedure. These proposals are communicated through the Netherland Government to the contracting Powers, which will consider together as to the measures to be taken.

PART III.—FINAL PROVISIONS

ART. 34. The present Convention shall be ratified as soon as possible.

The ratifications shall be deposited at The Hague.

A *procès-verbal* of the deposit of each ratification shall be drawn up, of which a duly certified copy shall be sent through the diplomatic channel to all the signatory Powers.

ART. 35. The Convention shall come into force six months after its ratification.

It shall remain in force for twelve years, and shall be tacitly renewed for periods of twelve years, unless denounced.

The denunciation must be notified, at least two years before the expiration of each period, to the Netherland Government, which will inform the other Powers.

The denunciation shall only have effect in regard to the notifying Power. The Convention shall continue in force as far as the other Powers are concerned.

APPENDIX 6 (c)

CONVENTION (XII) RELATIVE TO THE CREATION OF AN INTERNATIONAL PRIZE COURT[1]
(Signed at The Hague, October 18, 1907)

His Majesty, the German Emperor, King of Prussia; [etc.]:

Animated by the desire to settle in an equitable manner the differences which sometimes arise in the course of a naval war in connection with the decisions of national prize courts;

Considering that, if these courts are to continue to exercise their functions in the manner determined by national legislation, it is desirable that in certain cases an appeal should be provided under conditions conciliating, as far as possible, the public and private interests involved in matters of prize;

Whereas, moreover, the institution of an International Court, whose jurisdiction and procedure would be carefully defined, has seemed to be the best method of attaining this object;

Convinced, finally, that in this manner the hardships consequent on naval war would be mitigated; that, in particular, good relations will be more easily maintained between belligerents and neutrals and peace better assured;

Desirous of concluding a Convention to this effect, have appointed the following as their plenipotentiaries:

[Here follow the names of plenipotentiaries.]

Who, after depositing their full powers, found in good and due form, have agreed upon the following provisions:

PART I.—GENERAL PROVISIONS

ART. 1. The validity of the capture of a merchant ship or its cargo is decided before a prize court in accordance with

[1] Treaties of the United States. Edited by Charles 3:248–265.

the present Convention when neutral or enemy property is involved.

ART. 2. Jurisdiction in matters of prize is exercised in the first instance by the prize courts of the belligerent captor.

The judgments of these courts are pronounced in public or are officially notified to parties concerned who are neutrals or enemies.

ART. 3. The judgments of national prize courts may be brought before the International Prize Court—

1. When the judgment of the national prize courts affects the property of a neutral Power or individual;

2. When the judgment affects enemy property and relates to—

(a) Cargo on board a neutral ship;

(b) An enemy ship captured in the territorial waters of a neutral Power, when that Power has not made the capture the subject of a diplomatic claim;

(c) A claim based upon the allegation that the seizure has been effected in violation, either of the provisions of a Convention in force between the belligerent Powers, or of an enactment issued by the belligerent captor.

The appeal against the judgment of the national court can be based on the ground that the judgment was wrong either in fact or in law.

ART. 4. An appeal may be brought—

1. By a neutral Power, if the judgment of the national tribunals injuriously affects its property or the property of its nationals (Article 3, No. 1), or if the capture of an enemy vessel is alleged to have taken place in the territorial waters of that Power (Article 3, No. 2b).

2. By a neutral individual, if the judgment of the national court injuriously affects his property (Article 3, No. 1), subject, however, to the reservation that the Power to which he belongs may forbid him to bring the case before the Court, or may itself undertake the proceedings in his place;

3. By an individual subject or citizen of an enemy Power, if the judgment of the national court injuriously affects his property in

the cases referred to in Article 3, No. 2, except that mentioned in paragraph *b*.

ART. 5. An appeal may also be brought on the same conditions as in the preceding article, by persons belonging either to neutral States or to the enemy, deriving their rights from and entitled to represent an individual qualified to appeal, and who have taken part in the proceedings before the national court. Persons so entitled may appeal separately to the extent of their interest.

The same rule applies in the case of persons belonging either to neutral States or to the enemy who derive their rights from and are entitled to represent a neutral Power whose property was the subject of the decision.

ART. 6. When, in accordance with the above Article 3, the International Court has jurisdiction, the national courts can not deal with a case in more than two instances. The municipal law of the belligerent captor shall decide whether the case may be brought before the International Court after judgment has been given in first instance or only after an appeal.

If the national courts fail to give final judgment within two years from the date of capture, the case may be carried direct to the International Court.

ART. 7. If a question of law to be decided is covered by a treaty in force between the belligerent captor and a Power which is itself or whose subject or citizen is a party to the proceedings, the Court is governed by the provisions of the said treaty.

In the absence of such provisions, the Court shall apply the rules of international law. If no generally recognized rule exists, the Court shall give judgment in accordance with the general principles of justice and equity.

The above provisions apply equally to questions relating to the order and mode of proof.

If, in accordance with Article 3, No. 2*c*, the ground of appeal is the violation of an enactment issued by the belligerent captor, the Court will enforce the enactment.

The Court may disregard failure to comply with the procedure laid down in the enactments of the belligerent captor, when it is of opinion that the consequences of complying therewith are unjust and inequitable.

ART. 8. If the Court pronounces the capture of the vessel or cargo to be valid, they shall be disposed of in accordance with the laws of the belligerent captor.

If it pronounces the capture to be null, the Court shall order restitution of the vessel or cargo, and shall fix, if there is occasion, the amount of the damages. If the vessel or cargo have been sold or destroyed, the Court shall determine the compensation to be given to the owner on this account.

If the national court pronounced the capture to be null, the Court can only be asked to decide as to the damages.

ART. 9. The contracting Powers undertake to submit in good faith to the decisions of the International Prize Court and to carry them out with the least possible delay.

PART II.—CONSTITUTION OF THE INTERNATIONAL PRIZE COURT

ART. 10. The International Prize Court is composed of judges and deputy judges, who will be appointed by the contracting Powers, and must all be jurists of known proficiency in questions of international maritime law, and of the highest moral reputation.

The appointment of these judges and deputy judges shall be made within six months after the ratification of the present Convention.

ART. 11. The judges and deputy judges are appointed for a period of six years, reckoned from the date on which the notification of their appointment is received by the Administrative Council established by the Convention for the pacific settlement of international disputes of the 29th July, 1899. Their appointments can be renewed.

Should one of the judges or deputy judges die or resign, the same procedure is followed for filling the vacancy as was followed for appointing him. In this case, the appointment is made for a fresh period of six years.

ART. 12. The judges of the International Prize Court are all equal in rank and have precedence according to the date on which the notification of their appointment was received (Article 11, paragraph 1), and if they sit by rota (Article 15, paragraph 2), according to the date on which they entered upon their duties. When the date is the same the senior in age takes precedence.

The deputy judges when acting are assimilated to the judges. They rank, however, after them.

ART. 13. The judges enjoy diplomatic privileges and immunities in the performance of their duties and when outside their own country.

Before taking their seat, the judges must swear, or make a solemn promise before the Administrative Council, to discharge their duties impartially and conscientiously.

ART. 14. The Court is composed of fifteen judges; nine judges constitute a quorum.

A judge who is absent or prevented from sitting is replaced by the deputy judge.

ART. 15.[1] The judges appointed by the following contracting Powers: Germany, the United States of America, Austria-Hungary, France, Great Britain, Italy, Japan, and Russia, are always summoned to sit.

The judges and deputy judges appointed by the other contracting Powers sit by rota as shown in the table annexed[2] to the present

---

[1] Reservation of this article was made by Chile, Cuba, Ecuador, Guatemala, Haiti, Persia, Salvador, Siam, Turkey, and Uruguay.

[2] ANNEX TO ARTICLE 15

Distribution of Judges and Deputy Judges by Countries for Each Year of the Period of Six Years

JUDGES	DEPUTY JUDGES	JUDGES	DEPUTY JUDGES
First Year		*Second Year*	
1 Argentine	Paraguay	Argentine	Panama
2 Colombia	Bolivia	Spain	Spain
3 Spain	Spain	Greece	Roumania
4 Greece	Roumania	Norway	Sweden
5 Norway	Sweden	Netherlands	Belgium
6 Netherlands	Belgium	Turkey	Luxemburg
7 Turkey	Persia	Uruguay	Costa Rica

Convention; their duties may be performed successively by the same person. The same judge may be appointed by several of the said Powers.

ART. 16. If a belligerent Power has, according to the rota, no judge sitting in the Court, it may ask that the judge appointed by it should take part in the settlement of all cases arising from the war. Lots shall then be drawn as to which of the judges entitled to sit according to the rota shall withdraw. This arrangement does not affect the judge appointed by the other belligerent.

ART. 17. No judge can sit who has been a party, in any way whatever, to the sentence pronounced by the national courts, or has taken part in the case as counsel or advocate for one of the parties.

No judge or deputy judge can, during his tenure of office, appear as agent or advocate before the International Prize Court nor act for one of the parties in any capacity whatever.

ART. 18. The belligerent captor is entitled to appoint a naval officer of high rank to sit as assessor, but with no voice in the decision. A neutral Power, which is a party to the proceedings or whose subject or citizen is a party, has the same right of appointment; if as the result of this last provision more than one Power is concerned, they must agree among themselves, if necessary by lot, on the officer to be appointed.

JUDGES	DEPUTY JUDGES	JUDGES	DEPUTY JUDGES
Third Year		*Fourth Year*	
1 Brazil	Dominican Rep.	Brazil	Guatemala
2 China	Turkey	China	Turkey
3 Spain	Portugal	Spain	Portugal
4 Netherlands	Switzerland	Peru	Honduras
5 Roumania	Greece	Roumania	Greece
6 Sweden	Denmark	Sweden	Denmark
7 Venezuela	Haiti	Switzerland	Netherlands
Fifth Year		*Sixth Year*	
1 Belgium	Netherlands	Belgium	Netherlands
2 Bulgaria	Montenegro	Chile	Salvador
3 Chile	Nicaragua	Denmark	Norway
4 Denmark	Norway	Mexico	Ecuador
5 Mexico	Cuba	Portugal	Spain
6 Persia	China	Servia	Bulgaria
7 Portugal	Spain	Siam	China

ART. 19. The Court elects its president and vice-president by an absolute majority of the votes cast. After two ballots, the election is made by a bare majority, and, in case the votes are equal, by lot.

ART. 20. The judges on the International Prize Court are entitled to traveling allowances in accordance with the regulations in force in their own country, and in addition receive, while the Court is sitting or while they are carrying out duties conferred upon them by the Court, a sum of 100 Netherland florins *per diem*.

These payments are included in the general expenses of the Court dealt with in Article 47, and are paid through the International Bureau established by the Convention of the 29th July, 1899.

The judges may not receive from their own Government or from that of any other Power any remuneration in their capacity of members of the Court.

ART. 21. The seat of the International Prize Court is at The Hague and it can not, except in the cases of *force majeure*, be transferred elsewhere without the consent of the belligerents.

ART. 22. The Administrative Council fulfils, with regard to the International Prize Court, the same functions as to the Permanent Court of Arbitration, but only representatives of contracting Powers will be members of it.

ART. 23. The International Bureau acts as registry to the International Prize Court and must place its offices and staff at the disposal of the Court. It has charge of the archives and carries out the administrative work.

The secretary general of the International Bureau acts as registrar.

The necessary secretaries to assist the registrar, translators and shorthand writers, are appointed and sworn in by the Court.

ART. 24. The Court determines which language it will itself use and what languages may be used before it.

In every case the official language of the national courts which have had cognizance of the case may be used before the Court.

ART. 25. Powers which are concerned in a case may appoint special agents to act as intermediaries between themselves and the

Court. They may also engage counsel or advocates to defend their rights and interests.

ART. 26. A private person concerned in a case will be represented before the Court by an attorney, who must be either an advocate qualified to plead before a court of appeal or a high court of one of the contracting States, or a lawyer practising before a similar court, or lastly a professor of law at one of the higher teaching centers of those countries.

ART. 27. For all notices to be served, in particular on the parties, witnesses, or experts, the Court may apply direct to the Government of the State on whose territory the service is to be carried out. The same rule applies in the case of steps being taken to procure evidence.

The requests for this purpose are to be executed so far as the means at the disposal of the Power applied to under its municipal law allow. They can not be rejected unless the Power in question considers them calculated to impair its sovereign rights or its safety. If the request is complied with, the fees charged must only comprise the expenses actually incurred.

The Court is equally entitled to act through the Power on whose territory it sits.

Notices to be given to parties in the place where the Court sits may be served through the International Bureau.

PART III.—PROCEDURE IN THE INTERNATIONAL PRIZE COURT

ART. 28. An appeal to the International Prize Court is entered by means of a written declaration made in the national court which has already dealt with the case or addressed to the International Bureau; in the latter case the appeal can be entered by telegram.

The period within which the appeal must be entered is fixed at 120 days, counting from the day the decision is delivered or notified (Article 2, paragraph 2).

ART. 29. If the notice of appeal is entered in the national court, this Court, without considering the question whether the appeal was entered in due time, will transmit within seven days the record of the case to the International Bureau.

If the notice of the appeal is sent to the International Bureau, the Bureau will immediately inform the national court, when possible by telegraph. The latter will transmit the record as provided in the preceding paragraph.

When the appeal is brought by a neutral individual the International Bureau at once informs by telegraph the individual's Government, in order to enable it to enforce the rights it enjoys under Article 4, paragraph 2.

ART. 30. In the case provided for in Article 6, paragraph 2, the notice of appeal can be addressed to the International Bureau only. It must be entered within thirty days of the expiration of the period of two years.

ART. 31. If the appellant does not enter his appeal within the period laid down in Article 28 or 30, it shall be rejected without discussion.

Provided that he can show that he was prevented from so doing by *force majeure*, and that the appeal was entered within sixty days after the circumstances which prevented him entering it before had ceased to operate, the Court can, after hearing the respondent, grant relief from the effect of the above provision.

ART. 32. If the appeal is entered in time, a certified copy of the notice of appeal is forthwith officially transmitted by the Court to the respondent.

ART. 33. If in addition to the parties who are before the Court, there are other parties concerned who are entitled to appeal, or if, in the case referred to in Article 29, paragraph 3, the Government who has received notice of an appeal has not announced its decision, the Court will await before dealing with the case the expiration of the period laid down in Article 28 or 30.

ART. 34. The procedure before the International Court includes two distinct parts: the written pleadings and oral discussions.

The written pleadings consist of the deposit and exchange of cases, counter-cases, and, if necessary, of replies, of which the order is fixed by the Court, as also the periods within which they must be delivered. The parties annex thereto all papers and documents of which they intend to make use.

A certified copy of every document produced by one party must be communicated to the other party through the medium of the Court.

ART. 35. After the close of the pleadings, a public sitting is held on a day fixed by the Court.

At the sitting the parties state their view of the case both as to the law and as to the facts.

The court may, at any stage of the proceedings, suspend speeches of counsel, either at the request of one of the parties, or on their own initiative, in order that supplementary evidence may be obtained.

ART. 36. The International Court may order the supplementary evidence to be taken either in the manner provided by Article 27, or before itself, or one or more of the members of the Court, provided that this can be done without resort to compulsion or the use of threats.

If steps are to be taken for the purpose of obtaining evidence by members of the Court outside the territory where it is sitting, the consent of the foreign Government must be obtained.

ART. 37. The parties are summoned to take part in all stages of the proceedings and receive certified copies of the minutes.

ART. 38. The discussions are under the control of the president or vice-president, or, in case they are absent or can not act, of the senior judge present.

The judge appointed by a belligerent party can not preside.

ART. 39. The discussions take place in public, subject to the right of a Government who is a party to the case to demand that they be held in private.

Minutes are taken of these discussions and signed by the president and registrar, and these minutes alone have an authentic character.

ART. 40. If a party does not appear, despite the fact that he has been duly cited, or if a party fails to comply with some step within the period fixed by the Court, the case proceeds without that party, and the Court gives judgment in accordance with the material at its disposal.

ART. 41. The Court officially notifies to the parties decrees or decisions made in their absence.

ART. 42. The Court takes into consideration in arriving at its decision all the facts, evidence, and oral statements.

ART. 43. The Court considers its decision in private and the proceedings are secret.

All questions are decided by a majority of the judges present. If the number of judges is even and equally divided, the vote of the junior judge in the order of precedence laid down in Article 12, paragraph 1, is not counted.

ART. 44. The judgment of the Court must give the reasons on which it is based. It contains the names of the judges taking part in it, and also of the assessors, if any; it is signed by the president and registrar.

ART. 45. The sentence is pronounced in public sitting, the parties concerned being present or duly summoned to attend; the sentence is officially communicated to the parties.

When this communication has been made, the Court transmits to the national prize court the record of the case, together with copies of the various decisions arrived at and of the minutes of the proceedings.

ART. 46. Each party pays its own costs.

The party against whom the Court decides bears, in addition, the costs of the trial, and also pays 1 per cent of the value of the subject-matter of the case as a contribution to the general expenses of the International Court. The amount of these payments is fixed in the judgment of the Court.

If the appeal is brought by an individual, he will furnish the International Bureau with security to an amount fixed by the Court, for the purpose of guaranteeing eventual fulfilment of the two obligations mentioned in the preceding paragraph. The Court is entitled to postpone the opening of the proceedings until the security has been furnished.

ART. 47. The general expenses of the International Prize Court are borne by the contracting Powers in proportion to their share in the composition of the Court as laid down in Article 15 and in the annexed table. The appointment of deputy judges does not involve any contribution.

The Administrative Council applies to the Powers for the funds requisite for the working of the Court.

ART. 48. When the Court is not sitting, the duties conferred upon it by Article 32, Article 34, paragraphs 2 and 3, Article 35, paragraph 1, and Article 46, paragraph 3, are discharged by a delegation of three judges appointed by the Court. This delegation decides by a majority of votes.

ART. 49. The Court itself draws up its own rules of procedure, which must be communicated to the contracting Powers.

It will meet to elaborate these rules within a year of the ratification of the present Convention.

ART. 50. The Court may propose modifications in the provisions of the present Convention concerning procedure. These proposals are communicated, through the medium of the Netherland Government, to the contracting Powers, which will consider together as to the measures to be taken.

PART IV.—FINAL PROVISIONS

ART. 51. The present Convention does not apply as of right except when the belligerent Powers are all parties to the Convention.

It is further fully understood that an appeal to the International Prize Court can only be brought by a contracting Power or the subject or citizen of a contracting Power.

In the cases mentioned in Article 5, the appeal is only admitted when both the owner and the person entitled to represent him are equally contracting Powers or the subjects or citizens of contracting Powers.

ART. 52. The present Convention shall be ratified and the ratifications shall be deposited at The Hague as soon as all the Powers mentioned in Article 15 and in the table annexed are in a position to do so.

The deposit of the ratifications shall take place, in any case, on the 30th June, 1909, if the Powers which are ready to ratify furnish nine judges and nine deputy judges to the Court, qualified to validly constitute a Court. If not, the deposit shall be postponed until this condition is fulfilled.

A minute of the deposit of ratifications shall be drawn up, of which a certified copy shall be forwarded, through the diplomatic channel, to each of the Powers referred to in the first paragraph.

ART. 53. The Powers referred to in Article 15 and in the table annexed are entitled to sign the present Convention up to the deposit of the ratifications contemplated in paragraph 2 of the preceding article.

After this deposit, they can at any time adhere to it, purely and simply. A Power wishing to adhere, notifies its intention in writing to the Netherland Government transmitting to it, at the same time, the act of adhesion, which shall be deposited in the archives of the said Government. The latter shall send, through the diplomatic channel, a certified copy of the notification and of the act of adhesion to all the Powers referred to in the preceding paragraph, informing them of the date on which it has received the notification.

ART. 54. The present Convention shall come into force six months from the deposit of the ratifications contemplated in Article 52, paragraphs 1 and 2.

The adhesions shall take effect sixty days after notification of such adhesion has been received by the Netherland Government, or as soon as possible on the expiration of the period contemplated in the preceding paragraph.

The International Court shall, however, have jurisdiction to deal with prize cases decided by the national courts at any time after the deposit of the ratifications or of the receipt of the notification of the adhesions. In such cases, the period fixed in Article 28, paragraph 2, shall only be reckoned from the date when the Convention comes into force as regards a Power which has ratified or adhered.

ART. 55. The present Convention shall remain in force for twelve years from the time it comes into force, as determined by Article 54, paragraph 1, even in the case of Powers which adhere subsequently.

It shall be renewed tacitly from six years to six years unless denounced.

Denunciation must be notified in writing, at least one year before the expiration of each of the periods mentioned in the two preceding paragraphs, to the Netherland Government, which will inform all the other contracting Powers.

Denunciation shall only take effect in regard to the Power which has notified it. The Convention shall remain in force in the case of the other contracting Powers, provided that their participation in the appointment of judges is sufficient to allow of the composition of the Court with nine judges and nine deputy judges.

ART. 56. In case the present Convention is not in operation as regards all the Powers referred to in Article 15 and the annexed table, the Administrative Council shall draw up a list on the lines of that article and table of the judges and deputy judges through whom the contracting Powers will share in the composition of the Court. The times allotted by the said table to judges who are summoned to sit in rota will be redistributed between the different years of the six-year period in such a way that, as far as possible, the number of the judges of the Court in each year shall be the same. If the number of deputy judges is greater than that of the judges, the number of the latter can be completed by deputy judges chosen by lot among those powers which do not nominate a judge.

The list drawn up in this way by the Administrative Council shall be notified to the contracting Powers. It shall be revised when the number of these Powers is modified as the result of adhesions or denunciations.

The change resulting from an adhesion is not made until the 1st January after the date on which the adhesion takes effect, unless the adhering Power is a belligerent Power, in which case it can ask to be at once represented in the Court, the provision of Article 16 being, moreover, applicable if necessary.

When the total number of judges is less than eleven, seven judges form a quorum.

ART. 57. Two years before the expiration of each period referred to in paragraphs 1 and 2 of Article 55 any contracting Power can demand a modification of the provisions of Article 15 and of the annexed table, relative to its participation in the composition of the Court. The demand shall be addressed to the Administrative Council, which will examine it and submit to all the Powers proposals as to the measures to be adopted. The Powers shall inform the Administrative Council of their decision with the least possible delay. The result shall be at once, and at least one year and thirty days before the expiration of the said period of two years, communicated to the Power which made the demand.

When necessary, the modifications adopted by the Powers shall come into force from the commencement of the fresh period.

In faith whereof the plenipotentiaries have appended their signatures to the present Convention.

Done at The Hague, the 18th October, 1907, in a single copy, which shall remain deposited in the archives of the Netherland Government, and duly certified copies of which shall be sent, through the diplomatic channel, to the Powers designated in Article 15 and in the table annexed.

[Here follow signatures.]

ADDITIONAL PROTOCOL TO THE CONVENTION RELATIVE TO THE ESTABLISHMENT OF AN INTERNATIONAL COURT OF PRIZE

(Signed at The Hague, September 19, 1910.)

Germany, the United States of America, the Argentine Republic, Austria-Hungary, Chile, Denmark, Spain, France, Great Britain, Japan, Norway, the Netherlands, Sweden,

Powers signatory to the Hague Convention dated October 18, 1907, for the establishment of an International Court of Prize,

Considering that for some of these Powers difficulties of a constitutional nature prevent the acceptance of the said Convention, in its present form,

Have deemed it expedient to agree upon an additional protocol taking into account these difficulties without jeopardizing any legitimate interest and have, to that end, appointed as their plenipotentiaries, to wit:

[Here follow the names of plenipotentiaries.]

Who, after depositing their full powers, found to be in good and due form, have agreed upon the following:

ART. 1. The Powers signatory or adhering to the Hague Convention of October 18, 1907, relative to the establishment of an International Court of Prize, which are prevented by difficulties of a constitutional nature from accepting the said Convention in its present form, have the right to declare in the instrument of ratification or adherence that in prize cases, whereof their national courts have jurisdiction, recourse to the International Court of Prize can only be exercised against them in the form of an action in damages for the injury caused by the capture.

ART. 2. In the case of recourse to the International Court of Prize, in the form of an action for damages, Article 8 of the Convention is not applicable; it is not for the Court to pass upon the validity or the nullity of the capture, nor to reserve or affirm the decision of the national tribunals.

If the capture is considered illegal, the Court determines the amount of damages to be allowed, if any, to the claimants.

ART. 3. The conditions to which recourse to the International Court of Prize is subject by the Convention are applicable to the action in damages.

ART. 4. Under reserve of the provisions hereinafter stated the rules of procedure established by the Convention for recourse to the International Court of Prize shall be observed in the action in damages.

ART. 5. In derogation of Article 28, paragraph 1, of the Convention, the suit for damages can only be brought before the International Court of Prize by means of a written declaration addressed to the International Bureau of the Permanent Court of Arbitration; the case may even be brought before the Bureau by telegram.

ART. 6. In derogation of Article 29 of the Convention the International Bureau shall notify directly, and if possible by telegram, the Government of the belligerent captor of the declaration of action brought before it.

The Government of the belligerent captor, without considering whether the prescribed periods of time have been observed, shall, within seven days of the receipt of the notification, transmit to the International Bureau the case, appending thereto a certified copy of the decision, if any, rendered by the national tribunal.

ART. 7. In derogation of Article 45, paragraph 2, of the Convention the Court rendering its decision and notifying it to the parties to the suit shall send directly to the Government of the belligerent captor the record of the case submitted to it, appending thereto a copy of the various intervening decisions as well as a copy of the minutes of the preliminary proceedings.

ART. 8. The present additional protocol shall be considered as forming an integral part of and shall be ratified at the same time as the Convention.

If the declaration provided for in Article 1 herein above is made in the instrument of the ratification, a certified copy thereof shall be inserted in the *procès-verbal* of the deposit of ratifications referred to in Article 52, paragraph 3, of the Convention.

ART. 9. Adherence to the Convention is subordinated to adherence to the present additional protocol.

In faith of which the plenipotentiaries have affixed their signatures to the present additional protocol.

Done at The Hague on the 19th day of September, 1910, in a single copy, which shall remain deposited in the archives of the Government of the Netherlands and of which duly certified copies shall be forwarded through diplomatic channels to the Powers designated in Article 15 of the Convention relative to the establishment of an International Court of Prize of October 18, 1907, and in its appendix.

[Here follow signatures.]

APPENDIX

TREATY FOR THE ADVANCEMENT [OF PEACE BETWEEN THE]
UNITED STATES AND [...]

The United States of America and the Republic of [...] being desirous to strengthen the bonds of amity that bind them together and also to advance the cause of general peace, have resolved to enter into a treaty for that purpose and to that end have appointed as their plenipotentiaries:

[Names of Plenipotentiaries.]

ART. 1. The high contracting parties agree that all disputes between them, of every nature whatsoever, which diplomacy shall fail to adjust, shall be submitted for investigation and report to an International Commission, to be constituted in the manner prescribed in the next succeeding Article; and they agree not to declare war or begin hostilities during such investigation and report.

ART. 2. The International Commission shall be composed of five members, to be appointed as follows: One member shall be chosen from each country, by the Government thereof; one member shall be chosen by each Government from some third country; the fifth member shall be chosen by common agreement between the two Governments. The expenses of the Commission shall be paid by the two Governments in equal proportion.

The International Commission shall be appointed within four months after the exchange of the ratifications of this treaty; and vacancies shall be filled according to the manner of the original appointment.

ART. 3. In case the high contracting parties shall have failed to adjust a dispute by diplomatic methods, they shall at once refer it to the International Commission for investigation and report. The

---
[1] United States. Treaty Series, no. 598.

APPENDIX

...l Commission may, however, act upon its own in[...]nd in such case it shall notify both Governments and re[...] ...eir co-operation in the investigation.

...e report of the International Commission shall be completed [...]hin one year after the date on which it shall declare its investiga-...ion to have begun, unless the high contracting parties shall extend the time by mutual agreement. The report shall be prepared in triplicate; one copy shall be presented to each Government, and the third retained by the Commission for its files.

The high contracting parties reserve the right to act independently on the subject-matter of the dispute after the report of the Commission shall have been submitted.

ART. 4. The present treaty shall be ratified by the President of the United States of America, by and with the advice and consent of the Senate thereof; and by the President of the Republic of Guatemala, with the approval of the Congress thereof; and the ratifications shall be exchanged as soon as possible. It shall take effect immediately after the exchange of ratifications, and shall continue in force for a period of five years; and it shall thereafter remain in force until twelve months after one of the high contracting parties have given notice to the other of an intention to terminate it.

In witness whereof the respective plenipotentiaries have signed the present treaty and have affixed thereunto their seals.

Done in Washington on the 20th day of September, in the year of our Lord nineteen hundred and thirteen.

APPENDIX 8

BIBLIOGRAPHY

I. Fundamental Concepts

a.—THE STATE

BROWN, PHILIP M.
  Rights of states under international law.
  (Yale law journal, 26:85-93, December, 1916.)
DICKINSON, EDWIN D.
  Analogy between natural persons and international persons in the law of nations.
  (Yale law journal, 26:564-591, May, 1917.)
FOLLETT, M. P.
  The new state; group organization the solution of popular government. New York, Longmans, Green & Co., 1918.
  8°. vii, 373 p.
GIDDINGS, FRANKLIN H.
  The responsible state; a reëxamination of fundamental political doctrines in the light of world war and the menace of anarchism. Boston, Houghton Mifflin Co., 1918
  12°. x, 107 p.
HILL, DAVID J.
  World organization, as affected by the nature of the modern state. New York, Columbia university press, 1911.
  8°. ix, 214 p.
SCOTT, JAMES B.
  The American institute of international law; its declaration of the rights and duties of nations. Washington, American institute of international law, 1916.
  8°. 125 p.

WILLOUGHBY, WESTEL W.
An examination of the nature of the state; a study in political philosophy. New York, Macmillan Co., 1903.
8°. xii, 448 p.

WILLOUGHBY, W. W., and CRANE, R. T.
Juristic conception of the state.
(American political science review, 12:192–214, May, 1918.)

b.—SOVEREIGNTY

BALDWIN, SIMEON E.
Division of sovereignty.
(International law notes, 3:57–59, July, 1918.)

BALDWIN, SIMEON E.
The vesting of sovereignty in a league of nations.
(Yale law review, 28:209–218, January, 1919.)

LANSING, ROBERT
A unique international problem.
(American journal of international law, 11:763–771, October, 1917.)

Deals with the problem of governing the islands of Spitzbergen, over which no nation has yet asserted sovereignty. The questions of territorial and personal sovereignty are involved.

LASKI, HAROLD J.
Studies in the problem of sovereignty. New Haven, Yale university press, 1917.
8°. xi, 297 p.

MERRIAM, CHARLES E.
History of the theory of sovereignty since Rousseau. New York, Columbia university press, 1900.
8°. 233 p.

c.—EQUALITY

BARBOSA, RUY
Equality of sovereign states.
(Independent, 64:75–82, January 9, 1908.)

An address delivered by one of the delegates of Brazil at the Second Hague conference, in support of the traditional doctrine of the equality of states.

BROWN, PHILIP M.
  The theory of the independence and equality of states.
  (American journal of international law, 9:305–335, April, 1915.)

DICKINSON, EDWIN D.
  League of nations and international law.
  (American political science review, 12:304–311, May, 1918.)

  Author believes that the success of a league of nations requires a drastic revision of the theories on which international law is based; particularly the theory of the equality of states.

HICKS, FREDERICK C.
  The equality of states and the Hague conferences.
  (American journal of international law, 2:530–561, July, 1908.)

LOUGHLIN, HARRY H.
  Rating the several sovereign nations on a basis equitable for the allotment of representatives to a world parliament.
  (Scientific monthly, 3:579–584, December, 1916.)

  Three schemes are worked out for proportional representation of states.
  "Small nations will argue that all sovereign nations should be equally represented; yet equitability, not necessarily equality, is the only basis of representation in governing bodies generally."

MYERS, DENYS P.
  Representation in public international organs.
  (American journal of international law, 8:81–108, January, 1914.)

  A study of the actual basis of representation in forty-five official international conferences and organizations.

d.—NATIONALITY

BUTLER, NICHOLAS MURRAY
  Nationality and beyond.
  (International conciliation, No. 107, October, 1916. 10 p.)

DESTRÉE, JULES
  Belgium and the principle of nationality. Translated by H. Clay. London, Council for the study of international relations, 1917.
  8°. 45 p.

KREHBIEL, EDWARD
  Nationalism, war and society. A study of nationalism and its concomitant, war, in their relation to civilization; and of the fundamentals and the progress of the opposition to war. New York, Macmillan Co., 1916.
  12°. xxxv, 276 p.

LAMBERT, HENRI
  National self-determination.
  (North American review, 207:541–548, April, 1918.)

MCMURRAY, ORRIN K.
  Inter-citizenship: a basis for world peace.
  (Yale law journal, 27:299–316, January, 1918.)

MASARYK, THOMAS G.
  The problem of small nations in the European crisis; inaugural lecture at the University of London, King's College. London, Council for the study of international relations, 1916.
  8°. 32 p.

MUIR, RAMSAY
  Nationalism and internationalism. The culmination of modern history. Boston, Houghton Mifflin & Co., 1916.
  12°. 229 p.

PERLA, LEO
  What is "national honor." With introduction by Norman Angell. New York, Macmillan Co., 1918.
  8°. xxxiv, 211 p.

"National honor is the fundamental *casus belli* and the challenge of the reconstruction. To define it is to lay the corner-stone for universal, all-inclusive arbitration without which the peace of the future must rest as a house upon sands."—*Preface*.

PIGGOTT, FRANCIS T.
  Nationality, including naturalization and English law on the high seas and beyond the realm. London, W. Clowes & Sons, 1907.
  8°. 2 v.

RUYSSEN, THEODORE
  The principle of nationality.

(International conciliation. No. 109, December, 1916; No. 112, March, 1917; No. 118, September, 1917.)
1. The world war and the principle of nationality.
2. Small states and nationalities.
3. What is a nationality?
4. The problems of nationality.

e.—SANCTION FOR INTERNATIONAL LAW

BALDWIN, SIMEON E.
 Suspension from the society of nations, a sufficient sanction for a world-court judgment.
 (American law review, 52:695-700, September-October, 1918.)

HILL, DAVID J.
 The possible means of increasing the effectiveness of international law.
 (American society of international law. Proceedings, 1916, p. 11-17.)

SPENCER, ARTHUR W.
 The organization of international force.
 (American journal of international law, 9:45-71, January, 1915.)

WRIGHT, PHILIP Q.
 Enforcement of international law through municipal law in the United States. Urbana, University of Illinois, 1916.
 8°. 264 p.

II. BALANCE OF POWER

BERNARD, MONTAGUE
 Systems of policy.
 (*In his* Four lectures on subjects connected with diplomacy, 1868; Lecture 2, p. 61-109.)

BRANDYCE, HARRY D.
 Balance of power in 1915.
 (Forum, 46:129-141, August, 1911.)

DONNADIEU, LÉONCE
 Essai sur la théorie de l'équilibre. Étude d'histoire diplomatique et de droit international. Paris, A. Rousseau, 1900.
 8°. xx, 293 p.

DUPUIS, CHARLES
  Le principe d'équilibre et le concert européen de la paix de Westphalie à l'acte d'Algesiras. Paris, Perrin et cie, 1909.
  8°. 525 p.
GENTZ, FRIEDRICH VON
  Fragments upon the balance of power in Europe. Translated from the German. London, M. Peltier, 1806.
  8°. 335 p.
HASSALL, ARTHUR
  The balance of power, 1715-1789. New York, Macmillan Co., 1898.
  8°. viii, 433 p.
HUME, DAVID
  Of the balance of power.
  (*In his* Philosophical works, London, 1882, v. 3, Essay 7, p. 348-356.)
LECKIE, GOULD F.
  An historical research into the nature of the balance of power in Europe. London, Taylor & Hessey, 1817.
  8°. ix, 371 p.
SINGER, ARTHUR
  Histoire de la Triple alliance; avec une annexe de Hans F. Helmolt: Le contenu de la Triple alliance, étude diplomatique; tr. de l'allemand par Louis Suret . . . Paris, Giard, 1915.
  8°. vii-viii, 370 p.

III. EARLY PROPOSALS FOR INTERNATIONAL ORGANIZATION

DARBY, W. EVANS
  International tribunals; a collection of the various schemes which have been propounded, and of instances since 1815. Third ed. London, J. M. Dent, 1900.
  8°. x, 516 p.
MEULEN, JACOB TER
  Der Gedanke der internationalen Organisation in seiner Ent-

wicklung 1300–1800. Haag, Martinus Nijhoff, 1917.
8°. xi, 397 p.

1306
DUBOIS, PIERRE
De recuperatione Terre Sancte; traité de politique générale. Pub. d'après le manuscrit du Vatican par Ch.-V. Langlois. Paris, A. Picard, 1891.
8°. xxiv, 144 p.

1601
THE GREAT DESIGN of Henry IV, from the memoirs of the Duke of Sully; and the United States of Europe, by Edward Everett Hale. With introduction by Edwin D. Mead, Boston, Ginn & Co., 1909.
12°. xxi, 91 p.

Contains also "Passages illustrating the history of the Great Design," pp. 54-76. Dr. Hale's article was written in 1871.

DAVIS, HAYNE
The Grand Design of Henry the Great.
(Independent, 56:1497–9, June 30, 1904.)

PYLE, JOSEPH GILPIN.
An earlier league to enforce peace.
(Unpopular review, 10:244–54, October–December, 1918.)
An account of the Grand Design of Henry IV.

1623
CRUCÉ, ÉMERIC
Le nouveau Cynée, ou discours d'estat représentant les occasions et moyens d'establir une paix générale et la liberté du commerce par tout le monde. Edited and translated from the original French text of 1623. Philadelphia, Allen, Lane & Scott, 1909.
4°. xxxi, 363 p.

BALCH, THOMAS W.
Eméric Crucé. Philadelphia, Allen, Lane & Scott, 1900.
8°. 74 p.

1693

PENN, WILLIAM

Essay towards the present and future peace of Europe. London, 1693. 12°.

An essay towards the present and future peace of Europe, by the establishment of an European dyet, parliament, or estates. London, 1696.

William Penn's plan for a general European union.

(In Memoirs of the Historical Society of Pennsylvania. Philadelphia, 1858. v. 6, p. 265–281.)

Plan for the peace of Europe, an essay towards the present and future peace of Europe by the establishment of an European diet, parliament, or estates. Boston, 1896.

8°. 20 p. (Old South leaflets, general series, No. 75.)

An essay towards the present and future peace of Europe. First published in 1693–94. Washington, D. C., The American peace society, 1912.

8°. 21 p.

The peace of Europe: The fruits of solitude, and other writings. London & Toronto, J. M. Dent & Sons; New York, E. P. Dutton & Co. [1916]

8°. 292 p. (Everyman's library No. 724.)

1710.

BELLERS, JOHN

Some reasons for an European State proposed to the Powers of Europe. By an universal guarantee, and an annual Congress, Senate, Dyet, or Parliament, to settle any disputes about the bounds and rights of princes and states hereafter. With an abstract of a scheme form'd by King Henry the fourth of France, upon the same subject, and also a proposal for a general council or convocation of all the different religious perswasions in Christendom, (not to dispute what they differ about, but) to settle the general principles they agree in: By which it will appear, that they may be good subjects and neighbours, tho' of different

apprehensions of the way to heaven. In order to prevent broils
& war at home, when foreign wars are ended. London, 1710.

1712

SAINT-PIERRE, CHARLES, ABBÉ DE
Mémoires pour rendre la paix perpétuelle en Europe. Cologne,
chez Jacques le Pacifique, 1712.
12°. 36, 448 p.
Projet pour rendre la paix perpétuelle en Europe. Utrecht,
A. Schouten, 1713.
8°. 2v. port.
A project for settling an everlasting peace in Europe. First proposed by Henry IV of France and approved by Queen Elizabeth and most of the then princes of Europe, and now discussed at large, and made practicable. London, printed for J. W., 1714.
12°. x, 177 p.

1761

ROUSSEAU, JEAN JACQUES, 1712-1778.
A lasting peace through the federation of Europe. Translated
by C. E. Vaughan. London, Constable & Co., 1917.
12°. 128 p.

1789

BENTHAM, JEREMY
A plan for an universal and perpetual peace.
(*In his* Works. Edinburgh, 1843. v. 2, p. 546-560.)
Grundsätze für ein künftiges Völkerrecht und einen dauernden
Frieden, übersetzt von Camill Klatscher (mit einer Einleitung
über Bentham, Kant und Wundt von Oskar Kraus). Halle,
1915.

1795

KANT, IMMANUEL
Eternal peace and other international essays. Boston, World
peace foundation, 1914.
12°. xxiv, 179 p.

Kant's principles of politics, including his essay on Perpetual peace. A contribution to political science. Edited and translated by W. Hastie. . . . Edinburgh, T. &. T. Clark, 1891.
12°. xliv, 148 p.

Perpetual peace, a philosophical essay by Immanuel Kant, published in 1795; tr. by Benjamin F. Trueblood. Boston, The American Peace Society 1897.
12°. 53 p.

Perpetual peace; a philosophical essay by Immanuel Kant, 1795. Translated, with introduction and notes, by M. Campbell Smith, with a preface by Professor Latta. New York, Macmillan Co.; London, G. Allen & Unwin (1917).
12°. xi (2) 203 p.

1840

LADD, WILLIAM

The essays of Philanthropos (pseud.) on peace and war, which first appeared in the Christian Mirror, printed at Portland, Maine. Rev. and cor. by the author. 2d ed. . . . Exeter, N. H., J. T. Burnham in behalf of the Exeter, and other peace societies, 1827.
12°. 173 p.

A dissertation on a congress of nations. By Philanthropos (pseud.). Published by order of the American Peace Society. (Boston?) Press of J. Loring, 1832.
8°. 28 p.

An essay on a congress of nations, for the adjustment of international disputes without resort to arms . . . 3d thousand. London, T. Ward & Co., 1840.
8°. 32 p.

Essay on a congress of nations, for the adjustment of international disputes and for the promotion of universal peace, without resort to arms.

(*In* Prize essays on a congress of nations. Boston, Whipple & Damrell, 1840. p. 509–700.)

An essay on a congress of nations, for the adjustment of international disputes without resort to arms. Reprinted from the original edition of 1840, with an introduction by J. B. Scott. New York, Oxford University Press, 1916.
8°. L, 162 p.

IV. FORMER LEAGUES OF NATIONS

1518

A SIXTEENTH-CENTURY league of nations.
(The Nation. International Relations section. v. 108, p. 372, March 8, 1919).
Treaty between England and France negotiated by Thomas Wolsey, October 2, 1518.

1787

SCOTT, JAMES B.
James Madison's notes of debates in the Federal Convention of 1787 and their relation to a more perfect society of nations. New York, Oxford University press, 1918.
8°. xviii, 149 p.

1813–1823

ABBOTT, WILBUR C.
After Napoleon and after Wilhelm II
(Unpopular review, 11:233–245, April–June, 1919.)
DAVIS, HENRY W.
The war of Ormuzd and Ahriman in the nineteenth century. Baltimore, J. S. Waters, 1852.
8°. 450 p.
PHILLIPS, WALTER A.
The confederation of Europe; a study of the European alliance, 1813–1823, as an experiment in the international organization of peace. London, Longmans, Green & Co., 1914.
8°. xv, 315 p.
The peace movement and the Holy Alliance.
(Edinburgh Review, 215:405–433, April, 1912.)

V. ARGUMENTS FOR A NEW WORLD POLITY

ANITCHKOW, MICHAEL
 War and labor. Westminster, Archibald Constable & Co., 1900.
 8°. xii, 578 p.

BAILEY, LIBERTY H.
 Universal service; the hope of humanity. New York, Sturgis & Walton, 1918.
 8°. xii, 165 p.

BOLCE, HAROLD
 New internationalism. New York, Appleton & Co., 1907.
 12°. 309 p.

BOURNE, RANDOLPH S., *comp*.
 Towards an enduring peace; a symposium of peace proposals and programs, 1914-1916; with an introduction by Franklin H. Giddings. New York, American association for international conciliation, 1916.
 8°. xv, 336 p.

BUTLER, NICHOLAS MURRAY
 International mind, an argument for the judicial settlement of international disputes. New York, Scribner, 1912.
 8°. xi, 121 p.

 "The international mind is nothing else than that habit of thinking of foreign relations and business, and that habit of dealing with them, which regard the several nations of the civilized world as friendly and coöperating equals in aiding the progress of civilization, in developing commerce and industry and in spreading enlightenment and culture throughout the world."

BUTLER, NICHOLAS MURRAY
 World in ferment; interpretations of the war for a new world. New York, Scribner, 1917.
 12°. viii, 254 p.

FARIES, JOHN C.
 The rise of internationalism. New York, W. D. Gray, 1915.
 8°. 207 p.

HART, HEBER L.
 The bulwarks of peace. London, Methuen & Co., 1918.
 12°. xii, 221 p.

JORDAN, DAVID S., and KREHBIEL, EDWARD B.
  Syllabus of lectures on international conciliation given at Leland Stanford Junior University. Boston, World peace foundation, 1912.
  8°. iv, 244 p.
  "Outline of thirty-seven lectures, with references to books and periodical articles under each subject."

LANE, RALPH NORMAN ANGELL
  The great illusion. A study of the relation of military power in nations to their economic and social advantage. New edition. New York, G. P. Putnam's Sons, 1912.
  8°. xvi, 428 p.

MACFARLANE, CHARLES W.
  The economic basis of an enduring peace. Philadelphia, G. W. Jacobs & Co., 1918.
  8°. 79 p.

MARSHALL, HENRY R.
  War and the ideal of peace. New York, Duffield & Co., 1915.
  12°. 234 p.

MOORE, JOHN BASSETT
  The peace problem.
  (Columbia University quarterly, 18:210–225, June, 1916; reprinted in North American Review, July, 1916.)

MORRIS, ROBERT T.
  The way out of war. Notes on the biology of the subject. New York, Doubleday, Page & Co., 1918.
  12°. vi, 166 p.

NOVICOW, JACQUES
  War and its alleged benefits. Translated by T. Seltzer. New York, H. Holt & Co., 1911.
  16°. 130 p.

PAPERS on inter-racial problems communicated to the first Universal Races Congress, held at the University of London, July 26–29, 1911. Edited by G. Spiller. Boston, World peace foundation, 1911.
  8°. xlvi, 485 p.

TENNEY, ALVAN A.
Theories of social organization and the problem of international peace.
(Political science quarterly, 30:1-14, March, 1915.)

TRUEBLOOD, BENJAMIN F.
The federation of the world. Third edition. Boston, Houghton, Mifflin & Co., 1908.
12°. ix, 162 p.

VI. PROGRESS TOWARD THE IDEAL OF INTERNATIONAL ORGANIZATION

a.—INTERNATIONAL CONGRESSES, COMMISSIONS, AND UNIONS

BALDWIN, SIMEON E.
The international congresses and conferences of the last century as forces working toward the solidarity of the world.
(American journal of international law. 1:565-578, July, 1907; 1:808-829, October, 1907.)

Pages 808-829 contain:
1. List of memorable international conferences, congresses, or associations of official representatives of governments, exclusive of those mainly concerned in dealing with the results of a particular war.
2. List of the more important international congresses, etc., composed of private individuals.

BARRETT, JOHN
Pan-American union: peace, friendship, commerce. Washington, D. C., Pan-American union, 1911.
8°. 253 p.

LOWE, BOUTELLE E.
International aspects of the labor problem. New York, W. D. Gray, 1918.
8°. 128 p.

MCADOO, WILLIAM G.
International high commission and Pan-American coöperation.
(American journal of international law, 11:772-789, October, 1917.)

Pan-American scientific congress. 2d., Washington, D. C., 1915-1916.
> The final act and interpretative commentary thereon, prepared by James Brown Scott, reporter general of the congress. Washington, Government printing office, 1916.
> 8°. 516 p.

Reinsch, Paul S.
> Public international unions. 2d. ed. Boston, World peace foundation, 1916.
> 8°. viii, 189 p.

b.—Hague Conferences

Choate, Joseph H.
> The two Hague conferences. Princeton, Princeton university press, 1913.
> 12°. xiv, 109 p.

Higgins, A. Pearce
> The Hague peace conferences and other international conferences concerning the laws and usages of war. Texts of conventions with commentaries. Cambridge, University press, 1909.
> 8°. xiv, 632 p.

Hull, William I.
> The two Hague conferences and their contributions to international law. Boston, Ginn & Co., 1908.
> 12°. xiv, 516 p.

Lawrence, Thomas J.
> International problems and Hague conferences. London, J. M. Dent & Co., 1908.
> 12°. x, 210 p.

Schücking, Walther
> The international union of the Hague conferences. Translated from the German by Charles G. Fenwick. New York, Oxford university press, 1918.
> 8°. xiv, 341 p.
> Issued by the Carnegie Endowment for International Peace.

SCOTT, JAMES B.
  The Hague peace conferences of 1899 and 1907; a series of lectures delivered before the Johns Hopkins University. Baltimore, Johns Hopkins press, 1909.
  8°. 2 v.
  v. 1, conferences; v. 2, documents.

C.—PERMANENT COURT OF ARBITRATION

BARCLAY, THOMAS
  New methods of adjusting international disputes and the future. London, Constable & Co., 1917.
  8°. xiv, 206 p.

This book deals with the whole question of arbitral and judicial settlement, and is an invaluable manual of consultation while reading more specific treatises.

MYERS, DENYS P.
  The origin of the Hague arbitral courts.
  (American journal of law, 8:769–801, October, 1914; 10:270–311, April, 1916.)

Relates both to the Permanent Court of Arbitration, and the proposed Court of Arbitral Justice.

SCOTT, JAMES B., *editor*
  The Hague court reports. New York, Oxford university press, 1916.
  8°. cxi, 664 p.

Issued by the Division of International Law, Carnegie Endowment for International Peace.

In addition to the compromis and awards, the arguments and other documents are given.

WILSON, GEORGE G., *editor*
  The Hague arbitration cases. Boston, Ginn & Co., 1915.
  8°. x, 525 p.

CALDWELL, WALLACE E.
  Hellenic conceptions of peace. New York, 1919.
  8°. 141 p.
  (Doctoral thesis, Columbia University.)

RAEDER, ANTON H.
L'arbitrage international chez les Hellènes. New York, G. P. Putnam's Sons, 1912.
8°. 322 p.

TODD, MARCUS N.
International arbitration among the Greeks. Oxford, Clarendon press, 1913.
8°. xii, 196 p.

d.—COURT OF ARBITRAL JUSTICE

AMERICAN society for judicial settlement of international disputes.
Proceedings, 1910–1916. Baltimore, Waverly press, 1911–1917.
8°. 6 v.

BALCH, THOMAS W.
A world court in the light of the United States Supreme Court. Philadelphia, Allen, Lane & Scott, 1918.
8°. 163 p.

JUDICIAL settlement of international disputes.
Published quarterly by the American society for judicial settlement of international disputes. Baltimore, The Preston.

The society was formed in 1910 "for the purpose of promoting the establishment of a judicial tribunal which would perform for the nations of the civilized world a similar service to that which is given by ordinary courts to individuals, and of encouraging recourse to such a tribunal after its establishment."

WEHBERG, HANS
The problem of an international court of justice. Translated from the German by Charles G. Fenwick. New York, Oxford university press, 1918.
8°. xxxiii, 251 p.

Issued by the Carnegie Endowment for International Peace.

e.—INTERNATIONAL PRIZE COURT AND THE INTERNATIONAL NAVAL CONFERENCE

BENTWICH, NORMAN
The declaration of London. London, E. Wilson, 1911.
8°. vii, 179 p.

Discusses each article in detail. The author finds himself in disagreement with Bowles' Sea Law, listed below, which "has provided me," he says, "with arguments to controvert rather than with material to embody."

BOWLES, THOMAS G.
Sea law and sea power as they would be affected by recent proposals; with reasons against those proposals. London, J. Murray, 1910.
8°. xv, 296 p.

Discusses the probable operation of an international prize court, administering the law as stated in the Declaration of London.

THE DECLARATION of London, 1909.
(World peace foundation. Pamphlet series. v. 5, No. 3, pt. 2, App. I., June, 1915.)

An annotated text of the Declaration.

HIGGINS, A. PEARCE
Establishment of an International Prize Court.
(*In his* Hague peace conferences and other international conferences. p. 407-444.)

The text of the unratified convention, with comment on the need and the probable operation of an international prize court.

U. S. NAVAL war college, Newport.
International law topics. The declaration of London of February 26, 1909. Washington, Government printing office, 1910.
8°. 193 p.

Discussions of the Declaration, by officers of the United States Navy, under the guidance of Prof. George G. Wilson, who was a member of the International Naval Conference.

WHITE, THOMAS R.
Constitutionality of the proposed international prize court, considered from the standpoint of the United States.
(American journal of international law, 2:490-506, July, 1908.)

f.—CENTRAL AMERICAN COURT OF JUSTICE

CENTRAL American league of nations.
(World peace foundation. Pamphlet series. v. 7, No. 1. February, 1917. p. 110-151, i-xxi.)

Events leading up to the Peace Conference of 1907; and the inauguration of the Central American Court of Justice. The appendices contain the texts of the documents involved.

CORTE de justicia centroamericana, Cartago, Costa Rica.

Annales. San José, A. Alsina, 1911–1917.

8°. 12 v.

REGLAMENTO de la Corte de justicia centroamericana, diciembre de 1911. San José de Costa Rica, A. Alsina, 1911.

8°. 19 p.

COSTA RICA v. NICARAGUA. Central American Court of Justice, September 30, 1916.

(American Journal of International Law, 11:181–229, Jan. 1917.)

GONZÁLEZ, SALVADOR RODRÍGUEZ

The neutrality of Honduras and the question of the Gulf of Fonseca.

(American journal of international law, 10:509–542, July, 1916.)

REPUBLIC of El Salvador v. The Republic of Nicaragua.

Central American Court of Justice, March 9, 1917.

(American Journal of International Law, 11:674–730, July, 1917.)

g.—CODIFICATION OF INTERNATIONAL LAW

1876

FIELD, DAVID D.

Outlines of an international code. Second edition. New York, Baker, Voorhis & Co., 1876.

8°. 712 p.

"It aims to give a scheme of international law, such as publicists would recommend to governments, and at the same time, by pointing out in the notes the difference between existing rules and those recommended, to show what the former really are at the present time."—*Preface*.

1887

LEVI, LEONE

International law: with materials for a code of international law. New York, D. Appleton & Co., 1897.

12°. xii, 346 p.

First published in 1887.

"I have undertaken this work under the conviction that it would be of great advantage to reduce into the form of a code the leading principles of the law of nations; that the greater diffusion of knowledge of such law would often prevent disputes; and that, on the occurrence of differences between states, a collection of the well-established rules . . . would facilitate a resort to international arbitration."—*Preface*.

Includes positive international law as shown in treaties and conventions.

1890

FIORE, PASQUALE
International law codified and its legal sanction; or, the legal organization of the society of states. Translated from the fifth Italian edition, with an introduction by Edwin M. Borchard. New York, Baker, Voorhis & Co., 1918.
8°. xix, 750 p.

First published in 1890.

"The book does not purport to be a code of existing international law, but a systematic body of rules evolved by the author out of his accurate knowledge of positive law and of the defects of the prevailing system and submitted for adoption to the nations of the world for the better legal regulation of their mutual interests and relations."—EDITOR.

1911

NYS, ERNEST
Codification of international law.
(American journal of international law, 5:871–900, October, 1911.)

1911

ROOT, ELIHU
Function of private codification in international law.
(American journal of international law, 5:577–589, July, 1911; Proceedings, 5:19–32, 1911.)

h.—INTERNATIONAL ADMINISTRATION

CHAMBERLAIN, JOSEPH P.
The Danube. Nov. 1, 1918. Washington, Gov't. Print. off., 1918.
8°. 122 p. 5 maps.

International supervision of world trade routes. Two reports presented to the Final Settlements Committee of the New York Peace Society.

(The messenger of the New York Peace Society, v. 2, no. 2, p. 1–8, Jan., 1919.)

I. International trade routes, by J. P. Chamberlain and S. P. Duggan.
II. International control of communications on trade routes of the world as a pre-requisite for international coöperation, by Calvin Tomkins.

KAECKENBEECK, G.

International rivers, a monograph based on diplomatic documents . . . with an introductory note by Henry Goudy. London, Sweet & Maxwell, 1918.

8°. xxvi, 255 p.

KREHBIEL, EDWARD

European commission of the Danube; an experiment in international administration.

(Political science quarterly, 33:38–55, March, 1918; reprinted in International conciliation, No. 131, October, 1918.)

MOORE, FREDERICK

The control of foreign loans and concessions in China. A report presented to the Final Settlements Committee of the New York Peace Society, July 17, 1918.

(The Messenger of the New York Peace Society, v. 2, no. 1, p. 1–15, December, 1918.)

OGILVIE, PAUL M.

International waterways. New York, Macmillan Co., 1920.

8°. 424 p.

OVERLACH, T. W.

Foreign financial control in China. New York, Macmillan Co., 1919.

8°. xiii, 295 p.

REEVES, JESSE S.

The international beginnings of the Congo Free State. Baltimore, Johns Hopkins Press, 1894.

8°. 95 p. (Johns Hopkins University Studies in Historical and Political Science. 12th Series, nos. xi–xii.)

SAYRE, FRANCIS B.
Experiments in international administration. New York, Harper & Bros., 1919.
12°. xvi, 201 p.

VII. RECENT PROPOSALS AND DISCUSSIONS

ADAMS, GEORGE BURTON
The British Empire and a league of peace, together with an analysis of federal government, its functions and its method. New York, G. P. Putnam's sons, 1919.
12°. iii, 115 p.

ALLIN, C. D.
Representation on the Council of the League of Nations.
(Minnesota Law Review, 4:117-154, January, 1920.)

ASHBEE, CHARLES R.
The American League to enforce peace; an English interpretation, with an introduction by G. Lowes Dickinson. London, Allen & Unwin, 1917.
8°. 92 p.

BERRY, TREVOR T.
The hope of the world. An appreciation of the League of Nations scheme. London, P. S. King & Son, 1919.
12°. 192 p.

BRAILSFORD, Henry N.
League of nations. New York, Macmillan Co., 1917.
12°. vii, 332 p.

BRIDGMAN, RAYMOND L.
World organization. Boston, for the International union, by Ginn, 1905.
8°. vi, 172 p.

BRYCE, JAMES
Proposals for the prevention of future wars. London, Allen & Unwin, 1917.
8°. 54 p.

BUTLER, SIR GEOFFREY
  A handbook to the League of Nations. London, Longmans, Green & Co., 1919.
  8°. x, 80 p.
CENTRAL organization for a durable peace. The Hague.
  Recueil de rapports sur les differents points du programme-minimum. La Haye, Nijhoff, 1916–.
  8°.
  v. 1-4 already published.
COSMOS, *pseud*.
  Basis of durable peace. New York, Scribner, 1917.
  12°. ix, 144 p.
THE COVENANTER: an American exposition of the Covenant of the League of Nations, by William H. Taft, George W. Wickersham, A. Lawrence Lowell, and Henry W. Taft. New York, Doubleday, Page & Co., 1919.
  12°. ix, 188 p.
CROZIER, ALFRED O.
  Nation of nations; the way to permanent peace. A supreme constitution for the government of governments. Cincinnati, Stewart & Kidd, 1915.
  8°. 128 p.
DICKINSON, GOLDSWORTHY L.
  Choice before us. New York, Dodd, Mead & Co., 1917.
  8°. xiii, 268 p.
  The foundations of a league of peace.
  (World peace foundation. Pamphlet series, v. 5, No. 2, April, 1915. 20 p.)
DUGGAN, STEPHEN P., *editor*
  The League of Nations; the principle and the practice. Boston, Atlantic Monthly Press, 1919.
  8°. xviii, 357 p.
  A symposium by sixteen American writers.
EDMUNDS, STERLING E.
  International law applied to the treaty of peace, being a comparative analysis of the covenant and Treaty of Versailles of June 28,

1919, with the articles of the settlement and the applicable principles of the law of nations set out in parallel columns. [St. Louis?] 1919.
4°. 71 p.

ERZBERGER, MATTHIAS
The league of nations, the way to the world's peace; tr. by Bernard Miall. New York, Henry Holt, 1919.
8°. vi, 331 p.

FAYLE, C. ERNEST
The fourteenth point; a study of the league of nations. London, J. Murray, 1919.
12°. xi, 140 p.

GOLDSMITH, ROBERT
League to enforce peace; with a special introduction by A. Lawrence Lowell. New York, Macmillan Co., 1917.
12°. xxvi, 331 p.

HANSEN, H.
The adventures of the Fourteen Points. New York, Century Co., 1919.
8°. xxiii, 185 p.

HILL, DAVID J.
Present problems in foreign policy. New York, D. Appleton & Co., 1919.
8°. xiii, 385 p.

HISTORICAL light on the League to enforce peace.
(World peace foundation. Pamphlet series. v. 6, No. 6, December, 1916. 27 p.)

HOBSON, JOHN A.
Towards international government. London, Allen & Unwin, 1915.
12°. 216 p.

HYDE, H. E.
The international solution. London, Allen & Unwin, 1918.
12°. xviii, 93 p.

KALLEN, HORACE MEYER
  The league of nations, today and tomorrow. Boston, Marshall Jones Company, 1919.
  8°. xx, 181 p.

KEEN, FRANK N.
  The world in alliance; a plan for preventing future wars. London, W. Southwood & Co., 1915.
  12°. 60 p.

  Hammering out the details. London, A. C. Fifield, 1917.
  12°. 32 p.

Comparing the scheme of the League of Nations society in England with the League to Enforce Peace, American branch, and the Central Organization for a Durable Peace, and defining the essentials of a league of nations.

KEYNES, JOHN MAYNARD
  The economic consequences of the peace. London, Macmillan & Co., 1920.
  8°. vii, 279 p.

KOCOUREK, ALBERT
  Some reflections on the problem of a society of nations.
  (American journal of international law. 12:498–518, July, 1918.)

LAFONTAINE, HENRI
  The great solution—magnissima charta; essay on evolutionary and constructive pacifism. Boston, World peace foundation, 1916.
  8°. x, 177 p.

LANE, RALPH NORMAN ANGELL
  America and the new world-state; a plea for American leadership in international organization. New York, G. P. Putnam, 1915.
  8°. x, 305 p.

LAWRENCE, THOMAS J.
  The society of nations, its past, present and possible future. New York, Oxford university press, 1919.
  8°. xi, 194 p.

THE LEAGUE Bulletin, issued weekly by the League to Enforce Peace, 130 West Forty-second Street, New York.

The *Bulletin* was first issued on mimeographed sheets. Its successive numbers indicate events in the progress of the movement.

A LEAGUE of nations. Boston, World peace foundation, 1917–.
Vol. 1, No. 1, is dated October, 1917.
Supersedes World Peace Foundation. Pamphlet series.

THE LEAGUE of nations.
(International conciliation, No. 131, October, 1918. 65 p.)
1. The League of Nations, by Viscount Grey of Falloden.
2. A League of Nations, by Nicholas Murray Butler.
3. Labor and the League of Nations, by Ordway Tead.
4. The European Commission of the Danube: an experiment in international administration, by Edward Krehbiel.
5. Address of President Wilson at the Metropolitan Opera House, New York, September 27, 1918.

LEAGUE of nations society. Monthly report for members. London, 1 Central Buildings, Westminster.
No. 1 is dated January, 1918.

LEAGUE of nations society. Publications. London, 1 Central Buildings, Westminster, 1916.
Publication No. 1 was issued in March, 1916.

THE LEAGUE of Nations Covenant; the new international obligations of the United States under the proposed covenant of the League of Nations.
(Academy of Political Science. Proceedings, v. 8, No. 3, July, 1919.)
A series of addresses and papers presented at the national conference held in New York City, June 5, 1910.

LEAGUE to enforce peace.
A reference book for speakers: Win the war: Make the world safe by the defeat of German militarism: Keep the world safe by a league of nations. New York, The League, 1917.
12°. 64 p.
Bibliography, pp. 63–64.

LEAGUE to enforce peace. American branch. Independence Hall conference held in the city of Philadelphia, Bunker Hill Day (June 17), 1915, together with the speeches made at a public banquet in the Bellevue-Stratford hotel on the preceding evening. New York City, printed by the League to enforce peace, 1915.
12°. xii, 65 p.

Contains addresses by Wm. H. Short, Wm. H. Taft, A. Lawrence Lowell, Oscar S. Straus, George Gray, Hamilton Holt, Theodore Marburg, John B. Clark, and Edward A. Filene.

LEAGUE to enforce peace.
Enforced peace. Proceedings of the first annual national assemblage of the League to enforce peace, Washington, May 26–27, 1916. With an introductory chapter and appendices giving the proposals of the league, its officers and committees. New York, The League, 1916.
12°. vi, 204 p.

LEAGUE to enforce peace.
Win the war for permanent peace. Addresses made at the national convention of the League to enforce peace, in the city of Philadelphia, May 16 and 17, 1918. Convention and Governors' declaration. New York, The League, 1918.
8°. 253 p.

LOWELL, ABBOTT L.
A league to enforce peace.
(World peace foundation. Pamphlet series, v. 5, No. 5, pt. 1, October, 1915, 18 p.)

MARBURG, THEODORE
Draft convention for league of nations, by group of American jurists and publicists. Description and comment by Theodore Marburg. New York, Macmillan Co., 1918.
12°. 46 p.

The draft is the work of a private study group of twenty-one men, and is the result of a year's conferences and investigation. It is based on the program of the League to Enforce Peace, and represents a considerable development since the publication of Mr. Marburg's "League of Nations."

League of nations. New York, Macmillan Co., 1917-1918.

12°. 2 v.

Vol. 1, a chapter in the history of the movement; Vol. 2, its principles examined.

MARRIOTT, J. A. R.

The European commonwealth; problems historical and diplomatic. Oxford, Clarendon Press, 1918.

8°. xi, 370 p.

MINOR, RALEIGH C.

A republic of nations. A study of the organization of a federal league of nations. New York, Oxford university press, 1918.

12°. xxxix, 316 p.

MORROW, DWIGHT W.

The society of free states. New York, Harper & Bros., 1919.

12°. 224 p.

MYERS, DENYS P.

The conciliation plan of the league to enforce peace, with American treaties in force.

(World peace foundation. Pamphlet series. v. 6, No. 5, October, 1916. 35 p.)

OPPENHEIM, LASSA

The League of Nations and its problems. Three lectures. London, Longmans, Green & Co., 1919.

8°. xii, 84 p.

PAISH, GEORGE

A permanent League of Nations. London, T. Fisher Unwin, 1918.

12°. 139 p.

PHILLIPS, W. ALLISON

National federations and world federation.

(Edinburgh Review, 226: 1-27, July, 1917.)

POWELL, LYMAN P. and HODGINS, FRED B., Comp.

America and the league of nations; addresses in Europe, Woodrow Wilson. Chicago, Rand, McNally & Co. (1919).

12°. viii, 208 p.

RANDALL, H. L.
　The legal antecedents of a league of nations.
　(Yale law journal. 28: 301-313, Feb., 1919.)

(1) The enforcement of rights, (2) The position of international law, (3) The development of law, (4) The problem, (5) A partnership of nations, (6) The enforcement of public right.

THE RECOMMENDATIONS of Habana concerning international organization, adopted by the American Institute of International Law at Habana, January 23, 1917. New York, Oxford university press, 1917.
　8°. 100 p.

SAROLEA, CHARLES
　Europe and the League of nations. London, G. Bell & Sons, 1919.
　12°. vi, 317 p.

SCELLE, GEORGES
　Le pacte des nations et sa liaison avec le Traité de paix. Paris, Sirey, 1919.
　12°. x, 459 p.

SHORT, WILLIAM H.
　Program and policies of the League to enforce peace; a handbook for officers, speakers, and editors. New York, The League, 1916.
　12°. viii, 53 p.

SLAYDEN, JAMES L.
　Disarmament and international courts prerequisites to a durable peace.
　(Annals, American Academy of political and social science, 72: 92-100, July, 1917.

SMUTS, JAN C.
　The league of nations; a practical suggestion. London, Hodder & Stoughton, 1918.
　12°. 71 p.

STALLYBRASS, W. T. S.
　A society of states; or, Sovereignty, independence, and equality in a league of nations. London, G. Routledge & Sons, ltd. (1918).
　12°. 176 p.

STOWELL, ELLERY C.
Plans for world organization.
(Columbia University quarterly, 18:226-240, June, 1916.)

SYDENHAM, LORD, of Combe
The greatest "League of Nations."
(Nineteenth century and after, 84:251-259, August, 1918.)

TAFT, WILLIAM H. and BRYAN, WILLIAM J.
The proposal for a league to enforce peace.
(International conciliation, No. 106, September, 1916.   35 p.)
Mr. Taft for the affirmative, and Mr. Bryan for the negative.
An enlarged edition was published by the George H. Doran Co., in 1917.

TCHERNOFF, J.
Les nations et la Société des nations dans la politique moderne.
Paris, Alcan, 1919.
12°.   xxvii, 200 p.   (Bibliothèque d'histoire contemporaine.)

TEAD, ORDWAY
The people's part in peace; an inquiry into the basis for a sound internationalism.   New York, H. Holt & Company, 1918.
12°.   ix, 156 p.

THOMAS, ALBERT
The league of nations.
(Atlantic Monthly, 122:677-687, November, 1918.)
"Here is a question of stabilizing the various categories of inter-Allied institutions which are already functioning and growing more effective as the war goes on."

WALKER, JAMES, and PETRE, M. D.
State morality and a League of Nations.   London, T. Fisher Unwin, 1919.
12°.   121 p.

WALSTON, SIR CHARLES
The English-speaking brotherhood and the league of nations.
Cambridge, University press, 1919.
12°.   xxi, 224 p.

WAR OBVIATED by an international police; a series of essays written in various countries. The Hague, M. Nijhoff, 1915.
8°. iv, 223 p.

Articles representing points of view by publicists in Holland, Finland, United States, Austria, France, Germany, and Great Britain.

WELLS, H. G., and others

The idea of a league of nations. Boston, The Atlantic monthly press (1919).
8°. 44 p.

WILSON, GEORGE G.

The Monroe doctrine and the program of the League to enforce peace.
(World peace foundation. Pamphlet series. v. 6, No. 4, August, 1916. 15 p.)

WOOD, T. McKINNON

A necessary guarantee of the peace.
(Contemporary review, 114:477-483.)

WOOLF, LEONARD S.

The framework of a lasting peace. London, Allen & Unwin, 1917.
8°. 154 p.

Comparison of the projects of the League to Enforce Peace; minimum program of the Central Organization for a durable peace, The Hague; The League of Nations Society; proposals of Lord Bryce's group; the Fabian Society draft treaty; the community of nations; preliminary draft of a general treaty for the pacific settlement of international disputes, by a Dutch committee.

International government. New York, Brentano's, 1916.
4°. xxiii, 412 p.

This volume consists of two reports prepared for the Research Department of the Fabian Society, with an introduction by Bernard Shaw, together with a project by a Fabian committee for a supernational authority that will prevent war.

YORK, ELIZABETH

Leagues of nations: ancient, mediæval, and modern. London, The Swarthmore press, 1919.
12°. vi, 337 p.

INDEX

INDEX

Accretion, 124
Administration, *see* International administration
Ador, Gustave, 157
Agadir, 28
Agriculture, 266-267
Air, 124, 128
Aix-la-Chapelle, Conference of, 85
Albania, 27
Alexander I (Russia), 80-87
Alexander VI, Pope, 126
Algeciras conference, 28
Aliens, 125, 128, 222-225
Allegiance, 124
Alliances, 19, 21, 52, 79
Allied and Associated Powers, 37
Allied Maritime Transport Council, 204-209
Alsace-Lorraine, 124
American Peace Society, 74
Armistice, 36
Armistice commission, 41
Asylum, 231
Austin, John, 96-97

Balance of power, 12, 17-33, 36, 52, 81
Balch, Thos. W., 68, 152
Baldwin, Simeon E., 281
Balkan wars, 26
Barclay, Thomas, 151
Bays, 124
Bellers, John, 71
Belligerent Powers with general interests, *see* Allied and Associated Powers
Belligerent Powers with particular interests, 37
Bentham, Jeremy, 3, 72
Benton, Senator, 233
Bernard, Montague, 19, 216
Big Five, 41
Big Four, 41, 82
Big Ten, *see* Supreme council
Big Three, 41

Bills of exchange, 244-245
Bismarck, 214
Blair, Senator, 217
Borchard, Edward, 129, 222, 251
Bosnia, 27
Boycott, International, 113, 132, 138
British Dominions, 5, 34, 38, 47, 54-56, 138
British Empire, 4, 34-35, 55, 79
British War Cabinet, 35
Bucharest, Treaty of, 27
Bynkershoek, 127

Camouna (ship), 142
Carnegie, Andrew, 173
Caroline case, 123
Casablanca affair, 28
Castlereagh, 85
Central America Bureau, 260-261
Central American Court of Justice, 171-175
Central American League of Nations, 87-91
Central American Peace Conference (1907), 89
Central Rhine Commission, 196
Cession, 124
Chamberlain, J. P., 196
Charlton case, 247
Chaumont, Treaty of, 81-85
China, 125
Chinese consortium, 17
Citizenship, 249
Civil War, 138
Clemenceau, Premier, 30
Coast navigation, 128
Commissions of Inquiry, 134-146
 Bryan treaties, 143-145
 Hague, 140-142
 Labor charter, 274-275
 Taft treaties, 142-143
Common consent, 97
"Complaint of Peace," 67-68
Compromis, 160

491

INDEX

Concert of Europe, 23-33
Confederation of Europe, 23, 80-87, 90
Confederation of the Rhine, 81
Conflict of laws, 242-255
Conquest, 124
Conscription, 34
Constitutions, 53-54, 119
Consuls, 218-219
Contracts, 100
Corinto, Treaty of (1902), 88
Corporations, 15, 52
Courts, National, 166
Covenant, definition, 53-54; *see also* League of Nations Covenant
Cremer, Sir W. R., 290
Crucé, Emeric, 68
Crusades, 99
Cuba, 11
Custom, 96-97

Danube River, 195-196
Declaration of the rights and duties of nations, 10
Diplomacy
 Definition, 217
 Origin, 220
Diplomatic congresses, 228
Diplomatic intercourse, 56, 212-226
Diplomatic officers, 216, 218
Diplomatic protection, 129, 222-225
Diplomatic rupture, 131
Disarmament, 109
Display of force, 132
Dogger Bank affair, 140-141
Domain, 124
Domestic jurisdiction, 118, 135, 138, 151
Drummond, Sir James E., 44
Dunant, Henri, 283

Embargo, 131
Ems dispatch, 214
Equality of states, 7-12, 42, 122, 169, 171
Erasmus, 67
European Danube Commission, 195-196
European war
 Coöperation during, 201-211
 Outbreak of, 29, 34
Executive power, 176
Expatriation, 249-254

Extradition, 89, 230-236
 Laws, 245-249
Extraterritoriality, 130

Family of nations, *see* Society of Nations
Feudalism, 21
Fishing, 128
Fontaine, Arthur, 279
Franco-American alliance, Proposed, 303
Franz, Ferdinand, Archduke, Assassination of, 28
Freedom of the Seas, 111

Geneva Convention, 284-285
Gentz, Friedrich von, 82
German colonies, 125, 178
Gladstone, 49
Good offices, 112, 137, 140
Governments, 4
"Great Design of Henry IV," *see* Henry IV
Great Powers, 11, 15, 17, 36, 52, 125
Grotius, Hugo, 8, 111-112, 127

Hague Conference, Third, 106-107
Hague Conferences, 103
Hague Conventions, 104-106, 140, 149
Hague Conventions on private international law, 244-245
Hague International Bureau, 260
Hall, W. E., 155
Henry IV, 69-70, 83
Herzegovina, *see* Bosnia
Hiero, King of Syracuse, 20
Hill, David J., 52
Holy Alliance, 83-87
Holy Roman Empire, 6, 21, 69
Hostilities, Opening of, 132
Hume, David, 20

Immigration, 118, 249
Imperial Conferences (British), 35
Imperial War Cabinet (British), 35
Imperial War Conference (British), 35
Independence, 7
Inland waters, 126
Inter-Allied Conference, *see* Paris Conference (1917)
Inter-Allied Supreme Economic Council, 41
Intercourse, 130-131

INDEX

International administration, 176-198, 256
International anarchy, 7
International arbitration, 61, 68, 112, 147-163
  Disregard of awards, 155
  Judicial character, 151-154
  Procedure, 156
  Subjects suitable for, 149-151
International Association for the Legal Protection of Labor, 288
International bureaus, 257-264
International conferences, Private, 281-282
International coöperation, vi, 15, 52, 54, 89, 199-293
  European war, 35, 201-211
International crime, 95, 111, 166
International Institute of Agriculture, 266-267
International Labor Conference, 271-273, 278
International Labor Office, 271, 279, 288
International Labor Organization, 236-237, 254, 270-279, 289
International law, 6, 95-198
  Definition, 97
  General, 101, 108
  History, 98-99
  Peace, 121-133
  Universal, 101
International law and the League, 108-120
International legislature, 6, 116-119
International Maritime Committee, 240
International Naval Conference (London), 103
International organization, 3-91
International police, 117
International rivers, 108, 126, 192-197
International Sugar Commission, 267-269
International Trades Union Congress (1919), 289
International unions
  Private, 256, 280-293
  Public, 256-269
Interparliamentary Union, 143, 289-292
  Bureau, 292
Intervention, 23, 86-87, 122

Japan, 125
Jay treaty (1794), 150, 232
Joint administration, *see* International administration
Judicial Arbitration Court (Hague), 154, 168-170
Judicial Settlement, 152
Jurisdiction, 124-130
  Exemption from, 129
Jus gentium, 8
Jus naturale, 8
Jus sanguinis, 250
Jus soli, 250
Justiciable questions, 151

Kant, Immanuel, 73
Kaunitz, Count, 23
Kiao-Chau, 125
Knox, Senator, 43
Krüdener, Baroness von, 84

La Harpe, 83
Labor, 236-239, 254-255, 270-279, 286-289
Labor Charter, 270-279
Ladd, William, 74
Laibach, Conference of, 87
Lange, C. L., 144
Law-making treaties, 101-107
League of Nations
  Admittance to membership, 55
  Assembly, 57
    General powers, 58
    Representation in, 57
    Specific powers, 58-59, 135
    Voting in, 57
  Automatic form, 64
  Characteristics, 52
  Commission to draft covenant, 41-44
  Commissions under, 55, 61
  Conditions of success, 90
  Council, 44-45, 52-53
    Duties, 51, 109, 134-139
    General powers, 53, 58
    Meetings, 45, 47
    Members, 57
    Representation in, 57
    Specific powers, 59-60
    Voting in, 51, 57
  Covenant, 50-51
    Amendments, 119
    Article X, 110

INDEX

League of Nations—*Continued*
    As a law-making treaty, 108-116
    Drafts of, 43-44
    Preamble, 54, 94
    Salient features, 49-65
  Definition, 79
  Delegated form, 64
  How it was born, 34-48, 51
  Legal department, 167
  Majority vote, 58
  Members, 47, 50, 55
    Teutonic allies, 50
    Other members, 55
  Non-members, 136-139, 147-149
  Obligations of members, 55, 61-63
  Organization Committee, 45-47
  Organs of, 56, 79
  Permanent Court of International Justice, 61
  Representatives of members, 56
  Seat, 45
  Secretariat, 60-61, 257-259
  Secretary-General, 44
  Unanimity rule, 58, 137
  Withdrawal from, 55-56, 61
League of Red Cross Societies, 286
League to Enforce Peace, 76-77
Leagues of Nations of the past, 79-91
Leased territory, 125
Legal questions, 151
Legislature, 116
Legitimacy, 23, 82
Legrand, Daniel, 238
Leibnitz, 71
Liberty, 8
Lodge, Senator, 43
London, Declaration of (1909), 105-106
London, Treaty of (1518), 67
Louis XVIII (France), 82
Lowell, A. L., 64

Macaulay, 201-202
Mandatories, 60-61, 78, 115-116, 125, 178-183
Marblehead, Peace of the, 88
Marginal waters, *see* Three-mile limit
Measures short of war, *see* Non-hostile redress
Meditation, 137, 140, 153
Metternich, 85
Minor powers, 10
Mixed Arbitration Tribunal, 156

Monroe Doctrine, 18, 23, 43, 87, 90, 114-115, 119
Moore, J. B., 153, 158, 230, 246, 248-249
Morocco, 28
Morrow, Dwight, 206-209
Moynier, Gustav, 283
Munro, H. F., vi
Myers, D., 220

Napoleon Bonaparte, 6, 22, 80-84
Nation, 3
National honor, 16, 150-151, 172
National legislation, 242-255
Nationality, 4, 124, 129, 249-254
Naturalization, 129, 249-254
Nature, state of, 8
Neutrality, 121
Neutrals, 37, 44
New Hebrides, 188-190
New Orleans lynching case, 224-225
Nicholas II (Russia), 103
Non-hostile redress, 131-132
Non-intercourse, 132
Non-sovereign territories, 184-185
"Nouveau Cynée," 68
Novosiltsov, 83
Nys, Ernest, 68

Occupation, 124
Open covenants, 214
Open sea, 124, 126-127
Oppenheim, L., 32
Owen, Robert, 238

Pacific blockade, 132
Panama Canal Zone, 125
Pan-Serbian movement, 28
Paris, Treaty of (May 30, 1814), 82
  2d Treaty of (Nov. 20, 1815), 82
Paris conference (1917), 35, 203
Pax Romana, 20
Panama republic, 10
Peace conference (Paris), 36-45
  Commissions, 41
  Regulations, 37
Peace Congress (Versailles), 45-46
Peloponnesian wars, 20
Penn, William, 66, 70-71
Permanent Court of Arbitration (Hague), 142, 147, 154, 158-162, 164
  Cases decided, 162

INDEX

Permanent Court of International Justice (League), 164-168, 275
Personnel of international courts, 164-175
Pirates, 128
Pitt, 81, 84
Platt amendment, 11
Poland, 6
Polarized law, 244
Political crimes, 231-234, 236
Political questions, 151
Polybius, 21
Prescription, 124
Primacy of the Great Powers, 12, 17, 36
Prize courts
  International, 105, 170-171
  National, 170
Property, 123-124
Proposed leagues of nations, 66-78
Protectorates, 184
Public international unions, *see* International unions, Public
Public utilities, 109
Publicity, 139, 229
Pyrrhus, King, 68

Quadruple Alliance, 82-85

Races, 4
Ralston, J. H., 153
Rebus sic stantibus, 100
Recognition, 6
Red Cross, 116, 283-286
Reinsch, Paul, 262, 268
Reparation Commission, 123
Reprisal, 131
Retorsion, 131
Revolution, 13
Rhine courts, 197
Rhine River, 196-197
  Left bank, 31
Richelieu, 85
Right to exist, 7, 19, 110
Rohan, Cardinal de, 71
Roman empire, 6, 99
Rousseau, 72, 83
Rozhdestvensky, Admiral, 141
Russo-Japanese war, 26, 140

Saint-Pierre, 71, 83
Samoa, 185-188
San José, Treaty of, 88

Satow, E. M., 217
Scott, J. B., 152
Sea laws, 99, 239
Secret diplomacy, 214
Secret treaties, *see* Treaties, Secret
Selden, John, 127
Self-help, 122
Serajevo, 28
Slavery, 233
Smith, Munro, 178
Smuts, J. C., 78, 181-183
Society of nations, 3-16, 56, 79, 95
Southey, Robert, 71
Sovereignty, 7, 16, 53, 122, 125, 138, 177
Spanish America, 86-91
Spanish succession war, 21
Spheres of influence, 184
Spitzbergen, 190-192
Stare decisis, 96, 153
State, definition, 3
States, *de facto*, 5
  de jure, 5
Statute law, 96
Sugar Commission, 267-269
Sully, M. B., duc de, 69
Sumner, Chas., 68
Supreme Council, 37, 40-41
Supreme War Council, 35-37, 205
Suzerainty, 184
Switzerland, 4, 21
Sylvagius, John, 67

Talleyrand, 22, 82
Tavignano (ship), 142
Territory, 124
Thomas, Albert, 279
Three-mile limit, 124, 127-128
Tilsit, Treaty of, 81
Treaties, 95-107, 227-241
  Abrogation, 113
  Arbitration, 156
  As contracts, 100
  Extradition, 230-236
  Labor, 236-239, 277
  Maritime, 239-241
  Non-political, 228
  Political, 228
  Publication by League, 229
  Revision, 113
  Secret, 113
Triple alliance, 24, 34
Triple entente, 25

INDEX

Troppau, Conference of, 86
Turco-Italian war, 26, 142

Uniform state laws, 242
U. S. Articles of Confederation, 157
U. S. Constitution, 49
Universal Postal Union, 258-259, 264-266
Usage, 97
Utrecht, Peace of, 21

Vattel, 111
Verona, Conference of, 87
Versailles, Peace Congress, *see* Peace Congress (Versailles)
Versailles, Treaty of, 45
    Ratification, 46-47
    River commissions, 193-195
    Signing, 46
    U. S. fails to ratify, v, 46

Vessels
    Private, 128, 130
    Public, 123, 128, 130
Vienna, Congress of, 82
Vital interests, *see* National honor
Vollenhoven, C. van, 111
Voting trust, 53

Walton, Isaak, 215
War, 139
War, Prevention of, 20, 219-222
War, Right to declare, 7, 11, 13, 110
Webster, Daniel, 122
Webster-Ashburton treaty, 232
Westphalia, Peace of, 21
Wheat Executive, 208
Wilson, G. G., 161, 165
Wilson, President, 29-30, 40, 42-44
Wolsey, Cardinal, 67-68
Wotton, Sir Henry, 215